# THE HYMNAL

PUBLISHED BY AUTHORITY OF

## THE GENERAL ASSEMBLY

OF THE

## PRESBYTERIAN CHURCH
## IN THE UNITED STATES
## OF AMERICA ⸜ 1933

PHILADELPHIA

PRESBYTERIAN BOARD OF CHRISTIAN
EDUCATION

CLARENCE DICKINSON, M.A., MUS.D., LITT.D., EDITOR
CALVIN WEISS LAUFER, M.A., D.D., ASSISTANT EDITOR

Copyright, 1933, by
the Presbyterian Board of Christian Education

*Thirty-fifth Printing, 1980*

Printed in the United States of America

# PREFACE

THIS Hymnal has been compiled in response to a very general demand from the Church and in an endeavor to meet certain needs in devotional expression which are peculiar to our time.

The editors have tried to make the book as compact as is compatible with a certain measure of completeness. Those hymns have been omitted, therefore, which, upon careful investigation, have been found to be seldom, if ever, used. On the other hand, old hymns which through years of association have become fixed in the affections of many people have been retained, even though they may, in some cases, fall below the general standard set for the Hymnal. The rich treasure of the heritage hymns of the Church has been carefully preserved and their representation considerably enlarged by the inclusion of such ancient, stately hymn tunes as the fifteenth century English "Deo Gracias," the French "Rouen Church Melody," the "Chartres Church Melody," and others. In response to requests a few plain song melodies have been associated with the hymns for which they were written, or to which they are inherently suited: St. Ambrose' "O Splendor of God's Glory Bright," St. Gregory's "Father We Praise Thee, Now the Night Is Over," and Aurelius Prudentius' "Of the Father's Love Begotten." Many fine old tunes have been included from Calvin's "Genevan Psalter" and the English and Scottish Psalters, as well as several noble Lutheran chorales, Bohemian hymns and tunes, Wesleyan hymns, and others representative of notable religious movements in the Church.

Mindful of the various nationalities so largely represented in the Presbyterian Church in this country, the editors have sought out and included a number of cherished Welsh, Irish, and Scandinavian hymns and tunes, which in their beauty and universal appeal are a very real enrichment of the Hymnal. Representative folk song tunes have also been included, as the most spontaneous outpourings of the hearts of the people.

Considerable new poetic material has been added to give expression to certain new emphases in the religious thought of the present day, which concerns itself in such large measure, on the one hand, with social service, the brotherhood of man and world friendship and, on the other, with the inner life, that mystical conception of the Christian life as "hid with Christ in God." Here, especially, the editors have availed themselves of beautiful modern tunes which are peculiarly suited to the texts.

Probably no one church will use all the hymns in the book, but the editors have earnestly sought to make the hymns included so representative and so

# Preface

varied that every church will find in it a sufficient number to suit its particular needs and preferences.

A widespread desire for the enrichment of our services of worship has led to the inclusion of responses suitable for use at the opening of a service; before or after the reading of Scripture; upon the presentation of the offering; before or after prayer, either spoken or silent; and at the close of the service. Also a number of short prayer hymns, or orisons, have been introduced, which may be found to add beauty to the service; they are particularly suited for use at the close of a vesper or evening service. They may be sung as choir hymns for a time, until the congregation becomes familiar with them.

The words of the hymns have been placed between the staves of music because of a general and urgent demand.

The editors cannot adequately express their appreciation of the tireless labor and self-sacrifice of the Committees on Content and on Music, who insist upon remaining anonymous. They have given without stint and with deep devotion of their time and strength and thought and counsel.

The Hymnal is offered to the Church in the hope and with the prayer that, in spite of its imperfections and limitations, it may bring worshiping congregations into closer communion with God as they "speak to him in song," and into closer fellowship with one another as together they sing his praise.

# ACKNOWLEDGMENTS

GRATEFUL acknowledgment is made to the many authors, composers, and publishers, who have helped substantially to make this hymnal possible. We record our obligation to the officers of The Beacon Press, Inc.; The Century Company; The Pilgrim Press; The Board of Publication of the United Lutheran Church in America; The Church Pension Fund; Houghton Mifflin Company; The United Church Publishing House, Toronto, Canada; Novello and Company, Limited; and the Oxford University Press.

Where any hymns and tunes appear without proper acknowledgment, it is to be understood that diligent search is still being made and that, upon further information, due credit will be given in future editions.

For permission to use hymns and tunes our gratitude is recorded to the following persons and publishing houses:

| | HYMN | TUNE |
|---|---|---|
| The Very Reverend the Abbot of Downside | | 110, 368, 403, Response 7 |
| American Peace Society | 402 | |
| American Tract Society | 341 | |
| Association for Promotion of Christian Knowledge | 300 | 133 |
| Miss Emily Aston | 147 | |
| Mr. Edward Shippen Barnes | | 70, Response 3 |
| Mr. Clifford Bax | 424 | |
| The Beacon Press | 84, 90, 101, 176, 320, 323, 363, 370, 425, 471, 486 | |
| Mr. Clifford Booth | | 375 |
| Rev. Walter Russell Bowie | 409 | |
| Mrs. Bridges | Response 82 | Responses 84, 86 |
| Miss Honor Brooke | 74, 141, 303, 444 | |
| Mr. J. Rutherford Brownlie | 187 | |
| Mrs. George S. Burgess | 411 | |
| Mr. E. M. Butler | 258 | |
| Calvinist Methodist Book Agency | | 183 |
| Mr. Kyrle Chatfield | 239 | |
| The Chautauqua Institution | 39, 216 | 39, 216 |
| The Churchman Monthly | 489 | |
| William Clowes and Sons, Ltd. | | 498 |
| Rev. Joseph Simpson Cook | 453 | |

# Acknowledgments

|  | HYMN | TUNE |
|---|---|---|
| Mrs. Julia Cady Cory | 461 | |
| Mr. Vernon B. Coster | 273 | |
| Rev. Allen Eastman Cross | 494 | |
| Mr. E. T. Davies | | 250 |
| Mrs. Grace Davis | 179 | |
| Rev. Robert Davis | 397 | |
| Mr. Leopold L. Dix | | 508 |
| Canon Charles Winfred Douglas | | 276, Response 85 |
| Mr. Francis Duckworth | | 32, 72 |
| Rev. F. Llewellyn Edwards | | 323 |
| The Epworth Press | | 504 |
| Dr. David Evans | | 177 |
| W. Gwenlyn Evans and Sons | | 373 |
| The Governors of the Repton School | | 509 |
| Mrs. John H. Gower | | 157 |
| Mr. W. Greatorex | | 148, 258 |
| Rev. Marion Franklin Ham | 370 | |
| Harper & Brothers | | 487 |
| Dr. Basil Harwood | | 156, 422 |
| Miss Beatrice Hatch | 213 | |
| The Heidelberg Press | 219 | |
| W. H. Hewlett | Response 25 | |
| The Homiletic Review | 85, 496 | |
| The Hope Publishing Company | | 47, 126 |
| Miss M. Morley Horder | | 82, 140, 219, Response 43 |
| Houghton Mifflin Company | 22, 87, 107, 178, 208, 282, 302, 344, 373, 403, 499 | |
| Mr. F. D. How | 170 | |
| Mrs. John Hughes | | 104 |
| Messrs. Hughes and Sons | | 233 |
| Miss Eleanor Hull | 325 | |
| Canon L. S. Hunter | 507 | |
| The Hymn Society of America | 181 | |
| Mr. Philip James | | Response 92 |
| Mrs. Robert F. Jefferys | 32, 138, 359, 400, 433, 490, Response 84 | 433 |
| Miss N. D. Jenkins | | 247 |
| Mrs. J. W. Jones | | 511 |
| Messrs. Keith, Blake and Company | | 238 |
| Rev. Hugh T. Kerr | 88 | |
| Rev. Shepherd Knapp | 368 | |
| Rev. Calvin W. Laufer | 13, 367 | 245, 324, 350, 367, Response 5 |
| The Leyda Publishing Company | 493 | |
| Charlotte Mathewson Lockwood | | 4 |

# Acknowledgments

| | HYMN | TUNE |
|---|---|---|
| Mr. George Lomas | | 277 |
| Hon. Mrs. Lowry | 393 | |
| Mrs. Mary Runyon Lowry | 332, 396 | 332, 396 |
| Messrs. McClure, Naismith Brodie and Company | 247 | |
| Prof. Robert G. McCutchan | | 423 |
| The Macmillan Company | 432, 438 | |
| Dr. Ernest MacMillan | | 453 |
| Miss Helen Macnicol | 234 | |
| Marshall, Morgan and Scott, Ltd. | | 327 |
| Mr. Henry Lowell Mason | | 181 |
| Rev. John Howard Masterman | 405 | |
| Mr. Hamish Hemington Mathams | 277 | |
| Miss Mary E. Maude | 248 | |
| Rev. William P. Merrill | 416 | 415 |
| Rev. John J. Moment | 4, 290 | |
| Miss Florence Monk | | 171 |
| Mr. John Murray | 423 | |
| National Council of the Young Men's Christian Association | 477 | |
| National Board of the Young Woman's Christian Association | Response 7 | |
| National Sunday School Union of Great Britain | 445 | |
| James Nisbet and Company, Ltd. | 227 | |
| Dr. T. Tertius Noble | | 366 |
| Rev. Frank Mason North | 410 | |
| Novello and Company, Ltd. | 155, 307, 466 | 48, 111, 123, 128, 149, 155, 161, 168, 170, 174, 247, 268, 270, 307, 365, 376, 384, 402, 438, 441, 455, 457, 466. 473, 484, 495, 500 Responses 8, 48, 53, 56 |
| Major E. F. Oakeley | | 46, 101 |
| Mr. John Oxenham | 322, 341 | |
| Oxford University Press | 24, 55, 66, 170, 177, 187, 213, 258, 330, 386, 417, 419, 420, 509, Responses 14, 42, 82, 86 | 9, 12, 13, 24, 30, 44, 80, 95, 100, 102, 138, 165, 177, 182, 189, 191, 196, 213, 222, 248, 276, 282, 284, 294, 298, 299, 300, 319, 320, 323, 325, 328, 330, 344, 368, 371, 388, 416, 417, 419, 429, 439, 442, 444, 447, 451, 471, 486, 512, Responses 11, 31, 33, 16, 37, 39, 40, 42, 84, 86 |
| The Parish Press | | Response 72 |
| Mrs. Horatio W. Parker | 379 | 19, 193, 270, 370, 404 |
| W. Paxton and Company, Ltd. | | 303 |

# Acknowledgments

| | HYMN | TUNE |
|---|---|---|
| Miss Emily S. Perkins | 67 | 67 |
| Mr. A. D. Peters | 424 | |
| The Pilgrim Press | 140 | |
| Messrs. Pinker and Morrison | 322 | |
| The Presbyterian Advance | 401 | |
| The Presbyterian Board of National Missions | 418 | 418 |
| The Psalms and Hymn Trust | | 29, 73, 302 |
| | | |
| Mrs. Irene Martin Ramsay | | 153 |
| Fleming H. Revell Company | 276 | 276 |
| A. W. Ridley and Company | 35, 345 | 494 |
| Rev. Robert Rowland Roberts | 183 | |
| Dr. W. H. C. Romanis | 502 | |
| Prof. Julius Rontgen | | 93, 393 |
| | | |
| Miss Margaret E. Sangster | 387 | |
| Charles Scribner's Sons | 70, 72, 488 | |
| Mr. Geoffrey T. Shaw | | 265 |
| Messrs. John F. Shaw and Co., Ltd. | | 469 |
| Society for Promoting Christian Knowledge | 133, 439, 504 | 133, 395 |
| Sir Arthur Somervell | | Response 31 |
| "Songs of Syon" | 226, 503, 505 | 503 |
| Mr. J. F. R. Stainer | | Response 83 |
| Messrs. Stainer and Bell | | 145, 510 |
| | | |
| Miss Alice Tarrant | 408, 441, 491 | |
| Mrs. Ethel Taylor | | 84, 213, 246 |
| Mr. George Thalben-Ball | | 76 |
| | | |
| The Board of Publication of the United Lutheran Church | | 27, 51 |
| The United Presbyterian Board of Publication | 102 | |
| | | |
| Rev. Henry van Dyke | 5, 415 | |
| The Vicar of St. Albans, Birmingham, England | 238 | |
| | | |
| Miss Clara S. Walmsley | 40 | |
| Rev. Lauchlan MacLean Watt | 243 | |
| The Wesleyan Methodist Sunday School Department, London | | 446 |
| Dr. Healey Willan | | Responses 65, 73, 75 |
| Rev. George R. Woodward | 226, 331, 503, 505, 513 | 119, 331, 503, 513 |
| | | |
| "The Yattendon Hymnal" | | Responses 82, 84, 86 |

# CONTENTS

## HYMNS

# Contents

## VIII. THE LIFE IN CHRIST

# Index of First Lines

xi

# Index of First Lines

# Index of First Lines

# Index of First Lines

xiv

# Index of First Lines

xv

# Index of First Lines

# Index of Responses

# Index of Ancient Hymns and Canticles

# Alphabetical Index of Tunes

# Alphabetical Index of Tunes

# Metrical Index of Tunes

# Topical Index

# Topical Index

# Topical Index

# Topical Index

# Topical Index

# Topical Index

# Topical Index

# Topical Index

# Topical Index

xxxii

# Index of Authors

# Index of Authors

# Index of Composers

# Index of Composers

Dykes, Rev. John Bacchus (1823–1876), 53, 57, 99, 150, 159, 205, 206, 218, 224, 233, 236, 255, 275, 289, 309, 322, 323, 356, 392, 398, 426, 427, 440, 485, 492.

Ebeling, Johann Georg (1620–1676), 125.
Edwards, E., Response 6.
Edwards, Rev. F. Llewellyn, 323.
Elliott, James William (1833–1915), 268, 473.
Elvey, Sir George Job (1816–1893), 109, 175, 190, 230, 460; Chant 68.
Emerson, L. O., 41.
"Essay on the Church Plain Chant" (1782), 304.
"Este's Psalter" (1592), 91, 229, 503; Response 24.
Evans, David, 177, 325
Evans, David Emlyn (1843–1913), 511.
Evans, D., "Hymnau a Thonau" (1865), 222, 371, 419.
Ewing, Lt. Col. Alexander (1830–1895), 435.

Farrant, Richard (c. 1530–1580), Response 9; Chant 48.
Felton, Rev. William (c. 1715–1769), Chant 61.
Filitz, Rev. Friedrich (1804–1876), 252; Response 13.
Fink, Rev. Gottfried Wilhelm (1783–1846), 478.
Fischer, William Gustavus (1835–1912), 443.
Flemming, Friedrich Ferdinand (1778–1813), 306.
"Foundery Collection" (Rev. John Wesley's) (1742), 264, 288; Response 17.
"Freylinghausen's Gesangbuch," Halle (1704), 27, 30.

Gardiner, William (1770–1853), 410.
Gastorius, Severus (fl. 1675), 291.
Gauntlett, Henry John (1805–1876), 454.
"Geistliche Kirchengesäng," Cologne (1623), 13, 388.
"Geistliche Lieder," Leipzig (1539), 118, 351, 506.
"Geistliche Lieder," Wittenberg (1535), 342.
"Genevan Psalter" (1549), Chant 82.
"Genevan Psalter" (1551), 185, 386, 481; Doxologies 94, 95.
"Geneva Psalter" (1552), 424.
"Gesangbuch der Herzogl. Wirtembergischen Katholischen Hofkapelle" (1784), 65, 147.
Giardini, Felice de (1716–1796), 52, 378, 483.
Gibbons, Orlando (1583–1625), 68, 240, 488.
Gläser, Carl Gotthilf (1784–1829), 179.
Goodson, Richard, Chant 47.
Goss, Sir John (1800–1880), 14, 272, 273.
Gottschalk, Louis Moreau (1829–1869), 208.
Goudimel, Claude (c. 1510–1572), 227.
Gould, John Edgar (1822–1875), 225, 286.
Gounod, Charles François (1818–1893), 26, 38.

Gower, John Henry (1855–1922), 157.
Greatorex, Henry Wellington (1811–1858), "Collection" (1851), 94.
Greatorex, Walter (1877–    ), 148, 258.
Greene, Maurice (1696–1755), 16.
Grenoble Church Melody, Response 29.
Grüber, Franz (1787–1863), 132.
Gwyllt, Ieuan (see Rev. John Roberts) (1822–1877), 183.

Handel, George Frederick (1685–1759), 120, 122, 278, 313, 421.
Harding, John P. (1850–1911), 136.
Harrington, Karl Pomeroy, 497.
Hassler, Hans Leo (1564–1612), 151.
Hastings, Thomas (1784–1872), 197, 237.
Hatton, John C. (d. 1793), 377, 462.
Havergal, Frances Ridley (1836–1879), 56, 169, 456.
Havergal, Rev. William Henry (1793–1870), 97; Chant 49.
Haweis, Rev. Thomas (1734–1820), 199, 363.
Haydn, Franz Joseph (1732–1809), 69, 339.
Haydn, Johann Michael (1737–1806), 198, 400.
Hayes, William (1706–1777), 482.
Hayne, Rev. Leighton George (1836–1883), 425.
"Heilige Seelenlust" (1657), 43.
Hemy, Henri Frederick (1818–1888), 267.
Hewlett, William Henry, Response 25.
Hews, George (1806–1873), 209.
Hiles, Henry (1826–1904), 36.
Hill, G. Everett, 201.
"Hirschberg Gesangbuch" (1741), 79, 397.
Hodges, Rev. John Sebastian Bach (1830–1915), 353.
Holbrook, Joseph Perry (1822–1888), 62, 280.
Holden, Oliver (1765–1844), 192.
Hopkins, Edward John (1818–1901), 55, 71.
Horsley, William (1774–1858), 157.
Howard, Samuel (1710–1782), 188, 294, 383.
Hoyte, W. Stevenson, 467.
Hughes, John (1873–1932), 104.
Hullah, John (1812–1884), 284, 296.
Hurst, William, 498.
Husband, Rev. Edward (1843–1908), 228.
"Hymnau a Thonau" (D. Evans') (1865), 222, 371, 419.
"Hymns and Sacred Poems, A Collection of," Dublin (1749), 49, 340.

Isaak, Heinrich (c. 1455–1517), 505.
Isalaw (John Richards) (1843–1908), 15.

Jackson, Robert (1842–1914), 84, 213, 246.
Jacob, B., "National Psalmody" (1819), 400.
James, Philip, 496; Amen 92.
Jeffery, J. Albert (1851–1928), 58.
Jenkins, David (1849–1915), 247.
Jones, John (Talysarn) (1797–1857), 247.
Jones, Rev. William (1726–1800), 187, 232.
Joseph, Georg (17th century), 43.
Jowett, Rev. Joseph (1784–1856), 511.
Jude, William Herbert (1851–1892), 223.

# Index of Composers

# Index of Composers

# Brief Statement of the Reformed Faith

ADOPTED, MAY 22, 1902, BY THE GENERAL ASSEMBLY OF THE PRES-
BYTERIAN CHURCH IN THE UNITED STATES OF AMERICA

## Article I.  Of God

We believe in the ever-living God, who is a Spirit and the Father of our spirits; infinite, eternal, and unchangeable in His being and perfections; the Lord Almighty, most just in all His ways, most glorious in holiness, unsearchable in wisdom and plenteous in mercy, full of love and compassion, and abundant in goodness and truth.  We worship Him, Father, Son, and Holy Spirit, three persons in one Godhead, one in substance and equal in power and glory.

## Article II.  Of Revelation

We believe that God is revealed in nature, in history, and in the heart of man; that He has made gracious and clearer revelations of Himself to men of God who spoke as they were moved by the Holy Spirit; and that Jesus Christ, the Word made flesh, is the brightness of the Father's glory and the express image of His person.  We gratefully receive the Holy Scriptures, given by inspiration, to be the faithful record of God's gracious revelations and the sure witness to Christ, as the Word of God, the only infallible rule of faith and life.

## Article III.  Of the Eternal Purpose

We believe that the eternal, wise, holy, and loving purpose of God embraces all events, so that while the freedom of man is not taken away nor is God the author of sin, yet in His providence He makes all things work together in the fulfillment of His sovereign design and the manifestation of His glory; wherefore, humbly acknowledging the mystery of this truth, we trust in His protecting care and set our hearts to do His will.

## Article IV.  Of the Creation

We believe that God is the creator, upholder, and governor of all things; that He is above all His works and in them all; and that He made man in His own image, meet for fellowship with Him, free and able to choose between good and evil, and forever responsible to his Maker and Lord.

## Article V.  Of the Sin of Man

We believe that our first parents, being tempted, chose evil, and so fell away from God and came under the power of sin, the penalty of which is eternal death; and we confess that, by reason of this disobedience, we and all men are born with a sinful nature, that we have broken God's law, and that no man can be saved but by His grace.

## Article VI.  Of the Grace of God

We believe that God, out of His great love for the world, has given His only begotten Son to be the Saviour of sinners, and in the Gospel freely offers His all-sufficient salvation to all men.  And we praise Him for the unspeakable grace wherein He has provided a way of eternal life for all mankind.

## Article VII.  Of Election

We believe that God, from the beginning, in His own good pleasure, gave to His Son a people, an innumerable multitude, chosen in Christ unto holiness, service, and salvation; we believe that all who come to years of discretion can receive this salvation only through faith and repentance; and we believe that all who die in infancy, and all others given by the Father to the Son who are beyond the reach of the outward means of grace, are regenerated and saved by Christ through the Spirit, who works when and where and how He pleases.

## Article VIII.  Of Our Lord Jesus Christ

We believe in and confess the Lord Jesus Christ, the only Mediator between God and man, who, being the Eternal Son of God, for us men and for our salvation became truly man, being conceived by the Holy Ghost and born of the Virgin Mary, without sin; unto us He has revealed the Father, by His Word and Spirit making known the perfect will of God; for us He fulfilled all righteousness and satisfied eternal justice, offering Himself a perfect sacrifice upon the cross to take away the sin of the world; for us He rose from the dead and ascended into heaven, where He ever intercedes for us; in our hearts, joined to Him by faith, He abides forever as the indwelling Christ; over us, and over all for us, He rules: wherefore, unto Him we render love, obedience, and adoration as our Prophet, Priest, and King forever.

## Article IX.  Of Faith and Repentance

We believe that God pardons our sins and accepts us as righteous solely on the ground of the perfect obedience and sacrifice of Christ received by faith alone; and that this saving faith is always accompanied by repentance, wherein we confess and forsake our sins with full purpose of, and endeavor after, a new obedience to God.

## Article X. Of the Holy Spirit

We believe in the Holy Spirit, the Lord and Giver of Life, who moves everywhere upon the hearts of men, to restrain them from evil and to incite them unto good, and whom the Father is ever willing to give unto all who ask Him. We believe that He has spoken by holy men of God in making known His truth to men for their salvation; that, through our exalted Saviour, He was sent forth in power to convict the world of sin, to enlighten men's minds in the knowledge of Christ, and to persuade and enable them to obey the call of the Gospel; and that He abides with the Church, dwelling in every believer as the spirit of truth, of holiness, and of comfort.

## Article XI. Of the New Birth and the New Life

We believe that the Holy Spirit only is the author and source of the new birth; we rejoice in the new life, wherein He is given unto us as the seal of sonship in Christ, and keeps loving fellowship with us, helps us in our infirmities, purges us from our faults, and ever continues His transforming work in us until we are perfected in the likeness of Christ, in the glory of the life to come.

## Article XII. Of the Resurrection and the Life to Come

We believe that in the life to come the spirits of the just, at death made free from sin, enjoy immediate communion with God and the vision of His glory; and we confidently look for the general resurrection in the last day, when the bodies of those who sleep in Christ shall be fashioned in the likeness of the glorious body of their Lord, with whom they shall live and reign forever.

## Article XIII. Of the Law of God

We believe that the law of God, revealed in the Ten Commandments, and more clearly disclosed in the words of Christ, is forever established in truth and equity, so that no human work shall abide except it be built on this foundation. We believe that God requires of every man to do justly, to love mercy, and to walk humbly with his God;

and that only through this harmony with the will of God shall be fulfilled that brotherhood of man wherein the kingdom of God is to be made manifest.

## Article XIV. Of the Church and the Sacraments

We believe in the Holy Catholic Church of which Christ is the only Head. We believe that the Church Invisible consists of all the redeemed, and that the Church Visible embraces all who profess the true religion together with their children. We receive to our communion all who confess and obey Christ as their divine Lord and Saviour, and we hold fellowship with all believers in Him.

We receive the sacraments of Baptism and the Lord's Supper, alone divinely established and committed to the Church, together with the Word, as means of grace; made effectual only by the Holy Spirit, and always to be used by Christians with prayer and praise to God.

## Article XV. Of the Last Judgment

We believe that the Lord Jesus Christ will come again in glorious majesty to judge the world and to make a final separation between the righteous and the wicked. The wicked shall receive the eternal award of their sins, and the Lord will manifest the glory of His mercy in the salvation of His people and their entrance upon the full enjoyment of eternal life.

## Article XVI. Of Christian Service and the Final Triumph

We believe that it is our duty, as servants and friends of Christ, to do good unto all men, to maintain the public and private worship of God, to hallow the Lord's Day, to preserve the sanctity of the family, to uphold the just authority of the State, and so to live in all honesty, purity, and charity, that our lives shall testify of Christ. We joyfully receive the word of Christ, bidding His people go into all the world and make disciples of all nations, and declare unto them that God was in Christ reconciling the world unto Himself, and that He will have all men to be saved and to come to the knowledge of the truth. We confidently trust that by His power and grace, all His enemies and ours shall be finally overcome, and the kingdoms of this world shall be made the kingdom of our God and of His Christ. In this faith we abide; in this service we labor; and in this hope we pray, Even so,, come, Lord Jesus.

# The Lord's Prayer

OUR FATHER WHO ART IN HEAVEN, HALLOWED BE THY NAME. THY KINGDOM COME. THY WILL BE DONE IN EARTH, AS IT IS IN HEAVEN. GIVE US THIS DAY OUR DAILY BREAD. AND FORGIVE US OUR DEBTS, AS WE FORGIVE OUR DEBTORS. AND LEAD US NOT INTO TEMPTATION, BUT DELIVER US FROM EVIL: FOR THINE IS THE KINGDOM, AND THE POWER, AND THE GLORY, FOR EVER. AMEN.

# The Ten Commandments

GOD spake all these words, saying, I am the LORD thy God, which have brought thee out of the land of Egypt, out of the house of bondage.

**I.** Thou shalt have no other gods before me.

**II.** Thou shalt not make unto thee any graven image, or any likeness of any thing that is in heaven above, or that is in the earth beneath, or that is in the water under the earth; thou shalt not bow down thyself to them, nor serve them: for I, the LORD thy God, am a jealous God, visiting the iniquity of the fathers upon the children unto the third and fourth generation of them that hate me; and showing mercy unto thousands of them that love me, and keep my commandments.

**III.** Thou shalt not take the name of the LORD thy God in vain: for the LORD will not hold him guiltless that taketh his name in vain.

**IV.** Remember the Sabbath-day, to keep it holy. Six days shalt thou labor, and do all thy work: but the seventh day is the Sabbath of the LORD thy God; in it thou shalt not do any work, thou, nor thy son, nor thy daughter, thy manservant, nor thy maidservant, nor thy cattle, nor thy stranger that is within thy gates: for in six days the LORD made heaven and earth, the sea, and all that in them is, and rested the seventh day; wherefore the LORD blessed the Sabbath-day and hallowed it.

**V.** Honor thy father and thy mother; that thy days may be long upon the land which the LORD thy God giveth thee.

**VI.** Thou shalt not kill.

**VII.** Thou shalt not commit adultery.

**VIII.** Thou shalt not steal.

**IX.** Thou shalt not bear false witness against thy neighbor.

**X.** Thou shalt not covet thy neighbor's house, thou shalt not covet thy neighbor's wife, nor his manservant, nor his maidservant, nor his ox, nor his ass, nor any thing that is thy neighbor's.

HEAR also the words of our Lord Jesus, how He saith: Thou shalt love the Lord thy God with all thy heart, and with all thy soul, and with all thy mind. This is the first and great commandment. And the second is like unto it, Thou shalt love thy neighbor as thyself. On these two commandments hang all the law and the prophets.

# The Apostles' Creed

I BELIEVE in GOD THE FATHER Almighty, Maker of heaven and earth:

And in JESUS CHRIST his only Son, our Lord; who was conceived by the Holy Ghost, born of the Virgin Mary, suff:red under Pontius Pilate, was crucified, dead, and buried; he descended into hell *; the third day he rose again from the dead; he ascended into heaven, and sitteth on the right hand of God the Father Almighty; from thence he shall come to judge the quick and the dead.

I believe in the HOLY GHOST; the holy Catholic Church; the communion of saints; the forgiveness of sins; the resurrection of the body; and the life everlasting. Amen.

*i. e.* Continued in the state of the dead, and under the power of death, until the third day.

# Opening Sentences

THE Lord is in his holy temple: let all the earth keep silence before him.

God is a Spirit: and they that worship him must worship him in spirit and in truth.

O come, let us worship and bow down: let us kneel before the Lord our maker.

For he is our God; and we are the people of his pasture, and the sheep of his hand.

---

LET Israel hope in the Lord: for with the Lord there is mercy, and with him is plenteous redemption.

My voice shalt thou hear in the morning, O Lord; in the morning will I direct my prayer unto thee, and will look up.

---

I WILL come into thy house in the multitude of thy mercy: and in thy fear will I worship toward thy holy temple.

Let the words of my mouth, and the meditation of my heart, be acceptable in thy sight, O Lord, my strength, and my redeemer.

---

OUR help is in the name of the Lord, who made heaven and earth.

Where two or three are gathered together in my name, there am I in the midst of them.

---

THE Lord is in his holy temple: let all the earth keep silence before him.

O worship the Lord in the beauty of holiness: fear before him, all the earth.

---

IT IS a good thing to give thanks unto the Lord, and to sing praises unto thy name, O most High:

To shew forth thy lovingkindness in the morning, and thy faithfulness every night.

Delight thyself also in the Lord; and he shall give thee the desires of thine heart.

---

THE Lord is nigh unto all them that call upon him, to all that call upon him in truth.

He will fulfil the desire of them that fear him: he also will hear their cry, and will save them.

O thou that hearest prayer, unto thee shall all flesh come.

---

THE hour cometh, and now is, when the true worshippers shall worship the Father in spirit and in truth: for the Father seeketh such to worship him. God is a Spirit: and they that worship him must worship him in spirit and in truth.

---

BLESSED is the man whom thou choosest, and causest to approach unto thee, that he may dwell in thy courts: we shall be satisfied with the goodness of thy house, even of thy holy temple.

---

HUMBLE yourselves in the sight of the Lord, and he shall lift you up. Draw nigh to God, and he will draw nigh to you.

I was glad when they said unto me, Let us go into the house of the Lord. This is the day which the Lord hath made; we will rejoice and be glad in it.

---

WE HAVE not an high priest which cannot be touched with the feeling of our infirmities; but was in all points tempted like as we are, yet without sin. Let us therefore come boldly unto the throne of grace, that we may obtain mercy, and find grace to help in time of need.

---

FROM the rising of the sun unto the going down of the same the Lord's name is to be praised.

Let my prayer be set forth before thee as incense; and the lifting up of my hands as the evening sacrifice.

The day goeth away, for the shadows of the evening are stretched out.

But it shall come to pass, that at evening time it shall be light.

# HYMNS

## Adoration

Psalm c. Rev. William Kethe, 1561  L. M.

OLD HUNDREDTH
Louis Bourgeois, 1551
(English form of final line)

*With dignity*

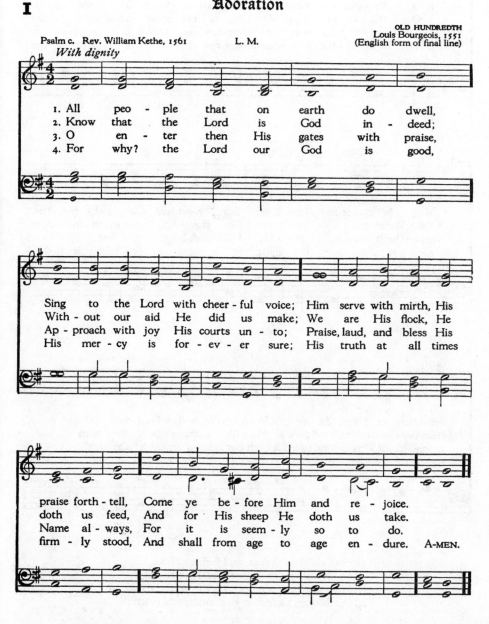

1. All peo - ple that on earth do dwell,
2. Know that the Lord is God in - deed;
3. O en - ter then His gates with praise,
4. For why? the Lord our God is good,

Sing to the Lord with cheer - ful voice; Him serve with mirth, His
With - out our aid He did us make; We are His flock, He
Ap - proach with joy His courts un - to; Praise, laud, and bless His
His mer - cy is for - ev - er sure; His truth at all times

praise forth - tell, Come ye be - fore Him and re - joice.
doth us feed, And for His sheep He doth us take.
Name al - ways, For it is seem - ly so to do.
firm - ly stood, And shall from age to age en - dure. A-MEN.

# Adoration

From Psalm civ.  Robert Grant, 1833   10. 10. 11. 11.   HANOVER  William Croft (1678-1727)

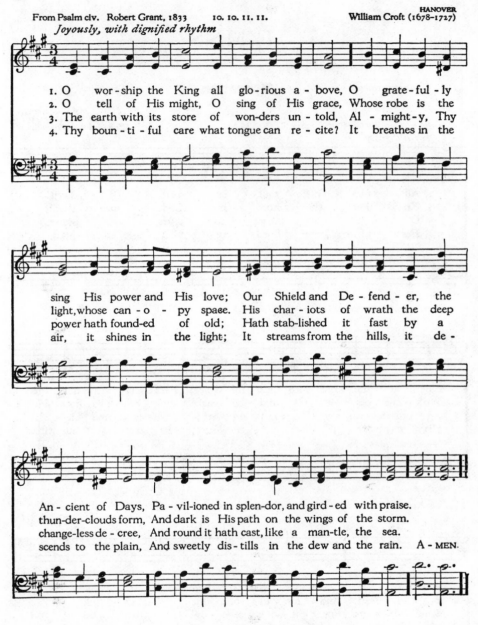

1. O wor-ship the King all glo-rious a-bove, O grate-ful-ly sing His power and His love; Our Shield and De-fend-er, the An-cient of Days, Pa-vil-ioned in splen-dor, and gird-ed with praise.

2. O tell of His might, O sing of His grace, Whose robe is the light, whose can-o-py space. His char-iots of wrath the deep thun-der-clouds form, And dark is His path on the wings of the storm.

3. The earth with its store of won-ders un-told, Al-might-y, Thy power hath found-ed of old; Hath stab-lished it fast by a change-less de-cree, And round it hath cast, like a man-tle, the sea.

4. Thy boun-ti-ful care what tongue can re-cite? It breathes in the air, it shines in the light; It streams from the hills, it de-scends to the plain, And sweetly dis-tills in the dew and the rain. A-MEN.

5. Frail children of dust, and feeble as frail,
In Thee do we trust, nor find Thee to fail;
Thy mercies how tender, how firm to the end,
Our Maker, Defender, Redeemer, and Friend!

German, c. 1800
Trans. by Rev. Edward Caswall, 1853    6. 6. 6. 6. 6. 6.    LAUDES DOMINI
Joseph Barnby, 1868

*Joyously and with dignity*

1. When morn - ing gilds the skies, My heart a - wak - ing cries
2. Does sad - ness fill my mind? A sol - ace here I find,
3. Ye na - tions of man - kind, In this your con - cord find,

May Je - sus Christ be praised: A - like at work and prayer
May Je - sus Christ be praised: Or fades my earth - ly bliss?
May Je - sus Christ be praised: Let all the earth a - round

To Je - sus I re - pair; May Je - sus Christ be praised!
My com - fort still is this, May Je - sus Christ be praised!
Ring joy - ous with the sound, May Je - sus Christ be praised! A-MEN.

4. Be this, while life is mine,
My canticle divine,
May Jesus Christ be praised:
Be this the eternal song,
Through all the ages long,
May Jesus Christ be praised!

# Adoration

Rev. John J. Moment, 1930  
7. 7. 7. 7. 5. 7. with Refrain  
ROCK OF AGES  
Ancient Hebrew melody; arr. by  
Charlotte Mathewson Lockwood

*Majestically*

1. Men and chil-dren ev-ery-where, With sweet mu-sic fill the air!
2. Morn-ing, eve-ning, bless His name, Skies with crim-son clouds a-flame,
3. Storm and flood and o-cean's roar, Break-ers crash-ing on the shore,

Na-tions, come, your voi-ces raise To the Lord in hymns of praise!
Rain-bow arch, His cove-nant sign, Countless stars by night that shine!
Wa-ter-falls that nev-er sleep, Towering moun-tain, can-yon deep,

Join the an-gel song, All the worlds to Him be-long!
Through His far do-main, Love is King where He doth reign!
Tell ye forth His might, Lord of life and truth and right!

REFRAIN

Ho-ly, ho-ly, To our God all glo-ry be! A-MEN.

# Adoration

Rev. Henry van Dyke, 1907   8. 7. 8. 7. D.   HYMN TO JOY
Ludwig van Beethoven, 1824

*With exultation*

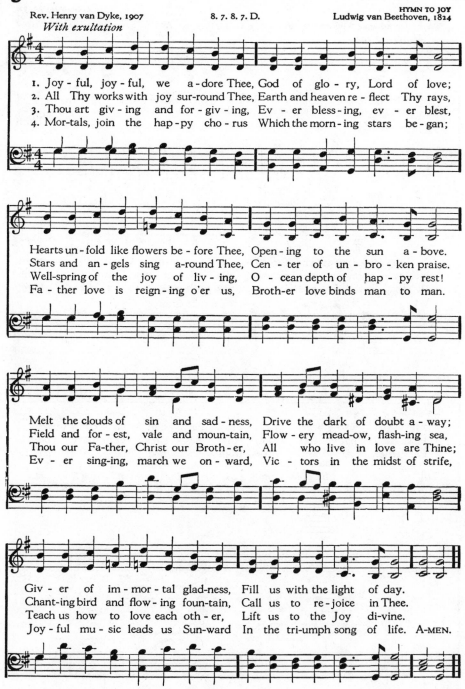

1. Joy - ful, joy - ful, we a - dore Thee, God of glo - ry, Lord of love;
2. All Thy works with joy sur-round Thee, Earth and heaven re - flect Thy rays,
3. Thou art giv - ing and for - giv - ing, Ev - er bless - ing, ev - er blest,
4. Mor-tals, join the hap - py cho - rus Which the morn - ing stars be - gan;

Hearts un - fold like flowers be - fore Thee, Open - ing to the sun a - bove.
Stars and an - gels sing a-round Thee, Cen - ter of un - bro - ken praise.
Well-spring of the joy of liv - ing, O - cean depth of hap - py rest!
Fa - ther love is reign - ing o'er us, Broth-er love binds man to man.

Melt the clouds of sin and sad - ness, Drive the dark of doubt a - way;
Field and for - est, vale and moun-tain, Flow - ery mead-ow, flash-ing sea,
Thou our Fa-ther, Christ our Broth - er, All who live in love are Thine;
Ev - er sing-ing, march we on - ward, Vic - tors in the midst of strife,

Giv - er of im - mor - tal glad-ness, Fill us with the light of day.
Chant-ing bird and flow - ing foun-tain, Call us to re - joice in Thee.
Teach us how to love each oth - er, Lift us to the Joy di - vine.
Joy - ful mu - sic leads us Sun-ward In the tri-umph song of life. A-MEN.

# 6 Adoration

Joachim Neander, 1680
Trans. by Catherine Winkworth, 1863    14. 14. 4. 7. 8.

LOBE DEN HERREN
" Stralsund Gesangbuch," 1665
Arr. in " Praxis Pietatis Melica," 1668

*Majestically*

1. Praise ye the Lord, the Al - might - y, the King of cre - a - tion!
2. Praise ye the Lord, who o'er all things so won-drous - ly reign - eth,
3. Praise ye the Lord! O let all that is in me a - dore Him!

O my soul, praise Him, for He is thy health and sal - va - tion!
Shel - ters thee un - der His wings, yea, so gen - tly sus - tain - eth!
All that hath life and breath, come now with prais - es be - fore Him!

All ye who hear, Now to His tem - ple draw near;
Hast thou not seen How thy de - sires e'er have been
Let the A - men Sound from His peo - ple a - gain:

Join me in glad ad - o - ra - - - tion!
Grant - ed in what He or - dain - - - eth?
Glad - ly for aye we a - dore . . . . Him. A - MEN.

# Adoration

WAS LEBET, WAS SCHWEBET
From the "Reinhardt MS.,"
Üttingen, 1754

Rev. John S. B. Monsell (1811-1875)　　13. 10. 13. 10.

*Moderately slow, but with flowing rhythm*

1. O wor - ship the Lord in the beau - ty of ho - li - ness!
2. Low at His feet lay thy bur - den of care - ful - ness,
3. Fear not to en - ter His courts in the slen - der - ness
4. O wor - ship the Lord in the beau - ty of ho - li - ness!

Bow down be - fore Him, His glo - ry pro - claim;
High on His heart He will bear it for thee,
Of the poor wealth thou wouldst reck - on as thine:
Bow down be - fore Him, His glo - ry pro - claim;

With gold of o - be - dience, and in - cense of low - li - ness,
Com - fort thy sor - rows, and an - swer thy prayer - ful - ness,
Truth in its beau - ty, and love in its ten - der - ness,
With gold of o - be - dience, and in - cense of low - li - ness,

Kneel and a - dore Him: the Lord is His name!
Guid - ing thy steps as may best for thee be.
These are the of - ferings to lay on His shrine.
Kneel and a - dore Him: the Lord is His name! A - MEN.

# Adoration

Daniel Ben Judah, 14th century
Revised version of "The Yigdal"

6. 6. 8. 4. D.

YIGDAL (LEONI)
Hebrew melody

*Majestically*

1. The God of Abra-ham praise, All prais-ed be His Name,
2. His spir-it flow-eth free, High sur-ging where it will:
3. He hath e-ter-nal life Im-plant-ed in the soul;

Who was, and is, and is to be, And still the same!
In proph-et's word He spoke of old— He speak-eth still.
His love shall be our strength and stay, While a-ges roll.

The one e-ter-nal God, Ere aught that now ap-pears;
Es-tab-lished is His law, And changeless it shall stand,
Praise to the liv-ing God! All prais-ed be His Name

The First, the Last: be-yond all thought His time-less years!
Deep writ up-on the hu-man heart, On sea, or land.
Who was, and is, and is to be, And still the same! A-MEN.

# Adoration

9

Rev. George Herbert (1593–1632)    10. 4. 6. 6. 6. 6. 10. 4.    Robert Alexander Stewart Macalister

ST. DARERCA

1. Let all the world in ev - ery cor - ner sing, "My God and King!"
2. Let all the world in ev - ery cor - ner sing, "My God and King!"

The heavens are not too high, His praise may thith - er fly;
The Church with psalms must shout, No door can keep them out;

The earth is not too low, His prais - es there may grow.
But a - bove all, the heart Must bear the lar - gest part.

Let all the world in ev - ery cor - ner sing, "My God and King!"
Let all the world in ev - ery cor - ner sing, "My God and King!" A-MEN.

From "The Church Hymnary," Revised. By permission of the Oxford University Press. Copyright, 1927, by the Oxford University Press.

# Adoration

**10**

Stanzas 1 and 2, "Foundling Hospital Collection," 1796
Stanza 3, Edward Osler, 1836

8. 7. 8. 7. D.
(FIRST TUNE)

ALLELUIA (WESLEY)
Samuel Sebastian Wesley (1810-1876)

*In moderate time*

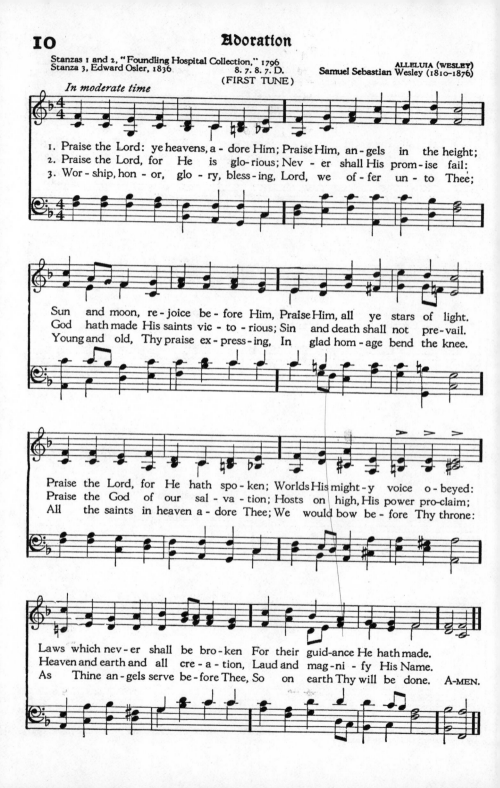

1. Praise the Lord: ye heavens, a - dore Him; Praise Him, an - gels in the height;
2. Praise the Lord, for He is glo - rious; Nev - er shall His prom - ise fail:
3. Wor - ship, hon - or, glo - ry, bless - ing, Lord, we of - fer un - to Thee;

Sun and moon, re - joice be - fore Him, Praise Him, all ye stars of light.
God hath made His saints vic - to - rious; Sin and death shall not pre - vail.
Young and old, Thy praise ex - press - ing, In glad hom - age bend the knee.

Praise the Lord, for He hath spo - ken; Worlds His might - y voice o - beyed:
Praise the God of our sal - va - tion; Hosts on high, His power pro - claim;
All the saints in heaven a - dore Thee; We would bow be - fore Thy throne:

Laws which nev - er shall be bro - ken For their guid-ance He hath made.
Heaven and earth and all cre - a - tion, Laud and mag - ni - fy His Name.
As Thine an - gels serve be - fore Thee, So on earth Thy will be done. A-MEN.

# Adoration

Stanzas 1 and 2, "Foundling Hospital Collection," 1796
Stanza 3, Edward Osler, 1836

8. 7. 8. 7. D.
(SECOND TUNE)

FABEN
John H. Willcox, 1849

*In stately rhythm*

1. Praise the Lord: ye heavens, a - dore Him; Praise Him, an - gels in the height;
2. Praise the Lord, for He is glo - rious; Nev - er shall His prom - ise fail:
3. Wor - ship, hon - or, glo - ry, bless - ing, Lord, we of - fer un - to Thee;

Sun and moon, re - joice be - fore Him, Praise Him, all ye stars of light.
God hath made His saints vic - to - rious; Sin and death shall not pre - vail.
Young and old, Thy praise ex - press - ing, In glad hom - age bend the knee.

Praise the Lord, for He hath spo - ken; Worlds His might - y voice o - beyed;
Praise the God of our sal - va - tion; Hosts on high, His power pro - claim;
All the saints in heaven a - dore Thee; We would bow be - fore Thy throne:

Laws which nev - er shall be bro - ken For their guid-ance He hath made.
Heaven and earth and all cre - a - tion, Laud and mag - ni - fy His Name.
As Thine an - gels serve be - fore Thee, So on earth Thy will be done. A-MEN.

James Montgomery, 1819        7. 7. 7. 7. D.        MENDELSSOHN
Felix Mendelssohn, 1840

*Joyously*

1. Songs of praise the an-gels sang, Heaven with al - le - lu - ias rang,
2. Saints be - low, with heart and voice, Still in songs of praise re - joice;

When Cre - a - tion was be - gun, When God spake and it was done.
Learn-ing here, by faith and love, Songs of praise to sing a - bove.

Songs of praise a - woke the morn When the Prince of Peace was born;
Borne up - on their lat - est breath, Songs of praise shall con-quer death;

Songs of praise a - rose when He Cap - tive led cap - tiv - i - ty,
Then, a - midst e - ter - nal joy, Songs of praise their powers em-ploy,

Songs of praise a - rose when He Cap - tive led cap-tiv - i - ty.
Then, a - midst e - ter - nal joy, Songs of praise their powers employ. A-MEN.

*organ pedal*

From Psalm cl
Rev. Henry Francis Lyte (1793–1847)    7. 7. 7. 7. with Alleluias       LLANFAIR
Robert Williams (c. 1781–1821)

1. Praise the Lord, His glo - ries show, Al – – le - lu - ia!
2. Earth to heaven, and heaven to earth, Al – – le - lu - ia!
3. Praise the Lord, His mer - cies trace, Al – – le - lu - ia!

Saints with - in His courts be - low, Al – – le - lu - ia!
Tell His won - ders, sing His worth, Al – – le - lu - ia!
Praise His prov - i - dence and grace, Al – – le - lu - ia!

An - gels round His throne a - bove, Al – – le - lu - ia!
Age to age and shore to shore, Al – – le - lu - ia!
All that He for man hath done, Al – – le - lu - ia!

All that see and share His love. Al – le - lu - ia!
Praise Him, praise Him ev - er - more! Al – le - lu - ia!
All He sends us through His Son. Al – le - lu - ia! A-MEN.

Tune from "The Church Hymnary." Revised. Used by permission of the Oxford University Press.

# 13
## Adoration

Rev. Calvin W. Laufer, 1931     8. 8. 4, 4. 8. 8. with Alleluias

LASST UNS ERFREUEN
"Geistliche Kirchengesäng,"
Cologne, 1623

*In unison. With feeling*

1. Thee, ho - ly Fa - ther, we a - dore; We sing Thy prais-es o'er and o'er:
2. Thou fill-est heaven and earth and sea With sov-ereign power and maj-es - ty:
3. Our souls on wings of rap-ture rise To swell the choirs of Par - a - dise:

*Harmony*     *Unison*

Al - le - lu - ia, Al - le - lu - ia! With ser-aph throngs join heart and voice,
Al - le - lu - ia, Al - le - lu - ia! Yet where the poor in spir - it meet,
Al - le - lu - ia, Al - le - lu - ia! En-thralled and thrilled, we Thee a - dore,

*Harmony*

Ac - claim Thy glo - ry, and re - joice: Al - le - lu - ia, Al - le -
There is Thy bless - ed mer - cy seat: Al - le - lu - ia, Al - le -
Who art our God for - ev - er - more. Al - le - lu - ia, Al - le -

*Unison*

lu - ia, Al - le - lu - ia, Al - le - lu - ia, Al - le - lu - ia!
lu - ia, Al - le - lu - ia, Al - le - lu - ia, Al - le - lu - ia!
lu - ia, Al - le - lu - ia, Al - le - lu - ia, Al - le - lu - ia! A-MEN.

Words copyright, 1933, by Calvin W. Laufer. Used by permission.
Tune from "Songs of Praise." Used by permission of the Oxford University Press.

# Adoration

**14**

From Psalm ciii
Rev. Henry Francis Lyte, 1834

8. 7. 8. 7. 8. 7.

BENEDIC ANIMA MEA
John Goss, 1867

*With dignity and joy*

1. Praise, my soul, the King of heav - en, To His feet thy
2. Praise Him for His grace and fa - vor To our fa - thers
3. Fa - ther - like, He tends and spares us; Well our fee - ble
4. An - gels, help us to a - dore Him— Ye be - hold Him

trib - ute bring; Ran - somed, healed, re - stored, for - giv - en,
in dis - tress; Praise Him, still the same for - ev - er,
frame He knows, In His hands He gen - tly bears us,
face to face; Sun and moon, bow down be - fore Him;

Who, like me, His praise should sing? Praise Him! praise Him!
Slow to chide, and swift to bless. Praise Him! praise Him!
Res - cues us from all our foes. Praise Him! praise Him!
Dwell - ers all in time and space, Praise Him! praise Him!

Praise Him! praise Him! Praise the Ev - er - last - ing King!
Praise Him! praise Him! Glo - rious in His faith - ful - ness!
Praise Him! praise Him! Wide - ly as His mer - cy flows!
Praise Him! praise Him! Praise with us the God of grace! A-MEN.

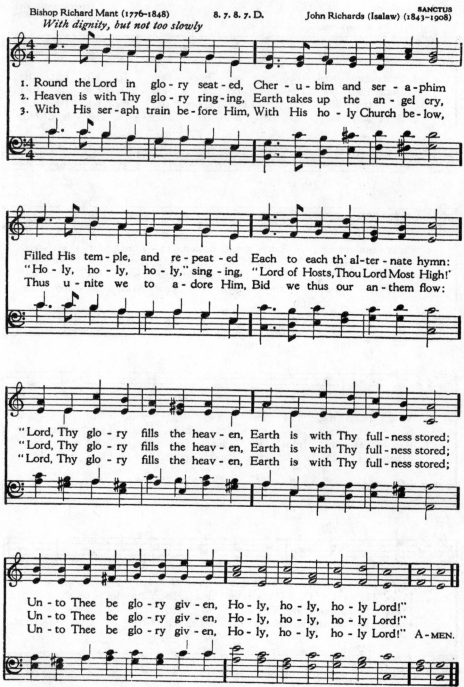

Bishop Richard Mant (1776-1848)     8. 7. 8. 7. D.     John Richards (Isalaw) (1843-1908)    SANCTUS

*With dignity, but not too slowly*

1. Round the Lord in glo-ry seat-ed, Cher-u-bim and ser-a-phim
2. Heaven is with Thy glo-ry ring-ing, Earth takes up the an-gel cry,
3. With His ser-aph train be-fore Him, With His ho-ly Church be-low,

Filled His tem-ple, and re-peat-ed Each to each th' al-ter-nate hymn:
"Ho-ly, ho-ly, ho-ly," sing-ing, "Lord of Hosts, Thou Lord Most High!"
Thus u-nite we to a-dore Him, Bid we thus our an-them flow:

"Lord, Thy glo-ry fills the heav-en, Earth is with Thy full-ness stored;
"Lord, Thy glo-ry fills the heav-en, Earth is with Thy full-ness stored;
"Lord, Thy glo-ry fills the heav-en, Earth is with Thy full-ness stored;

Un-to Thee be glo-ry giv-en, Ho-ly, ho-ly, ho-ly Lord!"
Un-to Thee be glo-ry giv-en, Ho-ly, ho-ly, ho-ly Lord!"
Un-to Thee be glo-ry giv-en, Ho-ly, ho-ly, ho-ly Lord!" A-MEN.

**16**

Psalm ciii. "Scottish Psalter," 1650     C. M.     Maurice Greene (1696-1755)
(FIRST TUNE)

*With majesty*

1. O thou my soul, bless God the Lord; And all that in me is
2. Bless, O my soul, the Lord thy God, And not for - get - ful be
3. All thine in - iq - ui - ties who doth Most gra - cious - ly for - give;
4. Who doth re - deem thy life, that thou To death mayst not go down;
5. Who with a - bun-dance of good things Doth sat - is - fy thy mouth;

Be stir - red up His ho - ly Name To mag - ni - fy and bless.
Of all His gra - cious ben - e - fits He hath be-stowed on thee:
Who thy dis - eas - es all and pains Doth heal, and thee re - lieve:
Who thee with lov - ing - kind-ness doth And ten - der mer - cies crown:
So that, even as the ea - gle's age, Re - new - ed is thy youth. A - MEN.

**16**

Psalm ciii. "Scottish Psalter," 1650     C. M.     Hugh Wilson (1766-1824)
(SECOND TUNE)

*With dignity and flowing rhythm*

1. O thou my soul, bless God the Lord; And all that in me is
2. Bless, O my soul, the Lord thy God, And not for - get - ful be
3. All thine in - iq - ui - ties who doth Most gra - cious - ly for - give;
4. Who doth re - deem thy life, that thou To death mayst not go down;
5. Who with a - bun - dance of good things Doth sat - is - fy thy mouth;

Be stir - red up His ho - ly Name To mag - ni - fy and bless.
Of all His gra - cious ben - e - fits He hath be-stowed on thee:
Who thy dis - eas - es all and pains Doth heal, and thee re - lieve:
Who thee with lov - ing-kind-ness doth And ten - der mer - cies crown:
So that, even as the ea - gle's age, Re - new - ed is thy youth. A - MEN.

# 17 Adoration

Johann Olaf Wallin (1779–1839)
Trans. by Charles Wharton Stork

8. 8. 10. 10.

WALLIN
Melody of 1529

*In unison, and stately rhythm*

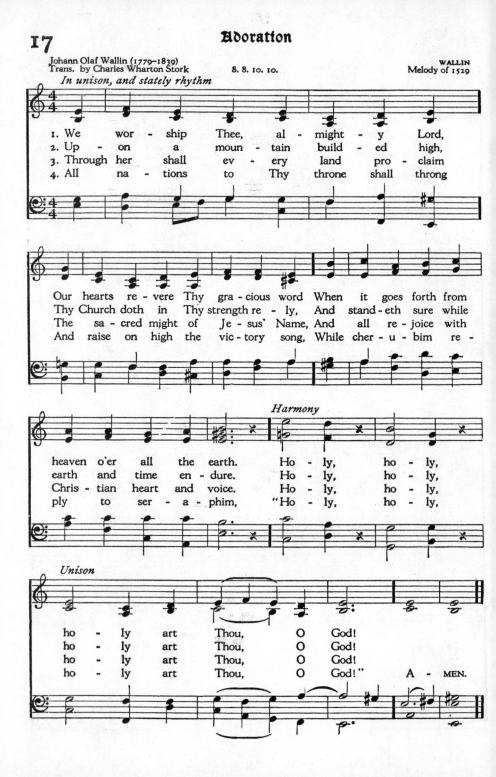

1. We wor - ship Thee, al - might - y Lord,
2. Up - on a moun - tain build - ed high,
3. Through her shall ev - ery land pro - claim
4. All na - tions to Thy throne shall throng

Our hearts re - vere Thy gra - cious word When it goes forth from
Thy Church doth in Thy strength re - ly, And stand - eth sure while
The sa - cred might of Je - sus' Name, And all re - joice with
And raise on high the vic - tory song, While cher - u - bim re -

*Harmony*

heaven o'er all the earth. Ho - ly, ho - ly,
earth and time en - dure. Ho - ly, ho - ly,
Chris - tian heart and voice. Ho - ly, ho - ly,
ply to ser - a - phim, "Ho - ly, ho - ly,

*Unison*

ho - ly art Thou, O God!
ho - ly art Thou, O God!
ho - ly art Thou, O God!
ho - ly art Thou, O God!" A - MEN.

MENDEBRAS
Old German melody
Arr. by Lowell Mason, 1839

Bishop Christopher Wordsworth, 1862      7. 6. 7. 6. D.

*With joy*

1. O day of rest and glad-ness, O day of joy and light,
2. On thee, at the Cre-a-tion, The light first had its birth;
3. New gra-ces ev-er gain-ing From this our day of rest,

O balm of care and sad-ness, Most beau-ti-ful, most bright;
On thee, for our sal-va-tion, Christ rose from depths of earth;
We reach the rest re-main-ing To spir-its of the blest.

On thee the high and low-ly, Through a-ges joined in tune,
On thee our Lord, vic-to-rious, The Spir-it sent from heaven;
To Ho-ly Ghost be prais-es, To Fa-ther, and to Son;

Sing ho-ly, ho-ly, ho-ly, To the great God Tri-une.
And thus on thee, most glo-rious, A tri-ple light was given.
The Church her voice up-rais-es To Thee, blest Three in One. A-MEN.

# The Lord's Day

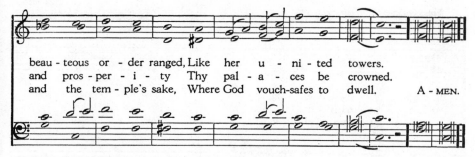

beau - teous or - der ranged, Like her u - ni - ted towers.
and pros - per - i - ty Thy pal - a - ces be crowned.
and the tem - ple's sake, Where God vouch-safes to dwell. A - MEN.

Tune copyright by Mrs. Horatio Parker. Used by permission.

## 20

Rev. John Ellerton, 1867

S. M.

Johann M. Spiess, 1745

SWABIA

*In moderate time*

1. This is the day of light: Let there be light to - day;
2. This is the day of rest: Our fail - ing strength re - new;
3. This is the day of peace: Thy peace our spir - its fill;
4. This is the day of prayer: Let earth to heaven draw near:

O Day-spring, rise up - on our night, And chase its gloom a - way.
On wea - ry brain and trou - bled breast Shed Thou Thy freshening dew.
Bid Thou the blasts of dis - cord cease, The waves of strife be still.
Lift up our hearts to seek Thee there; Come down to meet us here. A-MEN.

5. This is the first of days:
   Send forth Thy quickening breath,
   And wake dead souls to love and praise,
   O Vanquisher of death!

LIEBSTER JESU

Rev. Benjamin Schmolck, 1714
Trans. by Catherine Winkworth, 1858

Melody by Johann R. Ahle (1625–1673)
7. 8. 7. 8. 7. 7.   Arr. by Johann Sebastian Bach (1685–1750)
(FIRST TUNE)

*In moderate time*

1. Light of light, en - light - en me, Now a - new the
2. Let me with my heart to - day, Ho - ly, ho - ly,
3. Hence all care, all van - i - ty! For the day to

day is dawn - ing; Sun of grace, the shad - ows flee;
ho - ly, sing - ing, Rapt a - while from earth a - way,
God is ho - ly; Come, Thou glo - rious Maj - es - ty,

Bright - en Thou my Sab - bath morn - ing; With Thy joy - ous
All my soul to Thee up - spring - ing, Have a fore - taste
Deign to fill this tem - ple low - ly; Naught to - day my

sun - shine blest, Hap - py is my day of rest.
in - ly given How they wor - ship Thee in heaven.
soul shall move, Sim - ply rest - ing in Thy love.        A-MEN.

# The Lord's Day

Rev. Benjamin Schmolck, 1714
Trans. by Catherine Winkworth, 1858

7. 8. 7. 8. 7. 7.
(SECOND TUNE)

HINCHMAN
Uzziah C. Burnap, 1869

*With dignity*

1. Light of light, en-light-en me, Now a-new the day is dawn-ing; Sun of grace, the shad-ows flee; Bright-en Thou my Sab-bath morn-ing; With Thy joy-ous sun-shine blest, Hap-py is my day of rest.

2. Let me with my heart to-day, Ho-ly, ho-ly, ho-ly, sing-ing, Rapt a-while from earth a-way, All my soul to Thee up-spring-ing, Have a fore-taste in-ly given How they wor-ship Thee in heaven.

3. Hence all care, all van-i-ty! For the day to God is ho-ly; Come, Thou glo-rious Maj-es-ty, Deign to fill this tem-ple low-ly; Naught to-day my soul shall move, Sim-ply rest-ing in Thy love. A-MEN.

**22**

From Psalm xcii
Rev. Isaac Watts, 1719

L. M.

GRACE CHURCH
Ignaz J. Pleyel, 1815

*In flowing rhythm*

1. Sweet is the work, my God, my King, To praise Thy Name, give thanks and sing;
2. Sweet is the day of sa - cred rest; No mor - tal cares shall seize my breast;
3. My heart shall tri-umph in my Lord, And bless His works, and bless His word;
4. Then shall I see and hear and know All I de - sired or wished be - low;

To show Thy love by morn-ing light, And talk of all Thy truth at night.
O may my heart in tune be found, Like Da-vid's harp of sol - emn sound.
Thy works of grace, how bright they shine! How deep Thy counsels, how di-vine!
And ev-ery power find sweet em-ploy In that e - ter-nal world of joy. A-MEN.

**23**

From Psalm cxviii
Rev. Isaac Watts, 1719

C. M.

ARLINGTON
Thomas A. Arne, 1762

*With joy*

1. This is the day the Lord hath made; He calls the hours His own;
2. To - day He rose and left the dead, And Sa-tan's em - pire fell;
3. Ho - san - na to th' a-noint - ed King, To Da-vid's ho - ly Son!
4. Ho - san - na in the high - est strains The Church on earth can raise!

Let heaven re - joice, let earth be glad, And praise sur-round the throne.
To - day the saints His tri-umphs spread, And all His won-ders tell.
Help us, O Lord; de-scend and bring Sal - va-tion from the throne.
The high - est heavens in which He reigns Shall give Him no - bler praise. A-MEN.

Gregory the Great (540-604)
Trans. by Percy Dearmer

11. 11. 11. 5.

CHRISTE SANCTORUM
La Feillée's "Méthode du
Plain Chant," 1808

*To be sung in unison; in moderate time*

1. Fa - ther, we praise Thee, now the night is o - ver;
2. Mon - arch of all things, fit us for Thy man - sions;
3. All - ho - ly Fa - ther, Son, and Ho - ly Spir - it,

Ac - tive and watch - ful, stand we all be - fore Thee;
Ban - ish our weak - ness, health and whole - ness send - ing;
Trin - i - ty bless - ed, send us Thy sal - va - tion;

Sing - ing, we of - fer prayer and med - i -
Bring us to heav - en, where Thy saints u -
Thine is the glo - ry, gleam - ing and re -

*Harmony*

ta - tion: Thus we a - dore Thee.
nit - ed Joy with - out end - ing.
sound - ing Through all cre - a - tion. A - MEN.

From "The Church Hymnary," Revised. Used by permission of the Oxford University Press.
Words from "The English Hymnal." Used by permission of the Oxford University Press.

Latin; trans. by "O. B. C."
Recast by Horatio Nelson, 1864

7. 7. 7. 7.

INNOCENTS
Arr. from 13th century French melody in
"The Parish Choir," 1850

*In moderate time*

1. As the sun doth dai - ly rise, Bright-ening all the
2. Day by day pro - vide us food, For from Thee come
3. Be our Guard in sin and strife; Be the Lead - er
4. Quick-ened by the Spir - it's grace All Thy ho - ly

morn - ing skies, So to Thee with one ac - cord
all things good; Strength un - to our souls af - ford
of our life; Lest from Thee we stray a - broad,
will to trace While we dai - ly search Thy Word,

Lift we up our hearts, O Lord!
From Thy liv - ing Bread, O Lord!
Stay our way - ward feet, O Lord!
Wis - dom true im - part, O Lord! A - MEN.

5. Praise we, with the heavenly host,
Father, Son, and Holy Ghost;
Thee would we with one accord
Praise and magnify, O Lord!

Rev. Charles Wesley, 1740     7. 7. 7. 7. 7. 7.     LUX PRIMA   Charles F. Gounod, 1872

*In moderate time*

1. Christ, whose glo - ry fills the skies, Christ the true, the on - ly Light, Sun of Right - eous - ness, a - rise, Tri - umph o'er the shades of night; Day - spring from on high, be near; Day - Star, in my heart ap - pear.

2. Dark and cheer - less is the morn Un - ac - com - pa - nied by Thee; Joy - less is the day's re - turn Till Thy mer - cy's beams I see; Till they in - ward light im - part, Glad my eyes and warm my heart.

3. Vis - it, then, this soul of mine; Pierce the gloom of sin and grief; Fill me, Ra - dian - cy di - vine; Scat - ter all my un - be - lief; More and more Thy - self dis - play, Shin - ing to the per - fect day. A - MEN.

**27**

From Psalm xix
Joachim Neander (1650–1680)

7. 7. 7. 7.

GOTT SEI DANK DURCH ALLE WELT
"Freylinghausen's Gesangbuch,"
Halle, 1704

*May be sung in unison. With spirit*

1. Heaven and earth, and sea and air, All their Mak-er's praise de-clare;
2. See the glo-rious orb of day Breaking through the clouds his way;
3. See how He hath ev-ery-where Made this earth so rich and fair;
4. Lord, great won-ders work-est Thou! To Thy sway all crea-tures bow;

Wake, my soul, a-wake and sing: Now thy grate-ful prais-es bring.
Moon and stars with sil-very light Praise Him through the si-lent night.
Hill and vale and fruit-ful land, All things liv-ing, show His hand.
Write Thou deep-ly in my heart What I am, and what Thou art. A-MEN.

**28**

From Psalm v
Rev. Isaac Watts, 1719

C. M.

KILMARNOCK
Neil Dougall (1776–1862)

*In moderate time*

1. Lord, in the morn-ing Thou shalt hear My voice as-cend-ing high;
2. Up to the hills, where Christ is gone To plead for all His saints,
3. Thou art a God be-fore whose sight The wick-ed shall not stand;
4. But to Thy house will I re-sort, To taste Thy mer-cies there;
5. O may Thy Spir-it guide my feet In ways of right-eous-ness;

To Thee I will di-rect my prayer, To Thee lift up mine eye:
Pre-sent-ing at His Fa-ther's throne Our songs and our complaints.
Sin-ners shall ne'er be Thy de-light, Nor dwell at Thy right hand.
I will fre-quent Thy ho-ly court, And wor-ship in Thy fear.
Make ev-ery path of du-ty straight And plain be-fore my face. A-MEN.

# Morning

Rev. Louis F. Benson, 1897

8. 4. 8. 4. 8. 4.

WENTWORTH
Frederick C. Maker, 1876

*In moderate time*

1. The sun is on the land and sea,
2. Thy love was ev - er in our view,
3. We do not know what grief or care
4. All glo - ry to the Fa - ther be,

The day be - gun; Our morn - ing hymn be
Like stars, by night; Thy gifts are ev - ery
The day may bring: The heart shall find some
With Christ the Son, And, Ho - ly Spir - it,

gins with Thee, Blest Three in One; Our praise shall rise con -
morn - ing new, O God of light; Thy mer - cy, like the
glad - ness there That loves its King; The life that serves Thee
un - to Thee, For - ev - er One; All glo - ry to the

tin - ual - ly Till day is done.
heav - ens' blue, Fills all our sight.
ev - ery - where Can al - ways sing.
Trin - i - ty While a - ges run!

A - MEN.

Christian Knorr von Rosenroth (1636–1689)
Trans. by Jane Laurie Borthwick (1813–1897)

7. 7. 7. 7. 7. 3.

MORGENGLANZ DER EWIGKEIT
"Freylinghausen's Gesangbuch,"
Halle, 1704

In moderate time

1. Je - sus, Sun of Right - eous-ness, Bright - est Beam of
2. As on droop - ing herb and flower Falls the soft, re -
3. Like the sun's re - viv - ing ray, May Thy love, with
4. O our on - ly Hope and Guide, Nev - er leave us,

love di - - - vine, With the ear - ly
fresh - ing dew, Let Thy Spir - it's
ten - der glow, All our cold - ness
nor for - - - sake; Keep us ev - er

morn - ing rays Do Thou on our dark - ness shine,
grace and power All our wea - ry souls re - new,
melt a - way, Warm and cheer us forth to go,
at Thy side Till th' e - ter - nal morn - ing break,

And dis - pel with pur - est light All our night.
Showers of bless - ing o - ver all Soft - ly fall.
Glad - ly serve Thee and o - bey, All the day.
Mov - ing on to Zi - on hill, Home - ward still. A-MEN.

From "The Church Hymnary," Revised. Used by permission of the Oxford University Press.

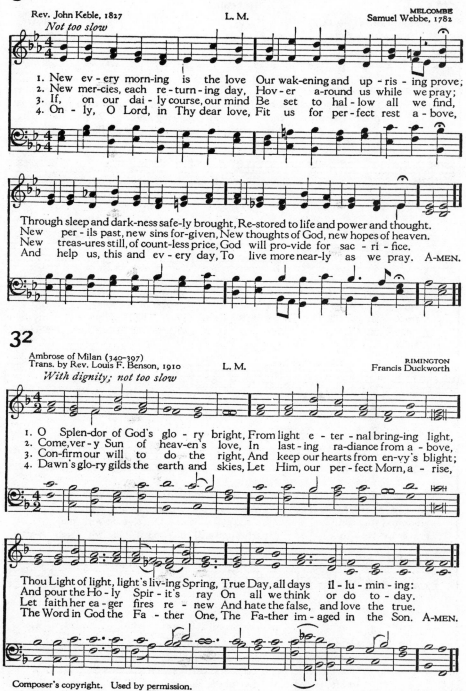

**31**

**Morning**

Rev. John Keble, 1827    L. M.    MELCOMBE
Samuel Webbe, 1782

*Not too slow*

1. New ev - ery morn-ing is the love Our wak-ening and up - ris - ing prove;
2. New mer-cies, each re - turn-ing day, Hov - er a-round us while we pray;
3. If, on our dai - ly course, our mind Be set to hal - low all we find,
4. On - ly, O Lord, in Thy dear love, Fit us for per - fect rest a - bove,

Through sleep and dark-ness safe-ly brought, Re-stored to life and power and thought.
New per - ils past, new sins for-given, New thoughts of God, new hopes of heaven.
New treas-ures still, of count-less price, God will pro-vide for sac - ri - fice.
And help us, this and ev - ery day, To live more near-ly as we pray. A-MEN.

**32**

Ambrose of Milan (340–397)
Trans. by Rev. Louis F. Benson, 1910    L. M.    RIMINGTON
Francis Duckworth

*With dignity; not too slow*

1. O Splen-dor of God's glo - ry bright, From light e - ter - nal bring-ing light,
2. Come, ver - y Sun of heav-en's love, In last - ing ra-diance from a - bove,
3. Con-firm our will to do the right, And keep our hearts from en-vy's blight;
4. Dawn's glo-ry gilds the earth and skies, Let Him, our per - fect Morn, a - rise,

Thou Light of light, light's liv-ing Spring, True Day, all days il - lu - min - ing:
And pour the Ho - ly Spir - it's ray On all we think or do to - day.
Let faith her ea - ger fires re - new And hate the false, and love the true.
The Word in God the Fa - ther One, The Fa-ther im - aged in the Son. A-MEN.

Composer's copyright.   Used by permission.

Rev. Henry Francis Lyte, 1847     10. 10. 10. 10.     EVENTIDE (MONK)
William H. Monk, 1861

*In moderate time*

1. A - bide with me: fast falls the e - ven - tide; The dark-ness
2. Swift to its close ebbs out life's lit - tle day; Earth's joys grow
3. I need Thy pres - ence ev - ery pass - ing hour; What but Thy
4. I fear no foe, with Thee at hand to bless: Ills have no

deep - ens; Lord, with me a - bide: When oth - er help - ers
dim, its glo - ries pass a - way; Change and de - cay in
grace can foil the Tempt - er's power? Who like Thy - self my
weight, and tears no bit - ter - ness. Where is death's sting? Where,

fail, and com-forts flee, Help of the help-less, O a - bide with me.
all a - round I see; O Thou who chang-est not, a - bide with me.
guide and stay can be? Through cloud and sunshine, O a - bide with me.
grave, thy vic - to - ry? I tri-umph still, if Thou a - bide with me. A-MEN.

5. Hold Thou Thy cross before my closing eyes;
   Shine through the gloom, and point me to the skies:
   Heaven's morning breaks, and earth's vain shadows flee:
   In life, in death, O Lord, abide with me.

# 34
## Evening

Bishop George W. Doane, 1824      7. 7. 7. 7.      SEYMOUR      Carl M. von Weber, 1826

*Not too fast*

1. Soft - ly now the light of day Fades up - on my sight a - way;
2. Thou, whose all - per - vad - ing eye Naught es - capes, with - out, with - in,
3. Soon for me the light of day Shall for - ev - er pass a - way;
4. Thou who, sin - less, yet hast known All of man's in - fir - mi - ty;

Free from care, from la - bor free, Lord, I would com-mune with Thee.
Par - don each in - fir - mi - ty, O - pen fault, and se - cret sin.
Then, from sin and sor - row free, Take me, Lord, to dwell with Thee.
Then, from Thine e - ter - nal throne, Je - sus, look with pity-ing eye. A - MEN.

# 35

Rev. Sabine Baring-Gould, 1865      6. 5. 6. 5.      MERRIAL      Joseph Barnby, 1868

*With graceful rhythm*

1. Now the day is o - ver, Night is draw - ing nigh,
2. Je - sus, give the wea - ry Calm and sweet re - pose;
3. Grant to lit - tle chil - dren Vi - sions bright of Thee;
4. Through the long night watch - es, May Thine an - gels spread
5. When the morn - ing wak - ens, Then may I a - rise

Shad - ows of the eve - ning Steal a - cross the sky.
With Thy ten - derest bless - ing May mine eye - lids close.
Guard the sail - ors toss - ing On the deep blue sea.
Their white wings a - bove me, Watch-ing round my bed.
Pure, and fresh, and sin - less In Thy ho - ly eyes. A - MEN.

Words used by permission of A. W. Ridley and Company.

Adelaide A. Procter, 1861
Stanza 3, line 7, alt.

C. M. D.

ST. LEONARD (HILES)
Henry Hiles, 1867

*In moderate time*

1. The shad-ows of the eve-ning hours Fall from the dark-ening sky;
2. The sor-rows of Thy serv-ants, Lord, O do not Thou de-spise,
3. Let peace, O Lord, Thy peace, O God, Up-on our souls de-scend;

Up-on the fra-grance of the flowers The dews of eve-ning lie:
But let the in-cense of our prayers Be-fore Thy mer-cy rise.
From mid-night fears and per-ils, Thou Our trem-bling hearts de-fend:

Be-fore Thy throne, O Lord of heaven, We kneel at close of day;
The bright-ness of the com-ing night Up-on the dark-ness rolls;
Give us a res-pite from our toil, Calm and sub-due our woes;

Look on Thy chil-dren from on high, And hear us while we pray.
With hopes of fu-ture glo-ry chase The shad-ows from our souls.
Through the long day we la-bor, Lord, O give us now re-pose. A-MEN.

EVENING PRAISE

Mary A. Lathbury, 1877  7. 7. 7. 7. 4. with Refrain  William F. Sherwin, 1877

*Quietly and reverently*

1. Day is dy - ing in the west; Heaven is touch - ing
2. Lord of life, be - neath the dome Of the u - ni -
3. While the deep - ening shad - ows fall, Heart of Love, en -
4. When for - ev - er from our sight Pass the stars, the

earth with rest: Wait and wor - ship while the night
verse, Thy home, Gath - er us who seek Thy face
fold - ing all, Through the glo - ry and the grace
day, the night, Lord of an - gels, on our eyes

Sets her eve - ning lamps a - light Through all the sky.
To the fold of Thy em - brace, For Thou art nigh.
Of the stars that veil Thy face, Our hearts as - cend.
Let e - ter - nal morn - ing rise, And shad - ows end.

REFRAIN

Ho - ly, ho - ly, ho - ly Lord God of Hosts! Heaven and earth are full of Thee!

Heaven and earth are prais - ing Thee, O Lord Most High! A - MEN.

Used by permission of the Chautauqua Institution.

# Evening

Robert Walmsley, 1893      8. 4. 8. 4. D.      VINCENT
Horatio Richmond Palmer (1834-1907)

*In moderate time ; quietly*

1. The sun de-clines; o'er land and sea Creeps on the night;
2. For-give the wrong this day we've done, Or thought, or said;

The twin-kling stars come one by one To shed their light;
Each mo-ment with its good or ill To Thee has fled;

With Thee there is no dark-ness, Lord; With us a-bide,
O Fa-ther, in Thy mer-cy great Will we con-fide;

And 'neath Thy wings we rest se-cure This e-ven-tide.
Thy ben-e-dic-tion now be-stow This e-ven-tide. A-MEN.

Words used by permission of Miss Clara S. Walmsley.

Bishop Reginald Heber (1783–1826)
Rev. William Mercer, 1864, stanza 2
Rev. Richard Whately (1787–1863), stanza 3
8. 4. 8. 4. 8. 8. 8. 4.

AR HYD Y NOS
Welsh traditional melody
Harmonized by L. O. Emerson, 1906

*In flowing rhythm*

1. God, that mad - est earth and heav - en, Dark - ness and light;
2. And when morn a - gain shall call us To run life's way,
3. Guard us wak - ing, guard us sleep - ing, And when we die,

Who the day for toil hast giv - en, For rest the night;
May we still, what - e'er be - fall us, Thy will o - bey.
May we in Thy might - y keep - ing All peace - ful lie;

May Thine an - gel guards de - fend us, Slum - ber sweet Thy mer - cy send us;
From the power of e - vil hide us, In the nar - row path - way guide us,
When the last dread call shall wake us, Do not Thou, our God, for - sake us

Ho - ly dreams and hopes at - tend us, This live - long night.
Nor Thy smile be e'er de - nied us The live - long day.
But to reign in glo - ry take us With Thee on high. A-MEN.

Bishop Thomas Ken (1637–1711)          L. M.          TALLIS' CANON
Thomas Tallis (c. 1520–1585)

*With dignity*

1. All praise to Thee, my God, this night,
2. For - give me, Lord, for Thy dear Son,
3. Teach me to live, that I may dread
4. O may my soul on Thee re - pose.

For all the bless - ings of the light; Keep me, O keep me,
The ill that I this day have done, That with the world, my -
The grave as lit - tle as my bed; Teach me to die, that
And with sweet sleep mine eye - lids close; Sleep that may me more

King of kings, Be - neath Thine own al - might - y wings.
self, and Thee, I, ere I sleep, at peace may be.
so I may Rise glo - rious at the aw - ful day.
vig - orous make To serve my God when I a - wake.  A-MEN.

5. Praise God, from whom all blessings flow;
   Praise Him, all creatures here below;
   Praise Him above, ye heavenly host;
   Praise Father, Son, and Holy Ghost.

43

ANGELUS
Georg Joseph
"Heilige Seelenlust," 1657

Rev. Henry Twells, 1868    L. M.

*In moderate time*

1. At e - ven, when the sun was set, The sick, O
2. Once more 'tis e - ven - tide, and we, Op - pressed with
3. O Sav - iour Christ, our woes dis - pel: For some are
4. And none, O Lord, have per - fect rest, For none are

Lord, a - round Thee lay; O in what di - vers
va - rious ills, draw near: What if Thy form we
sick, and some are sad, And some have nev - er
whol - ly free from sin; And they who fain would

pains they met! O with what joy they went a - way!
can - not see? We know and feel that Thou art here.
loved Thee well, And some have lost the love they had;
serve Thee best Are con - scious most of wrong with - in.    A - MEN.

5. O Saviour Christ, Thou too art man;
    Thou hast been troubled, tempted, tried;
    Thy kind but searching glance can scan
    The very wounds that shame would hide.

6. Thy touch has still its ancient power;
    No word from Thee can fruitless fall;
    Hear in this solemn evening hour,
    And in Thy mercy heal us all.

# 44 Evening

From a Greek service, 6th or 7th century
Trans. by Rev. John M. Neale, 1853, 1862  7. 6. 7. 6. 8. 8.

ST. ANATOLIUS (BROWN)
Arthur H. Brown, 1862

*In moderate time*

1. The day is past and o - ver: All thanks, O Lord, to Thee;
2. The joys of day are o - ver: I lift my heart to Thee,
3. The toils of day are o - ver: I raise the hymn to Thee,
4. Be Thou my soul's Pre - serv - er, O God, for Thou dost know

I pray Thee that of - fense - less The hours of dark may be.
And call on Thee that sin - less The hours of night may be.
And ask that free from per - il The hours of fear may be.
How man - y are the per - ils Through which I have to go.

O Je - sus, keep me in Thy sight,
O Je - sus, make their dark - ness light,
O Je - sus, keep me in Thy sight,
Lov - er of men, O hear my call,

And save me through the com - ing night.
And save me through the com - ing night.
And guard me through the com - ing night.
And guard and save me from them all.  A-MEN.

Music from "The Church Hymnary," Revised. Used by permission of the Oxford University Press.

# 45

Rev. John Ellerton, 1870
9. 8. 9. 8.
ST. CLEMENT
Rev. Clement C. Scholefield, 1874

*In moderate time; with flowing rhythm*

1. The day Thou gav - est, Lord, is end - ed, The dark - ness
2. We thank Thee that Thy Church un - sleep - ing, While earth rolls
3. As o'er each con - ti - nent and is - land The dawn leads
4. The sun that bids us rest is wak - ing Our breth - ren

falls at Thy be - hest; To Thee our morn - ing hymns as -
on - ward in - to light, Through all the world her watch is
on an - oth - er day, The voice of prayer is nev - er
'neath the west - ern sky, And hour by hour fresh lips are

cend - ed, Thy praise shall hal - low now our rest.
keep - ing, And rests not now by day or night.
si - lent, Nor dies the strain of praise a - way.
mak - ing Thy won - drous do - ings heard on high. A - MEN.

5. So be it, Lord; Thy throne shall never,
   Like earth's proud empires, pass away;
   But stand, and rule, and grow forever,
   Till all Thy creatures own Thy sway.

Francis T. Palgrave, 1865       L. M.       ABENDS
Herbert S. Oakeley, 1874

*In moderate time*

1. O Light of life, O Sav-iour dear, Be-fore we sleep, bow down Thine ear;
2. Oft from Thy roy-al road we part, Lost in the maz-es of the heart:
3. What sud-den sun-beams cheer our sight! What dawn-ing risen up-on the night!
4. Through day and dark-ness, Sav-iour dear, A-bide with us, more near-ly near;

Through dark and day, o'er land and sea, We have no oth-er hope but Thee.
Our lamps put out, our course for-got, We seek for God, and find Him not.
Thou giv'st Thy-self to us, and we Find guide and path and all in Thee.
Till on Thy face we lift our eyes, The Sun of God's own Par-a-dise. A-MEN.

*org.*

**47**

James Edmeston, 1820       8. 7. 8. 7.       EVENING PRAYER
George C. Stebbins, 1878

*Rather slowly*

1. Sav-iour, breathe an eve-ning bless-ing, Ere re-pose our spir-its seal;
2. Though de-struc-tion walk a-round us, Though the ar-row past us fly,
3. Though the night be dark and drear-y, Dark-ness can-not hide from Thee;
4. Should swift death this night o'er-take us, And our couch be-come our tomb,

Sin and want we come con-fess-ing: Thou canst save, and Thou canst heal.
An-gel guards from Thee surround us: We are safe if Thou art nigh.
Thou art He who, nev-er wea-ry, Watch-est where Thy peo-ple be.
May the morn in heaven a-wake us, Clad in light and death-less bloom. A-MEN.

Copyright, 1919, by George C. Stebbins. Renewal, Hope Publishing Company, owner.

Lucy E. G. Whitmore, 1824   10. 10. 10. 10.   Joseph Barnby, 1872

LONGWOOD

*In moderate time.   With dignity*

1. Fa - ther, a - gain in Je - sus' Name we meet,
2. O we would bless Thee for Thy cease - less care,
3. A - las, un - wor - thy of Thy bound - less love,
4. O by that Name in whom all full - ness dwells,

And bow in pen - i - tence be - neath Thy feet;
And all Thy works from day to day de - clare:
Too oft with care - less feet from Thee we rove;
O by that love which ev - ery love ex - cels,

A - gain to Thee our fee - ble voi - ces raise,
Is not our life with hour - ly mer - cies crowned?
But now, en - cour - aged by Thy voice, we come,
O by that blood so free - ly shed for sin,

To sue for mer - cy, and to sing Thy praise.
Does not Thine arm en - cir - cle us a - round?
Re - turn - ing sin - ners to a Fa - ther's home.
O - pen blest mer - cy's gate, and take us in!   A - MEN.

Music copyright.   Used by permission of Novello and Company, Ltd.

**Opening**

Psalm xcv
"Scottish Psalter," 1650

C. M.
(THE VENITE)

Melody from "A Collection of
Hymns and Sacred Poems," Dublin, 1749

1. O come, let us sing to the Lord,
   To Him our voices raise; With joyful noise let
   us the Rock Of our salvation praise.

2. Let us before His presence come
   With praise, and thankful voice; Let us sing psalms to
   Him with grace, And make a joyful noise.

3. For God's a great God, and great King;
   Above all gods He is. The depths of earth are
   in His hand; The heights of hills are His.

4. To Him the spacious sea belongs,
   For He the same did make; The dry land also
   from His hands Its form at first did take. A - MEN.

5. O come, and let us worship Him;
Let us bow down withal,
And on our knees before the Lord,
Our Maker, let us fall.

From Psalm lxxxiv
Rev. Isaac Watts, 1719
Stanza 4 alt.

6. 6. 6. 6. 8. 8.

DARWALL'S 148TH
Rev. John Darwall, 1770

*Joyously*

1. Lord of the worlds a - bove, How pleas - ant and how fair
2. O hap - py souls that pray Where God ap - points to hear!
3. They go from strength to strength, Through this dark vale of tears,
4. God is our Sun and Shield, Our Light and our De - fense;

The dwell - ings of Thy love, Thine earth - ly
O hap - py men that pay Their con - stant
Till each ar - rives at length, Till each in
With gifts His hands are filled: We draw our

tem - ples, are! To Thine a - bode my heart as - pires,
serv - ice there! They praise Thee still; and hap - py they
heaven ap - pears: O glo - rious seat, when God, our King,
bless - ings thence. Thrice hap - py he, O God of Hosts,

With warm de - sires to see my God.
That love the way to Zi - on's hill.
Shall thith - er bring our will - ing feet!
Whose spir - it trusts a - lone in Thee! A-MEN.

# 51

Gerhard Tersteegen, 1729
Trans. by Frederick W. Foster (1760-1835)
and Rev. John Miller, 1789; alt., 1932    6. 6. 8. D. 3. 3. 6. 6.

ARNSBERG
Rev. Joachim Neander's
"Bundes-Lieder," 1680

*Not too fast; reverently*

1. God Him-self is with us: Let us now a-dore Him, And with awe ap-
pear be-fore Him. God is in His tem-ple— All with-in keep
si — lence, Pros-trate lie with deep-est rev-erence. Him a-lone God we own,
Him, our God and Sav-iour; Praise His Name for-ev - er.

2. God Him-self is with us: Hear the harps re-sound - ing! See the crowds the
throne sur-round-ing! "Ho-ly, ho-ly, ho - ly"— Hear the hymn as-
cend - ing, An-gels, saints, their voices blend-ing! Bow Thine ear To us here:
Hear, O Christ, the prais-es That Thy Church now rais - es.

3. O Thou Fount of bless-ing, Pu-ri-fy my spir - it; Trust-ing on-ly
in Thy mer - it, Like the ho-ly an - gels Who be-hold Thy
glo - ry, May I cease-less-ly a-dore Thee, And in all, Great and small,
Seek to do most near - ly What Thou lov-est dear - ly.    A-MEN.

Anon., c. 1757  6. 6. 4. 6. 6. 6. 4.  TRINITY (ITALIAN HYMN)
Felice de Giardini, 1769

*Joyously, but with dignity*

1. Come, Thou Al - might - y King, Help us Thy
2. Come, Thou In - car - nate Word, Gird on Thy
3. Come, Ho - ly Com - fort - er, Thy sa - cred
4. To the great One in Three The high - est

Name to sing, Help us to praise: Fa - ther, all -
might - y sword, Our prayer at - tend: Come, and Thy
wit - ness bear In this glad hour: Thou who al -
prais - es be, Hence ev - er - more! His sov - ereign

glo - ri - ous, O'er all vic - to - ri - ous, Come, and reign
peo - ple bless, And give Thy word suc - cess; Spir - it of
might - y art, Now rule in ev - ery heart, And ne'er from
maj - es - ty May we in glo - ry see, And to e -

o - ver us, An - cient of Days.
ho - li - ness, On us de - scend.
us de - part, Spir - it of power.
ter - ni - ty Love and a - dore. A - MEN.

Bishop Reginald Heber, 1811    L. M. with Refrain    HOSANNA  Rev. John B. Dykes, 1865

*With jubilant movement*

1. Ho - san - na to the liv - ing Lord! Ho - san - na to th' In-
2. "Ho - san - na, Lord!" Thine an - gels cry; "Ho - san - na, Lord!" Thy
3. O Sav - iour, with pro - tect - ing care, Re - turn to this Thy
4. But, chief - est, in our cleans - ed breast, E - ter - nal, bid Thy

car - nate Word! To Christ, Cre - a - tor, Sav - iour, King,
saints re - ply; A - bove, be - neath us, and a - round,
house of prayer; As - sem - bled in Thy sa - cred Name,
Spir - it rest, And make our se - cret soul to be

Let earth, let heaven, Ho - san - na sing! Ho - san - na, Lord! Ho -
The dead and liv - ing swell the sound: "Ho - san - na, Lord! Ho -
Now we Thy part - ing prom - ise claim: Ho - san - na, Lord! Ho -
A temp - ple pure, and wor - thy Thee: Ho - san - na, Lord! Ho -

san - na in the high - - est!
san - na in the high - - est!"
san - na in the high - - est!
san - na in the high - - est!    A - MEN.

Ascribed to Rev. John Fawcett (1740–1817)
Stanza 1, line 6, alt.; stanza 3 recast by
Rev. Godfrey Thring (1823–1903)     8. 7. 8. 7. 8. 7.     SICILIAN MARINERS
Arr. from a Sicilian melody

*In moderate time*

1. Lord, dis - miss us with Thy bless - ing; Fill our hearts with
2. Thanks we give and ad - o - ra - tion For Thy gos - pel's
3. So that when Thy love shall call us, Sav - iour, from the

joy and peace; Let us each, Thy love pos - sess - ing,
joy - ful sound; May the fruits of Thy sal - va - tion
world a - way, Let no fear of death ap - pall us,

Tri - umph in re - deem - ing grace: O re - fresh us,
In our hearts and lives a - bound: Ev - er faith - ful,
Glad Thy sum - mons to o - bey: May we ev - er,

O re - fresh us, Trav - eling through this wil - der - ness.
Ev - er faith - ful To the truth may we be found;
May we ev - er Reign with Thee in end - less day. A-MEN.

# Closing

**55**

Rev. John Ellerton, 1866      10. 10. 10. 10.      ELLERS   Edward J. Hopkins, 1869

*Not too fast. With flexible rhythm*

1. Sav - iour, a - gain to Thy dear Name we raise
2. Grant us Thy peace up - on our home - ward way;
3. Grant us Thy peace, Lord, through the com - ing night;
4. Grant us Thy peace through - out our earth - ly life,

With one ac - cord our part - ing hymn of praise;
With Thee be - gan, with Thee shall end the day:
Turn Thou for us its dark - ness in - to light;
Our balm in sor - row, and our stay in strife;

We stand to bless Thee ere our wor - ship cease;
Guard Thou the lips from sin, the hearts from shame,
From harm and dan - ger keep Thy chil - dren free,
Then, when Thy voice shall bid our con - flict cease,

Then, low - ly kneel - ing, wait Thy word of peace.
That in this house have called up - on Thy Name.
For dark and light are both a - like to Thee.
Call us O Lord, to Thine e - ter - nal peace. A-MEN.

Words from "The Church Hymnary," Revised. Used by permission of the Oxford University Press.

# Times of Worship

Rev. John S. B. Monsell, 1863, 1873
Stanza 1 alt.

6. 5. 6. 5. D. with Refrain

HERMAS
Frances R. Havergal, 1871

*In march rhythm*

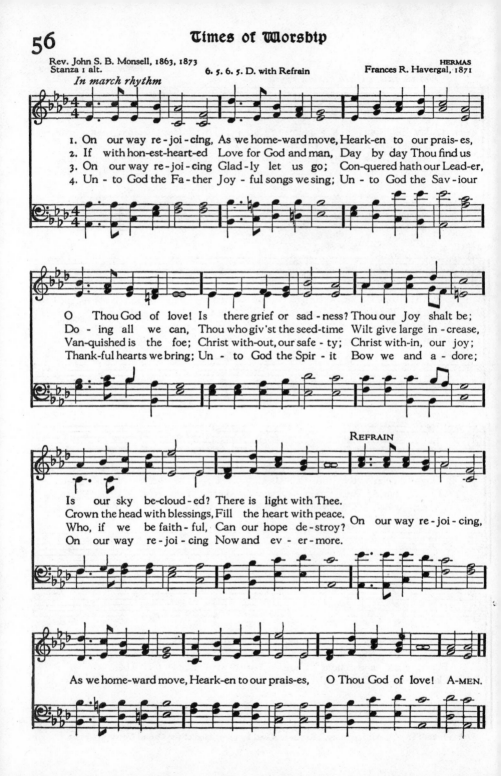

1. On our way re-joi-cing, As we home-ward move, Heark-en to our prais-es,
2. If with hon-est-heart-ed Love for God and man, Day by day Thou find us
3. On our way re-joi-cing Glad-ly let us go; Con-quered hath our Lead-er,
4. Un-to God the Fa-ther Joy-ful songs we sing; Un-to God the Sav-iour

O Thou God of love! Is there grief or sad-ness? Thou our Joy shalt be;
Do-ing all we can, Thou who giv'st the seed-time Wilt give large in-crease,
Van-quished is the foe; Christ with-out, our safe-ty; Christ with-in, our joy;
Thank-ful hearts we bring; Un-to God the Spir-it Bow we and a-dore;

Is our sky be-cloud-ed? There is light with Thee.
Crown the head with blessings, Fill the heart with peace.
Who, if we be faith-ful, Can our hope de-stroy?
On our way re-joi-cing Now and ev-er-more.

REFRAIN

On our way re-joi-cing,

As we home-ward move, Heark-en to our prais-es, O Thou God of love! A-MEN.

Bishop Reginald Heber; pub. 1826
11. 12. 12. 10.
NICÆA
Rev. John B. Dykes, 1861

*With exaltation*

1. Ho - ly, Ho - ly, Ho - ly! Lord God Al - might - y!
2. Ho - ly, Ho - ly, Ho - ly! All the saints a - dore Thee,
3. Ho - ly, Ho - ly, Ho - ly! Though the dark - ness hide Thee,
4. Ho - ly, Ho - ly, Ho - ly! Lord God Al - might - y!

Ear - ly in the morn - ing our song shall rise to Thee;
Cast - ing down their gold - en crowns a - round the glass - y sea;
Though the eye of sin - ful man Thy glo - ry may not see,
All Thy works shall praise Thy Name, in earth and sky and sea;

Ho - ly, Ho - ly, Ho - ly! Mer - ci - ful and Might - y!
Cher - u - bim and ser - a - phim fall - ing down be - fore Thee,
On - ly Thou art ho - ly; there is none be - side Thee
Ho - ly, Ho - ly, Ho - ly! Mer - ci - ful and Might - y!

God in Three Per - sons, bless - ed Trin - i - ty!
Who wert, and art, and ev - er - more shalt be.
Per - fect in power, in love, and pu - ri - ty.
God in Three Per - sons, bless - ed Trin - i - ty!

A-MEN.

Bishop William C. Doane, 1886

11. 10. 11. 10.

ANCIENT OF DAYS
J. Albert Jeffery, 1886

*With marked rhythm.* Voices

1. An - cient of Days, who sit - test throned in glo - ry;
2. O Ho - ly Fa - ther, who hast led Thy chil - dren
3. O Ho - ly Je - sus, Prince of Peace and Sav - iour,
4. O Ho - ly Ghost, the Lord and the Life Giv - er,
5. O Tri - une God, with heart and voice a - dor - ing,

*Introduction 1st stanza*

*Accomp.*

To Thee all knees are bent, all voi - ces pray; Thy love has blest the
In all the a - ges, with the fire and cloud, Through seas dry-shod, through
To Thee we owe the peace that still pre-vails, Still - ing the rude wills
Thine is the quick-ening power that gives in-crease; From Thee have flowed, as
Praise we the good - ness that doth crown our days; Pray we that Thou wilt

# The Holy Trinity

wide world's won-drous sto-ry With light and life since E-den's dawn-ing day.
wea - ry wastes be-wild'ring; To Thee, in rev-erent love, our hearts are bowed.
of men's wild be-hav - ior, And calm-ing pas-sion's fierce and storm-y gales.
from a pleas-ant riv - er, Our plen - ty, wealth, pros-per-i-ty, and peace.
hear us, still im-plor-ing Thy love and fa-vor, kept to us al - ways. A-MEN.

**59**

Ambrose of Milan (340–397)
Trans. by Rev. John M. Neale

ADESTO SANCTA TRINITAS
Chartres church melody
Arr. for this book

L. M.

*May be sung in unison. In moderate time*

1. O Trin - i - ty of bless - ed light, O U - ni - ty of
2. To Thee our morn - ing song of praise, To Thee our eve - ning
3. All laud to God the Fa - ther be; All praise, e - ter - nal

prince - ly might, The fier - y sun now goes his way;
prayer we raise; Thy glo - ry sup - pliant we a - dore
Son, to Thee; All glo - ry, as is ev - er meet,

Shed Thou with - in our hearts Thy ray.
For - ev - er and for - ev - er - more.
To God the ho - ly Par - a - clete. A - - MEN.

Rev. Horatius Bonar (1808–1889)     8. 7. 8. 7. 8. 7.     ST. PETER'S WESTMINSTER
James Turle (1802–1882)

*With marked and joyous rhythm*

1. Glo - ry be to God the Fa - ther, Glo - ry be to
2. Glo - ry be to Him who loved us, Washed us from each
3. Glo - ry to the King of an - gels, Glo - ry to the
4. "Glo - ry, bless - ing, praise e - ter - nal!" Thus the choir of

God the Son, Glo - ry be to God the Spir - it—
spot and stain, Glo - ry be to Him who bought us,
Church's King, Glo - ry to the King of na - tions!
an - gels sings; "Hon - or, rich - es, power, do - min - ion!"

Great Je - ho - vah, Three in One! Glo - ry, glo - ry,
Made us kings with Him to reign! Glo - ry, glo - ry,
Heaven and earth, your prais - es bring; Glo - ry, glo - ry,
Thus its praise cre - a - tion brings; Glo - ry, glo - ry,

Glo - ry, glo - ry, While e - ter - nal a - ges run!
Glo - ry, glo - ry, To the Lamb that once was slain!
Glo - ry, glo - ry, To the King of glo - ry bring!
Glo - ry, glo - ry, Glo - ry to the King of kings! A-MEN.

# 61

## God the Father
### His Eternity and Power

From Psalm xciii
Rev. John Keble, 1839

8. 7. 8. 7. 8. 7.

REGENT SQUARE
Henry Smart, 1867

*Jubilantly*

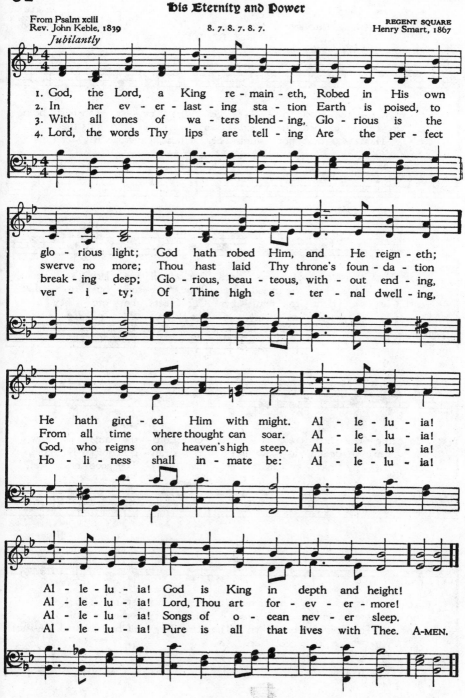

1. God, the Lord, a King re - main - eth, Robed in His own glo - rious light; God hath robed Him, and He reign - eth; He hath gird - ed Him with might. Al - le - lu - ia! Al - le - lu - ia! God is King in depth and height!

2. In her ev - er - last - ing sta - tion Earth is poised, to swerve no more; Thou hast laid Thy throne's foun - da - tion From all time where thought can soar. Al - le - lu - ia! Al - le - lu - ia! Lord, Thou art for - ev - er - more!

3. With all tones of wa - ters blend - ing, Glo - rious is the break - ing deep; Glo - rious, beau - teous, with - out end - ing, God, who reigns on heaven's high steep. Al - le - lu - ia! Al - le - lu - ia! Songs of o - cean nev - er sleep.

4. Lord, the words Thy lips are tell - ing Are the per - fect ver - i - ty; Of Thine high e - ter - nal dwell - ing, Ho - li - ness shall in - mate be: Al - le - lu - ia! Al - le - lu - ia! Pure is all that lives with Thee. A-MEN.

# God the Father

Bishop Edward H. Bickersteth, 1860

7. 6. 7. 6. D.
(FIRST TUNE)

PEARSALL
R. L. de Pearsall (1795-1856)
"St. Gall Gesangbuch," 1863

*In moderate time; with spirit*

1. O God, the Rock of A - ges, Who ev - er - more hast been,
2. Our years are like the shad - ows On sun - ny hills that lie,
3. O Thou who dost not slum - ber, Whose light grows nev - er pale,

What time the tem - pest ra - ges, Our dwell - ing place se - rene:
Or grass - es in the mead - ows That blos - som but to die;
Teach us a - right to num - ber Our years be - fore they fail;

Be - fore Thy first cre - a - tions, O Lord, the same as now,
A sleep, a dream, a sto - ry By stran - gers quick - ly told,
On us Thy mer - cy light - en, On us Thy good - ness rest,

To end - less gen - er - a - tions The Ev - er - last - ing Thou!
An un - re - main - ing glo - ry Of things that soon are old.
And let Thy Spir - it bright - en The hearts Thy - self hast blessed. A-MEN.

# 62

## His Eternity and Power

Bishop Edward H. Bickersteth, 1860 — 7. 6. 7. 6. D. (SECOND TUNE) — Joseph P. Holbrook, 1865

MIRIAM

*With dignity*

1. O God. the Rock of A - ges, Who ever-more hast been,
What time the tem - pest ra - ges, Our dwell - ing place se - rene:
Be - fore Thy first cre - a - tions, O Lord, the same as now,
To end - less gen - er - a - tions The Ev - er - last - ing Thou!

2. Our years are like the shad - ows On sun - ny hills that lie,
Or grass - es in the mead - ows That blos - som but to die;
A sleep, a dream, a sto - ry By stran - gers quick - ly told,
An un - re-main - ing glo - ry Of things that soon are old.

3. O Thou, who dost not slum - ber, Whose light grows nev - er pale,
Teach us a - right to num - ber Our years be - fore they fail;
On us Thy mer - cy light - en, On us Thy good - ness rest,
And let Thy Spir - it bright - en The hearts Thy-self hast blessed. A-MEN.

**63**

From Psalm c. Rev. Isaac Watts, 1705, 1719
Stanza 1 alt. by Rev. John Wesley
L. M.
PARK STREET
Frederick M. A. Venua, c. 1810

*With majesty but not too slowly*

1. Be - fore Je - ho - vah's aw - ful throne, Ye na-tions, bow with sa - cred joy; Know that the
2. His sov-ereign power, with-out our aid, Made us of clay, and formed us men; And when like
3. We'll crowd His gates with thank-ful songs, High as the heavens our voi - ces raise; And earth, with
4. Wide as the world is His com-mand, Vast as e - ter - ni - ty His love; Firm as a

Lord is God a-lone, He can cre-ate, and He de-stroy; He can cre-ate, and He de-stroy.
wan-dering sheep we strayed, He brought us to His fold again, He brought us to His fold a - gain.
her ten thou-sand tongues, Shall fill His courts with sound-ing praise, Shall fill His courts with sound-ing praise.
rock His truth shall stand, When roll-ing years shall cease to move, When roll-ing years shall cease to move. A-MEN.

**64**

From Psalm cxxxvi
John Milton, 1624; alt.
7. 7. 7. 7.
MONKLAND
Arr. by John B. Wilkes, 1861

*Joyously*

1. Let us with a glad - some mind Praise the Lord, for He is kind:
2. Let us sound His Name a - broad, For of gods He is the God:
3. He, with all - com - mand-ing might, Filled the new - made world with light:
4. All things liv - ing He doth feed; His full hand sup - plies their need:
5. Let us then with glad - some mind Praise the Lord, for He is kind:

For His mer - cies shall en - dure, Ev - er faith - ful, ev - er sure. A-MEN.

# His Eternity and Power

Rev. Isaac Watts, 1709
Stanza 3 alt.

C. M. D.

ELLACOMBE
"Gesangbuch der Herzogl. Wirtembergischen
Katholischen Hofkapelle," 1784

*In marked rhythm*

1. I sing the might-y power of God, That made the moun-tains rise;
2. I sing the good-ness of the Lord, That filled the earth with food;
3. There's not a plant or flower be-low, But makes Thy glo-ries known;

That spread the flow-ing seas a-broad, And built the loft-y skies.
He formed the crea-tures with His word, And then pro-nounced them good.
And clouds a-rise, and tem-pests blow, By or-der from Thy throne;

I sing the Wis-dom that or-dained The sun to rule the day;
Lord, how Thy won-ders are dis-played, Wher-e'er I turn my eye:
While all that bor-rows life from Thee Is ev-er in Thy care,

The moon shines full at His com-mand, And all the stars o-bey.
If I sur-vey the ground I tread, Or gaze up-on the sky!
And ev-ery-where that man can be, Thou, God, art pres-ent there. A-MEN.

Rev. Walter Chalmers Smith (1824–1908)  11. 11. 11. 11.

JOANNA
Welsh hymn melody

*In moderate time, rhythmically*

1. Im - mor - tal, in - vis - i - ble, God on - ly wise,
2. Un - rest - ing, un - hast - ing, and si - lent as light,
3. To all, life Thou giv - est— to both great and small;
4. Great Fa - ther of Glo - ry, pure Fa - ther of Light,

In light in - ac - ces - si - ble hid from our eyes,
Nor want - ing, nor wast - ing, Thou rul - est in might;
In all life Thou liv - est, the true life of all;
Thine an - gels a - dore Thee, all veil - ing their sight;

Most bless - ed, most glo - rious, the An - cient of Days,
Thy jus - tice like moun - tains high soar - ing a - bove,
We blos - som and flour - ish as leaves on the tree,
All praise we would ren - der; O help us to see

Al - might - y, vic - to - rious, Thy great Name we praise.
Thy clouds which are foun - tains of good - ness and love.
And with - er and per - ish— but naught chan - geth Thee.
'Tis on - ly the splen - dor of light hid - eth Thee! A - MEN.

From "The Church Hymnary," Revised. Used by permission of Mr. William Galbraith and the Oxford University Press.

67

Emily S. Perkins, 1921; alt.  8. 7. 8. 7.  Iambic  BURG
Emily S. Perkins, 1921

*May be sung in unison; in moderate time*

1. Thou art, O God, the God of might: Thy power is nev-er-fail-ing;
2. Thou art, O God, the God of truth: Thy word re-mains un-shak-en;
3. Thou art, O God, the God of love: Thy mer-cy is un-end-ing;
4. Thou art, O God, the God of grace: Though sin our hearts hath hard-ened,

Thou safe-ly lead-est in the fight, 'Gainst ev-ery foe pre-vail-ing.
Thy jus-tice and Thy right-eous-ness Have ev-ery strong-hold tak-en.
Thou guard-est us with ten-der care, Each day our souls de-fend-ing.
Thy grace can wash a-way the stain, And heaven re-ceive us, par-doned. A-MEN.

Copyright, 1921, by Emily S. Perkins.

68

Psalm xcvi. "Scottish Psalter," 1650  C. M.
SONG 67 (GIBBONS)
Orlando Gibbons (1583–1625)
Arr. by Henry Smart (1813–1879)

*Moderately slow*

1. O sing a new song to the Lord: Sing all the earth to God,
2. Great hon-or is be-fore His face, And maj-es-ty di-vine;
3. Do ye as-cribe un-to the Lord, Of peo-ple ev-ery tribe,
4. Give ye the glo-ry to the Lord That to His Name is due;
5. In beau-ty of His ho-li-ness, O do the Lord a-dore;

To God sing, bless His Name, show still His sav-ing health a-broad.
Strength is with-in His ho-ly place, And there doth beau-ty shine.
Glo-ry do ye un-to the Lord And might-y power as-cribe.
Come ye in-to His courts, and bring An of-fer-ing with you.
Like-wise let all the earth through-out Trem-ble His face be-fore. A-MEN.

# God the Father

Joseph Addison, 1712

L. M. D.

CREATION
Franz Joseph Haydn, 1798

*Joyously*

1. The spa-cious fir-ma-ment on high, With all the blue e-the-re-al sky, And span-gled heavens, a shin-ing frame, Their great O-rig-i-nal pro-claim: Th' un-wea-ried sun, from day to day, Does his Cre-a-tor's power dis-play, And pub-lish-es to ev-ery land The work of an al-might-y hand.

2. Soon as the eve-ning shades pre-vail, The moon takes up the won-drous tale, And night-ly to the lis-tening earth Re-peats the sto-ry of her birth; Whilst all the stars that round her burn, And all the plan-ets in their turn, Con-firm the ti-dings as they roll, And spread the truth from pole to pole.

3. What though in sol-emn si-lence all Move round this dark ter-res-tri-al ball? What though no re-al voice nor sound A-midst their ra-diant orbs be found? In rea-son's ear they all re-joice, And ut-ter forth a glo-rious voice; For-ev-er sing-ing, as they shine, "The hand that made us is di-vine." A-MEN.

# God in Nature

TERRA PATRIS
Melody by Franklin L. Sheppard, 1915
This Arr. by Edward Shippen Barnes, 1926

Rev. Maltbie D. Babcock, 1901                    S. M. D.

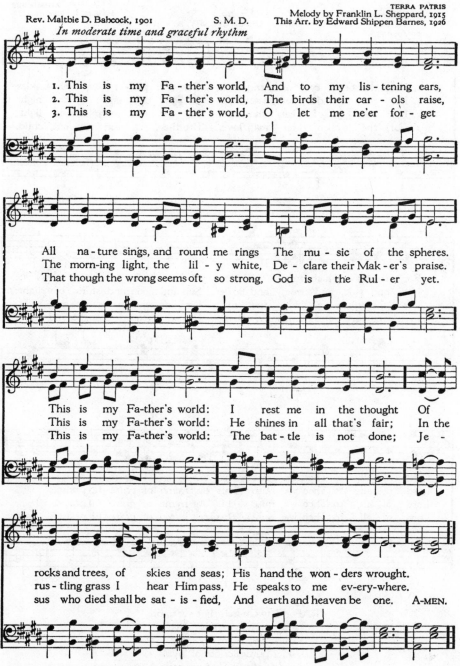

*In moderate time and graceful rhythm*

1. This is my Fa-ther's world, And to my lis-tening ears,
2. This is my Fa-ther's world, The birds their car-ols raise,
3. This is my Fa-ther's world, O let me ne'er for-get

All na-ture sings, and round me rings The mu-sic of the spheres.
The morn-ing light, the lil-y white, De-clare their Mak-er's praise.
That though the wrong seems oft so strong, God is the Rul-er yet.

This is my Fa-ther's world: I rest me in the thought Of
This is my Fa-ther's world: He shines in all that's fair; In the
This is my Fa-ther's world: The bat-tle is not done; Je-

rocks and trees, of skies and seas; His hand the won-ders wrought.
rus-tling grass I hear Him pass, He speaks to me ev-ery-where.
sus who died shall be sat-is-fied, And earth and heaven be one. A-MEN.

Music copyright, 1927, by Edward Shippen Barnes.
Words from "Thoughts for Every-Day Living." Copyright, 1901, by Charles Scribner's Sons.

# God the Father

Folliott S. Pierpoint, 1864

7. 7. 7. 7. 7. 7.
(FIRST TUNE)

ST. ATHANASIUS
Edward J. Hopkins, 1872

*Joyously*

1. For the beau - ty of the earth; For the glo - ry of the skies;
2. For the won - der of each hour Of the day and of the night,
3. For the joy of ear and eye; For the heart and mind's de - light;
4. For the joy of hu - man love, Broth-er, sis - ter, par - ent, child,

For the love which from our birth O - ver and a - round us lies:
Hill and vale, and tree and flower, Sun and moon, and stars of light:
For the mys - tic har - mo - ny Link-ing sense to sound and sight:
Friends on earth, and friends a - bove; For all gen - tle thoughts and mild:

Lord of all, to Thee we raise This our hymn of grate - ful praise.
Lord of all, to Thee we raise This our hymn of grate - ful praise.
Lord of all, to Thee we raise This our hymn of grate - ful praise.
Lord of all, to Thee we raise This our hymn of grate - ful praise. A-MEN.

5. For Thy Church that evermore
Lifteth holy hands above,
Offering up on every shore
Her pure sacrifice of love:
Lord of all, to Thee we raise
This our hymn of grateful praise.

# God in Nature

Folliott S. Pierpoint, 1864

7. 7. 7. 7. 7. 7.
(SECOND TUNE)

DIX
Abridged from a chorale by
Conrad Kocher, 1838

*Joyously*

1. For the beau-ty of the earth; For the glo-ry of the skies;
2. For the won-der of each hour Of the day and of the night,
3. For the joy of ear and eye; For the heart and mind's de-light;
4. For the joy of hu-man love, Broth-er, sis-ter, par-ent, child,

For the love which from our birth O-ver and a-round us lies:
Hill and vale, and tree and flower, Sun and moon, and stars of light:
For the mys-tic har-mo-ny Link-ing sense to sound and sight:
Friends on earth, and friends a-bove; For all gen-tle thoughts and mild:

Lord of all, to Thee we raise This our hymn of grate-ful praise.
Lord of all, to Thee we raise This our hymn of grate-ful praise.
Lord of all, to Thee we raise This our hymn of grate-ful praise.
Lord of all, to Thee we raise This our hymn of grate-ful praise. A-MEN.

5. For Thy Church that evermore
Lifteth holy hands above,
Offering up on every shore
Her pure sacrifice of love:
Lord of all, to Thee we raise
This our hymn of grateful praise.

Rev. Maltbie D. Babcock, 1901      **L. M.**      ST. VENANTIUS
          (FIRST TUNE)    Rouen church melody

*May be sung in unison*
*In moderate time, with majesty and reverence*

1. When the great sun sinks to his rest, His gold-en glo-ries thrill-ing me, And voice-less long-ings stir my breast, Then teach me, Lord, to wor-ship Thee.
2. And when the stars— the day-light fled— In ser-ried, shin-ing ranks I see, Fill-ing the splen-did vault o'er-head, Then teach me, Lord, to wor-ship Thee.
3. Or if in sol-emn for-est shades The calm of na-ture steals o'er me, And si-lence all my soul per-vades, Then teach me, Lord, to wor-ship Thee. A - - MEN.

4. Not in the sacred shrines alone,
   Which chime their summons unto me,
  Would I look upward to Thy throne,
   But everywhere would worship Thee.

Words copyright, 1901, by Charles Scribner's Sons.

# God in Nature

Rev. Maltbie D. Babcock, 1901

L. M.
(SECOND TUNE)

RIMINGTON
Francis Duckworth

*Reverently and in moderate time*

1. When the great sun sinks to his rest,
2. And when the stars — the day-light fled —
3. Or if in sol - emn for - est shades

His gold - en glo - ries thrill - ing me, And voice-less long - ings
In ser - ried, shin - ing ranks I see, Fill - ing the splen - did
The calm of na - ture steals o'er me, And si - lence all my

stir my breast, Then teach me, Lord, to wor - ship Thee.
vault o'er - head, Then teach me, Lord, to wor - ship Thee.
soul per - vades, Then teach me, Lord, to wor - ship Thee. A-MEN.

4. Not in the sacred shrines alone,
   Which chime their summons unto me:
   Would I look upward to Thy throne,
   But everywhere would worship Thee.

Composer's copyright.
Words copyright, 1901, by Charles Scribner's Sons.

**73**

Adelaide A. Procter, 1858        8. 4. 8. 4. 8. 4.        WENTWORTH
Frederick C. Maker, 1876

*With dignity and joy*

1. My God, I thank Thee, who hast made The earth so bright,
2. I thank Thee, too, that Thou hast made Joy to a-bound;
3. I thank Thee, Lord, that Thou hast kept The best in store;

So full of splen-dor and of joy, Beau-ty and light;
So man-y gen-tle thoughts and deeds Cir-cling us round,
We have e-nough, yet not too much To long for more:

So man-y glo-rious things are here, No-ble and right.
That in the dark-est spot of earth Some love is found.
A yearn-ing for a deep-er peace Not known be-fore. A-MEN.

4. I thank Thee, Lord, that here our souls,
 Though amply blest,
Can never find, although they seek,
 A perfect rest;
Nor ever shall, until they lean
 On Jesus' breast.

# 74

Rev. Stopford A. Brooke (1832–1916)  7. 7. 7. 7.  Arr. by John B. Wilkes (1785–1869)

MONKLAND

*Jubilantly*

1. Let the whole cre - a - tion cry, "Glo - ry to the Lord on high!"
2. Praise Him, all ye hosts a - bove, Ev - er bright and fair in love!
3. Men and wom - en, young and old, Raise the an - them man - i - fold;
4. From the north to south - ern pole Let the might - y cho - rus roll:

Heaven and earth, a - wake and sing, "God is good and there-fore King."
Sun and moon, up - lift your voice, Night and stars, in God re - joice!
And let chil-dren's hap - py hearts In this wor - ship bear their parts.
Ho - ly, ho - ly, ho - ly One! Glo - ry be to God a - lone! A-MEN.

Words used by permission of Miss Honor Brooke.

# 75

From Psalm cxlvii
Rev. Isaac Watts, 1719  C. M.  William Wheale, c. 1723

BEDFORD

*Not too slow*

1. With songs and hon - ors sound - ing loud, Ad - dress the Lord on high;
2. He sends His showers of bless - ing down To cheer the plains be - low;
3. His stead - y coun - sels change the face Of the de - clin - ing year;
4. He sends His word, and melts the snow; The fields no long - er mourn;
5. The chan - ging wind, the fly - ing cloud, O - bey His might - y word:

O - ver the heavens He spreads His cloud, And wa - ters veil the sky.
He makes the grass the moun-tains crown, And corn in val - leys grow.
He bids the sun cut short his race, And win - try days ap - pear.
He calls the warm - er gales to blow, And bids the spring re - turn.
With songs and hon - ors sound - ing loud Praise ye the sov - ereign Lord! A-MEN.

John Stuart Blackie, 1840      8. 7. 8. 8. 7.      LLANHERNE   George Thalben-Ball

*Joyously*

1. An - gels ho - ly, high and low - ly, Sing the prais - es of the Lord!
2. O - cean hoar - y, tell His glo - ry, Cliffs, where tum-bling seas have roared!
3. Rock and high-land, wood and is - land, Crag where ea - gle's pride hath soared,

Earth and sky, all liv - ing na - ture, Man, the stamp of
Pulse of wa - ters blithe-ly beat - ing, Wave ad - van - cing,
Might - y moun-tains, pur - ple-breast - ed, Peaks cloud-cleav - ing,

thy Cre - a - tor, Praise ye, praise ye, God the Lord!
wave re - treat - ing, Praise ye, praise ye, God the Lord!
snow - y - crest - ed, Praise ye, praise ye, God the Lord! A-MEN.

Music used by permission of George Thalben-Ball.

4. Praise Him ever, bounteous Giver!
    Praise Him, Father, Friend, and Lord!
Each glad soul its free course winging,
Each glad voice its free song singing,
    Praise the great and mighty Lord!

**77**

From Psalm xc
Rev. Isaac Watts, 1719

C. M.

ST. ANNE
Probably by William Croft, 1708
"Supplement to the New Version"

*With majesty*

1. Our God, our Help in a - ges past, Our Hope for years to come,
2. Be - fore the hills in or - der stood, Or earth re - ceived her frame,
3. A thou - sand a - ges in Thy sight Are like an eve - ning gone;
4. Time, like an ev - er - roll - ing stream, Bears all its sons a - way;
5. Our God, our Help in a - ges past, Our Hope for years to come,

Our Shel - ter from the storm - y blast, And our e - ter - nal Home:
From ev - er - last - ing Thou art God, To end - less years the same.
Short as the watch that ends the night Be - fore the ris - ing sun.
They fly for - got - ten, as a dream Dies at the o - pening day.
Be Thou our Guard while life shall last, And our e - ter - nal Home. A-MEN.

**78**

Rev. Isaac Watts, 1709

L. M.

CANONBURY
Robert Schumann, 1839

*In moderate time*

1. My God, how end - less is Thy love! Thy gifts are ev - ery eve - ning new;
2. Thou spread'st the cur - tains of the night, Great Guard-ian of my sleep - ing hours;
3. I yield my powers to Thy com - mand, To Thee I con - se - crate my days;

And morn - ing mer - cies from a - bove Gen - tly dis - till like ear - ly dew.
Thy sov-ereign word re-stores the light, And quick-ens all my wak-ing powers.
Per - pet-ual bless - ings from Thy hand De - mand per-pet - ual songs of praise. A-MEN.

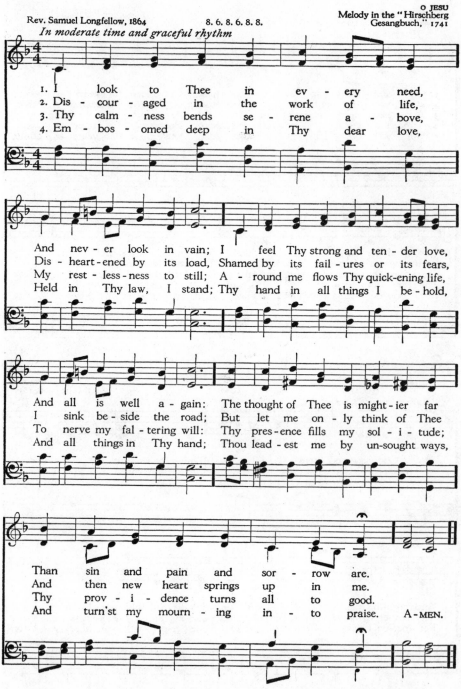

Rev. Samuel Longfellow, 1864          8. 6. 8. 6. 8. 8.

O JESU
Melody in the "Hirschberg
Gesangbuch," 1741

*In moderate time and graceful rhythm*

1. I look to Thee in ev - ery need,
2. Dis - cour - aged in the work of life,
3. Thy calm - ness bends se - rene a - bove,
4. Em - bos - omed deep in Thy dear love,

And nev - er look in vain; I feel Thy strong and ten - der love,
Dis - heart-ened by its load, Shamed by its fail - ures or its fears,
My rest - less-ness to still; A - round me flows Thy quick-ening life,
Held in Thy law, I stand; Thy hand in all things I be - hold,

And all is well a - gain: The thought of Thee is might - ier far
I sink be - side the road; But let me on - ly think of Thee
To nerve my fal - tering will: Thy pres - ence fills my sol - i - tude;
And all things in Thy hand; Thou lead - est me by un-sought ways,

Than sin and pain and sor - row are.
And then new heart springs up in me.
Thy prov - i - dence turns all to good.
And turn'st my mourn - ing in - to praise. A - MEN.

**80**

John Bowring (1792–1872)      8. 7. 8. 7.      SUSSEX
English traditional melody

*With marked rhythm*

1. God is Love; His mer - cy bright-ens All the path in which we rove;
2. Chance and change are bus - y ev - er; Man de - cays, and a - ges move;
3. E'en the hour that dark - est seem-eth Will His change-less good-ness prove;
4. He with earth - ly cares en - twin - eth Hope and com - fort from a - bove;

Bliss He wakes, and woe He light-ens: God is Wis - dom, God is Love.
But His mer - cy wan - eth nev - er: God is Wis - dom, God is Love.
From the mist His bright-ness stream-eth: God is Wis - dom, God is Love.
Ev - ery-where His glo - ry shin - eth: God is Wis - dom, God is Love. A-MEN.

Tune from " The English Hymnal." Used by permission of the Oxford University Press.

**81**

Joseph Addison, 1712      C. M.      ST. PETER
Alexander R. Reinagle, 1836

*In moderate time. With dignity*

1. When all Thy mer - cies, O my God, My ris - ing soul sur - veys,
2. Un - num-bered com - forts to my soul Thy ten - der care be - stowed,
3. Ten thou-sand thou-sand pre - cious gifts My dai - ly thanks em - ploy;
4. Through all e - ter - ni - ty to Thee A joy - ful song I'll raise:

Trans - port - ed with the view, I'm lost In won - der, love, and praise.
Be - fore my in - fant heart con-ceived From whom those comforts flowed.
Nor is the least a cheer - ful heart That tastes those gifts with joy.
For O e - ter - ni - ty's too short To ut - ter all Thy praise! A-MEN.

# 82     God the Father

Rev. Thomas Toke Lynch (1818–1871)     C. M. D.     PETERSHAM   Clement William Poole (1828–1924)

*In moderate time*

1. The Lord is rich and mer-ci-ful; The Lord is ver-y kind;
2. The Lord is glo-ri-ous and strong; Our God is ver-y high;
3. The Lord is won-der-ful and wise, As all the a-ges tell;

O come to Him, come now to Him, With a be-liev-ing mind.
O trust in Him, trust now in Him, And have se-cur-i-ty.
O learn of Him, learn now of Him, Then with thee it is well.

His com-forts, they shall strength-en thee, Like flow-ing wa-ters cool;
He shall be to thee like the sea, And thou shalt sure-ly feel
And with His light thou shalt be blest, There-in to work and live;

And He shall for thy spir-it be A foun-tain ev-er full.
His wind, that blow-eth health-i-ly Thy sick-ness-es to heal.
And He shall be to thee a rest When eve-ning hours ar-rive.    A-MEN.

Tune used by permission of The Misses Horder.

**83**

# His Love and Fatherhood

From Psalm xxxiv. Tate and Brady's
"New Version," 1696, 1698          C. M.          WILTSHIRE
George T. Smart (1776–1867)

*Joyously but in moderate time*

1. Through all the chan-ging scenes of life, In trou-ble and in joy,
2. O     mag-ni-fy the Lord with me, With me ex-alt His Name;
3. O     make but tri-al of His love; Ex-pe-rience will de-cide
4. To    Fa-ther, Son, and Ho-ly Ghost, The God whom we a-dore,

The prais-es of my God shall still My heart and tongue em-ploy.
When in dis-tress to Him I called, He to my res-cue came.
How blest they are, and on-ly they, Who in His truth con-fide.
Be glo-ry, as it was, is now, And shall be ev-er-more. A-MEN.

**84**

Rev. Oscar Clute (1840–1901)          S. M.          TRENTHAM
Robert Jackson, 1894

*In moderate time; reverently*

1. O   Love of God most full, O Love of God most free, Come warm my
2. Warm as the glow-ing sun So shines Thy love on me, It wraps me
3. The wild-est sea is calm, The tem-pest brings no fear, The dark-est
4. O   Love of God most full, O Love of God most free, Thou warm'st my

heart, come fill my soul, Come lead me un-to Thee!
'round with kind-ly care, It draws me un-to Thee.
night is full of light, Be-cause Thy love is near.
heart, Thou fill'st my soul, With might Thou strength-en'st me. A-MEN.

Tune used by permission of Mrs. Ethel Taylor.

# God the Father

Rev. Henry H. Tweedy, 1926      C. M. D.      "Anglo-Genevan Psalter," 1556

OLD. 22ND

*In moderate time.*   *With dignity*

1. O gra-cious Fa - ther of man-kind, Our spir - its' un-seen Friend,
2. Thou hear-est these, the good and ill, Deep bur - ied in each breast;
3. Thou seek-est us in love and truth More than our minds seek Thee;

High heav-en's Lord, our hearts' dear Guest, To Thee our prayers as - cend.
The se - cret thought, the hid-den plan, Wrought out or un - ex - pressed.
Through o - pen gates Thy power flows in Like flood tides from the sea.

Thou dost not wait till hu - man speech Thy gifts di - vine im-plore;
O cleanse our prayers from hu - man dross, At - tune our lives to Thee,
No more we seek Thee from a - far, Nor ask Thee for a sign,

Our dreams, our aims, our work, our lives Are prayers Thou lov-est more.
Un - til we la - bor for those gifts We ask on bend-ed knee.
Con-tent to pray in life and love And toil, till all are Thine. A-MEN.

This hymn, awarded first prize in a competition established by the Homiletic Review in 1925, is here printed by permission of the editor.

Psalm lxii. "Scottish Psalter," 1650          C. M.          ST. FLAVIAN
Adapted from "Day's Psalter," 1563

*Moderately slow*

1. My soul with ex - pec - ta - tion doth De - pend on God in - deed;
2. He on - ly my sal - va - tion is, And my strong Rock is He;
3. In God my glo - ry pla - ced is, And my sal - va - tion sure;
4. Ye peo - ple, place your con - fi - dence In Him con - tin - ual - ly;

My strength and my sal - va - tion do From Him a - lone pro - ceed.
He on - ly is my sure de - fense: I shall not mov - ed be.
In God the Rock is of my strength, My ref - uge most se - cure.
Be - fore Him pour ye out your heart: God is our ref - uge high. A - MEN.

**87**

Oliver Wendell Holmes, 1848          L. M.          LOUVAN
Virgil C. Taylor, 1847

*In moderate time*

1. Lord of all be - ing, throned a - far, Thy glo - ry flames from sun and star;
2. Sun of our life, Thy quick - ening ray Sheds on our path the glow of day;
3. Our mid - night is Thy smile with - drawn; Our noon - tide is Thy gra - cious dawn;
4. Grant us Thy truth to make us free, And kind - ling hearts that burn for Thee;

Cen - ter and soul of ev - ery sphere, Yet to each lov - ing heart how near!
Star of our hope, Thy soft - ened light Cheers the long watch - es of the night.
Our rain - bow arch, Thy mer - cy's sign; All, save the clouds of sin, are Thine.
Till all Thy liv - ing al - tars claim One ho - ly light, one heaven - ly flame. A - MEN.

# 88

## God the Father

Rev. Hugh T. Kerr, 1916

10. 4. 10. 4. 10. 10.

SANDON
Charles Henry Purday (1799-1885)

*In moderate time*

1. God of our life, through all the cir-cling years, We trust in Thee;
2. God of the past, our times are in Thy hand; With us a-bide.
3. God of the com-ing years, through paths un-known We fol-low Thee;

In all the past, through all our hopes and fears, Thy hand we see.
Lead us by faith to hope's true Prom-ised Land; Be Thou our guide.
When we are strong, Lord, leave us not a-lone; Our ref-uge be.

With each new day, when morn-ing lifts the veil,
With Thee to bless, the dark-ness shines as light,
Be Thou for us in life our Dai-ly Bread,

We own Thy mer-cies, Lord, which nev-er fail.
And faith's fair vi-sion chan-ges in-to sight.
Our heart's true Home when all our years have sped. A-MEN.

**89**

John Bowring, 1825      L. M.      QUEBEC
Henry Baker, 1862

*In moderate time*

1. Fa-ther and Friend! Thy light, Thy love, Beam-ing through all Thy works we see;
2. Thy voice we hear, Thy pres-ence feel, While Thou, too pure for mor-tal sight,
3. We know not in what hal-lowed part Of the wide heavens Thy throne may be,
4. Thy chil-dren shall not faint nor fear, Sus-tained by this ex-alt-ed thought:

Thy glo-ry gilds the heavens a-bove, And all the earth is full of Thee.
In-volved in clouds, in-vis-i-ble, Reign-est the Lord of life and light.
But this we know, that where Thou art, Strength, wis-dom, good-ness dwell with Thee.
Since Thou, their God, art ev-ery-where, They can-not be where Thou art not! A-MEN.

**90**

Thomas Wentworth Higginson, 1846      L. M.      FEDERAL STREET
Henry K. Oliver, 1832

*In moderate time*

1. To Thine e-ter-nal arms, O God, Take us, Thine err-ing chil-dren in;
2. Those arms were round our child-hood's ways, A guard through help-less years to be;
3. We trust-ed hope and pride and strength; Our strength proved false, our pride was vain,
4. A guide to trem-bling steps yet be! Give us of Thine e-ter-nal power!

From dan-gerous paths too bold-ly trod, From wan-dering thoughts and dreams of sin.
O leave not our ma-tur-er days! We still are help-less with-out Thee.
Our dreams have fad-ed all at length — We come to Thee, O Lord, a-gain!
So shall our paths all lead to Thee, And life still smile, like child-hood's hour. A-MEN.

# God the Father

**91**

Psalm xlvi. "Scottish Psalter," 1650     C. M.

WINCHESTER OLD
"Este's Psalter," 1592

*In moderate time*

1. God is our Ref - uge and our Strength, In straits a pres - ent aid;
2. Though hills a-midst the seas be cast; Though wa - ters roar - ing make
3. A riv - er is, whose streams make glad The Cit - y of our God;
4. God in the midst of her doth dwell; And noth - ing shall her move;

There-fore, al-though the earth re - move, We will not be a - fraid;
And trou - bled be; yea though the hills By swell-ing seas do shake.
The ho - ly place, where-in the Lord Most High hath His a - bode.
The Lord to her an help - er will, And that right ear - ly, prove. A-MEN.

**92**

From Psalm xxvii
James Montgomery, 1822     7. 6. 7. 6.

MEIN LEBEN
Melchior Vulpius (1560–1616)

*In moderate time and marked rhythm*

1. God is my strong Sal - va - tion; What foe have I to fear?
2. Though hosts en - camp a - round me, Firm to the fight I stand;
3. Place on the Lord re - li - ance, My soul, with cour - age wait;
4. His might thy heart shall strength-en, His love thy joy in - crease;

In dark-ness and temp - ta - tion My Light, my Help is near.
What ter - ror can con - found me, With God at my right hand?
His truth be thine af - fi - ance, When faint and des - o - late.
Mer - cy thy days shall length - en; The Lord will give thee peace. A-MEN.

# His Love and Fatherhood

Rev. Frederick W. Faber, 1854  8. 7. 8. 7. D.  
IN BABILONE  
Dutch traditional melody

*With dignity and graceful rhythm*  
*May be sung in unison*

1. There's a wide-ness in God's mer-cy, Like the wide-ness of the sea;
2. For the love of God is broad-er Than the meas-ure of man's mind;

There's a kind-ness in His jus-tice, Which is more than lib-er-ty.
And the heart of the E-ter-nal Is most won-der-ful-ly kind.

There is no place where earth's sor-rows Are more felt than up in heaven;
If our love were but more sim-ple, We should take Him at His word;

There is no place where earth's fail-ings Have such kind-ly judg-ment given.
And our lives would be all sun-shine In the sweet-ness of our Lord. A-MEN.

Tune used by permission of Professor Julius Rontgen.

MANOAH
Henry W. Greatorex's
"Collection," Boston, 1851

Rev. Isaac Watts, 1707                    C. M.

*In joyous mood*

1. Be - gin, my tongue, some heaven-ly theme, And speak some bound-less thing,
2. Tell of His won-drous faith - ful - ness, And sound His power a - broad;
3. His ver - y word of grace is strong As that which built the skies;
4. O might I hear Thy heaven-ly tongue But whis - per, "Thou art Mine,"

The might-y works, or might-ier Name, Of our e - ter - nal King.
Sing the sweet prom-ise of His grace, And our re-deem-ing God.
The voice that rolls the stars a - long Speaks all the prom - is - es.
Those gen - tle words should raise my song To notes al-most di - vine.    A-MEN.

**95**

Rev. Samuel Johnson, 1864                7. 7. 7. 7.

HORSHAM
English traditional melody

*Not too fast*

1. Life of a - ges, rich - ly poured, Love of God, un - spent and free,
2. Breath-ing in the think-er's creed; Puls-ing in the he - ro's blood;
3. Con - se - crat-ing art and song, Ho - ly book and pil - grim track;
4. Life of a - ges, rich - ly poured, Love of God, un - spent and free,

Flow - ing in the proph-et's word And the peo-ple's lib - er - ty;
Nerv - ing sim-plest thought and deed; Fresh-ening time with truth and good;
Hurl - ing floods of ty - rant wrong From the sa - cred lim - its back—
Flow still in the proph-et's word And the peo-ple's lib - er - ty!    A-MEN.

From "Songs of Praise." Used by permission of the Oxford University Press.

# 96 His Abiding Presence

From Psalm cxxi. John Campbell,
Duke of Argyll (1845–1914)   10. 4. 10. 4. 10. 10.   Charles Henry Purday (1799–1885)   SANDON

*In moderate time*

1. Un - to the hills a - round do I lift up My long - ing eyes;
2. He will not suf - fer that thy foot be moved: Safe shalt thou be.
3. Je - ho - vah is Him - self thy keep - er true, Thy change-less shade;
4. From ev - ery e - vil shall He keep thy soul, From ev - ery sin;

O whence for me shall my sal - va - tion come, From whence a - rise?
No care - less slum - ber shall His eye - lids close, Who keep - eth thee.
Je - ho - vah thy de-fense on thy right hand Him - self hath made.
Je - ho - vah shall pre-serve thy go - ing out, Thy com - ing in.

From God the Lord doth come my cer - tain aid,
Be - hold, He sleep - eth not, He slum - bereth ne'er,
And thee no sun by day shall ev - er smite;
A - bove thee watch - ing, He whom we a - dore

From God the Lord who heaven and earth hath made.
Who keep - eth Is - rael in His ho - ly care.
No moon shall harm thee in the si - lent night.
Shall keep thee hence - forth, yea, for - ev - er - more.   A-MEN.

**97**

Psalm xxiii. "Scottish Psalter," 1650
Based on Francis Rous and others

C. M.

EVAN
Rev. William H. Havergal, 1846

*With serenity; in moderate time*

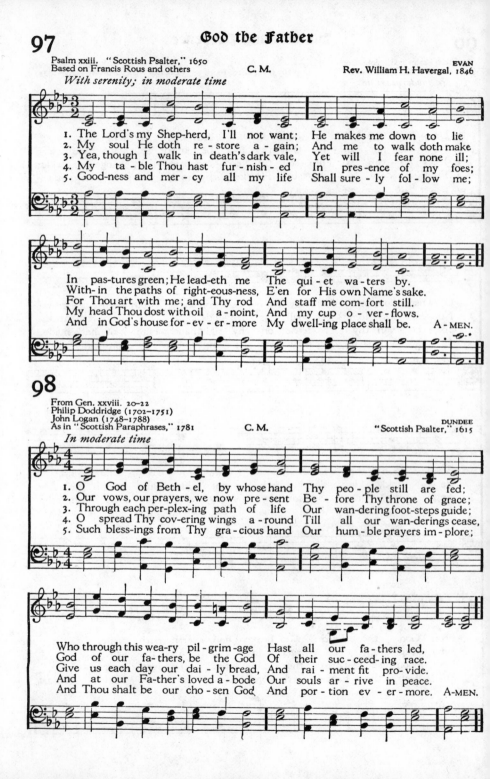

1. The Lord's my Shep-herd, I'll not want; He makes me down to lie
2. My soul He doth re - store a - gain; And me to walk doth make
3. Yea, though I walk in death's dark vale, Yet will I fear none ill;
4. My ta - ble Thou hast fur - nish - ed In pres-ence of my foes;
5. Good-ness and mer - cy all my life Shall sure - ly fol - low me;

In pas-tures green; He lead-eth me The qui - et wa-ters by.
With-in the paths of right-eous-ness, E'en for His own Name's sake.
For Thou art with me; and Thy rod And staff me com-fort still.
My head Thou dost with oil a-noint, And my cup o - ver-flows.
And in God's house for - ev - er-more My dwell-ing place shall be. A-MEN.

**98**

From Gen. xxviii. 20–22
Philip Doddridge (1702–1751)
John Logan (1748–1788)
As in "Scottish Paraphrases," 1781

C. M.

DUNDEE
"Scottish Psalter," 1615

*In moderate time*

1. O God of Beth - el, by whose hand Thy peo - ple still are fed;
2. Our vows, our prayers, we now pre - sent Be - fore Thy throne of grace;
3. Through each per-plex-ing path of life Our wan-dering foot-steps guide;
4. O spread Thy cov-ering wings a - round Till all our wan-derings cease,
5. Such bless-ings from Thy gra - cious hand Our hum - ble prayers im - plore;

Who through this wea-ry pil - grim-age Hast all our fa - thers led,
God of our fa - thers, be the God Of their suc - ceed-ing race.
Give us each day our dai - ly bread, And rai - ment fit pro-vide.
And at our Fa-ther's loved a - bode Our souls ar - rive in peace.
And Thou shalt be our cho - sen God And por - tion ev - er-more. A-MEN.

# 99 His Abiding Presence

Psalm xxiii
Rev. Henry W. Baker, 1868

8. 7. 8. 7. Iambic

DOMINUS REGIT ME
Rev. John B. Dykes, 1868

*In moderate time*

1. The King of love my Shep - herd is,
2. Where streams of liv - ing wa - ter flow
3. Per - verse and fool - ish oft I strayed,
4. In death's dark vale I fear no ill

Whose good - ness fail - eth nev - er; I noth - ing lack if
My ran - somed soul He lead - eth, And where the ver - dant
But yet in love He sought me, And on His shoul - der
With Thee, dear Lord, be - side me; Thy rod and staff my

I am His And He is mine for - ev - er.
pas - tures grow, With food ce - les - tial feed - eth.
gen - tly laid, And home, re - joi - cing, brought me.
com - fort still, Thy cross be - fore to guide me. A-MEN.

5. Thou spread'st a table in my sight;
   Thy unction grace bestoweth;
   And O what transport of delight
   From Thy pure chalice floweth.

6. And so through all the length of days
   Thy goodness faileth never:
   Good Shepherd, may I sing Thy praise
   Within Thy house forever.

RHIW
From "A Students' Hymnal,"
University of Wales, 1923

Rev. James D. Burns, 1857      S. M.

*Not too fast*

1. Still with Thee, O my God, I would de-sire to be;
2. With Thee when dawn comes in And calls me back to care,
3. With Thee a-mid the crowd That throngs the bus-y mart,
4. With Thee when dark-ness brings The sig-nal of re-pose,
5. With Thee, in Thee, by faith A-bid-ing, I would be;

By day, by night, at home, a-broad, I would be still with Thee.
Each day re-turn-ing to be-gin With Thee, my God, in prayer.
To hear Thy voice, where time's is loud, Speak soft-ly to my heart.
Calm in the shad-ow of Thy wings, Mine eye-lids I would close.
By day, by night, in life, in death, I would be still with Thee. A-MEN.

Tune from "A Students' Hymnal" (Hymns of the Kingdom). Used by permission of the Oxford University Press.

**101**

ABENDS
Herbert S. Oakeley, 1874

Rev. Seth Curtis Beach, 1866      L. M.

*In moderate time*

1. Mys-te-rious Pres-ence, source of all— The world with-out, the soul with-in,
2. Thou breath-est in the rush-ing wind; Thy spir-it stirs in leaf and flower;
3. Thy hand un-seen to ac-cents clear A-woke the psalm-ist's trem-bling lyre,
4. That touch di-vine, still, Lord, im-part; Still give the proph-et's burn-ing word;

Foun-tain of life, O hear our call, And pour Thy liv-ing wa-ters in!
Nor wilt Thou from the will-ing mind With-hold Thy light and love and power.
And touched the lips of ho-ly seer With flame from Thine own al-tar fire.
And, vo-cal in each wait-ing heart, Let liv-ing psalms of praise be heard. A-MEN.

Tune used by permission of Major E. F. Oakeley.

## His Abiding Presence

**102**

Psalm cxxxix
From "The Psalter Hymnal," 1927    L. M.    SOLDAU
"Wittenberg Gesangbuch," 1524

*In moderate time*

1. Lord, Thou hast searched me, and dost know Wher-e'er I rest, wher-e'er I go;
2. My words from Thee I can-not hide; I feel Thy power on ev-ery side;
3. Where can I go a-part from Thee, Or whith-er from Thy pres-ence flee?
4. If I the wings of morn-ing take, And far a-way my dwell-ing make,
5. If deep-est dark-ness cov-er me, The dark-ness hid-eth not from Thee;

Thou know-est all that I have planned, And all my ways are in Thy hand.
O won-drous know-ledge, a-w-ful might, Un-fath-omed depth, un-meas-ured height!
In heaven? It is Thy dwell-ing fair; In death's a-bode? Lo, Thou art there.
The hand that lead-eth me is Thine, And my sup-port Thy power di-vine.
To Thee both night and day are bright, The dark-ness shin-eth as the light. A-MEN.

Words copyright, 1927, by United Presbyterian Board of Publication. Used by permission.
Tune from "The Church Hymnary," Revised. Used by permission of the Oxford University Press.

**103**

William Cowper, 1774    C. M.    DUNDEE
"Scottish Psalter," 1615

*In moderate time*

1. God moves in a mys-te-rious way His won-ders to per-form;
2. Deep in un-fath-om-a-ble mines Of nev-er-fail-ing skill
3. Ye fear-ful saints, fresh cour-age take; The clouds ye so much dread
4. Blind un-be-lief is sure to err, And scan His work in vain;

He plants His foot-steps in the sea, And rides up-on the storm.
He treas-ures up His bright de-signs, And works His sov-ereign will.
Are big with mer-cy, and shall break In bless-ings on your head.
God is His own In-ter-pre-ter, And He will make it plain. A-MEN.

# God the Father

Rev. William Williams (Welsh), 1745
Stanza 1 trans. by Rev. Peter Williams, 1771
Stanzas 2, 3 trans. by Rev. William Williams, c. 1772

DISMISSAL
William L. Viner, 1845

8. 7. 8. 7. 8. 7.
(FIRST TUNE)

*In moderate time*

1. Guide me, O Thou great Je - ho - vah, Pil - grim through this
2. O - pen now the crys - tal foun - tain, Whence the heal - ing
3. When I tread the verge of Jor - dan, Bid my anx - ious

bar - ren land; I am weak, but Thou art might - y;
stream doth flow; Let the fire and cloud - y pil - lar
fears sub - side; Death of death, and hell's De - struc - tion,

Hold me with Thy power - ful hand; Bread of heav - en,
Lead me all my jour - ney through; Strong De - liv - erer,
Land me safe on Ca - naan's side; Songs of prais - es,

Bread of heav - en, Feed me till I want no more.
strong De - liv - erer, Be Thou still my Strength and Shield.
songs of prais - es I will ev - er give to Thee. A-MEN.

# His Abiding Presence

**104**

Rev. William Williams (Welsh), 1745
Stanza 1 trans. by Rev. Peter Williams, 1771
Stanzas 2, 3 trans. by Rev. William Williams, c. 1772

CWM RHONDDA
Welsh hymn melody
John Hughes (1873–1932)

8. 7. 8. 7. 8. 7.
(SECOND TUNE)

*In moderate time*

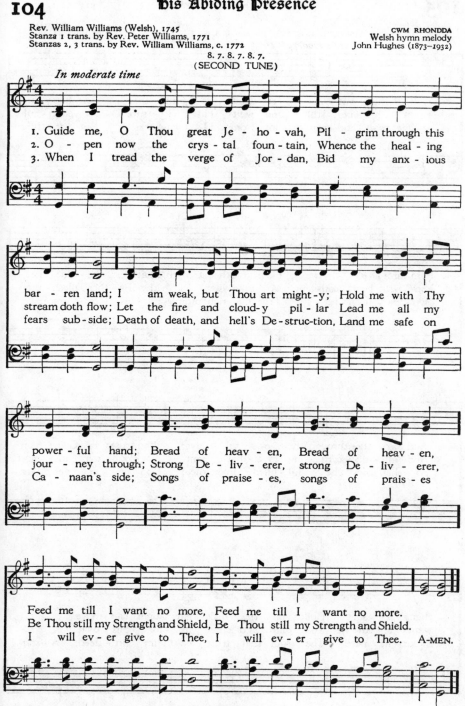

1. Guide me, O Thou great Je-ho-vah, Pil-grim through this bar-ren land; I am weak, but Thou art might-y; Hold me with Thy power-ful hand; Bread of heav-en, Bread of heav-en, Feed me till I want no more, Feed me till I want no more.

2. O-pen now the crys-tal foun-tain, Whence the heal-ing stream doth flow; Let the fire and cloud-y pil-lar Lead me all my jour-ney through; Strong De-liv-er-er, strong De-liv-er-er, Be Thou still my Strength and Shield, Be Thou still my Strength and Shield.

3. When I tread the verge of Jor-dan, Bid my anx-ious fears sub-side; Death of death, and hell's De-struc-tion, Land me safe on Ca-naan's side; Songs of praise-es, songs of prais-es I will ev-er give to Thee, I will ev-er give to Thee. A-MEN.

Tune copyrighted. Used by permission of Mrs. John Hughes.

# God the Father

Georg Neumark, 1657
Trans. by Catherine Winkworth, 1855, 1863    9. 8. 9. 8. 8. 8.

NEUMARK
Georg Neumark, 1657

*Confidently, but in moderate time*

1. If thou but suf - fer God to guide thee, And hope in
2. On - ly be still, and wait His lei - sure In cheer - ful
3. Sing, pray, and swerve not from His ways, But do thine

Him through all thy ways, He'll give thee strength, what-e'er be - tide thee,
hope, with heart con - tent To take what - e'er thy Fa - ther's pleas - ure
own part faith - ful - ly; Trust His rich prom - is - es of grace,

And bear thee through the e - vil days; Who trusts in God's un -
And all - dis - cern - ing love hath sent; Nor doubt our in - most
So shall they be ful - filled in thee; God nev - er yet for -

chang - ing love Builds on the rock that naught can move.
wants are known To Him who chose us for His own.
sook at need The soul that trust - ed Him in - deed. A - MEN.

# His Abiding Presence

Rev. Joseph H. Gilmore, 1862
Lines 3, 4 of refrain added

L. M. D.

HE LEADETH ME
William B. Bradbury, 1864

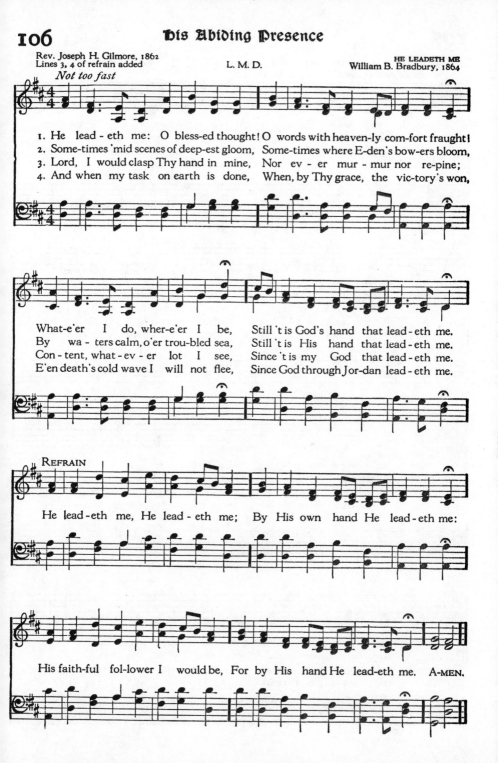

*Not too fast*

1. He lead-eth me: O bless-ed thought! O words with heaven-ly com-fort fraught!
2. Some-times 'mid scenes of deep-est gloom, Some-times where E-den's bow-ers bloom,
3. Lord, I would clasp Thy hand in mine, Nor ev - er mur - mur nor re-pine;
4. And when my task on earth is done, When, by Thy grace, the vic-tory's won,

What-e'er I do, wher-e'er I be, Still 't is God's hand that lead-eth me.
By wa - ters calm, o'er trou-bled sea, Still 't is His hand that lead-eth me.
Con - tent, what-ev - er lot I see, Since 't is my God that lead-eth me.
E'en death's cold wave I will not flee, Since God through Jor-dan lead-eth me.

**REFRAIN**

He lead-eth me, He lead - eth me; By His own hand He lead-eth me:

His faith-ful fol-lower I would be, For by His hand He lead-eth me. A-MEN.

**107**

# God the Father

Harriet Beecher Stowe (1812–1896)    11. 10. 11. 10.    CONSOLATION
Felix Mendelssohn (1809–1847)

*In moderate time*

1. Still, still with Thee, when pur - ple morn - ing break - eth,
2. A - lone with Thee, a - mid the mys - tic shad - ows,
3. Still, still with Thee! As to each new - born morn - ing
4. So shall it be at last, in that bright morn - ing,

When the bird wak - eth, and the shad - ows flee;
The sol - emn hush of na - ture new - ly born;
A fresh and sol - emn splen - dor still is given,
When the soul wak - eth and life's shad - ows flee;

Fair - er than morn - ing, love - li - er than day - light,
A - lone with Thee in breath - less ad - o - ra - tion,
So does this bless - ed con - scious - ness, a - wak - ing,
O in that hour, fair - er than day - light dawn - ing,

Dawns the sweet con - scious - ness, I am with Thee.
In the calm dew and fresh - ness of the morn.
Breathe each day near - ness un - to Thee and heaven.
Shall rise the glo - rious thought, I am with Thee. A-MEN.

John Bowring, 1825  
*In moderate time*  
7. 7. 7. 7. D.  
ST. GEORGE'S, WINDSOR  
George J. Elvey, 1859

1. Watch-man, tell us of the night, What its signs of prom-ise are:
2. Watch-man, tell us of the night; High-er yet that star as-cends:
3. Watch-man, tell us of the night, For the morn-ing seems to dawn:

Trav-eler, o'er yon moun-tain's height, See that glo-ry-beam-ing star!  
Trav-eler, bless-ed-ness and light, Peace and truth, its course por-tends.  
Trav-eler, dark-ness takes its flight; Doubt and ter-ror are with-drawn.

Watch-man, doth its beau-teous ray Aught of joy or hope fore-tell?  
Watch-man, will its beams a-lone Gild the spot that gave them birth?  
Watch-men, let thy wan-derings cease; Hie thee to thy qui-et home.

Trav-eler, yes; it brings the day, Prom-ised day of Is-ra-el.  
Trav-eler, a-ges are its own, And it bursts o'er all the earth!  
Trav-eler, lo, the Prince of Peace, Lo, the Son of God, is come! A-MEN.

Frederick William Henry Myers (1843-1901)

11. 10. 11. 10.

WELWYN

Alfred Scott-Gatty (1847-1918)

*In moderate time; with joyous reverence*

1. Hark, what a sound, and too di-vine for hear-ing,
2. Sure-ly He com-eth, and a thou-sand voi-ces
3. So ev-en I, and with a pang more thrill-ing,
4. Yea, through life, death, through sor-row and through sin-ning

Stirs on the earth and trem-bles in the air!
Shout to the saints and to the deaf are dumb;
So ev-en I, and with a hope more sweet,
He shall suf-fice me, for He hath suf-ficed;

Is it the thun-der of the Lord's ap-pear-ing?
Sure-ly He com-eth, and the earth re-joi-ces,
Yearn for the sign, O Christ, of Thy ful-fill-ing,
Christ is the end, for Christ was the be-gin-ning,

Is it the mu-sic of His peo-ple's prayer?
Glad in His com-ing who hath sworn, "I come."
Faint for the flam-ing of Thine ad-vent feet.
Christ the be-gin-ning, for the end is Christ. A-MEN.

Tune used by permission of The Very Reverend the Abbot of Downside.

# 111 Jesus Christ the Lord

From Psalm lxxii
James Montgomery, 1821, 1828      7. 6. 7. 6. D.      **TOURS**   Berthold Tours, 1872

*With joy*

1. Hail to the Lord's A - noint - ed, Great Da - vid's great - er Son!
2. He comes with suc - cor speed - y To those who suf - fer wrong;
3. He shall come down like show - ers Up - on the fruit - ful earth;
4. O'er ev - ery foe vic - to - rious, He on His throne shall rest,

Hail, in the time ap - point - ed, His reign on earth be - gun!
To help the poor and need - y, And bid the weak be strong;
And love, joy, hope, like flow - ers, Spring in His path to birth;
From age to age more glo - rious, All - bless - ing and all - blest;

He comes to break op - pres - sion, To set the cap - tive free,
To give them songs for sigh - ing, Their dark - ness turn to light,
Be - fore Him on the moun - tains Shall peace, the her - ald, go;
The tide of time shall nev - er His cov - e - nant re - move;

To take a - way trans - gres - sion, And rule in eq - ui - ty.
Whose souls, con - demned and dy - ing, Were pre - cious in His sight.
And right - eous - ness, in foun - tains, From hill to val - ley flow.
His Name shall stand for - ev - er— That Name to us is Love. A-MEN.

Tune used by permission of Novello and Company, Ltd.

# His Advent

From the Liturgy of St. James
Trans. by Rev. Gerard Moultrie (1829–1885)

8. 7. 8. 7. 8. 7.

PICARDY
French traditional carol

*Slowly and with reverence*

1. Let all mor-tal flesh keep si-lence, And with fear and trem-bling stand;
2. King of kings, yet born of Ma-ry, As of old on earth He stood,
3. Rank on rank the host of heav-en Spreads its van-guard on the way,
4. At His feet the six-winged ser-aph; Cher-u-bim, with sleep-less eye,

Pon-der noth-ing earth-ly-mind-ed, For with bless-ing in His hand,
Lord of lords, in hu-man ves-ture— In the bod-y and the blood—
As the Light of light de-scend-eth From the realms of end-less day,
Veil their fa-ces to the pres-ence, As with cease-less voice they cry,

Christ our God to earth de-scend-eth, Our full hom-age to de-mand.
He will give to all the faith-ful His own self for heaven-ly food.
That the powers of hell may van-ish As the dark-ness clears a-way.
Al-le-lu-ia, Al-le-lu-ia, Al-le-lu-ia, Lord Most High! A-MEN.

# Jesus Christ the Lord

Rev. Charles Wesley, 1744

8. 7. 8. 7. D.
(FIRST TUNE)

HYFRYDOL
Rowland Hugh Prichard (1811–1887)

*With joy and in moderate time*

1. Come, Thou long - ex - pect - ed Je - sus, Born to set Thy peo - ple free;
2. Born Thy peo - ple to de - liv - er, Born a child and yet a King,

From our fears and sins re - lease us; Let us find our rest in Thee.
Born to reign in us for - ev - er, Now Thy gra - cious King-dom bring.

Is - rael's Strength and Con - so - la - tion, Hope of all the earth Thou art;
By Thine own e - ter - nal Spir - it Rule in all our hearts a - lone;

Dear De - sire of ev - ery na - tion, Joy of ev - ery long - ing heart.
By Thine all - suf - fi - cient mer - it Raise us to Thy glo - rious throne. A-MEN.

**113**

Rev. Charles Wesley, 1744  8. 7. 8. 7.  Arr. from "Psalmodia Sacra," Gotha, 1715
STUTTGART
(SECOND TUNE)

*With joy and in moderate time*

1. Come, Thou long-ex-pect-ed Je-sus, Born to set Thy peo-ple free;
2. Is-rael's Strength and Con-so-la-tion, Hope of all the earth Thou art;
3. Born Thy peo-ple to de-liv-er, Born a child, and yet a King,
4. By Thine own e-ter-nal Spir-it Rule in all our hearts a-lone;

From our fears and sins re-lease us; Let us find our rest in Thee.
Dear De-sire of ev-ery na-tion, Joy of ev-ery long-ing heart.
Born to reign in us for-ev-er, Now Thy gra-cious King-dom bring.
By Thine all-suf-fi-cient mer-it Raise us to Thy glo-rious throne. A-MEN.

**114**

Rev. Georg Weissel, 1642
Trans. by Catherine Winkworth, 1855  L. M.  T. Williams' "Psalmodia Evangelica," 1789
TRURO

*In moderate time*

1. Lift up your heads, ye might-y gates, Be-hold, the King of glo-ry waits;
2. Fling wide the por-tals of your heart; Make it a tem-ple, set a-part
3. Re-deem-er, come! I o-pen wide My heart to Thee; here, Lord, a-bide.

The King of kings is draw-ing near; The Sav-iour of the world is here!
From earth-ly use for Heaven's em-ploy, A-dorned with prayer, and love, and joy.
Let me Thy in-ner pres-ence feel; Thy grace and love in me re-veal. A-MEN.

# 115 Jesus Christ the Lord

Laurentius Laurenti, 1700
Trans. by Sarah B. Findlater, 1854
7. 6. 7. 6. D.
LANCASHIRE
Henry Smart, 1836

*In joyous rhythm*

1. Re - joice, re - joice, be - liev - ers, And let your lights ap - pear;
2. See that your lamps are burn - ing; Re - plen - ish them with oil;
3. Our Hope and Ex - pec - ta - tion, O Je - sus, now ap - pear!

The eve - ning is ad - van - cing, And dark - er night is near:
And wait for your sal - va - tion, The end of earth - ly toil.
A - rise, Thou Sun so longed for, O'er this be - night - ed sphere!

The Bride-groom is a - ris - ing, And soon He draw - eth nigh;
The watch - ers on the moun - tain Pro - claim the Bride-groom near,
With hearts and hands up - lift - ed, We plead, O Lord, to see

Up, pray, and watch, and wres - tle: At mid - night comes the cry.
Go meet Him as He com - eth, With al - le - lu - ias clear.
The day of earth's re - demp - tion That brings us un - to Thee. A-MEN.

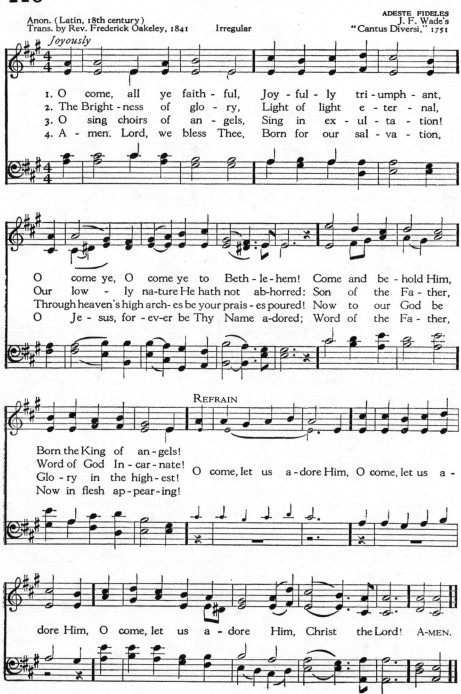

Anon. (Latin, 18th century)
Trans. by Rev. Frederick Oakeley, 1841    Irregular

ADESTE FIDELES
J. F. Wade's
"Cantus Diversi," 1751

*Joyously*

1. O come, all ye faith - ful, Joy - ful - ly tri - umph - ant,
2. The Bright - ness of glo - ry, Light of light e - ter - nal,
3. O sing choirs of an - gels, Sing in ex - ul - ta - tion!
4. A - men. Lord, we bless Thee, Born for our sal - va - tion,

O come ye, O come ye to Beth - le - hem! Come and be - hold Him,
Our low - ly na - ture He hath not ab - horred: Son of the Fa - ther,
Through heaven's high arch - es be your prais - es poured! Now to our God be
O Je - sus, for - ev - er be Thy Name a - dored; Word of the Fa - ther,

REFRAIN

Born the King of an - gels!
Word of God In - car - nate!
Glo - ry in the high - est!    O come, let us a - dore Him, O come, let us a -
Now in flesh ap - pear - ing!

dore Him, O come, let us a - dore Him, Christ the Lord! A-MEN.

MENDELSSOHN
Felix Mendelssohn, 1840
Arr. by William H. Cummings, 1850

Rev. Charles Wesley, 1739     7. 7. 7. 7. D. with Refrain

*With joy*

1. Hark! the her - ald an - gels sing, "Glo - ry to the new - born King;
2. Christ, by high - est heaven a - dored; Christ, the Ev - er - last - ing Lord!
3. Hail the heaven-born Prince of Peace! Hail the Sun of Right-eous-ness!

Peace on earth, and mer - cy mild, God and sin - ners rec - on - ciled!"
Late in time be - hold Him come, Off - spring of the Vir - gin's womb:
Light and life to all He brings, Risen with heal - ing in His wings.

Joy - ful, all ye na - tions, rise, Join the tri - umph of the skies;
Veiled in flesh the God - head see; Hail th' In - car - nate De - i - ty,
Mild He lays His glo - ry by, Born that man no more may die,

With th' an - gel - ic host pro - claim, "Christ is born in Beth - le - hem!"
Pleased as man with men to dwell, Je - sus, our Em - man - u - el.
Born to raise the sons of earth, Born to give them sec - ond birth.

Hark! the her - ald an - gels sing, "Glo - ry to the new-born King!" A - MEN.

# 118

## His Birth

Rev. Martin Luther, 1535
Trans. by Catherine Winkworth, 1855

L. M.

VOM HIMMEL HOCH
"Geistliche Lieder," Leipzig, 1539

*Moderately slow, in graceful rhythm*

1. Ah, dear-est Je-sus, ho-ly Child, Make Thee a bed, soft, un-de-filed
2. My heart for ver-y joy doth leap, My lips no more can si-lence keep;
3. Glo-ry to God in high-est heaven, Who un-to man His Son hath given,

With-in my heart, that it may be A qui-et cham-ber kept for Thee.
I, too, must sing with joy-ful tongue That sweet-est an-cient cra-dle song.
While an-gels sing with ten-der mirth, A glad new year to all the earth. A-MEN.

# 119

Rev. Martin Luther, 1524

L. M.

PUER NOBIS NASCITUR
Michael Praetorius, 1609
Harmonized by George R. Woodward, 1904

*In the style of a carol*

1. All praise to Thee, E-ter-nal Lord, Clothed in a garb of flesh and blood;
2. A lit-tle Child, Thou art our Guest, That wea-ry ones in Thee may rest;
3. Thou com-est in the dark-some night To make us chil-dren of the light,
4. All this for us Thy love hath done; By this to Thee our love is won:

Choos-ing a man-ger for Thy throne, While worlds on worlds are Thine a-lone.
For-lorn and low-ly is Thy birth, That we may rise to heaven from earth.
To make us, in the realms di-vine, Like Thine own an-gels round Thee shine.
For this we tune our cheer-ful lays, And sing our thanks in cease-less praise. A-MEN.

Tune used by permission of Rev. George R. Woodward.

Nahum Tate, 1703

C. M.

George Frederick Handel, 1728
CHRISTMAS

*With joyous rhythm*

1. While shep-herds watched their flocks by night,
2. "Fear not," said he — for might-y dread
3. "To you, in Da-vid's town this day,
4. "The heaven-ly Babe you there shall find

All seat-ed on the ground; The an-gel of the Lord came down,
Had seized their trou-bled mind— "Glad ti-dings of great joy I bring
Is born of Da-vid's line, The Sav-iour, who is Christ, the Lord,
To hu-man view dis-played, All mean-ly wrapped in swath-ing bands,

And glo-ry shone a-round, And glo-ry shone a-round.
To you and all man-kind, To you and all man-kind.
And this shall be the sign: And this shall be the sign:
And in a man-ger laid, And in a man-ger laid." A-MEN.

5. Thus spake the seraph, and forthwith
   Appeared a shining throng
   Of angels praising God, who thus
   Addressed their joyful song:

6. "All glory be to God on high,
   And to the earth be peace:
   Good will henceforth, from heaven to men,
   Begin and never cease!"

# 121

## His Birth

Bishop Phillips Brooks, 1868    8. 6. 8. 6. 7. 6. 8. 6.    ST. LOUIS
Lewis H. Redner, 1868

*With joy and serenity*

1. O lit - tle town of Beth - le - hem, How still we see thee lie;
2. For Christ is born of Ma - ry; And gath - ered all a - bove,
3. How si - lent - ly, how si - lent - ly The won - drous gift is given!
4. O ho - ly Child of Beth - le - hem, De - scend to us, we pray;

A - bove thy deep and dream-less sleep The si - lent stars go by.
While mor - tals sleep, the an - gels keep Their watch of won-dering love.
So God im - parts to hu - man hearts The bless - ings of His heaven.
Cast out our sin, and en - ter in, Be born in us to - day.

Yet in thy dark streets shin - eth The ev - er - last - ing Light;
O morn - ing stars, to - geth - er Pro - claim the ho - ly birth;
No ear may hear His com - ing, But in this world of sin,
We hear the Christ-mas an - gels The great glad ti - dings tell;

The hopes and fears of all the years Are met in thee to - night.
And prais - es sing to God the King, And peace to men on earth.
Where meek souls will re - ceive Him, still The dear Christ en - ters in.
O come to us, a - bide with us, Our Lord Em - man - u - el.    A-MEN.

From Psalm xcviii. Rev. Isaac Watts, 1719     C. M.      ANTIOCH
George Frederick Handel, 1742

*With joy and dignity*

1. Joy to the world! the Lord is come: Let earth re-
2. Joy to the earth! the Sav-iour reigns: Let men their
3. No more let sins and sor-rows grow, Nor thorns in-
4. He rules the world with truth and grace, And makes the

ceive her King; Let ev-ery heart pre-pare Him room,
songs em-ploy; While fields and floods, rocks, hills, and plains
fest the ground; He comes to make His bless-ings flow
na-tions prove The glo-ries of His right-eous-ness,

And heaven and na-ture sing, And heaven and na-ture
Re-peat the sound-ing joy, Re-peat the sound-ing
Far as the curse is found, Far as the curse is
And won-ders of His love, And won-ders of His

And heaven and na-ture sing, . . . . . . . . . .
Re-peat the sound-ing joy, . . . . . . . . . .
Far as the curse is found, . . . . . . . . . .
And won-ders of His love, . . . . . . . . . .

And
Re
Far
And

sing, And heaven, and heaven and na-ture sing.
joy, Re-peat, re-peat the sound-ing joy.
found, Far as, far as the curse is found.
love, And won-ders, won-ders of His love. A-MEN.

heaven and na-ture sing,
peat the sound-ing joy,
as the curse is found,
won-ders of His love.

# 123

Bishop Phillips Brooks (1835–1893)                    Rev. Timothy Richard Matthews (1826–1910)

CHENIES

7. 6. 7. 6. D.

*In the style of a carol*

1. The sky can still re-mem-ber   The ear-liest Christ-mas morn,
2. O nev-er-fail-ing splen-dor!   O nev-er-si-lent song!
3. O an-gels sweet and splen-did,   Throng in our hearts and sing

When in the cold De-cem-ber   The Sav-iour Christ was born.
Still keep the green earth ten-der,   Still keep the gray earth strong,
The won-ders which at-tend-ed   The com-ing of the King;

No star un-folds its glo-ry,   No trum-pet wind is blown,
Still keep the brave earth dream-ing   Of deeds that shall be done,
Till we too, bold-ly press-ing   Where once the shep-herds trod,

But tells the Christ-mas sto-ry   In mu-sic of its own.
While chil-dren's lives come stream-ing   Like sun-beams from the sun.
Climb Beth-lehem's Hill of Bless-ing,   And find the Son of God. A-MEN.

Tune used by permission of Novello and Company, Ltd.

# 124

## Jesus Christ the Lord

James Montgomery, 1816, 1825          8. 7. 8. 7. 8. 7.

REGENT SQUARE
Henry Smart (1813-1879)

*With joy and in moderate time*

1. An - gels, from the realms of glo - ry, Wing your flight o'er
2. Shep-herds, in the fields a - bid - ing, Watch - ing o'er your
3. Sa - ges, leave your con - tem - pla - tions, Bright - er vi - sions
4. Saints, be - fore the al - tar bend - ing, Watch - ing long in

all the earth; Ye who sang cre - a - tion's sto - ry,
flocks by night, God with man is now re - sid - ing,
beam a - far; Seek the great De - sire of na - tions;
hope and fear, Sud - den - ly the Lord, de - scend - ing,

Now pro - claim Mes - si - ah's birth: Come and wor - ship,
Yon - der shines the in - fant Light: Come and wor - ship,
Ye have seen His na - tal star: Come and wor - ship,
In His tem - ple shall ap - pear: Come and wor - ship,

Come and wor - ship, Wor - ship Christ, the new - born King!
Come and wor - ship, Wor - ship Christ, the new - born King!
Come and wor - ship, Wor - ship Christ, the new - born King!
Come and wor - ship, Wor - ship Christ, the new - born King!          A-MEN.

## 125

Rev. Paul Gerhardt, 1653
Trans. by Catherine Winkworth, 1858    8. 3. 3. 6. D.    EBELING (BONN)
Johann Georg Ebeling (1620–1676)

*In the style of a carol*

1. All my heart this night re - joi - ces, As I hear,
   Far and near, Sweet - est an - gel voi - ces;
   "Christ is born," the choirs are sing - ing, Till the air,
   Ev - ery - where, Now with joy is ring - ing.

2. Hark! a voice from yon - der man - ger, Soft and sweet,
   Doth en - treat, "Flee from woe and dan - ger;
   Breth - ren, come; from all that grieves you You are freed;
   All you need I will sure - ly give you."

3. Come, then, let us has - ten yon - der; Here let all,
   Great and small, Kneel in awe and won - der,
   Love Him who with love is yearn - ing; Hail the Star
   That from far Bright with hope is burn - ing. A-MEN.

Rev. Martin Luther, 1530

CRADLE SONG

Melody by William J. Kirkpatrick (1838–1921)

11. 11. 11. 11.

*Unison. In the style of a carol*

1. A - way in a man - ger, no crib for a bed,
2. The cat - tle are low - ing, the Ba - by a - wakes,
3. Be near me, Lord Je - sus; I ask Thee to stay

The lit - tle Lord Je - sus laid down His sweet head;
But lit - tle Lord Je - sus, no cry - ing He makes.
Close by me for - ev - er, and love me, I pray.

The stars in the bright sky looked down where He lay,
I love Thee, Lord Je - sus, look down from the sky,
Bless all the dear chil - dren in Thy ten - der care,

The lit - tle Lord Je - sus a - sleep on the hay.
And stay by my cra - dle till morn - ing is nigh.
And fit us for heav - en to live with Thee there. A - MEN.

Copyright 1923. Renewal. Hope Publishing Company, owner. Used by permission.

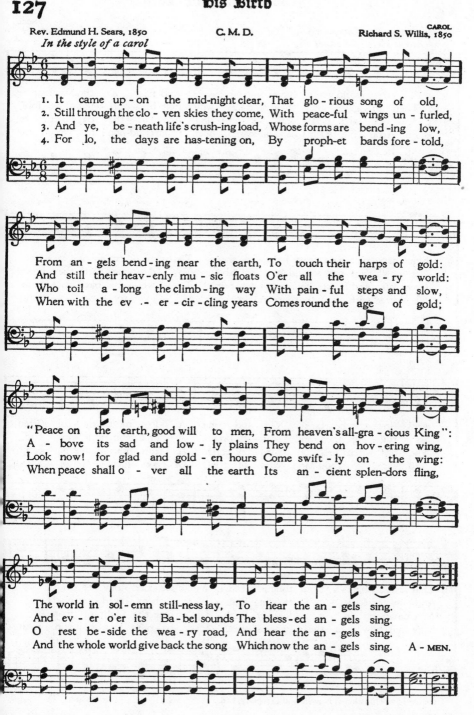

Rev. Edmund H. Sears, 1850      C. M. D.      Richard S. Willis, 1850 CAROL

*In the style of a carol*

1. It came up-on the mid-night clear, That glo-rious song of old,
2. Still through the clo-ven skies they come, With peace-ful wings un-furled,
3. And ye, be-neath life's crush-ing load, Whose forms are bend-ing low,
4. For lo, the days are has-tening on, By proph-et bards fore-told,

From an-gels bend-ing near the earth, To touch their harps of gold:
And still their heav-enly mu-sic floats O'er all the wea-ry world:
Who toil a-long the climb-ing way With pain-ful steps and slow,
When with the ev-er-cir-cling years Comes round the age of gold;

"Peace on the earth, good will to men, From heaven's all-gra-cious King":
A-bove its sad and low-ly plains They bend on hov-ering wing,
Look now! for glad and gold-en hours Come swift-ly on the wing:
When peace shall o-ver all the earth Its an-cient splen-dors fling,

The world in sol-emn still-ness lay, To hear the an-gels sing.
And ev-er o'er its Ba-bel sounds The bless-ed an-gels sing.
O rest be-side the wea-ry road, And hear the an-gels sing.
And the whole world give back the song Which now the an-gels sing. A-MEN.

Rev. Thomas Toke Lynch, 1868   C. M. D.   Arr. by Arthur S. Sullivan, 1871

NOEL

*In the style of a carol*

1. A thou-sand years have come and gone, And near a thou-sand more,
2. Then an-gels on their star-ry way Felt bliss un-felt be-fore,
3. And we are glad, and we will sing, As in the days of yore;
4. For trou-ble such as men must bear From child-hood to four-score,

Since hap-pier light from heav-en shone Than ev-er shone be-fore:
For news that men should be as they, To dark-ened earth they bore;
Come all, and hearts made read-y bring, To wel-come back once more
He shared with us, that we might share His joy for-ev-er-more;

And in the hearts of old and young A joy most joy-ful stirred,
So toil-ing men and spir-its bright A first com-mun-ion had,
The day when first on win-try earth A sum-mer change be-gan,
And twice a thou-sand years of grief, Of con-flict, and of sin,

That sent such news from tongue to tongue As ears had nev-er heard.
And in meek mer-cy's ris-ing light Were each ex-ceed-ing glad
And, dawn-ing in a low-ly birth, Up-rose the Light of man.
May tell how large the har-vest sheaf His pa-tient love shall win. A-MEN.

Tune used by permission of Novello and Company, Ltd.

THE FIRST NOWELL
Traditional melody in
Old English carol   Irregular, with Refrain   W. Sandys' "Christmas Carols," 1833

*In the style of a carol*

1. The first Now-ell the an-gel did say, Was to cer-tain poor
2. They look- ed up and they saw a star Shin-ing in the
3. And by the light of that same star, Three Wise Men
4. This star drew nigh to the north-west, O'er Beth-le-hem

shep-herds, in fields as they lay, In fields where they lay a - keep-ing their
east be - yond them far, And to the earth it gave great
came from a coun-try a - far, To seek for a king was their in -
then it took its rest, And there it did both stop and

REFRAIN

sheep, On a cold win-ter's night that was so deep. Now-ell, Now-
light, And so it con-tin-ued both day and night.
tent, And to fol-low the star wher-ev-er it went.
stay, Right o-ver the place where Je-sus lay.

ell, Now-ell, Now - ell, Born is the King of Is - ra - el! A-MEN.

5. Then entered in those Wise Men three
   Full reverently upon their knee,
   And offered there in His presence
   Their gold, and myrrh, and frankincense.

6. Then let us all with one accord
   Sing praises to our heavenly Lord;
   That hath made heaven and earth of naught,
   And with His blood mankind hath bought.

# Jesus Christ the Lord

Latin (medieval)
Trans. by Rev. John M. Neale, 1853

6. 6. 7. 9. 7. 8. 5. 5.

IN DULCI JUBILO
14th century German melody
Harmonized by John Stainer, 1867

*In jubilant style*

1. Good Chris-tian men, re - joice   With heart, and soul, and voice;
2. Good Chris-tian men, re - joice   With heart, and soul, and voice;
3. Good Chris-tian men, re - joice   With heart, and soul, and voice;

Give ye heed to what we say: News! news! Je - sus Christ is born to-day:
Now ye hear of end-less bliss; Joy! joy! Je - sus Christ was born for this!
Now ye need not fear the grave: Peace! peace! Je - sus Christ was born to save!

Ox and ass be-fore Him bow, And He is in the man-ger now.
He has oped the heaven-ly door, And man is bless-ed ev-er-more.
Calls you one and calls you all, To gain His ev-er-last-ing hall.

Christ is born to - day!    Christ is born to - day!
Christ was born for this!   Christ was born for this!
Christ was born to save!    Christ was born to save!    A - MEN.

GOD REST YOU MERRY, GENTLEMEN
Traditional melody
Harmonized by John Stainer, 1867

English traditional　　　7. 6. 7. 6. 7. 6. with Refrain

*In the style of a carol*

1. God rest you mer-ry, gen-tle-men, Let noth-ing you dis-may,
2. From God our heaven-ly Fa-ther A bless-ed an-gel came;
3. "Fear not, then," said the an-gel, "Let noth-ing you af-fright,
4. Now to the Lord sing prais-es, All you with-in this place,

Re-mem-ber Christ our Sav-iour Was born on Christ-mas Day;
And un-to cer-tain shep-herds Brought ti-dings of the same;
This day is born a Sav-iour Of a pure Vir-gin bright,
And with true love and broth-er-hood Each oth-er now em-brace;

To save us all from Sa-tan's power When we were gone a-stray.
How that in Beth-le-hem was born The Son of God by name.
To free all those who trust in Him From Sa-tan's power and might."
This ho-ly tide of Christ-mas All oth-ers doth de-face.

REFRAIN

O ti-dings of com-fort and joy, Com-fort and joy;

O ti-dings of com-fort and joy. A-MEN.

# 132 Jesus Christ the Lord

Rev. Joseph Mohr, 1818
Translation compiled
from several sources

6. 6. 8. 8. 6. 6.

STILLE NACHT
Ascribed to Franz Grüber, 1818

1. Si - lent night! ho - ly night! All is dark, save the light Yon - der, where they sweet vig - il keep O'er the Babe, who in si - lent sleep Rests in heav - en - ly peace, Rests in heav - en - ly peace.

2. Peace - ful night! ho - li - est night! Dark - ness flies, all is light; Shep - herds hear the an - gels sing: "Al - le - lu - ia! hail the King! Christ the Sav - iour is here! Je - sus the Sav - iour is here!"

3. Si - lent night! ho - li - est night! Child of heaven, O how bright Thou didst smile on us when Thou wast born! Blest in - deed that hap - py morn, Full of heav - en - ly joy! Full of heav - en - ly joy!

A - MEN.

**133**

Christina Rossetti (1830–1894)  6. 7. 6. 7.  HERMITAGE
R. O. Morris

*In unison.  Not too fast*

1. Love came down at Christ - mas, Love all love - ly, Love di - vine;
2. Wor - ship we the God - head, Love in - car - nate, Love di - vine;
3. Love shall be our to - ken, Love be yours and love be mine,

*Col 8va. ad lib.*

Love was born at Christ - mas, Stars and an - gels gave the sign.
Wor - ship we our Je - sus: But where - with for sa - cred sign?
Love to God and all men, Love for plea and gift and sign. A - MEN.

Used by permission of the Society for Promoting Christian Knowledge.

**134**

Dora Greenwell, 1874  L. M.  EIN KIND GEBOREN
Old German carol

*In the style of a carol.  Not too fast*

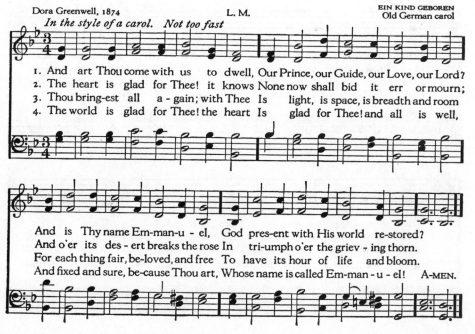

1. And art Thou come with us to dwell, Our Prince, our Guide, our Love, our Lord?
2. The heart is glad for Thee! it knows None now shall bid it err or mourn;
3. Thou bring-est all a - gain; with Thee Is light, is space, is breadth and room
4. The world is glad for Thee! the heart Is glad for Thee! and all is well,

And is Thy name Em-man-u - el, God pres-ent with His world re-stored?
And o'er its des - ert breaks the rose In tri-umph o'er the griev - ing thorn.
For each thing fair, be-loved, and free To have its hour of life and bloom.
And fixed and sure, be-cause Thou art, Whose name is called Em-man-u - el! A - MEN.

Bishop Reginald Heber, 1811      11. 10. 11. 10.      MORNING STAR
John P. Harding (1850–1911)

*In the style of a carol*

1. Bright - est and best of the sons of the morn - ing,
2. Cold on His cra - dle the dew - drops are shin - ing;
3. Say, shall we yield Him, in cost - ly de - vo - tion,
4. Vain - ly we of - fer each am - ple ob - la - tion,

Dawn on our dark - ness and lend us thine aid;
Low lies His head with the beasts of the stall:
O - dors of E - dom and of - ferings di - vine,
Vain - ly with gifts would His fa - vor se - cure;

Star of the East, the ho - ri - zon a - dorn - ing,
An - gels a - dore Him in slum - ber re - clin - ing,
Gems of the moun - tain and pearls of the o - cean,
Rich - er by far is the heart's ad - o - ra - tion,

Guide where our in - fant Re - deem - er is laid.
Mak - er and Mon - arch and Sav - iour of all.
Myrrh from the for - est, or gold from the mine?
Dear - er to God are the prayers of the poor. A - MEN.

5. Brightest and best of the sons of the morning,
     Dawn on our darkness, and lend us thine aid;
     Star of the East, the horizon adorning,
     Guide where our infant Redeemer is laid.

# Jesus Christ the Lord

Bishop William Walsham How, 1871   7. 6. 7. 6. D.   ROTTERDAM
Berthold Tours, 1875

*With joy, but with dignity*

1. O one with God the Fa - ther In maj - es - ty and might,
2. Yet, Lord, we see but dark - ly; O heaven - ly Light, a - rise,
3. O Je - sus, shine a - round us With ra - diance of Thy grace;

The Bright-ness of His glo - ry, E - ter - nal Light of light,
Dis - pel these mists that shroud us, And hide Thee from our eyes!
O Je - sus, turn up - on us The bright-ness of Thy face.

O'er this our home of dark - ness Thy rays are stream - ing now;
We long to track the foot - prints That Thou Thy - self hast trod;
We need no star to guide us, As on our way we press,

The shad-ows flee be - fore Thee; The world's true Light art Thou.
We long to see the path - way That leads to Thee, our God.
If Thou Thy light vouch-saf - est, O Sun of Right-eous-ness. A-MEN.

Rev. Louis F. Benson (1855-1930)   C. M. D.   KINGSFOLD
English traditional melody

*In the style of a carol*

1. O sing a song of Beth - le - hem, Of shep-herds watch-ing there,
2. O sing a song of Naz - a - reth, Of sun - ny days of joy,
3. O sing a song of Gal - i - lee, Of lake and woods and hill,
4. O sing a song of Cal - va - ry, Its glo - ry and dis - may;

And of the news that came to them From an - gels in the air:
O sing of fra - grant flow-ers' breath, And of the sin - less Boy:
Of Him who walked up - on the sea And bade its waves be still:
Of Him who hung up - on the tree, And took our sins a - way:

The light that shone on Beth - le - hem Fills all the world to - day;
For now the flowers of Naz - a - reth In ev - ery heart may grow;
For though, like waves on Gal - i - lee, Dark seas of trou - ble roll,
For He who died on Cal - va - ry Is ris - en from the grave,

Of Je - sus' birth and peace on earth The an - gels sing al - way.
Now spreads the fame of His dear Name On all the winds that blow.
When faith has heard the Mas - ter s word, Falls peace up - on the soul.
And Christ, our Lord, by heaven a - dored, Is might - y now to save. A-MEN.

Tune from "The English Hymnal." Used by permission of the Oxford University Press.

# 139

## Jesus Christ the Lord

15th century
Trans. by Benjamin Webb (1820-1885)     L. M.

DEO GRACIAS
"The Agincourt Song," 1415

*In unison; majestically*

1. O   Love,   how   deep,   how   broad,   how   high!
2. For   us   bap - tized,   for   us   He   bore
3. For   us   to   wick - ed   men   be - trayed,
4. For   us   He   rose   from   death   a - gain,

How   pass - ing   thought   and   fan - ta - sy,
His   ho - ly   fast,   and   hun - gered   sore;
Scourged,   mocked,   in   crown   of   thorns   ar - rayed;
For   us   He   went   on   high   to   reign;

That   God,   the   Son   of   God,   should   take
For   us   temp - ta - tions   sharp   He   knew;
For   us   He   bore   the   cross - 's   death;
For   us   He   sent   His   Spir - it   here

Our   mor - tal   form   for   mor - tals'   sake!
For   us   the   Temp - ter   o - ver - threw.
For   us   at   length   gave   up   His   breath.
To   guide,   to   strength - en,   and   to   cheer.   A - MEN.

Rev. Jay T. Stocking, 1912      C. M. D.      Clement William Poole (1828-1924)

PETERSHAM

*In moderate time*

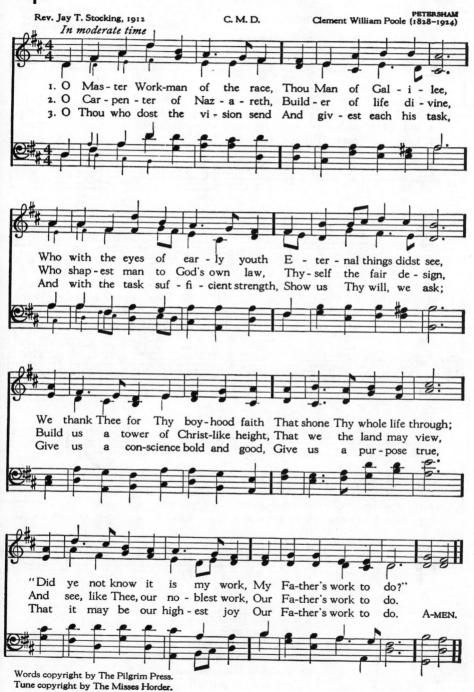

1. O Mas - ter Work-man of the race, Thou Man of Gal - i - lee,
2. O Car - pen - ter of Naz - a - reth, Build - er of life di - vine,
3. O Thou who dost the vi - sion send And giv - est each his task,

Who with the eyes of ear - ly youth E - ter - nal things didst see,
Who shap - est man to God's own law, Thy - self the fair de - sign,
And with the task suf - fi - cient strength, Show us Thy will, we ask;

We thank Thee for Thy boy - hood faith That shone Thy whole life through;
Build us a tower of Christ-like height, That we the land may view,
Give us a con - science bold and good, Give us a pur - pose true,

"Did ye not know it is my work, My Fa - ther's work to do?"
And see, like Thee, our no - blest work, Our Fa - ther's work to do.
That it may be our high - est joy Our Fa - ther's work to do. A - MEN.

Words copyright by The Pilgrim Press.
Tune copyright by The Misses Horder.

# Jesus Christ the Lord

Rev. Stopford Augustus Brooke (1832–1916)

7. 7. 5. D.

WINDRUSH
Rouen church melody
Adapted as in "School Worship," 1926

*Moderately fast. May be sung in unison*

1. When the Lord of Love was here, Hap-py hearts to Him were dear,
2. Meek and low-ly were His ways; From His lov-ing grew His praise,
3. When He walked the fields, He drew From the flowers, and birds, and dew,
4. Lord, be ours Thy power to keep, In the ver-y heart of grief,

Though His heart was sad; Worn and lone-ly for our sake,
From His giv-ing, prayer: All the out-casts thronged to hear;
Par-a-bles of God; For with-in His heart of love
And in tri-al, love; In our meek-ness to be wise,

Yet He turned a-side to make All the wea-ry glad.
All the sor-row-ful drew near To en-joy His care.
All the soul of man did move, God had His a-bode.
And through sor-row to a-rise To our God a-bove. A - MEN.

5. Fill us with Thy deep desire
All the sinful to inspire
With the Father's life;
Free us from the cares that press
On the heart of worldliness,
From the fret and strife.

Latin; trans. by Rev. John M. Neale, 1854    L. M.    "The Agincourt Song," 1415    DEO GRACIAS

*Unison. In moderate time; majestically*

1. O won - drous type, O vi - sion fair ;
2. With shin - ing face and bright ar - ray,
3. And faith - ful hearts are raised on high
4. O Fa - ther, with th' e - ter - nal Son,

Of glo - ry that the Church shall share,
Christ deigns to man - i - fest to - day
By this great vi - sion's mys - ter - y;
And Ho - ly Spir - it, ev - er One,

Which Christ up - on the moun - tain shows
What glo - ry shall be theirs a - bove
For which in joy - ful strains we raise
Vouch - safe to bring us by Thy grace

Where bright - er than the sun He glows.
Who joy in God with per - fect love.
The voice of prayer, the hymn of praise.
To see Thy glo - ry face to face.    A - MEN.

# 143

Edward Denny, 1839

C. M.

DALEHURST
Arthur Cottman, 1874

*In moderate time*

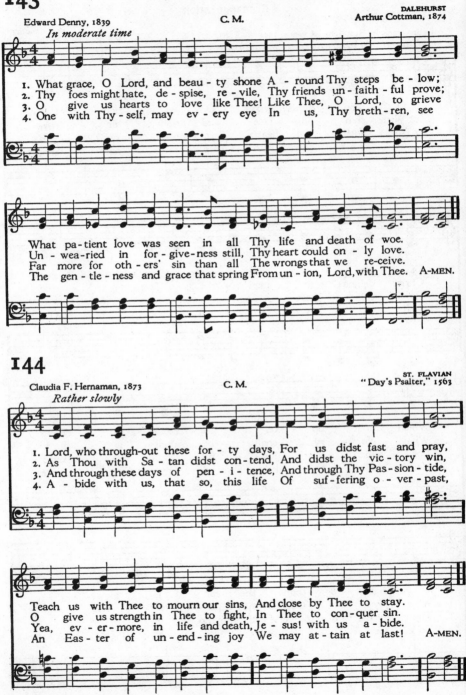

1. What grace, O Lord, and beau - ty shone A - round Thy steps be - low;
2. Thy foes might hate, de - spise, re - vile, Thy friends un - faith - ful prove;
3. O give us hearts to love like Thee! Like Thee, O Lord, to grieve
4. One with Thy - self, may ev - ery eye In us, Thy breth - ren, see

What pa - tient love was seen in all Thy life and death of woe.
Un - wea - ried in for - give - ness still, Thy heart could on - ly love.
Far more for oth - ers' sin than all The wrongs that we re - ceive.
The gen - tle - ness and grace that spring From un - ion, Lord, with Thee. A - MEN.

# 144

Claudia F. Hernaman, 1873

C. M.

ST. FLAVIAN
"Day's Psalter," 1563

*Rather slowly*

1. Lord, who through-out these for - ty days, For us didst fast and pray,
2. As Thou with Sa - tan didst con - tend, And didst the vic - tory win,
3. And through these days of pen - i - tence, And through Thy Pas - sion - tide,
4. A - bide with us, that so, this life Of suf - fering o - ver - past,

Teach us with Thee to mourn our sins, And close by Thee to stay.
O give us strength in Thee to fight, In Thee to con - quer sin.
Yea, ev - er - more, in life and death, Je - sus! with us a - bide.
An Eas - ter of un - end - ing joy We may at - tain at last! A - MEN.

Rev. John Hampden Gurney (1802–1862)

Old Irish melody; from Dr. Petrie's Collection

ST. COLUMBA (IRISH)

C. M.

*Not too fast. In flowing rhythm*

1. Lord, as to Thy dear cross we flee, And plead to be for - given, So let Thy life our pat - tern be, And form our souls for heaven.
2. Help us through good re - port and ill Our dai - ly cross to bear, Like Thee to do our Fa - ther's will, Our breth - ren's griefs to share.
3. Let grace our self - ish - ness ex - pel, Our earth - li - ness re - fine, And kind - ness in our bos - oms dwell, As free and true as Thine.
4. If joy shall at Thy bid - ding fly, And grief's dark day come on, We in our turn would meek - ly cry "Fa - ther, Thy will be done." A - MEN.

5. Kept peaceful in the midst of strife,
Forgiving and forgiven,
O may we lead the pilgrim's life,
And follow Thee to heaven.

Tune used by permission of Messrs. Stainer and Bell.

# 146 Jesus Christ the Lord

Theodulph of Orleans, c. 820; trans. by Rev. John M. Neale, 1854
Stanza 1, line 1; stanza 5, alt. in "Hymns Ancient and Modern"
7. 6. 7. 6. D.

ST. THEODULPH
Melchior Teschner, c. 1615

**ASCRIPTION**

{ All glo - ry, laud, and hon - or To Thee, Re - deem - er, King,
{ To whom the lips of chil - dren Made sweet ho - san - nas ring.

1. Thou art the King of Is - rael, Thou Da - vid's roy - al Son,
2. The com - pa - ny of an - gels Are prais - ing Thee on high,
3. The peo - ple of the He - brews With palms be - fore Thee went;
4. To Thee, be - fore Thy pas - sion, They sang their hymns of praise;
5. Thou didst ac - cept their prais - es; Ac - cept the prayers we bring,

Who in the Lord's Name com - est, The King and Bless - ed One.
And mor - tal men, and all things Cre - at - ed, make re - ply.
Our praise and prayer and an - thems Be - fore Thee we pre - sent,
To Thee, now high ex - alt - ed, Our mel - o - dy we raise.
Who in all good de - light - est, Thou good and gra - cious King.

**REFRAIN**

{ All glo - ry, laud, and hon - or To Thee, Re - deem - er, King,
{ To whom the lips of chil - dren Made sweet ho - san - nas ring. A-MEN.

# His Triumphal Entry

ELLACOMBE
"Gesangbuch der Herzogl. Wirtembergischen
Katholischen Hofkapelle," 1784

Jennette Threlfall (1821–1880)    7. 6. 7. 6. D.

*With joy*

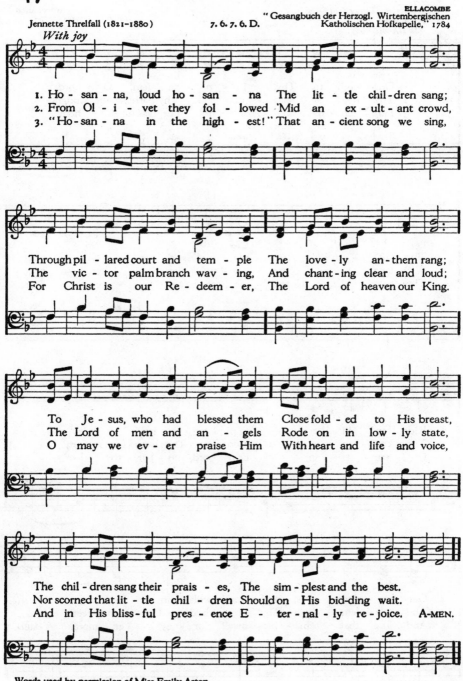

1. Ho - san - na, loud ho - san - na The lit - tle chil - dren sang;
2. From Ol - i - vet they fol - lowed 'Mid an ex - ult - ant crowd,
3. "Ho - san - na in the high - est!" That an - cient song we sing,

Through pil - lared court and tem - ple The love - ly an - them rang;
The vic - tor palm branch wav - ing, And chant - ing clear and loud;
For Christ is our Re - deem - er, The Lord of heaven our King.

To Je - sus, who had blessed them Close fold - ed to His breast,
The Lord of men and an - gels Rode on in low - ly state,
O may we ev - er praise Him With heart and life and voice,

The chil - dren sang their prais - es, The sim - plest and the best.
Nor scorned that lit - tle chil - dren Should on His bid - ding wait.
And in His bliss - ful pres - ence E - ter - nal - ly re - joice. A-MEN.

Words used by permission of Miss Emily Aston.

# 148

## Jesus Christ the Lord

Bishop Jeremy Taylor (1613-1667)
Stanza 3, alt.

10. 10. 10. 10.

WOODLANDS
Walter Greatorex (1877– )

*With majesty*

1. Draw nigh to Thy Je - ru - sa - lem, O Lord,
2. Thy road is read - y; and Thy paths, made straight,
3. Ho - san - na! wel - come to our hearts! for here

Thy faith - ful peo - ple cry with one ac - cord:
With long - ing ex - pec - ta - tion seem to wait
Thou hast a tem - ple, too, as Zi - on dear;

Ride on in tri - umph; Lord, be - hold we lay
The con - se - cra - tion of Thy beau - teous feet,
O en - ter in, dear Lord, un - bar the door

Our pas - sions, lusts, and proud wills in Thy way!
And si - lent - ly Thy prom - ised ad - vent greet!
And in that tem - ple dwell for - ev - er - more. A - MEN.

Tune used by permission of Mr. W. Greatorex.

# 149 His Triumphal Entry

Rev. John King, 1830 — 7. 6. 7. 6. D. — Berthold Tours, 1872

TOURS

*Moderately fast*

1. When, His sal - va - tion bring - ing, To Zi - on Je - sus came,
2. And since the Lord re - tain - eth His love for chil - dren still,
3. For should we fail pro - claim - ing Our great Re - deem - er's praise,

The chil - dren all stood sing - ing Ho - san - na to His Name:
Though now as King He reign - eth On Zi - on's heaven - ly hill,
The stones, our si - lence sham - ing, Would their ho - san - nas raise.

Nor did their zeal of - fend Him, But, as He rode a - long,
We'll flock a - round His ban - ner Who sits up - on His throne,
But shall we on - ly ren - der The trib - ute of our words?

He let them still at - tend Him, And smiled to hear their song.
And cry a - loud, "Ho - san - na To Da - vid's roy - al Son!"
No; while our hearts are ten - der, They, too, shall be the Lord's. A-MEN.

Tune used by permission of Novello and Company, Ltd.

**150**

Rev. Henry H. Milman, 1827
Stanza 1, line 3, alt.

L. M.
(FIRST TUNE)

ST. DROSTANE
Rev. John B. Dykes, 1862

*In majestic style*

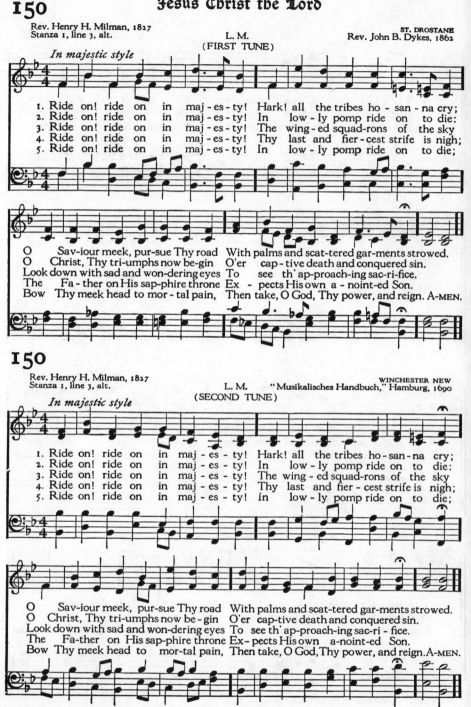

1. Ride on! ride on in maj-es-ty! Hark! all the tribes ho-san-na cry;
2. Ride on! ride on in maj-es-ty! In low-ly pomp ride on to die:
3. Ride on! ride on in maj-es-ty! The wing-ed squad-rons of the sky
4. Ride on! ride on in maj-es-ty! Thy last and fier-cest strife is nigh;
5. Ride on! ride on in maj-es-ty! In low-ly pomp ride on to die;

O Sav-iour meek, pur-sue Thy road With palms and scat-tered gar-ments strowed
O Christ, Thy tri-umphs now be-gin O'er cap-tive death and conquered sin.
Look down with sad and won-dering eyes To see th' ap-proach-ing sac-ri-fice.
The Fa-ther on His sap-phire throne Ex-pects His own a-noint-ed Son.
Bow Thy meek head to mor-tal pain, Then take, O God, Thy power, and reign. A-MEN.

**150**

Rev. Henry H. Milman, 1827
Stanza 1, line 3, alt.

L. M.
(SECOND TUNE)

WINCHESTER NEW
"Musikalisches Handbuch," Hamburg, 1690

*In majestic style*

1. Ride on! ride on in maj-es-ty! Hark! all the tribes ho-san-na cry;
2. Ride on! ride on in maj-es-ty! In low-ly pomp ride on to die:
3. Ride on! ride on in maj-es-ty! The wing-ed squad-rons of the sky
4. Ride on! ride on in maj-es-ty! Thy last and fier-cest strife is nigh;
5. Ride on! ride on in maj-es-ty! In low-ly pomp ride on to die;

O Sav-iour meek, pur-sue Thy road With palms and scat-tered gar-ments strowed.
O Christ, Thy tri-umphs now be-gin O'er cap-tive death and conquered sin.
Look down with sad and won-dering eyes To see th' ap-proach-ing sac-ri-fice.
The Fa-ther on His sap-phire throne Ex-pects His own a-noint-ed Son.
Bow Thy meek head to mor-tal pain, Then take, O God, Thy power, and reign. A-MEN.

# 151 His Passion

Ascribed to Bernard of Clairvaux (1091-1153)
Trans. (into German) by Rev. Paul Gerhardt, 1656
Trans. (from the German) by Rev. James W. Alexander, 1830
7. 6. 7. 6. D.

PASSION CHORALE
Hans Leo Hassler, 1601
Harmonized by Johann S. Bach, 1729

*With great dignity*

1. O sa-cred Head, now wound-ed, With grief and shame weighed down;
2. What Thou, my Lord, hast suf-fered Was all for sin-ners' gain:
3. What lan-guage shall I bor-row To thank Thee, dear-est Friend,

Now scorn-ful-ly sur-round-ed With thorns, Thine on-ly crown;
Mine, mine was the trans-gres-sion, But Thine the dead-ly pain.
For this Thy dy-ing sor-row, Thy pit-y with-out end?

O sa-cred Head, what glo-ry, What bliss till now was Thine!
Lo, here I fall, my Sav-iour! 'Tis I de-serve Thy place;
O make me Thine for-ev-er; And should I faint-ing be,

Yet, though de-spised and go-ry, I joy to call Thee mine.
Look on me with Thy fa-vor, Vouch-safe to me Thy grace.
Lord, let me nev-er, nev-er Out-live my love to Thee. A-MEN.

## 152

Rev. Isaac Watts, 1707

L. M.
(FIRST TUNE)

ROCKINGHAM OLD
Edward Miller, 1790

*In moderate time*

1. When I sur-vey the won-drous cross On which the Prince of Glo-ry died,
2. For-bid it, Lord, that I should boast, Save in the death of Christ my God:
3. See, from His head, His hands, His feet, Sor-row and love flow min-gled down:
4. Were the whole realm of na-ture mine, That were a pres-ent far too small;

My rich-est gain I count but loss, And pour con-tempt on all my pride.
All the vain things that charm me most, I sac-ri-fice them to His blood.
Did e'er such love and sor-row meet, Or thorns com-pose so rich a crown?
Love so a-maz-ing, so di-vine, De-mands my soul, my life, my all. A-MEN.

## 152

Rev. Isaac Watts, 1707

L. M.
(SECOND TUNE)

HAMBURG
Arr. from a Gregorian chant, by
Lowell Mason, 1824

*In moderate time*

1. When I sur-vey the won-drous cross On which the Prince of Glo-ry died,
2. For-bid it, Lord, that I should boast, Save in the death of Christ my God:
3. See, from His head, His hands, His feet, Sor-row and love flow min-gled down:
4. Were the whole realm of na-ture mine, That were a pres-ent far too small;

My rich-est gain I count but loss, And pour con-tempt on all my pride.
All the vain things that charm me most, I sac-ri-fice them to His blood.
Did e'er such love and sor-row meet, Or thorns com-pose so rich a crown?
Love so a-maz-ing, so di-vine, De-mands my soul, my life, my all. A-MEN.

# 153

Matthew Bridges, 1848     6. 6. 6. 4. 8. 8. 4.     ECCE AGNUS
George William Warren (1828–1902)

*In majestic style*

1. Be - hold the Lamb of God! O Thou for sin - ners slain,
2. Be - hold the Lamb of God! All hail, In - car - nate Word!
3. Be - hold the Lamb of God! Wor - thy is He a - lone

Let it not be in vain That Thou hast died.
Thou ev - er - last - ing Lord, Sav - iour most blest!
To sit up - on the throne Of God a - bove,

Thee for my Sav - iour let me take, My on - ly ref - uge
Fill us with love that nev - er faints, Grant us, with all Thy
One with the An - cient of all days, One with the Com - fort -

let me make Thy pier - ced side!
bless - ed saints, E - ter - nal rest.
er in praise, All Light, all Love! A - MEN.

Tune used by permission of Mrs. Irene Martin Ramsay.

# Jesus Christ the Lord

## 154

John Bowring, 1825      8. 7. 8. 7.      RATHBUN
Ithamar Conkey, 1851

*Not too slow*

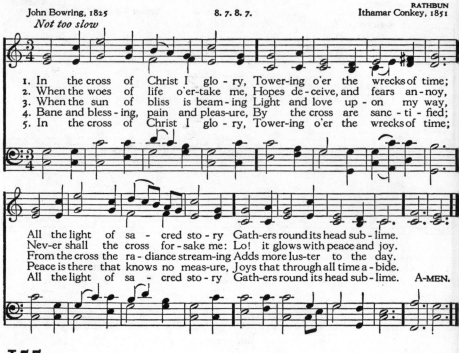

1. In the cross of Christ I glo - ry, Tower-ing o'er the wrecks of time;
2. When the woes of life o'er-take me, Hopes de - ceive, and fears an - noy,
3. When the sun of bliss is beam - ing Light and love up - on my way,
4. Bane and bless - ing, pain and pleas-ure, By the cross are sanc - ti - fied;
5. In the cross of Christ I glo - ry, Tower-ing o'er the wrecks of time;

All the light of sa - cred sto - ry Gath-ers round its head sub - lime.
Nev-er shall the cross for-sake me: Lo! it glows with peace and joy.
From the cross the ra - diance stream-ing Adds more lus-ter to the day.
Peace is there that knows no meas-ure, Joys that through all time a - bide.
All the light of sa - cred sto - ry Gath-ers round its head sub - lime. A-MEN.

## 155

Rev. William J. S. Simpson, 1886      8. 7. 8. 7.      CROSS OF JESUS
John Stainer, 1887

*In moderate time*

1. Cross of Je - sus, cross of sor - row, Where the blood of Christ was shed,
2. Here the King of all the a - ges, Throned in light ere worlds could be,
3. O mys - te - rious con - de - scend-ing! O a - ban - don-ment sub - lime!
4. Ev - er-more for hu - man fail - ure By His pas - sion we can plead;

Per-fect man on thee did suf - fer, Per - fect God on thee has bled!
Robed in mor-tal flesh is dy - ing, Cru - ci - fied by sin for me.
Ver-y God Him-self is bear-ing All the suf - fer - ings of time!
God has borne all mor - tal an - guish, Sure - ly He will know our need. A-MEN.

Used by permission of Novello and Company, Ltd.

Rev. Arthur T. Russell, 1851   7. 6. 7. 6. D.   MEIRIONYDD
Welsh hymn melody

*Not too fast. With great reverence*

1. O Je - sus, we a - dore Thee, Up - on the cross, our King!
2. Yet doth the world dis - dain Thee, Still pass - ing by the cross;
3. O glo - rious King, we bless Thee, No lon - ger pass Thee by;

We bow our hearts be - fore Thee, Thy gra - cious Name we sing.
Lord, may our hearts re - tain Thee; All else we count but loss.
O Je - sus, we con - fess Thee The Son en - throned on high.

That Name hath brought sal - va - tion, That Name in life our stay,
Ah, Lord, our sins ar - raigned Thee, And nailed Thee to the tree:
Lord, grant to us re - mis - sion; Life through Thy death re - store;

Our peace, our con - so - la - tion, When life shall fade a - way.
Our pride, our Lord, dis - dained Thee; Yet deign our Hope to be.
Yea, grant us the fru - i - tion Of life for - ev - er - more. A-MEN.

Tune used by permission of Dr. Basil Harwood.

**157**

Cecil Frances Alexander, 1848

C. M.
(FIRST TUNE)

MEDITATION
John H. Gower, 1890

*In moderate time*

1. There is a green hill far a-way, With-out a cit-y wall,
2. We may not know, we can-not tell, What pains He had to bear;
3. He died that we might be for-given, He died to make us good,
4. There was no oth-er good e-nough To pay the price of sin;
5. O dear-ly, dear-ly has He loved, And we must love Him, too,

Where the dear Lord was cru-ci-fied, Who died to save us all.
But we be-lieve it was for us He hung and suf-fered there.
That we might go at last to heaven, Saved by His pre-cious blood.
He on-ly could un-lock the gate Of heaven, and let us in.
And trust in His re-deem-ing blood, And try His works to do. A-MEN.

Copyright by John H. Gower.

**157**

Cecil Frances Alexander, 1848

C. M.
(SECOND TUNE)

HORSLEY
William Horsley, 1844

*Rather slowly*

1. There is a green hill far a-way, With-out a cit-y wall,
2. We may not know, we can-not tell, What pains He had to bear;
3. He died that we might be for-given, He died to make us good,
4. There was no oth-er good e-nough To pay the price of sin;
5. O dear-ly, dear-ly has He loved, And we must love Him, too,

Where the dear Lord was cru-ci-fied, Who died to save us all.
But we be-lieve it was for us He hung and suf-fered there.
That we might go at last to heaven, Saved by His pre-cious blood.
He on-ly could un-lock the gate Of heaven, and let us in.
And trust in His re-deem-ing blood, And try His works to do. A-MEN.

# His Passion

Rev. Johann Heermann, c. 1630
Trans. by Robert Bridges, 1899

11. 11. 11. 5.

HERZLIEBSTER JESU
Johann Crüger, 1640

*Rather slowly and solemnly*
*May be sung in unison*

1. Ah, dear - est Je - sus, how hast Thou of -
2. Who was the guilt - y? Who brought this up -
3. For me, dear Je - sus, was Thy in - car -
4. There - fore, dear Je - sus, since I can - not

fend - ed, That man to judge Thee hath in hate pre -
on Thee? A - las, my trea - son, Je - sus, hath un -
na - tion, Thy mor - tal sor - row, and Thy life's ob -
pay Thee, I do a - dore Thee, and will ev - er

tend - ed? By foes de - rid - ed, by Thine own re -
done Thee! 'Twas I, Lord Je - sus, I it was de -
la - tion; Thy death of an - guish and Thy bit - ter
pray Thee, Think on Thy pit - y and Thy love un -

ject - ed, O most af - flict - ed!
nied Thee: I cru - ci - fied Thee.
pas - sion, For my sal - va - tion.
swerv - ing, Not my de - serv - ing. A - MEN.

**Rev. Frederick William Faber (1814–1863)**     L. M.     **Rev. John B. Dykes (1823–1876)**   ST. CROSS

1. O come and mourn with me a - while; O come ye
2. Seven times He spake, seven words of love; And all three
3. O break, O break, hard heart of mine! Thy weak self -
4. A bro - ken heart, a fount of tears, Ask, and they

to the Sav - iour's side; O come, to - geth - er let us mourn:
hours His si - lence cried For mer - cy on the souls of men:
love and guilt - y pride His Pi - late and His Ju - das were:
will not be de - nied; A bro - ken heart love's cra - dle is:

Je - sus, our Lord, is cru - ci - fied!
Je - sus, our Lord, is cru - ci - fied!
Je - sus, our Lord, is cru - ci - fied!
Je - sus, our Lord, is cru - ci - fied!    A-MEN.

5. O love of God! O sin of man!
In this dread act your strength is tried,
And victory remains with love:
Jesus, our Lord, is crucified!

**160**

Bishop William Walsham How, 1854; alt.    L. M.    "St. Alban's Tune Book," 1875

PENITENCE

*Not too fast*

1. Lord Je - sus, when we stand a - far  And gaze up - on Thy ho - ly cross,
2. When we be - hold Thy bleed-ing wounds, And the rough way that Thou hast trod,
3. O  ho - ly Lord, up - lift - ed high,  With out-stretched arms, in mor-tal woe,
4. Give us an ev - er - liv - ing faith  To gaze be-yond the things we see;

In  love of Thee, and scorn of self, O may we  count the world as loss!
Make us to hate the load of sin  That lay so  heav - y  on  our God.
Thou dost em-brace in won-drous love The sin-ful  world that lies be-low.
And  in the mys-ter-y of Thy death Draw us and all  men un - to Thee. A - MEN.

**161**

Bishop William Walsham How (1823–1897)    6. 5. 6. 5.    Timothy Richard Matthews (1826–1910)

NORTH COATES

*Rather slowly*

1. O  my Sav - iour, lift - ed  From the  earth  for  me,
2. Lift  my earth - bound long - ings,  Fix  them, Lord, a - bove;
3. Lord, Thine arms are stretch - ing  Ev - er  far  and  wide,
4. And  I come, O  Je - sus:  Dare I  turn  a - way?
5. Bring - ing  all  my  bur - dens,  Sor - row, sin, and  care,

Draw me,  in Thy  mer - cy,  Near - er  un - to  Thee;
Draw me  with the  mag - net  Of Thy  might - y  love.
To  en - fold Thy  chil - dren  To Thy  lov - ing  side.
No! Thy  love hath  con - quered, And  I  come to - day;
At  Thy  feet  I  lay  them  And  I  leave them there.  A - MEN.

Tune by permission of Novello and Company, Ltd.

# Jesus Christ the Lord

Elizabeth C. Clephane, published 1872   7. 6. 8. 6. 8. 6. 8. 6.

ST. CHRISTOPHER
Frederick C. Maker, 1881

*Not too fast*

1. Be-neath the cross of Je - sus I fain would take my stand—
2. Up - on the cross of Je - sus Mine eye at times can see
3. I take, O cross, thy shad - ow For my a - bid - ing place:

The shad - ow of a might - y Rock With - in a wea - ry land;
The ver - y dy - ing form of One Who suf - fered there for me:
I ask no oth - er sun - shine than The sun - shine of His face;

A home with - in the wil - der - ness, A rest up - on the way,
And from my strick - en heart with tears Two won - ders I con - fess—
Con - tent to let the world go by, To know no gain nor loss:

From the burn-ing of the noon-tide heat, And the bur-den of the day.
The won-ders of re-deem-ing love And my un-worth-i-ness.
My sin-ful self my on-ly shame, My glo-ry all, the cross. A-MEN.

# His Resurrection

**163**

Based on the Latin, 14th century
Stanza 4, Rev. Charles Wesley, 1740   7. 7. 7. 7. with Alleluias

EASTER HYMN
"Lyra Davidica," 1708

*Jubilantly*

1. Je - sus Christ is risen to - day, Al - - - le - lu - ia!
2. Hymns of praise then let us sing, Al - - - le - lu - ia!
3. But the pains which He en - dured, Al - - - le - lu - ia!
4. Sing we to our God a - bove, Al - - - le - lu - ia!

Our tri - um - phant ho - ly day, Al - - - le - lu - ia!
Un - to Christ, our heaven-ly King, Al - - - le - lu - ia!
Our sal - va - tion have pro - cured; Al - - - le - lu - ia!
Praise e - ter - nal as His love; Al - - - le - lu - ia!

Who did once, up - on the cross, Al - - - le - lu - ia!
Who en - dured the cross and grave, Al - - - le - lu - ia!
Now a - bove the sky He's King, Al - - - le - lu - ia!
Praise Him, all ye heaven-ly host, Al - - - le - lu - ia!

Suf - fer to re - deem our loss. Al - - - le - lu - ia!
Sin - ners to re - deem and save. Al - - - le - lu - ia!
Where the an - gels ev - er sing. Al - - - le - lu - ia!
Fa - ther, Son, and Ho - ly Ghost. Al - - - le - lu - ia!   A-MEN.

# Jesus Christ the Lord

Latin; trans. by Rev. Francis Pott, 1861

8. 8. 8. 4. with Alleluias

PALESTRINA
Giovanni P. da Palestrina, 1591
Adapted by W. H. Monk

*Jubilantly. With majesty*

Al - le - lu - ia! Al - le - lu - ia! Al - le - lu - ia!

Org.

1. The strife is o'er, the bat - tle done;
2. The powers of death have done their worst,
3. The three sad days have quick - ly sped;
4. He closed the yawn - ing gates of hell;
5. Lord, by the stripes which wound - ed Thee,

The vic - to - ry of life is won; The song of
But Christ their le - gions hath dis - persed: Let shouts of
He ris - es glo - rious from the dead: All glo - ry
The bars from heaven's high por - tals fell: Let hymns of
From death's dread sting Thy serv - ants free, That we may

tri - umph has be - gun. Al - le - lu - ia!
ho - ly joy out - burst. Al - le - lu - ia!
to our ris - en Head! Al - le - lu - ia!
praise His tri - umphs tell. Al - le - lu - ia!
live and sing to Thee. Al - le - lu - ia! A - MEN.

# 165 His Resurrection

7. 7. 7. 7. with Alleluias

Rev. Charles Wesley (1707–1788)

LLANFAIR
Robert Williams (c. 1781–1821)

*Jubilantly*

1. "Christ the Lord is risen to-day," Al - le - lu - ia!
2. Vain the stone, the watch, the seal; Al - le - lu - ia!
3. Lives a - gain our glo - rious King; Al - le - lu - ia!
4. Soar we now where Christ has led, Al - le - lu - ia!
5. Hail, the Lord of earth and heaven! Al - le - lu - ia!

Sons of men and an - gels say; Al - le - lu - ia!
Christ has burst the gates of hell: Al - le - lu - ia!
Where, O death, is now thy sting? Al - le - lu - ia!
Fol - lowing our ex - alt - ed Head; Al - le - lu - ia!
Praise to Thee by both be given; Al - le - lu - ia!

Raise your joys and tri - umphs high; Al - le - lu - ia!
Death in vain for - bids His rise; Al - le - lu - ia!
Once He died, our souls to save; Al - le - lu - ia!
Made like Him, like Him we rise; Al - le - lu - ia!
Thee we greet tri - um - phant now; Al - le - lu - ia!

*In unison*

Sing, ye heavens, and earth, re - ply; Al - le - lu - ia!
Christ hath o - pened Par - a - dise. Al - le - lu - ia!
Where thy vic - to - ry, O grave? Al - le - lu - ia!
Ours the cross, the grave, the skies. Al - le - lu - ia!
Hail, the Res - ur - rec - tion Thou! Al - le - lu - ia! A-MEN.

May be sung to EASTER HYMN, Hymn 163.
From "The Church Hymnary," Revised. Used by permission of the Oxford University Press.

# 166 Jesus Christ the Lord

John of Damascus (8th century)
Trans. by Rev. John M. Neale, 1862

7. 6. 7. 6. D.

LANCASHIRE
Henry Smart, 1836

*Jubilantly*

1. The day of res - ur - rec - tion! Earth, tell it out a - broad
2. Our hearts be pure from e - vil, That we may see a - right
3. Now let the heavens be joy - ful, Let earth her song be - gin;

The Pass - o - ver of glad - ness, The Pass - o - ver of God.
The Lord in rays e - ter - nal Of res - ur - rec - tion light;
Let the round world keep tri - umph, And all that is there - in;

From death to life e - ter - nal, From this world to the sky,
And, lis - tening to His ac - cents, May hear, so calm and plain,
Let all things seen and un - seen, Their notes of glad - ness blend,

Our Christ hath brought us o - ver With hymns of vic - to - ry.
His own "All hail!" and, hear - ing, May raise the vic - tor strain.
For Christ the Lord hath ris - en, Our Joy that hath no end. A-MEN.

# 167 His Resurrection

Jean Tisserand, d. 1494
Trans. by Rev. John M. Neale, 1852   8. 8. 8. with Alleluias

O FILII ET FILIAE
French, 15th century

*May be sung in unison. With joy*

Al - le - lu - ia! Al - le - lu - ia! Al - le - lu - ia! Al -

le - lu - ia!

1. O sons and daugh - ters, let us sing!
2. That Eas - ter morn, at break of day,
3. An an - gel clad in white they see,
4. How blest are they who have not seen,
5. On this most ho - ly day of days,

The King of heaven, the glo - rious King, O'er death to - day rose
The faith - ful wom - en went their way To seek the tomb where
Who sat, and spake un - to the three, "Your Lord doth go to
And yet whose faith hath con - stant been; For they e - ter - nal
Our hearts and voi - ces, Lord, we raise To Thee, in ju - bi -

tri - umph - ing. Al - le - lu - ia! Al - le - lu - ia!
Je - sus lay. Al - le - lu - ia! Al - le - lu - ia!
Gal - i - lee." Al - le - lu - ia! Al - le - lu - ia!
life shall win. Al - le - lu - ia! Al - le - lu - ia!
lee and praise. Al - le - lu - ia! Al - le - lu - ia! A - MEN.

# 168 Jesus Christ the Lord

John of Damascus (8th century)
Trans. by Rev. John M. Neale, 1859          7. 6. 7. 6. D.

**ST. KEVIN**
Arthur Sullivan, 1872

*Jubilantly*

1. Come, ye faith-ful, raise the strain Of tri-um-phant glad-ness:
2. 'Tis the spring of souls to-day: Christ hath burst His pris-on,

God hath brought His peo-ple forth In-to joy from sad-ness.
And from three days' sleep in death As a sun hath ris-en;

Now re-joice, Je-ru-sa-lem, And with true af-fec-tion
All the win-ter of our sins, Long and dark, is fly-ing

Wel-come in un-wea-ried strains Je-sus' res-ur-rec-tion.
From His light, to whom we give Laud and praise un-dy-ing.  A-MEN.

Tune used by permission of Novello and Company, Ltd.

# His Resurrection

Bishop Venantius Fortunatus (530–609)
Trans. by John Ellerton (1826–1893)

Frances Ridley Havergal (1836–1879)

HERMAS

6. 5. 6. 5. D. with Refrain

*With joy*

1. "Wel-come, hap-py morn-ing!" Age to age shall say: "Hell to-day is van-quished,
2. Earth with joy con-fess-es, Cloth-ing her for spring, All good gifts re-turn with
3. Thou, of life the Au-thor, Death didst un-der-go, Tread the path of dark-ness,

Heaven is won to-day." Lo! the dead is liv-ing, God for-ev-er-more:
Her re-turn-ing King; Bloom in ev-ery mead-ow, Leaves on ev-ery bough,
Sav-ing strength to show; Come then, True and Faith-ful, Now ful-fill Thy word;

Him, their true Cre-a-tor, All His works a-dore. "Wel-come, hap-py morn-ing,"
Speak His sor-rows end-ed, Hail His tri-umph now.
'Tis Thine own third morn-ing; Rise, O bur-ied Lord!

REFRAIN

Age to age shall say: "Hell to-day is van-quished, Heaven is won to-day." A-MEN.

# 170

## Jesus Christ the Lord

Bishop William Walsham How, 1872    6. 6. 6. 6. 8. 8.    MANSFIELD
Joseph Barnby, 1893

*Jubilantly*

1. On wings of liv - ing light, At ear - liest
2. Then rose from death's dark gloom, Un - seen by
3. Ye chil - dren of the light, A - rise with
4. Leave in the grave be - neath The old things

dawn of day, Came down the an - gel bright, And rolled the
mor - tal eye, Tri - um-phant o'er the tomb, The Lord of
Him, a - rise: See, how the Day - Star bright Is burn-ing
passed a - way; Bur - ied with Him] in death, O live with

stone a - way. Your voi - ces raise with one ac - cord
earth and sky. Your voi - ces raise with one ac - cord
in the skies! Your voi - ces raise with one ac - cord
Him to - day! Your voi - ces raise with one ac - cord

To bless and praise your ris - en Lord.
To bless and praise your ris - en Lord.
To bless and praise your ris - en Lord.
To bless and praise your ris - en Lord.    A - MEN.

Tune used by permission of Novello and Company, Ltd.
Words from "The Church Hymnary," Revised. Used by permission of Mr. F. D. How and the Oxford University Press.

**171**

Rev. Charles Wesley (1707–1788)　　7. 7. 7. 7. with Alleluias　　William Henry Monk (1823–1889)

ASCENSION

*In jubilant style*

1. Hail the day that sees Him rise, Al - le - lu - ia!
2. There the glo - rious tri - umph waits: Al - le - lu - ia!
3. Him though high - est heaven re - ceives, Al - le - lu - ia!

Rav - ished from our wish - ful eyes! Al - le - lu - ia!
Lift your heads, e - ter - nal gates, Al - le - lu - ia!
Still He loves the earth He leaves; Al - le - lu - ia!

Christ, a - while to mor - tals given, Al - le - lu - ia!
Wide un - fold the ra - diant scene, Al - le - lu - ia!
Though re - turn - ing to His throne, Al - le - lu - ia!

Re - as - cends His na - tive heaven. Al - le - lu - ia!
Take the King of Glo - ry in! Al - le - lu - ia!
Still He calls man - kind His own. Al - le - lu - ia! A-MEN.

# Jesus Christ the Lord

Rev. Arthur Tozer Russell (1806-1874)    8. 8. 7. D.    Johann Gottfried Schicht (1753-1823)

ASCENDIT DEUS

*In moderate time, with dignity*

1. The Lord as-cend-eth up on high, The Lord hath tri-umphed glo-rious-ly, In power and might ex-cell-ing; The grave and hell are cap-tive led, Lo! He re-turns, our glo-rious Head, To His e-ter-nal dwell-ing.

2. The heavens with joy re-ceive their Lord, By saints, by an-gel hosts a-dored; O day of ex-ul-ta-tion! O earth, a-dore thy glo-rious King! His ris-ing, His as-cen-sion sing With grate-ful ad-o-ra-tion!

3. Our great High Priest hath gone be-fore, Now on His Church His grace to pour, And still His love He giv-eth; O may our hearts to Him as-cend; May all with-in us up-ward tend To Him who ev-er liv-eth! A-MEN.

Bishop Christopher Wordsworth, 1862     8. 7. 8. 7. D.     ST. ASAPH
      William S. Bambridge, 1872

*With dignity*

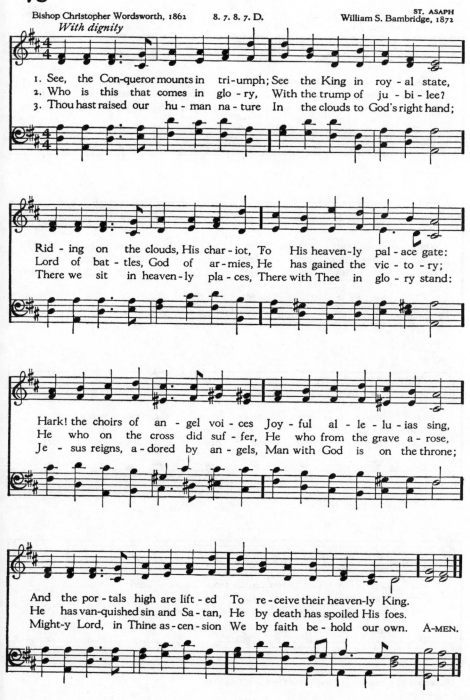

1. See, the Con-queror mounts in tri-umph; See the King in roy-al state,
2. Who is this that comes in glo-ry, With the trump of ju-bi-lee?
3. Thou hast raised our hu-man na-ture In the clouds to God's right hand;

Rid-ing on the clouds, His char-iot, To His heaven-ly pal-ace gate:
Lord of bat-tles, God of ar-mies, He has gained the vic-to-ry;
There we sit in heaven-ly pla-ces, There with Thee in glo-ry stand:

Hark! the choirs of an-gel voi-ces Joy-ful al-le-lu-ias sing,
He who on the cross did suf-fer, He who from the grave a-rose,
Je-sus reigns, a-dored by an-gels, Man with God is on the throne;

And the por-tals high are lift-ed To re-ceive their heaven-ly King.
He has van-quished sin and Sa-tan, He by death has spoiled His foes.
Might-y Lord, in Thine as-cen-sion We by faith be-hold our own. A-MEN.

Rev. Theodore Parker, 1846; arr.

10. 10. 10. 10.

LANGRAN
James Langran, 1862

*In moderate time*

1. O Thou great Friend to all the sons of men,
2. Thee would I sing: Thy truth is still the light
3. Yes, Thou art still the Life; Thou art the Way

Who once ap - pear'dst in hum - blest guise be - low,
Which guides the na - tions grop - ing on their way,
The ho - liest know — Light, Life, and Way of heaven;

Sin to re - buke, to break the cap - tive's chain,
Stum - bling and fall - ing in dis - as - trous night,
And they who dear - est hope and deep - est pray

To call Thy breth - ren forth from want and woe,
Yet hop - ing ev - er for the per - fect day.
Toil by the truth, life, way that Thou hast given. A-MEN.

Tune used by permission of Novello and Company, Ltd.

# 175

## His Living Presence

Alfred Tennyson, 1850      L. M.      ST. CRISPIN
George J. Elvey, 1862

*In moderate time and majestic style*

1. Strong Son of God, im-mor-tal Love, Whom we, that have not seen Thy face,
2. Thou seem-est hu-man and di-vine, The high-est, ho-liest man-hood, Thou:
3. Our lit-tle sys-tems have their day; They have their day and cease to be;
4. Let knowl-edge grow from more to more, But more of rev-erence in us dwell;

By faith, and faith a-lone, em-brace, Be-liev-ing where we can-not prove;
Our wills are ours, we know not how; Our wills are ours, to make them Thine.
They are but bro-ken lights of Thee, And Thou, O Lord, art more than they.
That mind and soul, ac-cord-ing well, May make one mu-sic as be-fore. A-MEN.

# 176

Rev. Frederick Lucian Hosmer, 1876      C. M.      KILMARNOCK
Neil Dougall (1776-1862)

*In moderate time, with dignity*

1. O Thou, in all Thy might so far, In all Thy love so near,
2. What heart can com-pre-hend Thy Name, Or, search-ing, find Thee out,
3. Yet though I know Thee but in part, I ask not, Lord, for more;
4. And dear-er than all things I know Is child-like faith to me,

Be-yond the range of sun and star, And yet be-side us here:
Who art with-in, a quick-ening Flame, A Pres-ence round a-bout.
E-nough for me to know Thou art, To love Thee and a-dore.
That makes the dark-est way I go An o-pen path to Thee. A-MEN.

# 177 Jesus Christ the Lord

Frank Fletcher, 1926

11. 10. 11. 10.

CHARTERHOUSE
David Evans

*Unison. In moderate time, with great dignity*

1. O Son of Man, our He - ro strong and ten - der, Whose serv-ants are the brave in all the earth, Our liv - ing sac - ri - fice to Thee we ren - der, Who shar-est all our sor-rows, all our mirth.

2. O feet so strong to climb the path of du - ty, O lips di - vine that taught the words of truth, Kind eyes that marked the lil - ies in their beau-ty, And heart that kin-dled at the zeal of youth;

3. Lov - er of chil - dren, boy-hood's in - spi - ra - tion, Of all man-kind the Serv - ant and the King; O Lord of joy and hope and con-so - la - tion, To Thee our fears and joys and hopes we bring.

4. Not in our fail - ures on - ly and our sad - ness We seek Thy pres-ence, Com - fort - er and Friend; O rich man's Guest, be with us in our glad - ness, O poor man's Mate, our low-li-est tasks at-tend. A-MEN.

Tune copyright, 1927, by David Evans. Used by permission.
Words from "The Church Hymnary," Revised. Used by permission of Mr. Frank Fletcher and the Oxford University Press.

# 178 His Living Presence

John G. Whittier, 1866     C. M.     Arr. from William Vincent Wallace, 1856

SERENITY

*In flowing rhythm, with dignity*

1. Im - mor - tal Love, for - ev - er full, For - ev - er flow - ing free,
2. We may not climb the heaven - ly steeps To bring the Lord Christ down;
3. But warm, sweet, ten-der, e - ven yet A pres - ent help is He;
4. The heal - ing of His seam - less dress Is by our beds of pain;
5. O Lord and Mas - ter of us all, What-e'er our name or sign,

For - ev - er shared, for - ev - er whole, A nev - er - ebb - ing sea!
In vain we search the low - est deeps, For Him no depths can drown:
And faith has still its Ol - i - vet, And love its Gal - i - lee.
We touch Him in life's throng and press, And we are whole a - gain.
We own Thy sway, we hear Thy call, We test our lives by Thine. A - MEN.

# 179

Rev. Ozora Stearns Davis, 1909     C. M.

AZMON
Carl G. Gläser
Arr. by Lowell Mason

*In moderate time*

1. We bear the strain of earth - ly care, But bear it not a - lone;
2. Through din of mar - ket, whirl of wheels, And thrust of driv - ing trade,
3. The com-mon hopes that make us men Were His in Gal - i - lee;
4. Our broth-er - hood still rests in Him, The Broth - er of us all,

Be - side us walks our Broth-er Christ And makes our task His own.
We fol - low where the Mas - ter leads, Se - rene and un - a - fraid.
The tasks He gives are those He gave Be - side the rest - less sea.
And o'er the cen-turies still we hear The Mas-ter's win-some call. A - MEN.

Rev. Edward H. Plumptre, 1864  8. 8. 8. 8. 8. 8.  ST. PETERSBURG
Dimitri Bortniansky, 1825

*In moderate time*

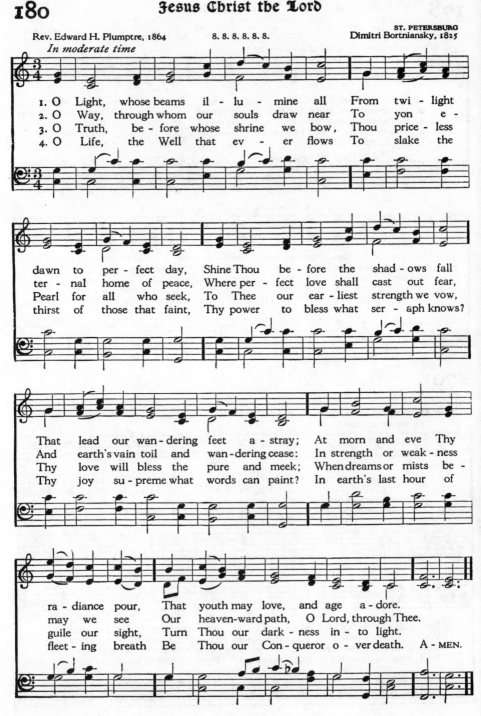

1. O Light, whose beams il - lu - mine all From twi - light
2. O Way, through whom our souls draw near To yon e -
3. O Truth, be - fore whose shrine we bow, Thou price - less
4. O Life, the Well that ev - er flows To slake the

dawn to per - fect day, Shine Thou be - fore the shad - ows fall
ter - nal home of peace, Where per - fect love shall cast out fear,
Pearl for all who seek, To Thee our ear - liest strength we vow,
thirst of those that faint, Thy power to bless what ser - aph knows?

That lead our wan - dering feet a - stray; At morn and eve Thy
And earth's vain toil and wan - dering cease: In strength or weak - ness
Thy love will bless the pure and meek; When dreams or mists be -
Thy joy su - preme what words can paint? In earth's last hour of

ra - diance pour, That youth may love, and age a - dore.
may we see Our heaven-ward path, O Lord, through Thee.
guile our sight, Turn Thou our dark - ness in - to light.
fleet - ing breath Be Thou our Con - queror o - ver death. A - MEN.

**181**

Rev. Harry Webb Farrington, 1910 · C. M. · Henry Lowell Mason · EXETER

*Not too fast*

1. I know not how that Beth-lehem's Babe Could in the God - head be;
2. I know not how that Cal - vary's cross A world from sin could free;
3. I know not how that Jo - seph's tomb Could solve death's mys-ter - y;

I on - ly know the Man-ger Child Has brought God's life to me.
I on - ly know its match-less love Has brought God's love to me.
I on - ly know a liv - ing Christ, Our im - mor - tal - i - ty. A-MEN.

Words copyright. Used by permission of the Hymn Society of America.
Tune copyright, 1924, by Henry Lowell Mason. Used by permission.

**182**

Nancy Byrd Turner, 1928 · L. M. · "Wittenberg Gesangbuch," 1524 · SOLDAU

*In moderate time; with flowing rhythm*

1. O Son of Man, who walked each day A hum - ble road se - rene and strong,
2. If light and joy should be my part, Then share with me the shin - ing hour;
3. So shall I walk in hap - pi - ness, So shall my task with love be fraught,
4. O Son of God, who came and shed A light for all the a - ges long,

Go with me now up - on life's way, My Com - rade all the jour - ney long.
If clouds should come, speak to my heart Thy word of com - fort, love, and power.
If Thou art near to mark and bless The la - bor done, the beau - ty wrought.
Thy com - pa - ny shall make me glad, Thy fel - low-ship shall keep me strong! A-MEN.

Words copyright, 1928, by the Presbyterian Board of Christian Education.
Tune from "The Church Hymnary," Revised. Used by permission of the Oxford University Press.

# 183 Jesus Christ the Lord

MOAB

Rev. Robert Rowland Roberts   6. 5. 6. 5. 6. 6. 6. 5.   Rev. John Roberts (Ieuan Gwyllt)
(1822–1877)

*In moderate time*

1. Far off I see the goal— O Sav-iour, guide me;
2. When-e'er Thy way seems strange, Go Thou be-fore me;
3. Should earth-ly pleas-ures wane, And joy for-sake me,
4. There, with the ran-somed throng Who praise for-ev-er

I feel my strength is small— Be Thou be-side me;
And, lest my heart should change, O Lord, watch o'er me;
And lone-ly hours of pain At length o'er-take me,
The love that made them strong To serve for-ev-er,

With vi-sion ev-er clear, With love that con-quers fear,
But, should my faith prove frail, And I through blind-ness fail,
My hand in Thine hold fast Till sor-row be o'er-past,
I, too, would seek Thy face, Thy fin-ished work re-trace,

And grace to per-se-vere, O Lord, pro-vide me.
O let Thy grace pre-vail, And still re-store me.
And gen-tle death at last For heaven a-wake me.
And mag-ni-fy Thy grace, Re-deemed for-ev-er. A-MEN.

Words used by permission of Rev. Robert R. Roberts.
Tune used by permission of Calvinist Methodist Book Agency.

Rev. Charles Wesley, 1758      8. 7. 8. 7. 8. 7.      J. F. Wade's "Cantus Diversi," 1751

HOLYWOOD

*Triumphantly*

1. Lo! He comes, with clouds de - scend - ing, Once for our sal -
2. Ev - ery eye shall now be - hold Him, Robed in dread-ful
3. Yea, A - men! Let all a - dore Thee, High on Thine e -

va - tion slain; Thou - sand thou - sand saints at - tend - ing
maj - es - ty; Those who set at naught and sold Him,
ter - nal throne; Sav - iour, take the power and glo - ry,

Swell the tri - umph of His train: Al - le - lu - ia!
Pierced, and nailed Him to the tree, Deep - ly wail - ing,
Claim the King - dom for Thine own: O come quick - ly!

Al - le - lu - ia! God ap - pears on earth to reign.
deep - ly wail - ing, Shall the true Mes - si - ah see.
O come quick - ly! Al - le - lu - ia! Come, Lord, come!   A-MEN.

# 185

## Jesus Christ the Lord

Psalms lxxxv; lxxxii; lxxxvi
John Milton (1608-1674)

C. M.
(FIRST TUNE)

OLD 107TH
"Scottish Psalter," 1635
Based on the "Genevan Psalter"

*May be sung in unison. With majesty*

1. The Lord will come and not be slow, His foot-steps can - not err;
2. Truth from the earth, like to a flower, Shall bud and blos - som then;
3. Rise, God, judge Thou the earth in might, This wick - ed earth re - dress;
4. For great Thou art, and won-ders great By Thy strong hand are done:

Be - fore Him right-eous-ness shall go, His roy - al har - bin - ger.
And jus - tice, from her heaven-ly bower, Look down on mor - tal men.
For Thou art He who shall by right The na - tions all pos - sess.
Thou in Thy ev - er - last - ing seat Re - main-est God a - lone. A-MEN.

## 185

Psalms lxxxv; lxxxii; lxxxvi
John Milton (1608-1674)

C. M.
(SECOND TUNE)

ST. MAGNUS
Jeremiah Clark (1670-1707)

*With majesty*

1. The Lord will come and not be slow, His foot-steps can - not err;
2. Truth from the earth, like to a flower, Shall bud and blos - som then;
3. Rise, God, judge Thou the earth in might, This wick - ed earth re - dress;
4. For great Thou art, and won-ders great By Thy strong hand are done:

Be - fore Him right-eous-ness shall go, His roy - al har - bin-ger.
And jus-tice, from her heaven - ly bower, Look down on mor - tal men.
For Thou art He who shall by right The na - tions all pos-sess.
Thou in Thy ev - er - last - ing seat Re - main-est God a - lone. A-MEN.

Frances R. Havergal, 1873          8. 7. 8. 8. 7. 7. 7. 7. 7.

GWALIA
Welsh hymn melody

*In stately rhythm*

1. Thou art com - ing, O my Sav - iour, Thou art com - ing, O my King,
2. Thou art com - ing, Thou art com - ing; We shall meet Thee on Thy way,
3. O the joy to see Thee reign - ing, Thee, my own be - lov - ed Lord!

In Thy beau - ty all re - splend-ent; In Thy glo - ry all tran - scend-ent;
We shall see Thee, we shall know Thee, We shall bless Thee, we shall show Thee
Ev - ery tongue Thy Name con - fess - ing, Wor - ship, hon - or, glo - ry, bless - ing

Well may we re - joice and sing: Com-ing! in the open - ing east
All our hearts could nev - er say: What an an-them that will be,
Brought to Thee with glad ac - cord; Thee, my Mas - ter and my Friend,

Her - ald bright-ness slow - ly swells; Com - ing! O my
Ring - ing out love to Thee, Pour - ing out our
Vin - di - cat - ed and en - throned; Un - to earth's re -

glo - rious Priest, Hear we not Thy gold - en bells?
rap - ture sweet At Thine own all - glo - rious feet!
mot - est end Glo - ri - fied, a - dored, and owned. A-MEN.

# 187 Jesus Christ the Lord

Based on the Greek
Trans. by Rev. John Brownlie, 1907

C. M.

ST. STEPHEN
Rev. William Jones, 1789

*In joyous tempo*

1. The King shall come when morn-ing dawns, And light tri-um-phant breaks;
2. Not as of old a lit-tle child To bear, and fight, and die,
3. O bright-er than the ris-ing morn When He, vic-to-rious, rose,
4. O bright-er than that glo-rious morn Shall this fair morn-ing be,
5. The King shall come when morn-ing dawns, And light and beau-ty brings:

When beau-ty gilds the east-ern hills, And life to joy a-wakes.
But crowned with glo-ry like the sun That lights the morn-ing sky.
And left the lone-some place of death, De-spite the rage of foes—
When Christ, our King, in beau-ty comes, And we His face shall see!
Hail, Christ the Lord! Thy peo-ple pray, Come quick-ly, King of kings! A-MEN.

Words from "Hymns of the Russian Church." Used by permission of the Oxford University Press.

# 188

Rev. Horatius Bonar, 1846

S. M.

ST. BRIDE
Samuel Howard, 1762

*In moderate time. With dignity*

1. Come, Lord, and tar-ry not; Bring the long-looked-for day;
2. Come, for Thy saints still wait; Dai-ly as-cends their sigh:
3. Come, for cre-a-tion groans, Im-pa-tient of Thy stay,
4. Come, and make all things new; Build up this ru-ined earth;
5. Come, and be-gin Thy reign Of ev-er-last-ing peace;

O why these years of wait-ing here, These a-ges of de-lay?
The Spir-it and the Bride say, "Come": Dost Thou not hear the cry?
Worn out with these long years of ill, These a-ges of de-lay.
Re-store our fad-ed Par-a-dise, Cre-a-tion's sec-ond birth.
Come, take the King-dom to Thy-self, Great King of Right-eous-ness. A-MEN.

Rev. John S. B. Monsell, 1863     8. 7. 8. 7. 8. 7.     **GWALIA** Welsh hymn tune

*In moderate time. With joy*

1. O'er the dis - tant moun - tains break - ing, Comes the red - dening dawn of day; Rise, my soul, from sleep a - wak-ing, Rise, and sing, and watch, and pray; 'T is thy Sav - iour, 'tis thy Sav - iour On His bright re - turn-ing way.

2. O Thou long - ex - pect - ed, wea - ry Waits my anx - ious soul for Thee; Life is dark, and earth is drear-y Where Thy light I do not see; O my Sav - iour, O my Sav - iour, When wilt Thou re - turn to me?

3. Near - er is my soul's sal - va - tion, Spent the night, the day at hand; Keep me, in my low - ly sta-tion, Watch-ing for Thee, till I stand, O my Sav - iour, O my Sav - iour, In Thy bright, Thy prom-ised land. A-MEN.

Tune from "A Students' Hymnal" (Hymns of the Kingdom). Used by permission of the Oxford University Press.

# Jesus Christ the Lord

Rev. Matthew Bridges, 1851     S. M. D.     DIADEMATA  
George J. Elvey, 1868

*Joyously, but with great dignity*

1. Crown Him with man - y crowns, The Lamb up - on His throne;
2. Crown Him the Lord of love: Be - hold His hands and side,
3. Crown Him the Lord of peace; Whose power a scep - ter sways
4. Crown Him the Lord of years, The Po - ten - tate of time;

Hark! how the heaven-ly an - them drowns All mu - sic but its own:
Rich wounds, yet vis - i - ble a - bove, In beau - ty glo - ri - fied:
From pole to pole, that wars may cease, Ab - sorbed in prayer and praise:
Cre - a - tor of the roll - ing spheres, In - ef - fa - bly sub - lime:

A - wake, my soul, and sing Of Him who died for thee,
No an - gel in the sky Can ful - ly bear that sight,
His reign shall know no end; And round His pier - ced feet
All hail, Re - deem - er, hail! For Thou hast died for me:

And hail Him as thy match-less King Through all e - ter - ni - ty.
But down-ward bends his burn-ing eye At mys - ter -ies so bright.
Fair flowers of Par - a - dise ex - tend Their fra-grance ev - er sweet.
Thy praise shall nev-er, nev - er fail Through-out e - ter - ni - ty. A-MEN.

# Praise to Christ the Lord

MADRID
Source unknown

Christian Henry Bateman (1813–1889)          6. 6. 6. 6. D.          Harmonized by David Evans

*With joy*

1. Come, Chris-tians, join to sing    Al - le - lu - ia!    A - men!
2. Come, lift   your hearts on high;   Al - le - lu - ia!    A - men!
3. Praise yet  our Christ a - gain;    Al - le - lu - ia!    A - men!

Loud praise to Christ our King;    Al - le - lu - ia!    A - men!
Let   prais-es   fill   the  sky;   Al - le - lu - ia!    A - men!
Life  shall not  end   the strain;  Al - le - lu - ia!    A - men!

Let    all,  with  heart and voice,  Be - fore  His   throne re - joice;
He    is    our   Guide and Friend;  To   us  He'll con - de - scend;
On   heav - en's  bliss - ful shore   His   good - ness we'll a - dore,

Praise is  His  gra-cious choice:   Al - le - lu - ia!    A - men!
His   love shall nev - er end:      Al - le - lu - ia!    A - men!
Sing - ing  for - ev - er-more,    "Al - le - lu - ia!    A - men!"  A-MEN.

Tune from "The Church Hymnary," Revised. Used by permission of the Oxford University Press.

# Jesus Christ the Lord

Rev. Edward Perronet, 1779, 1780
Stanza 1, line 4, alt.; stanza 3, recast
Stanza 4 added by Rev. John Rippon, 1787    C. M.

CORONATION
Oliver Holden, 1793

(FIRST TUNE)

*In moderate time*

1. All hail the power of Je - sus' Name! Let an - gels pros - trate fall;
2. Sin - ners, whose love can ne'er for - get The worm-wood and the gall,
3. Let ev - ery kin - dred, ev - ery tribe, On this ter - res - trial ball,
4. O that with yon - der sa - cred throng We at His feet may fall!

Bring forth the roy - al di - a - dem,
Go, spread your tro - phies at His feet,
To Him all maj - es - ty as - cribe,
We'll join the ev - er - last - ing song,

And crown Him Lord of all; Bring forth the roy - al
And crown Him Lord of all; Go, spread your tro - phies
And crown Him Lord of all; To Him all maj - es -
And crown Him Lord of all; We'll join the ev - er -

di - a - dem, And crown Him Lord of all.
at His feet, And crown Him Lord of all.
ty as - cribe, And crown Him Lord of all.
last - ing song, And crown Him Lord of all. A-MEN.

# 192 Praise to Christ the Lord

Rev. Edward Perronet, 1779, 1780
Stanza 1, line 4, alt.; stanza 3, recast
Stanza 4 added by Rev. John Rippon, 1787    C. M.

MILES LANE
William Shrubsole, 1779

(SECOND TUNE)

*With dignity; but in moderate time*

1. All hail the power of Je - sus' Name!
2. Sin - ners, whose love can ne'er for - get
3. Let ev - ery kin - dred, ev - ery tribe,
4. O that with yon - der sa - cred throng

Let an - gels pros - trate fall; Bring forth the roy - al
The worm - wood and the gall, Go, spread your tro - phies
On this ter - res - trial ball, To Him all maj - es -
We at His feet may fall! We'll join the ev - er -

di - a - dem, And crown Him, crown Him,
at His feet, And crown Him, crown Him,
ty as - cribe, And crown Him, crown Him,
last - ing song, And crown Him, crown Him,

crown Him, crown Him Lord of all.
crown Him, crown Him Lord of all.
crown Him, crown Him Lord of all.
crown Him, crown Him Lord of all.    A - MEN.

# 193 Jesus Christ the Lord

Rev. Charles Wesley, 1746

6. 6. 6. 6. 8. 8.
(FIRST TUNE)

DARWALL'S 148TH
Rev. John Darwall, 1770

*Jubilantly*

1. Re - joice, the Lord is King: Your Lord and King a - dore!
2. His King - dom can - not fail, He rules o'er earth and heaven;
3. He all His foes shall quell, Shall all our sins de - stroy,

Re - joice, give thanks, and sing, And tri - umph
The keys of death and hell Are to our
And ev - ery bos - om swell With pure se -

ev - er - more: Lift up your heart, lift up your voice!
Je - sus given: Lift up your heart, lift up your voice!
raph - ic joy: Lift up your heart, lift up your voice!

Re - joice, a - gain I say, re - joice!
Re - joice, a - gain I say, re - joice!
Re - joice, a - gain I say, re - joice! A-MEN.

# 193 Praise to Christ the Lord

Rev. Charles Wesley, 1746

6. 6. 6. 6. 8. 8.
(SECOND TUNE)

JUBILATE
Horatio Parker, 1894

*With joy*

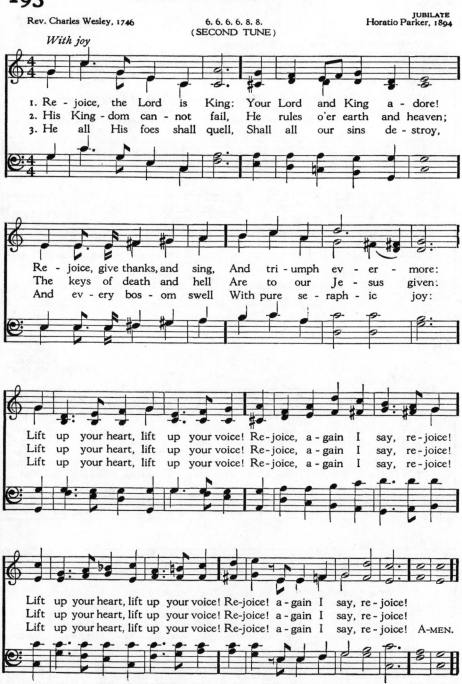

1. Re - joice, the Lord is King: Your Lord and King a - dore!
2. His King - dom can - not fail, He rules o'er earth and heaven;
3. He all His foes shall quell, Shall all our sins de - stroy,

Re - joice, give thanks, and sing, And tri - umph ev - er - more:
The keys of death and hell Are to our Je - sus given:
And ev - ery bos - om swell With pure se - raph - ic joy:

Lift up your heart, lift up your voice! Re - joice, a - gain I say, re - joice!
Lift up your heart, lift up your voice! Re - joice, a - gain I say, re - joice!
Lift up your heart, lift up your voice! Re - joice, a - gain I say, re - joice!

Lift up your heart, lift up your voice! Re - joice! a - gain I say, re - joice!
Lift up your heart, lift up your voice! Re - joice! a - gain I say, re - joice!
Lift up your heart, lift up your voice! Re - joice! a - gain I say, re - joice! A - MEN.

Tune copyright, 1894. Used by permission of Mrs. Horatio Parker.

**194**

German, 17th century

SCHÖNSTER HERR JESU
Silesian folk song, from "Schlesische Volkslieder,"
Leipzig, 1842

5. 6. 8. 5. 5. 8.

*In moderate time, and graceful rhythm*

1. Fair - est Lord Je-sus, Rul - er of all na-ture, O Thou of God and man the Son,
2. Fair are the mead-ows, Fair-er still the wood-lands, Robed in the bloom-ing garb of spring:
3. Fair is the sun-shine, Fair-er still the moon-light, And all the twink-ling, star-ry host:

Thee will I cher-ish, Thee will I hon-or, Thou, my soul's Glo-ry, Joy, and Crown.
Je - sus is fair - er, Je - sus is pur-er, Who makes the woe-ful heart to sing.
Je-sus shines bright-er, Je-sus shines pur-er, Than all the an-gels heaven can boast. A-MEN.

**195**

Rev. Thomas Kelly, 1820

C. M.

ST. MAGNUS
Jeremiah Clark, 1709

*With dignity*

1. The Head that once was crowned with thorns Is crowned with glo - ry now;
2. The high-est place that heaven af-fords Is His, is His by right,
3. The Joy of all who dwell a-bove, The Joy of all be - low
4. To them the cross, with all its shame, With all its grace, is given;
5. They suf - fer with their Lord be - low, They reign with Him a - bove;

A roy-al di-a-dem a-dorns The might-y Vic - tor's brow.
The King of kings, and Lord of lords, And heaven's e-ter - nal Light:
To whom He man - i - fests His love, And grants His Name to know.
Their name an ev - er - last-ing name, Their joy the joy of heaven.
Their prof - it and their joy to know The won-der of His love. A-MEN.

# 196 Praise to Christ the Lord

Rev. Horatius Bonar (1808-1889)

La Feillée's "Méthode du Plain Chant," 1808

O QUANTA QUALIA

10. 10. 10. 10. Dactylic

*In moderate time and with majestic rhythm*

1. Bless - ing and hon - or and glo - ry and power,
2. Sound - eth the heaven of the heavens with His Name;
3. Ev - er as - cend - eth the song and the joy;
4. Give we the glo - ry and praise to the Lamb;

Wis - dom and rich - es and strength ev - er - more
Ring - eth the earth with His glo - ry and fame;
Ev - er de - scend - eth the love from on high;
Take we the robe and the harp and the palm;

Give ye to Him who our bat - tle hath won,
O - cean and moun - tain, stream, for - est, and flower
Bless - ing and hon - or and glo - ry and praise —
Sing we the song of the Lamb that was slain,

Whose are the King - dom, the crown, and the throne.
Ech - o His prais - es and tell of His power.
This is the theme of the hymns that we raise.
Dy - ing in weak - ness, but ris - ing to reign.     A-MEN.

Tune from "The Church Hymnary," Revised. Used by permission of the Oxford University Press.

# Jesus Christ the Lord

**197**

NUN DANKET ALL' (GRÄFENBERG)
Johann Crüger's
"Praxis Pietatis Melica," 1653

Rev. Samuel Stennett, 1787

C. M.
(FIRST TUNE)

*May be sung in unison. Majestically*

1. Ma - jes - tic sweet-ness sits en-throned    Up - on the Sav - iour's    brow;
2. No    mor - tal can with Him com - pare    A - mong the sons    of    men;
3. To    Him I    owe my    life    and breath,    And all the joys    I    have;
4. To heaven, the place of His    a - bode,    He brings my wea - ry    feet;
5. Since from His boun - ty    I    re - ceive    Such proofs of love    di - vine,

His    head with ra - diant    glo - ries crowned,    His lips with grace o'er - flow.
Fair - er is He than    all    the fair    That fill the heaven - ly    train.
He makes me tri - umph o - ver death,    And saves me from    the    grave.
Shows me the glo - ries    of    my God,    And makes my joys com - plete.
Had    I    a thou-sand hearts to give,    Lord, they should all be    Thine.    A-MEN.

**197**

Rev. Samuel Stennett, 1787

C. M.
(SECOND TUNE)

ORTONVILLE
Thomas Hastings, 1837

*With dignity*

1. Ma-jes-tic sweet-ness sits en-throned Up-on the Sav-iour's brow; His head with ra-diant
2. No    mor-tal can with Him com-pare A-mong the sons of    men; Fair - er is He than
3. To    Him I owe my life and breath, And all the joys I    have; He makes me tri-umph
4. To heaven, the place of His    a - bode, He brings my wea-ry feet; Shows me the glo-ries
5. Since from His boun-ty I re-ceive Such proofs of love di-vine, Had I    a thou-sand

glo-ries crowned,    His lips with grace o'er-flow,    His lips with grace o'er-flow.
all    the fair    That fill the heaven-ly train,    That fill the heaven-ly train.
o - ver death,    And saves me from the    grave,    And saves me from the grave.
of    my God,    And makes my joys com-plete,    And makes my joys com-plete.
hearts to give,    Lord, they should all be Thine,    Lord, they should all be Thine. A-MEN.

# 198 Praise to Christ the Lord

Rev. Charles Wesley, 1744     10. 10. 11. 11.     J. Michael Haydn (1737–1806)

LYONS

*With joy and dignity*

1. Ye serv-ants of God, your Mas-ter pro-claim,
2. God rul-eth on high, al-might-y to save;
3. Sal-va-tion to God who sits on the throne!
4. Then let us a-dore, and give Him His right,

And pub-lish a-broad His won-der-ful Name;
And still He is nigh— His pres-ence we have:
Let all cry a-loud and hon-or the Son:
All glo-ry and power, and wis-dom and might,

The Name, all-vic-to-rious, of Je-sus ex-tol;
The great con-gre-ga-tion His tri-umph shall sing,
The prais-es of Je-sus the an-gels pro-claim,
All hon-or and bless-ing, with an-gels a-bove,

His King-dom is glo-rious, and rules o-ver all.
As-crib-ing sal-va-tion to Je-sus, our King.
Fall down on their fa-ces and wor-ship the Lamb.
And thanks nev-er ceas-ing, and in-fi-nite love. A-MEN.

RICHMOND
Adapted from T. Haweis (1734–1820)
by S. Webbe (the younger)

Rev. Charles Wesley, 1739                    C. M.

*With joy, but not too fast*

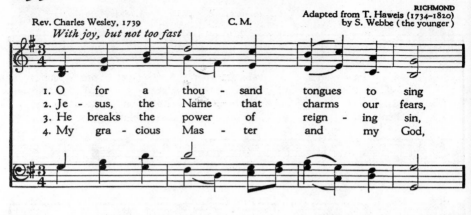

1. O for a thou - sand tongues to sing
2. Je - sus, the Name that charms our fears,
3. He breaks the power of reign - ing sin,
4. My gra - cious Mas - ter and my God,

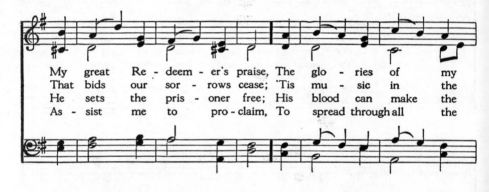

My great Re - deem - er's praise, The glo - ries of my
That bids our sor - rows cease; 'Tis mu - sic in the
He sets the pris - oner free; His blood can make the
As - sist me to pro - claim, To spread through all the

God and King, The tri - umphs of His grace.
sin - ner's ears, 'Tis life, and health, and peace.
sin - ful clean, His blood a - vailed for me.
earth a - broad, The hon - ors of Thy Name. A -MEN.

5. Glory to God and praise and love
   Be ever, ever given
   By saints below and saints above,
   The Church in earth and heaven.

Frances Ridley Havergal, 1870     7. 6. 7. 6. D.     ANGEL'S STORY
Arthur H. Mann, 1883

*With brightness*

1. O Sav - iour, pre - cious Sav - iour, Whom yet un - seen we love!
2. O Bring - er of sal - va - tion, Who won - drous - ly hast wrought,
3. In Thee all full - ness dwell - eth, All grace and power di - vine;

O Name of might and fa - vor, All oth - er names a - bove!
Thy - self the rev - e - la - tion Of love be - yond our thought!
The glo - ry that ex - cell - eth, O Son of God, is Thine;

We wor - ship Thee, we bless Thee, To Thee, O Christ, we sing;
We wor - ship Thee, we bless Thee, To Thee, O Christ, we sing;
We wor - ship Thee, we bless Thee, To Thee, O Christ, we sing;

We praise Thee, and con - fess Thee Our ho - ly Lord and King.
We praise Thee, and con - fess Thee Our gra - cious Lord and King.
We praise Thee, and con - fess Thee Our glo - rious Lord and King. A-MEN.

# Jesus Christ the Lord

Rev. Thomas Kelly, 1809

8. 7. 8. 7. 4. 7.
(FIRST TUNE)

CORONÆ
William H. Monk, 1871

*With exultation*

1. Look, ye saints! The sight is glo - rious:
2. Crown the Sav - iour! An - gels, crown Him!
3. Sin - ners in de - ri - sion crowned Him,
4. Hark, those bursts of ac - cla - ma - tion!

See the Man of Sor - rows now; From the fight re -
Rich the tro - phies Je - sus brings; In the seat of
Mock - ing thus the Sav - iour's claim; Saints and an - gels
Hark, those loud tri - um - phant chords! Je - sus takes the

turned vic - to - rious, Ev - ery knee to Him shall bow:
power en - throne Him, While the vault of heav - en rings:
crowd a - round Him, Own His ti - tle, praise His Name:
high - est sta - tion; O what joy the sight af - fords!

Crown Him! Crown Him! Crowns be - come the Vic - tor's brow.
Crown Him! Crown Him! Crown the Sav - iour King of kings.
Crown Him! Crown Him! Spread a - broad the Vic - tor's fame.
Crown Him! Crown Him! King of kings, and Lord of lords! A - MEN.

# 201 Praise to Christ the Lord

Rev. Thomas Kelly, 1809

8. 7. 8. 7. 4. 7.
(SECOND TUNE)

REX TRIUMPHANS
G. Everett Hill

*With exultation*

1. Look, ye saints! The sight is glo - rious:
2. Crown the Sav - iour! An - gels, crown Him!
3. Sin - ners in de - ri - sion crowned Him,
4. Hark, those bursts of ac - cla - ma - tion!

See the Man of Sor - rows now; From the fight re -
Rich the tro - phies Je - sus brings; In the seat of
Mock - ing thus the Sav - iour's claim; Saints and an - gels
Hark, those loud tri - um - phant chords! Je - sus takes the

turned vic - to - rious, Ev - ery knee to Him shall bow:
power en - throne Him, While the vault of heav - en rings:
crowd a - round Him, Own His ti - tle, praise His Name:
high - est sta - tion; O what joy the sight af - fords!

Crown Him! Crown Him! Crowns be - come the Vic - tor's brow.
Crown Him! Crown Him! Crown the Sav - iour King of kings.
Crown Him! Crown Him! Spread a - broad the Vic - tor's fame.
Crown Him! Crown Him! King of kings, and Lord of lords! A - MEN.

# Jesus Christ the Lord

Rev. Godfrey Thring, 1862      6. 5. 6. 5. D.      DAVID
Thomas Morley, 1867

*In moderate time*

1. Sav - iour, bless - ed Sav - iour, Lis - ten while we sing,
2. Near - er, ev - er near - er, Christ, we draw to Thee,
3. Clear - er still, and clear - er, Dawns the light from heaven,
4. Great, and ev - er great - er, Are Thy mer - cies here;

Hearts and voi - ces rais - ing Prais - es to our King.
Deep in ad - o - ra - tion Bend - ing low the knee:
In our sad - ness bring - ing News of sins for - given;
True and ev - er - last - ing Are the glo - ries there,

All we have we of - fer, All we hope to be,
Thou for our re - demp - tion Cam'st on earth to die;
Life has lost its shad - ows; Pure the light with - in;
Where no pain or sor - row, Toil or care, is known,

Bod - y, soul, and spir - it, All we yield to Thee.
Thou, that we might fol - low, Hast gone up on high.
Thou hast shed Thy ra - diance On a world of sin.
Where the an - gel le - gions Cir - cle round Thy throne. A-MEN.

# Praise to Christ the Lord

Rev. Samuel Medley, 1789        8. 8. 6. 8. 8. 6.        ARIEL
Arr. from Mozart
by Lowell Mason, 1836

*Moderately fast*

1. O could I speak the match - less worth,
2. I'd sing the char - ac - ters He bears,
3. Soon, the de - light - ful day will come

O could I sound the glo - ries forth Which in my Sav - iour shine,
And all the forms of love He wears, Ex - alt - ed on His throne:
When my dear Lord will bring me home, And I shall see His face;

I'd sing His glo - rious right-eous-ness, And mag - ni - fy the won-drous grace
In loft - iest songs of sweet-est praise, I would to ev - er - last-ing days
Then with my Sav-iour, Broth-er, Friend, A blest e - ter - ni - ty I'll spend,

Which made sal - va-tion mine, Which made sal-va - tion mine.
Make all His glo-ries known, Make all His glo - ries known.
Tri - um-phant in His grace, Tri - um-phant in His grace. A - MEN.

# The Holy Spirit

Rev. George Croly, 1854     10. 10. 10. 10.     Frederick C. Atkinson, 1870
MORECAMBE

*In moderate time, with deep reverence*

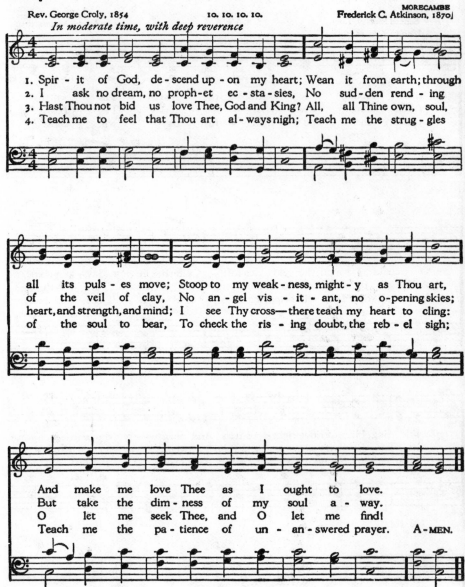

1. Spir - it of God, de - scend up - on my heart; Wean it from earth; through
2. I ask no dream, no proph-et ec - sta - sies, No sud - den rend - ing
3. Hast Thou not bid us love Thee, God and King? All, all Thine own, soul,
4. Teach me to feel that Thou art al - ways nigh; Teach me the strug - gles

all its puls - es move; Stoop to my weak - ness, might - y as Thou art,
of the veil of clay, No an - gel vis - it - ant, no o-pening skies;
heart, and strength, and mind; I see Thy cross—there teach my heart to cling:
of the soul to bear, To check the ris - ing doubt, the reb - el sigh;

And make me love Thee as I ought to love.
But take the dim - ness of my soul a - way.
O let me seek Thee, and O let me find!
Teach me the pa - tience of un - an - swered prayer. A - MEN.

5. Teach me to love Thee as Thine angels love,
    One holy passion filling all my frame;
    The baptism of the heaven-descended Dove,
    My heart an altar, and Thy love the flame.

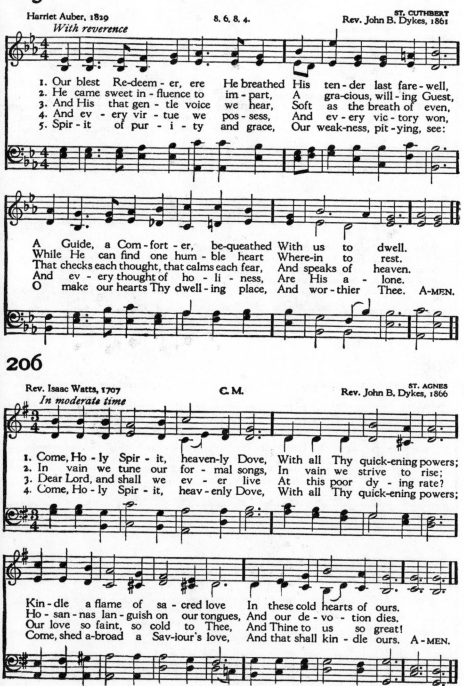

**205**

Harriet Auber, 1829
8. 6. 8. 4.
ST. CUTHBERT
Rev. John B. Dykes, 1861

*With reverence*

1. Our blest Re-deem-er, ere He breathed His ten-der last fare-well,
2. He came sweet in-fluence to im-part, A gra-cious, will-ing Guest,
3. And His that gen-tle voice we hear, Soft as the breath of even,
4. And ev-ery vir-tue we pos-sess, And ev-ery vic-to-ry won,
5. Spir-it of pur-i-ty and grace, Our weak-ness, pit-ying, see:

A Guide, a Com-fort-er, be-queathed With us to dwell.
While He can find one hum-ble heart Where-in to rest.
That checks each thought, that calms each fear, And speaks of heaven.
And ev-ery thought of ho-li-ness, Are His a-lone.
O make our hearts Thy dwell-ing place, And wor-thier Thee. A-MEN.

**206**

Rev. Isaac Watts, 1707
C. M.
ST. AGNES
Rev. John B. Dykes, 1866

*In moderate time*

1. Come, Ho-ly Spir-it, heaven-ly Dove, With all Thy quick-ening powers;
2. In vain we tune our for-mal songs, In vain we strive to rise;
3. Dear Lord, and shall we ev-er live At this poor dy-ing rate?
4. Come, Ho-ly Spir-it, heav-enly Dove, With all Thy quick-ening powers;

Kin-dle a flame of sa-cred love In these cold hearts of ours.
Ho-san-nas lan-guish on our tongues, And our de-vo-tion dies.
Our love so faint, so cold to Thee, And Thine to us so great!
Come, shed a-broad a Sav-iour's love, And that shall kin-dle ours. A-MEN.

**207**

James Montgomery, 1823    L. M.    MELCOMBE
Samuel Webbe, 1782

*In moderate time*

1. O    Spir-it of the liv-ing God,    In all Thy plen-i-tude of grace,
2. Give tongues of fire and hearts of love    To preach the rec-on-cil-ing word;
3. Be    dark-ness, at Thy com-ing, light;    Con-fu-sion, or-der in Thy path;
4. O    Spir-it of the Lord, pre-pare    All the round earth her God to meet;
5. Bap-tize the na-tions; far and nigh    The tri-umphs of the cross re-cord;

Wher-e'er the foot of man hath trod, De-scend on our a-pos-tate race.
Give power and unc-tion from a-bove, When-e'er the joy-ful sound is heard.
Souls with-out strength in-spire with might; Bid mer-cy tri-umph o-ver wrath.
Breathe Thou a-broad like morn-ing air, Till hearts of stone be-gin to beat.
The Name of Je-sus glo-ri-fy, Till ev-ery kin-dred call Him Lord. A-MEN.

**208**

Rev. Samuel Longfellow, 1864    7. 7. 7. 7.    MERCY
Arr. from Louis M. Gottschalk, 1867

*Not too fast*

1. Ho-ly    Spir-it, Truth di-vine,    Dawn up-on this soul of mine;
2. Ho-ly    Spir-it, Love di-vine,    Glow with-in this heart of mine;
3. Ho-ly    Spir-it, Power di-vine,    Fill and nerve this will of mine;
4. Ho-ly    Spir-it, Right di-vine,    King with-in my con-science reign;

Word of God, and in-ward Light, Wake my spir-it, clear my sight.
Kin-dle ev-ery high de-sire; Per-ish self in Thy pure fire.
By Thee may I strong-ly live, Brave-ly bear, and no-bly strive.
Be my Law, and I shall be Firm-ly bound, for-ev-er free. A-MEN.

**209**

Rev. Simon Browne, 1720
Ash and Evans' "Collection," 1769

HOLLEY
George Hews, 1835

*In moderate time*　　　　L. M.

1. Come, gra-cious Spir-it, heaven-ly Dove, With light and com-fort from a - bove;
2. The light of truth to us dis - play, And make us know and choose Thy way;
3. Lead us to ho - li - ness, the road Which we must take to dwell with God;
4. Lead us to God, our fi - nal rest, To be with Him for - ev - er blest;

Be Thou our Guard-ian, Thou our Guide; O'er ev - ery thought and step pre-side.
Plant ho - ly fear in ev - ery heart, That we from God may ne'er de-part.
Lead us to Christ, the liv - ing Way, Nor let us from His pas-tures stray.
Lead us to heaven, that we may share Full-ness of joy for-ev - er there. A-MEN.

**210**

Rev. Lawrence Tuttiett, 1864　　　　L. M.

QUEBEC
Henry Baker, 1862

*In moderate time*

1. O grant us light, that we may know The wis-dom Thou a - lone canst give;
2. O grant us light, that we may see Where er - ror lurks in hu - man lore,
3. O grant us light, that we may learn How dead is life from Thee a - part,
4. O grant us light, when, soon or late, All earth - ly scenes shall pass a - way,

That truth may guide wher-e'er we go, And vir-tue bless wher-e'er we live.
And turn our seek-ing minds to Thee, And love Thy ho - ly Word the more.
How sure is joy for all who turn To Thee an un - di - vid - ed heart.
In Thee to find the o - pen gate To death-less home and end-less day. A - MEN.

# 211
## The Holy Spirit

L. M.

Cecil Frances Alexander, 1858

MISSIONARY CHANT
Heinrich Christopher Zeuner, 1832

*In moderate time*

1. Thou Power and Peace, in whom we find  All  ho-liest strength, all pur-est love,
2. For - ev - er lend Thy sov-ereign aid,  And urge us  on, and keep us Thine;
3. Nor  let  us quench Thy sav-ing light;  But still with soft-est breath-ings stir

The  rush-ing  of  the might-y wind,  The brood-ing of the gen - tle dove:
Nor leave the hearts which Thou hast made, Fit tem-ples  of Thy grace di-vine;
Our  way-ward souls, and lead us right,  O  Ho - ly  Spir-it, Com-fort-er!  A-MEN.

# 212

C. M.

Rev. Andrew Reed, 1829

NUN DANKET ALL* (GRÄFENBERG)
Johann Crüger's
" Praxis Pietatis Melica," 1653

*Unison.  Rather slowly*

1. Spir - it  di - vine,  at - tend our prayers,  And  make this house Thy  home;
2. Come  as  the light:  to  us  re - veal  Our  emp - ti - ness and  woe;
3. Come  as  the fire:  and purge our hearts  Like  sac - ri - fi - cial  flame;
4. Come  as  the dove:  and spread Thy wings,  The  wings of peace - ful  love;
5. Spir - it  di - vine,  at - tend our prayers;  Make a  lost world Thy  home;

De - scend with all Thy gra-cious powers;  O  come, great Spir - it,  come!
And  lead us  in those paths of  life  Where all the right - eous  go.
Let  our whole soul an - of - fering be  To  our Re-deem-er's Name.
And  let Thy Church on earth be-come  Blest as  the Church a - bove.
De - scend with all Thy gra-cious powers;  O  come, great Spir - it,  come!  A - MEN.

**213**

Rev. Edwin Hatch, 1886

S. M.
(FIRST TUNE)

RHIW
From "A Students' Hymnal,"
University of Wales

*Rather slowly*

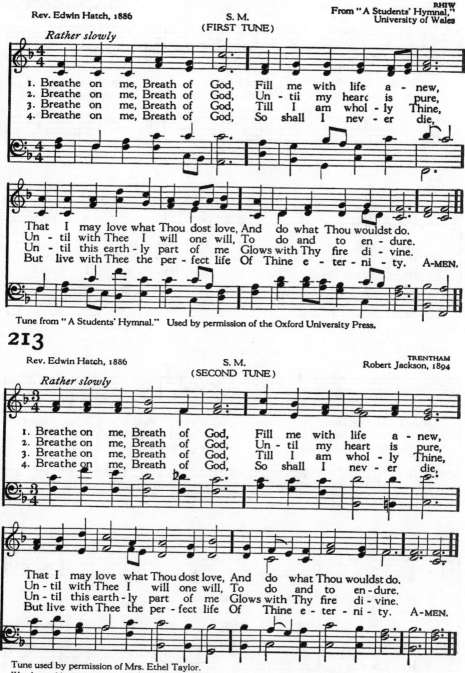

1. Breathe on me, Breath of God, Fill me with life a-new,
2. Breathe on me, Breath of God, Un-til my heart is pure,
3. Breathe on me, Breath of God, Till I am whol-ly Thine,
4. Breathe on me, Breath of God, So shall I nev-er die,

That I may love what Thou dost love, And do what Thou wouldst do.
Un-til with Thee I will one will, To do and to en-dure.
Un-til this earth-ly part of me Glows with Thy fire di-vine.
But live with Thee the per-fect life Of Thine e-ter-ni-ty. A-MEN.

Tune from "A Students' Hymnal." Used by permission of the Oxford University Press.

**213**

Rev. Edwin Hatch, 1886

S. M.
(SECOND TUNE)

TRENTHAM
Robert Jackson, 1894

*Rather slowly*

1. Breathe on me, Breath of God, Fill me with life a-new,
2. Breathe on me, Breath of God, Un-til my heart is pure,
3. Breathe on me, Breath of God, Till I am whol-ly Thine,
4. Breathe on me, Breath of God, So shall I nev-er die,

That I may love what Thou dost love, And do what Thou wouldst do.
Un-til with Thee I will one will, To do and to en-dure.
Un-til this earth-ly part of me Glows with Thy fire di-vine.
But live with Thee the per-fect life Of Thine e-ter-ni-ty. A-MEN.

Tune used by permission of Mrs. Ethel Taylor.
Words used by permission of Miss Beatrice Hatch and the Oxford University Press.

# 214 The Holy Spirit

Rev. Thomas Toke Lynch, 1855

REDHEAD NO. 76 (AJALON)
Richard Redhead, 1853

7. 7. 7. 7. 7. 7.

*In moderate time*

1. Gra - cious Spir - it, dwell with me; I my - self would
2. Truth - ful Spir - it, dwell with me; I my - self would
3. Ho - ly Spir - it, dwell with me; I my - self would

gra - cious be; And with words that help and heal
truth - ful be; And with wis - dom kind and clear
ho - ly be; Sep - a - rate from sin, I would

Would Thy life in mine re - veal; And with ac - tions
Let Thy life in mine ap - pear; And with ac - tions
Choose and cher - ish all things good, And what - ev - er

bold and meek Would for Christ my Sav - iour speak.
broth - er - ly Speak my Lord's sin - cer - i - ty:
I can be Give to Him who gave me Thee! A - MEN.

**215**

With joyous feeling

1. O Word of God In-car-nate, O Wis-dom from on high,
2. The Church from her dear Mas-ter Re-ceived the gift di-vine,
3. It float-eth like a ban-ner Be-fore God's host un-furled;
4. O make Thy Church, dear Sav-iour, A lamp of pur-est gold,

O Truth un-changed, un-chan-ging, O Light of our dark sky,
And still that light she lift-eth O'er all the earth to shine.
It shin-eth like a bea-con A-bove the dark-ling world.
To bear be-fore the na-tions Thy true light, as of old.

We praise Thee for the ra-diance That from the hal-lowed page,
It is the gold-en cas-ket, Where gems of truth are stored;
It is the chart and com-pass That o'er life's sur-ging sea,
O teach Thy wan-dering pil-grims By this their path to trace,

A lan-tern to our foot-steps, Shines on from age to age.
It is the heaven-drawn pic-ture Of Christ, the liv-ing Word.
'Mid mists and rocks and quick-sands, Still guides, O Christ, to Thee.
Till, clouds and dark-ness end-ed, They see Thee face to face. A-MEN.

Mary A. Lathbury, 1877          6. 4. 6. 4. D.          BREAD OF LIFE
William F. Sherwin, 1877

*Rather slowly, in flowing rhythm*

1. Break Thou the bread of life, Dear Lord, to me,
2. Bless Thou the truth, dear Lord, To me — to me,

As Thou didst break the loaves Be - side the sea;
As Thou didst bless the bread By Gal - i - lee;

Be - yond the sa - cred page I seek Thee, Lord;
Then shall all bond - age cease, All fet - ters fall;

My spir - it pants for Thee, O liv - ing Word.
And I shall find my peace, My All in all. A - MEN.

Courtesy of Chautauqua Institution.

**217**

Psalm xix. Rev. Isaac Watts, 1719    L. M.    UXBRIDGE
Lowell Mason, 1830

*With majestic movement*

1. The heavens de-clare Thy glo - ry, Lord; In ev - ery star Thy wis - dom shines;
2. The roll - ing sun, the chan-ging light, And nights and days, Thy power con-fess;
3. Sun, moon, and stars con-vey Thy praise Round the whole earth, and nev-er stand;
4. Nor shall Thy spread-ing gos-pel rest Till through the world Thy truth has run;

But when our eyes be-hold Thy Word, We read Thy Name in fair - er lines.
But the blest Vol-ume Thou hast writ Re-veals Thy jus-tice and Thy grace.
So when Thy truth be-gan its race, It touched and glanced on ev-ery land.
Till Christ has all the na-tions blest That see the light, or feel the sun. A-MEN.

**218**

Anne Steele, 1760    C. M.    BEATITUDO
Rev. John B. Dykes, 1875

*In moderate time*

1. Fa - ther of mer - cies, in Thy Word What end - less glo - ry shines;
2. Here the Re-deem-er's wel-come voice Spreads heaven-ly peace a - round;
3. O may these heaven-ly pa - ges be My ev - er dear de - light;
4. Di - vine In - struc - tor, gra - cious Lord, Be Thou for - ev - er near;

For - ev - er be Thy Name a - dored For these ce - les - tial lines.
And life and ev - er - last - ing joys At - tend the bliss-ful sound.
And still new beau-ties may I see, And still in - creas-ing light.
Teach me to love Thy sa - cred Word, And view my Sav-iour there. A - MEN.

Edwin Hodder, 1863                    C. M. D.                    Clement William Poole (1828-1924)

PETERSHAM

*In moderate time*

1. Thy Word is like a gar - den, Lord, With flow - ers bright and fair;
2. Thy Word is like an ar - mor - y, Where sol - diers may re - pair,

And ev - ery - one who seeks may pluck A love - ly clus - ter there.
And find for life's long bat - tle day All need - ful weap - ons there.

Thy Word is like a glo - rious choir, And loud its an - thems ring;
O may I find my ar - mor there: Thy Word my trust - y sword,

Though man-y tongues and parts u - nite, It is one song they sing.
I'll learn to fight with ev - ery foe The bat - tle of the Lord. A-MEN.

*Tune copyright by The Misses Horder. Used by permission.*

# The Life in Christ
## The Call of Christ

John M. Wigner, 1871　　　　　　6. 6. 6. 6. D.　　　　INVITATION
Frederick C. Maker, 1881

*Not too fast*

1. Come to the Sav - iour now, He gen - tly call - eth thee;
2. Come to the Sav - iour now, Ye who have wan - dered far;
3. Come to the Sav - iour, all, What - e'er your bur - dens be;

In true re - pent - ance bow, Be - fore Him bend the knee;
Re - new your sol - emn vow, For His by right you are;
Hear now His lov - ing call, "Cast all your care on Me."

He wait - eth to be - stow Sal - va - tion, peace, and love,
Come, like poor wan - dering sheep Re - turn - ing to His fold;
Come, and for ev - ery grief In Je - sus you will find

True joy on earth be - low, A home in heaven a - bove.
His arm will safe - ly keep, His love will ne'er grow cold.
A sure and safe re - lief, A lov - ing Friend and kind. A-MEN.

# 221 The Life in Christ

Rev. John M. Neale, 1862
Stanza 1, line 1; stanza 7, line 3, alt.

8. 5. 8. 3.
(FIRST TUNE)

BULLINGER
Rev. Ethelbert W. Bullinger, 1874

*In moderate time*

1. Art thou wea-ry, heav-y-lad-en, Art thou sore dis-trest? "Come to Me," saith One, "and com-ing, Be at rest."
2. Hath He marks to lead me to Him, If He be my Guide? "In His feet and hands are wound prints, And His side."
3. Is there di-a-dem, as Mon-arch, That His brow a-dorns? "Yea, a crown, in ver-y sure-ty, But of thorns."
4. If I find Him, if I fol-low, What His guer-don here? "Many a sor-row, many a la-bor, Many a tear." A-MEN.

5. If I still hold closely to Him,
     What hath He at last?
   "Sorrow vanquished, labor ended,
     Jordan passed."

6. If I ask Him to receive me,
     Will He say me nay?
   "Not till earth and not till **heaven**
     Pass away."

7. Finding, following, keeping, struggling,
     Is He sure to bless?
   "Saints, apostles, prophets, **martyrs,**
     Answer. 'Yes.'"

**221**

# The Call of Christ

Rev. John M. Neale, 1862
Stanza 1, line 1; stanza 7, line 3, alt.

8. 5. 8. 3.
(SECOND TUNE)

STEPHANOS
Rev. Henry W. Baker, 1868

*In moderate time*

1. Art thou wea - ry, heav - y - lad - en,
2. Hath He marks to lead me to Him,
3. Is there di - a - dem, as Mon - arch,
4. If I find Him, if I fol - low,

Art thou sore dis - trest? "Come to Me," saith
If He be my Guide? "In His feet and
That His brow a - dorns? "Yea, a crown, in
What His guer - don here? "Many a sor - row,

One, "and, com - ing, Be at rest."
hands are wound prints, And His side."
ver - y sure - ty, But of thorns."
many a la - bor, Many a tear." A - MEN.

5. If I still hold closely to Him,
   What hath He at last?
   "Sorrow vanquished, labor ended,
   Jordan passed."

6. If I ask Him to receive me,
   Will He say me nay?
   "Not till earth and not till heaven
   Pass away."

7. Finding, following, keeping, struggling,
   Is He sure to bless?
   "Saints, apostles, prophets, martyrs,
   Answer, 'Yes.'"

# The Life in Christ

LLANGLOFFAN
Welsh hymn melody
William Chatterton Dix, 1867; alt.      7. 6. 7. 6. D.      D. Evans' "Hymnau a Thonau," 1865

*In moderate time*

1. "Come un - to Me, ye wea - ry, And I will give you rest."
2. "Come un - to Me, ye wan - derers, And I will give you light."
3. "Come un - to Me, ye faint - ing, And I will give you life."
4. "And who - so - ev - er com - eth I will not cast him out."

O bless - ed voice of Je - sus, Which comes to hearts op - pressed!
O lov - ing voice of Je - sus, Which comes to cheer the night!
O cheer - ing voice of Je - sus, Which comes to aid our strife!
O wel - come voice of Je - sus, Which drives a - way our doubt;

It tells of ben - e - dic - tion, Of par - don, grace, and peace,
Our hearts were filled with sad - ness, And we had lost our way;
The foe is stern and ea - ger, The fight is fierce and long;
Which calls us, ver - y sin - ners, Un - worth - y though we be

Of joy that hath no end - ing, Of love which can - not cease.
But morn - ing brings us glad - ness, And songs, the break of day.
But Thou hast made us might - y, And strong-er than the strong.
Of love so free and bound - less, To come, dear Lord, to Thee!   A-MEN.

Tune from "The English Hymnal." Used by permission of the Oxford University Press.

**223**

Cecil Frances Alexander, 1852        8. 7. 8. 7.        GALILEE
William H. Jude, 1887

*In moderate time*

1. Je - sus calls us: o'er the tu - mult Of our life's wild, rest-less sea,
2. Je - sus calls us from the wor - ship Of the vain world's gold-en store,
3. In our joys and in our sor - rows, Days of toil and hours of ease,
4. Je - sus calls us: by Thy mer - cies, Sav - iour, may we hear Thy call,

Day by day His sweet voice sound-eth, Say-ing, "Chris-tian, fol - low Me."
From each i - dol that would keep us, Say-ing, "Chris-tian, love Me more."
Still He calls, in cares and pleas-ures, "Chris-tian, love Me more than these."
Give our hearts to Thine o - be-dience, Serve and love Thee best of all. A-MEN.

**224**

William Cowper, 1768        7. 7. 7. 7.        ST. BEES
Rev. John B. Dykes, 1862

*In moderate time*

1. Hark, my soul, it is the Lord! 'Tis thy Sav - iour, hear His word;
2. "I de - liv - ered thee when bound, And, when bleed-ing, healed thy wound;
3. "Can a wo-man's ten - der care Cease to - ward the child she bare?
4. "Mine is an un - chan-ging love, High - er than the heights a - bove,
5. Lord, it is my chief com-plaint That my love is weak and faint;

Je - sus speaks, and speaks to thee, "Say, poor sin - ner, lov'st thou Me?
Sought thee wan-dering, set thee right, Turned thy dark-ness in - to light.
Yes, she may for - get - ful be, Yet will I re - mem - ber thee.
Deep - er than the depths be-neath, Free and faith-ful, strong as death."
Yet I love Thee, and a - dore: O for grace to love Thee more! A-MEN.

## 225

Rev. Joseph Grigg, 1765
Stanza 2, line 2, alt.

L. M.

BERA
John E. Gould, 1849

*In moderate time*

1. Be - hold! a Stran-ger at the door; He gen-tly knocks, has knocked be-fore;
2. O love-ly at - ti - tude! He stands With melt-ing heart and lad - en hands:
3. But will He prove a friend in - deed? He will; the ver - y Friend you need:
4. Ad - mit Him, for the hu - man breast Ne'er en-ter-tained so kind a Guest;

Has wait-ed long, is wait-ing still: You treat no oth - er friend so ill.
O match-less kind-ness! and He shows This match-less kind-ness to His foes.
The Friend of sin-ners—yes, 't is He, With gar-ments dyed on Cal-va - ry.
No mor-tal tongue their joys can tell With whom He con-de-scends to dwell. A-MEN.

## 226

18th century
Trans. by Rev. E. Caswall and Rev. W. J. Blew

C. M.

BALLERMA
Old Spanish melody
Probably by F. H. Barthélémon (1741–1808)

*In moderate time*

1. All ye a cer - tain cure who seek In trou - ble and dis - tress,
2. Je - sus, who gave Him-self for men, Up - on the cross to die,
3. Ye hear His gra-cious voice and free, Ye hear His sum-mons blest:

What-ev - er griefs the spir - it break, Or sins the soul op - press:
For you un-locks His heart; O then Un - to that heart draw nigh!
"O all ye wea - ry, come to me, And I will give you rest!" A-MEN.

Words from "Songs of Syon." Used by permission.

# 227 The Call of Christ

Rev. Erdmann Neumeister (1671–1756)
Trans. by Emma Frances Bevan (1827–1909)

BERLIN
Claude Goudimel, d. 1572

7. 7. 7. 7. 7. 7.

1. Sin - ners Je - sus will re - ceive; Tell this
2. Shep - herds seek their wan - dering sheep O'er the
3. Sick and sor - row - ful and blind, I with
4. Christ re - ceiv - eth sin - ful men, E - ven

word of grace to all Who the heaven-ly path - way leave,
moun-tains bleak and cold; Je - sus such a watch doth keep
all my sins draw nigh; O my Sav - iour, Thou canst find
me with all my sin; O - p'neth to me heaven a - gain;

All who lin - ger, all who fall; This can
O'er the lost ones of His fold, Seek - ing
Help for sin - ners such as I; Speak that
With Him I may en - ter in. Death hath

bring them back a - gain: Christ re - ceiv - eth sin - ful men.
them o'er moor and fen: Christ re - ceiv - eth sin - ful men.
word of love a - gain: Christ re - ceiv - eth sin - ful men.
no more sting nor pain: Christ re - ceiv - eth sin - ful men. A-MEN.

Used by permission of James Nisbet and Company, Ltd.

Bishop William Walsham How, 1867    7. 6. 7. 6. D.    ST. EDITH
Justin H. Knecht, 1799
Rev. Edward Husband, 1871

*In moderate time*

1. O Je - sus, Thou art stand-ing Out-side the fast-closed door,
2. O Je - sus, Thou art knock-ing; And lo, that hand is scarred,
3. O Je - sus, Thou art plead-ing In ac - cents meek and low,

In low - ly pa-tience wait-ing To pass the thresh-old o'er:
And thorns Thy brow en-cir-cle, And tears Thy face have marred:
"I died for you, My chil-dren, And will ye treat Me so?"

Shame on us, Chris-tian broth-ers, His Name and sign who bear,
O love that pass-eth knowl-edge, So pa - tient-ly to wait!
O Lord, with shame and sor-row We o-pen now the door;

O shame, thrice shame up-on us, To keep Him stand-ing there!
O sin that hath no e-qual, So fast to bar the gate!
Dear Sav-iour, en - ter, en - ter, And leave us nev-er-more! A-MEN.

Frances Ridley Havergal (1836-1879)     6. 6. 6. 6. 6. 6.     Melody from "Este's Psalter," 1592

OLD 120TH

*In rather slow time*

1. Thy life was given for me; Thy blood, O Lord, was shed,
2. Long years were spent for me In wea - ri - ness and woe,
3. And Thou hast brought to me, Down from Thy home a - bove,

That I might ran - somed be, And quick - ened from the dead:
That through e - ter - ni - ty Thy glo - ry I might know:
Sal - va - tion full and free, Thy par - don and Thy love:

Thy life was given for me; What have I given for Thee?
Long years were spent for me; Have I spent one for Thee?
Great gifts Thou brought-est me; What have I brought to Thee? A-MEN.

4. O let my life be given,
    My years for Thee be spent,
   World fetters all be riven,
    And joy with suffering blent!
   Thou gav'st Thyself for me;
    I give myself to Thee.

Charlotte Elliott, 1836

L. M.
(FIRST TUNE)

ST. CRISPIN
George J. Elvey, 1862

*In rather slow time*

1. Just as I am, with-out one plea But that Thy
2. Just as I am, and wait-ing not To rid my
3. Just as I am, though tossed a-bout With many a
4. Just as I am, poor, wretch-ed, blind; Sight, rich-es,

blood was shed for me, And that Thou bidd'st me
soul of one dark blot, To Thee, whose blood can
con-flict, many a doubt, Fight-ings and fears with-
heal-ing of the mind, Yea, all I need, in

come to Thee, O Lamb of God, I come, I come!
cleanse each spot, O Lamb of God, I come, I come!
in, with-out, O Lamb of God, I come, I come!
Thee to find, O Lamb of God, I come, I come! A-MEN.

5. Just as I am! Thou wilt receive,
   Wilt welcome, pardon, cleanse, relieve;
   Because Thy promise I believe,
   O Lamb of God, I come!

6. Just as I am! Thy love unknown
   Has broken every barrier down;
   Now to be Thine, yea, Thine alone,
   O Lamb of God, I come!

Charlotte Elliott, 1836

L. M.
(SECOND TUNE)

WOODWORTH
William B. Bradbury, 1849

*In moderate time*

1. Just as I am, with-out one plea
2. Just as I am, and wait-ing not
3. Just as I am, though tossed a-bout
4. Just as I am, poor, wretch-ed, blind;

But that Thy blood was shed for me, And that Thou bidd'st me
To rid my soul of one dark blot, To Thee, whose blood can
With many a con-flict, many a doubt, Fight-ings and fears with-
Sight, rich-es, heal-ing of the mind, Yea, all I need, in

come to Thee, O Lamb of God, I come, I come!
cleanse each spot, O Lamb of God, I come, I come!
in, with-out, O Lamb of God, I come, I come!
Thee to find, O Lamb of God, I come, I come! A-MEN.

5. Just as I am! Thou wilt receive,
   Wilt welcome, pardon, cleanse, relieve;
   Because Thy promise I believe,
   O Lamb of God, I come!

6. Just as I am! Thy love unknown
   Has broken every barrier down;
   Now to be Thine, yea, Thine alone,
   O Lamb of God, I come!

**231**

# The Life in Christ

Emily E. S. Elliott, 1864        Irregular        Rev. Timothy R. Matthews, 1876

MARGARET

*In moderate time*

1. Thou didst leave Thy throne and Thy king - ly crown When Thou cam - est to
2. Heav - en's arch - es rang, when the an - gels sang, Pro - claim - ing Thy
3. Thou cam - est, O Lord, with the liv - ing Word That should set Thy
4. When the heavens shall ring, and the an - gels sing At Thy com - ing to

earth for me; But in Beth - le - hem's home there was found no room
roy - al de - gree; But in low - ly birth didst Thou come to earth,
chil - dren free; But with mock - ing scorn and with crown of thorn
vic - to - ry, Let Thy voice call me home, say - ing, "Yet there is room,

For Thy ho - ly na - tiv - i - ty. O come to my
And in great hu - mil - i - ty. O come to my
They bore Thee to Cal - va - ry. O come to my
There is room at My side for thee." And my heart shall re -

heart, Lord Je - sus: There is room in my heart for Thee!
heart, Lord Je - sus: There is room in my heart for Thee!
heart, Lord Je - sus: There is room in my heart for Thee!
joice, Lord Je - sus: There is room in my heart for Thee! A-MEN.

# Answering Christ's Call

Matthew Bridges, 1848

C. M.
(FIRST TUNE)

*Rather slowly*

1. My God, ac-cept my heart this day, And make it al-ways Thine,
2. Be-fore the cross of Him who died, Be-hold, I pros-trate fall;
3. A-noint me with Thy heaven-ly grace, A-dopt me for Thine own,
4. Let ev-ery thought, and work, and word, To Thee be ev-er given;

That I from Thee no more may stray, No more from Thee de-cline.
Let ev-ery sin be cru-ci-fied, Let Christ be all in all.
That I may see Thy glo-rious face, And wor-ship at Thy throne.
Then life shall be Thy serv-ice, Lord, And death the gate of heaven. A-MEN.

**232**

Matthew Bridges, 1848

C. M.
(SECOND TUNE)

ST. STEPHEN
Rev. William Jones, 1789

*In moderate time*

1. My God, ac-cept my heart this day, And make it al-ways Thine,
2. Be-fore the cross of Him who died, Be-hold, I pros-trate fall;
3. A-noint me with Thy heaven-ly grace, A-dopt me for Thine own,
4. Let ev-ery thought, and work, and word, To Thee be ev-er given;

That I from Thee no more may stray, No more from Thee de-cline.
Let ev-ery sin be cru-ci-fied, Let Christ be all in all.
That I may see Thy glo-rious face, And wor-ship at Thy throne.
Then life shall be Thy serv-ice, Lord, And death the gate of heaven. A-MEN.

# 233

## The Life in Christ

Rev. Charles Wesley, 1740

7. 7. 7. 7. D.
(FIRST TUNE)

MARTYN
Simeon B. Marsh, 1834

*In moderate time*

1. Je - sus, Lov - er of my soul, Let me to Thy bos - om fly,
2. Oth - er ref - uge have I none; Hangs my help - less soul on Thee;
3. Thou, O Christ, art all I want; More than all in Thee I find:
4. Plen - teous grace with Thee is found, Grace to cov - er all my sin;

While the near - er wa - ters roll, While the tem - pest still is high:
Leave, ah! leave me not a - lone, Still sup - port and com - fort me.
Raise the fall - en, cheer the faint, Heal the sick, and lead the blind:
Let the heal - ing streams a - bound; Make and keep me pure with - in.

Hide me, O my Sav - iour, hide, Till the storm of life is past;
All my trust on Thee is stayed, All my help from Thee I bring;
Just and ho - ly is Thy Name; I am all un - right - eous - ness;
Thou of life the Foun - tain art, Free - ly let me take of Thee;

Safe in - to the ha - ven guide; O re - ceive my soul at last!
Cov - er my de - fense - less head With the shad - ow of Thy wing.
False and full of sin I am, Thou art full of truth and grace.
Spring Thou up with - in my heart, Rise to all e - ter - ni - ty. A-MEN.

# Answering Christ's Call

HOLLINGSIDE

Rev. Charles Wesley, 1740

7. 7. 7. 7. D.
(SECOND TUNE)

Rev. John B. Dykes, 1861

*In moderate time*

1. Je - sus, Lov - er of my soul, Let me to Thy bos - om fly,
2. Oth - er ref - uge have I none; Hangs my help - less soul on Thee;
3. Thou, O Christ, art all I want; More than all in Thee I find:
4. Plen-teous grace with Thee is found, Grace to cov - er all my sin;

While the near - er wa - ters roll, While the tem - pest still is high:
Leave, ah! leave me not a - lone, Still sup - port and com - fort me.
Raise the fall - en, cheer the faint, Heal the sick, and lead the blind.
Let the heal - ing streams a - bound; Make and keep me pure with - in.

Hide me, O my Sav - iour, hide, Till the storm of life is past;
All my trust on Thee is stayed, All my help from Thee I bring;
Just and ho - ly is Thy Name; I am all un - right-eous - ness;
Thou of life the Foun - tain art, Free - ly let me take of Thee;

Safe in - to the ha - ven guide; O re - ceive my soul at last!
Cov - er my de-fense-less head With the shad - ow of Thy wing.
False and full of sin I am, Thou art full of truth and grace.
Spring Thou up with - in my heart, Rise to all e - ter - ni - ty. A-MEN.

# The Life in Christ

Rev. Charles Wesley, 1740

7. 7. 7. 7. D.
(THIRD TUNE)

ABERYSTWYTH
Joseph Parry, 1879

*In moderate time*

1. Je - sus, Lov - er of my soul, Let me to Thy bos - om fly,
2. Oth - er ref - uge have I none; Hangs my help-less soul on Thee;
3. Thou, O Christ, art all I want; More than all in Thee I find:
4. Plen - teous grace with Thee is found, Grace to cov - er all my sin;

While the near-er wa-ters roll, While the tem-pest still is high:
Leave, ah! leave me not a - lone, Still sup-port and com-fort me.
Raise the fall - en, cheer the faint, Heal the sick, and lead the blind.
Let the heal-ing streams a - bound; Make and keep me pure with - in.

Hide me, O my Sav - iour, hide, Till the storm of life is past;
All my trust on Thee is stayed, All my help from Thee I bring;
Just and ho - ly is Thy Name; I am all un - right - eous-ness;
Thou of life the Foun - tain art, Free-ly let me take of Thee;

Safe in - to the ha - ven guide; O re - ceive my soul at last!
Cov - er my de-fense-less head With the shad-ow of Thy wing.
False and full of sin I am, Thou art full of truth and grace.
Spring Thou up with-in my heart, Rise to all e - ter-ni - ty. A-MEN

Tune used by permission of Messrs. Hughes and Sons.

# Answering Christ's Call

From the "Marathi" of Narayan Vaman Tilak (1862–1919)
Trans. by Rev. Nicol Macnicol
C. M.

WIGTOWN
"Scottish Psalter," 1635

*Moderately slow*

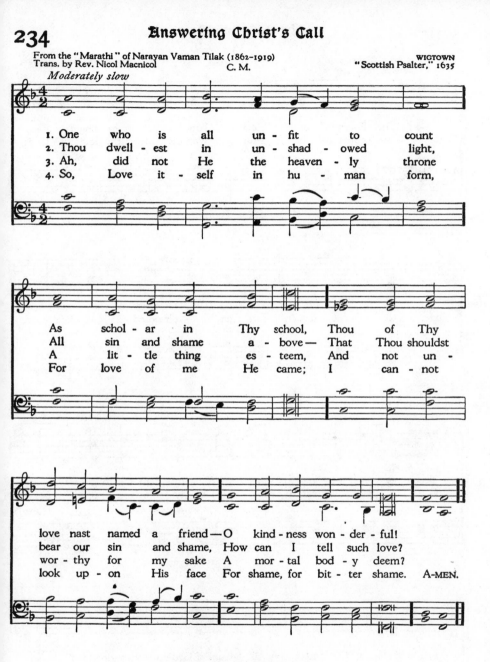

1. One who is all un - fit to count
   As schol - ar in Thy school, Thou of Thy
   love hast named a friend—O kind - ness won - der - ful!

2. Thou dwell - est in un - shad - owed light,
   All sin and shame a - bove— That Thou shouldst
   bear our sin and shame, How can I tell such love?

3. Ah, did not He the heaven - ly throne
   A lit - tle thing es - teem, And not un -
   wor - thy for my sake A mor - tal bod - y deem?

4. So, Love it - self in hu - man form,
   For love of me He came; I can - not
   look up - on His face For shame, for bit - ter shame. A-MEN.

5. If there is aught of worth in me,
   It comes from Thee alone;
   Then keep me safe, for so, O Lord,
   Thou keepest but Thine own.

Words copyright by Rev. Nicol Macnicol.   Used by permission of Miss Helen Macnicol.

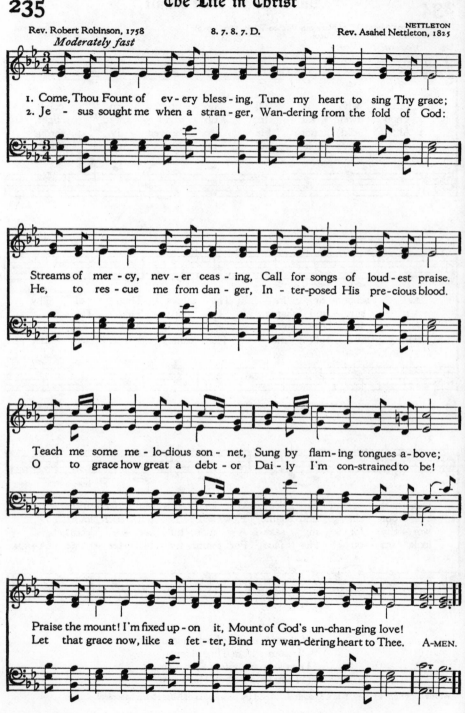

# 235

## The Life in Christ

Rev. Robert Robinson, 1758

*Moderately fast*

8. 7. 8. 7. D.

NETTLETON
Rev. Asahel Nettleton, 1825

1. Come, Thou Fount of ev-ery bless-ing, Tune my heart to sing Thy grace;
2. Je - sus sought me when a stran-ger, Wan-dering from the fold of God:

Streams of mer-cy, nev-er ceas-ing, Call for songs of loud-est praise.
He, to res-cue me from dan-ger, In - ter-posed His pre-cious blood.

Teach me some me - lo-dious son - net, Sung by flam-ing tongues a-bove;
O to grace how great a debt-or Dai-ly I'm con-strained to be!

Praise the mount! I'm fixed up-on it, Mount of God's un-chan-ging love!
Let that grace now, like a fet-ter, Bind my wan-dering heart to Thee. A-MEN.

Rev. Horatius Bonar, 1846

C. M. D.

VOX DILECTI
Rev. John B. Dykes, 1868

1. I heard the voice of Je-sus say, "Come un-to Me and rest;
2. I heard the voice of Je-sus say, "Be-hold, I free-ly give
3. I heard the voice of Je-sus say, "I am this dark world's Light;

Lay down, thou wea-ry one, lay down Thy head up-on My breast."
The liv-ing wa-ter; thirst-y one, Stoop down and drink, and live."
Look un-to Me, thy morn shall rise, And all thy day be bright."

I came to Je-sus as I was, Wea-ry and worn and sad,
I came to Je-sus, and I drank Of that life-giv-ing stream;
I looked to Je-sus, and I found In Him my Star, my Sun;

I found in Him a rest-ing place, And He has made me glad.
My thirst was quenched, my soul re-vived, And now I live in Him.
And in that Light of life I'll walk, Till trav-el-ing days are done. A-MEN.

# The Life in Christ

Rev. Augustus M. Toplady, 1776
Stanza 4, line 2, alt. by
Rev. Thomas Cotterill, 1815

7. 7. 7. 7. 7. 7.
(FIRST TUNE)

TOPLADY
Thomas Hastings, 1830

*In moderate time*

1. Rock of A - ges, cleft for me, Let me hide my - self in Thee; Let the wa - ter and the blood, From Thy riv - en side which flowed, Be of sin the dou - ble cure, Cleanse me from its guilt and power.

2. Not the la - bors of my hands Can ful - fill Thy law's de - mands; Could my zeal no res - pite know, Could my tears for - ev - er flow, All for sin could not a - tone; Thou must save, and Thou a - lone.

3. Noth - ing in my hand I bring, Sim - ply to Thy cross I cling; Na - ked, come to Thee for dress, Help - less, look to Thee for grace; Foul, I to the foun - tain fly; Wash me, Sav - iour, or I die.

4. While I draw this fleet - ing breath, When my eye - lids close in death, When I soar to worlds un - known, See Thee on Thy judg - ment throne, Rock of A - ges, cleft for me, Let me hide my - self in Thee. A-MEN.

Rev. Augustus M. Toplady, 1776
Stanza 4, line 2, alt. by
Rev. Thomas Cotterill, 1815

7. 7. 7. 7. 7. 7.
(SECOND TUNE)

REDHEAD NO. 76 (AJALON)
Richard Redhead, 1853

*In moderate time*

1. Rock of A - ges, cleft for me, Let me hide my -
2. Not the la - bors of my hands Can ful - fill Thy
3. Noth - ing in my hand I bring, Sim - ply to Thy
4. While I draw this fleet - ing breath, When my eye - lids

self in Thee; Let the wa - ter and the blood,
law's de - mands; Could my zeal no res - pite know,
cross I cling; Na - ked, come to Thee for dress,
close in death, When I soar to worlds un - known,

From Thy riv - en side which flowed, Be of sin the
Could my tears for - ev - er flow, All for sin could
Help - less, look to Thee for grace; Foul, I to the
See Thee on Thy judg - ment throne, Rock of A - ges,

dou - ble cure, Cleanse me from its guilt and power.
not a - tone; Thou must save, and Thou a - lone.
foun - tain fly; Wash me, Sav - iour, or I die.
cleft for me, Let me hide my - self in Thee. A - MEN.

Rev. Thomas Benson Pollock (1836–1896)    7. 7. 7. 6.      AGNES
                                         Edward Bunnett (1834–1923)

*Not too fast*

1. Je - sus, we are far a - way From the light of heaven - ly day;
2. Help us to be - wail our sin, And, in heaven - ly strength, be - gin
3. May Thy wis - dom be our guide, Com - fort, rest, and peace pro - vide
4. Fix our hearts on things on high; Let no e - vil thoughts come nigh;
5. May Thy grace with - in the soul Na - ture's way-ward-ness con - trol,

Lost in paths of sin we stray: Lord, in mer - cy hear us.
Dai - ly vic - to - ries to win: Lord, in mer - cy hear us.
Near to Thy pro - tect - ing side: Lord, in mer - cy hear us.
Purge from sin our mem - o - ry: Lord, in mer - cy hear us.
Guid-ing toward the heaven-ly goal: Lord, in mer - cy hear us. A - MEN.

Words used by permission of the Vicar of St. Albans, Birmingham.

239

Bishop Synesius of Cyrene (375–430)                  SOUTHWELL
Trans. by Rev. A. W. Chatfield (1808–1896)    S. M.       Damon's "Psalter," 1579
                                          (Later form of third line)

*In rather slow time*

1. Lord Je - sus, think on me, And purge a - way my sin;
2. Lord Je - sus, think on me, A - mid the bat - tle's strife;
3. Lord Je - sus, think on me, Nor let me go a - stray;
4. Lord Je - sus, think on me, That, when this life is past,

From earth-born pas-sions set me free, And make me pure with-in.
In all my pain and mis - er - y Be Thou my health and life.
Through dark-ness and per-plex - i - ty Point Thou the heaven-ly way.
I may th' e - ter - nal bright-ness see, And share Thy joy at last. A - MEN.

Words copyright by Kyrle Chatfield.

**240**

*In moderate time*

1. Lord, from the depths to Thee I cried: My voice, Lord, do Thou hear:
2. Lord, who shall stand, if Thou, O Lord, Shouldst mark in-iq-ui-ty?
3. I wait for God, my soul doth wait; My hope is in His word.
5. I say, more than they that do watch The morn-ing light to see.
5. Re-demp-tion al-so plen-te-ous Is ev-er found with Him:

Un-to my sup-pli-ca-tion's voice Give an at-ten-tive ear.
But yet with Thee for-give-ness is, That feared Thou may-est be.
More than they that for morn-ing watch, My soul waits for the Lord;
Let Is-ra-el hope in the Lord, For with Him mer-cies be.
And from all his in-iq-ui-ties He Is-rael shall re-deem. A-MEN.

**241**

William Cowper (1731-1800)     C. M.     COWPER
Lowell Mason, 1830

*In moderate time*

1. There is a foun-tain filled with blood Drawn from Em-man-uel's veins; And sin-ners, plunged be-
2. The dy-ing thief re-joiced to see That foun-tain in his day; And there may I, as
3. Dear dy-ing Lamb, Thy pre-cious blood Shall nev-er lose its power Till all the ran-somed
4. E'er since by faith I saw the stream Thy flow-ing wounds sup-ply, Re-deem-ing love has
5. When this poor lisp-ing, stammering tongue Lies si-lent in the grave, Then in a no-bler,

neath that flood, Lose all their guilt-y stains, Lose all their guilt-y stains.
vile as he, Wash all my sins a-way, Wash all my sins a-way.
Church of God Be saved, to sin no more, Be saved, to sin no more.
been my theme, And shall be till I die, And shall be till I die.
sweet-er song I'll sing Thy power to save, I'll sing Thy power to save. A-MEN.

**242**

Frances Ridley Havergal (1836–1879)  7. 7. 7. 7.  Adapted from Mozart (1756–1791)

MOZART

*In moderate time*

1. Take my life, and let it be Con - se-
2. Take my hands, and let them move At the
3. Take my voice, and let me sing, Al - ways,
4. Take my sil - ver and my gold; Not a

crat - ed, Lord, to Thee. Take my mo - ments
im - pulse of Thy love. Take my feet, and
on - ly, for my King. Take my lips, and
mite would I with - hold. Take my in - tel -

and my days; Let them flow in cease - less praise.
let them be Swift and beau - ti - ful for Thee.
let them be Filled with mes - sa - ges from Thee.
lect, and use Ev - ery power as Thou shalt choose. A - MEN.

5. Take my will, and make it Thine;
   It shall be no longer mine.
   Take my heart, it is Thine own;
   It shall be Thy royal throne.

6. Take my love; my Lord, I pour
   At Thy feet its treasure store.
   Take myself, and I will be
   Ever, only, all for Thee.

**243**

# Dedication and Consecration

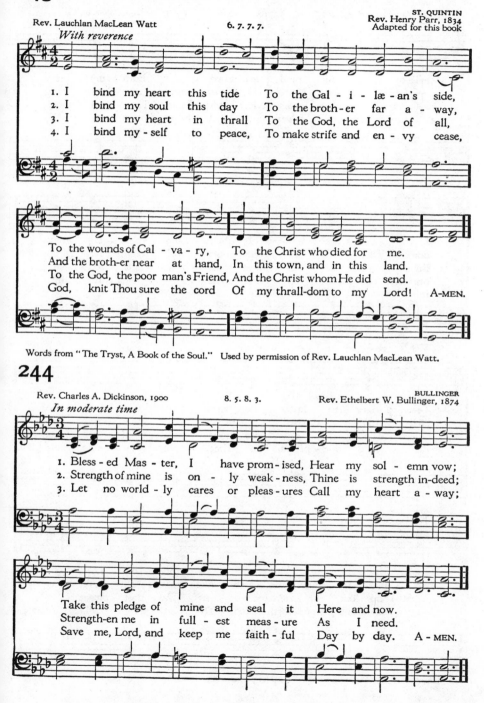

ST. QUINTIN
Rev. Henry Parr, 1834
Adapted for this book

Rev. Lauchlan MacLean Watt

6. 7. 7. 7.

*With reverence*

1. I bind my heart this tide To the Gal - i - læ - an's side,
2. I bind my soul this day To the broth - er far a - way,
3. I bind my heart in thrall To the God, the Lord of all,
4. I bind my - self to peace, To make strife and en - vy cease,

To the wounds of Cal - va - ry, To the Christ who died for me.
And the broth-er near at hand, In this town, and in this land.
To the God, the poor man's Friend, And the Christ whom He did send.
God, knit Thou sure the cord Of my thrall-dom to my Lord! A-MEN.

Words from "The Tryst, A Book of the Soul." Used by permission of Rev. Lauchlan MacLean Watt.

**244**

Rev. Charles A. Dickinson, 1900

8. 5. 8. 3.

BULLINGER
Rev. Ethelbert W. Bullinger, 1874

*In moderate time*

1. Bless - ed Mas - ter, I have prom - ised, Hear my sol - emn vow;
2. Strength of mine is on - ly weak - ness, Thine is strength in-deed;
3. Let no world - ly cares or pleas - ures Call my heart a - way;

Take this pledge of mine and seal it Here and now.
Strength-en me in full - est meas - ure As I need.
Save me, Lord, and keep me faith - ful Day by day. A - MEN.

# 245

## The Life in Christ

Rev. William H. Foulkes, 1918  10. 10. 10. 10.  Rev. Calvin W. Laufer, 1918

HALL

*In moderate time*

1. Take Thou our minds, dear Lord, we hum - bly pray;
2. Take Thou our hearts, O Christ, they are Thine own;
3. Take Thou our wills, Most High! Hold Thou full sway;
4. Take Thou our - selves, O Lord, heart, mind, and will;

Give us the mind of Christ each pass - ing day;
Come Thou with - in our souls and claim Thy throne;
Have in our in - most souls Thy per - fect way;
Through our sur - ren - dered souls Thy plans ful - fill.

Teach us to know the truth that sets us free;
Help us to shed a - broad Thy death - less love;
Guard Thou each sa - cred hour from self - ish ease;
We yield our - selves to Thee— time, tal - ents, all;

Grant us in all our thoughts to hon - or Thee.
Use us to make the earth like heaven a - bove.
Guide Thou our or - dered lives as Thou dost please.
We hear, and hence - forth heed, Thy sov - ereign call.  A-MEN.

Copyright, 1918, by Calvin W. Laufer.  Used by permission.

Rev. Henry Harbaugh, c. 1861

S. M.
(FIRST TUNE)

LAKE ENON (MERCERSBURG)
Isaac B. Woodbury

*In rather slow time*

1. Je - sus, I live to Thee, The Love - li - est and Best;
2. Je - sus, I die to Thee, When - ev - er death shall come;
3. Wheth - er to live or die, I know not which is best;
4. Liv - ing or dy - ing, Lord, I ask but to be Thine;

My life in Thee, Thy life in me, In Thy blest love I rest.
To die in Thee is life to me In my e - ter - nal home.
To live in Thee is bliss to me, To die is end - less rest.
My life in Thee, Thy life in me, Makes heaven for - ev - er mine. A-MEN.

Rev. Henry Harbaugh, c. 1861

S. M.
(SECOND TUNE)

TRENTHAM
Robert Jackson, 1894

*In moderate time*

1. Je - sus, I live to Thee, The Love - li - est and Best; My life in
2. Je - sus, I die to Thee, When-ev - er death shall come; To die in
3. Wheth-er to live or die, I know not which is best; To live in
4. Liv - ing or dy - ing, Lord, I ask but to be Thine; My life in

Thee, Thy life in me, In Thy blest love I rest.
Thee is life to me, In my e - ter - nal home.
Thee is bliss to me, To die is end - less rest.
Thee, Thy life in me, Makes heaven for - ev - er mine. A - MEN.

Tune used by permission of Mrs. Ethel Taylor.

# 247
## The Life in Christ

LLANLLYFNI

Rev. George Matheson (1842-1906)

S. M. D.
(FIRST TUNE)

John Jones (Talysarn) (1797-1857)
Arr. by David Jenkins (1849-1915)

*Moderately slow*

1. Make me a cap-tive, Lord, And then I shall be free;
2. My heart is weak and poor Un-til it mas-ter find;
3. My power is faint and low Till I have learned to serve;
4. My will is not my own Till Thou hast made it Thine;

Force me to ren-der up my sword, And I shall con-queror be.
It has no spring of ac-tion sure— It va-ries with the wind.
It wants the need-ed fire to glow, It wants the breeze to nerve;
If it would reach a mon-arch's throne It must its crown re-sign;

I sink in life's a-larms When by my-self I stand;
It can-not free-ly move Till Thou hast wrought its chain;
It can-not drive the world Un-til it-self be driven;
It on-ly stands un-bent A-mid the clash-ing strife,

Im-pris-on me with-in Thine arms, And strong shall be my hand.
En-slave it with Thy match-less love, And death-less it shall reign.
Its flag can on-ly be un-furled When Thou shalt breathe from heaven.
When on Thy bos-om it has leant And found in Thee its life. A-MEN.

Words used by permission of Messrs. McClure Naismith Brodie and Company.
Tune used by permission of Miss Nellie D. Jenkins.

# 247 Dedication and Consecration

Rev. George Matheson (1842-1906)

S. M. D.
(SECOND TUNE)

LEOMINSTER
George W. Martin, 1862
Harmonized by Arthur Sullivan, 1874

*In moderate time*

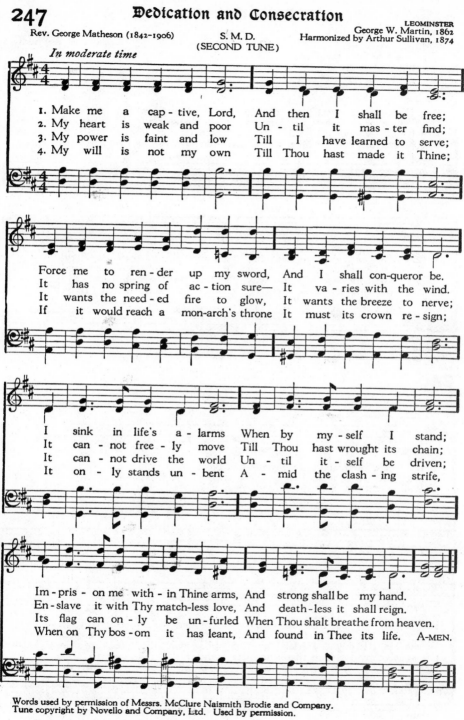

1. Make me a cap-tive, Lord, And then I shall be free;
2. My heart is weak and poor Un-til it mas-ter find;
3. My power is faint and low Till I have learned to serve;
4. My will is not my own Till Thou hast made it Thine;

Force me to ren-der up my sword, And I shall con-queror be.
It has no spring of ac-tion sure— It va-ries with the wind.
It wants the need-ed fire to glow, It wants the breeze to nerve;
If it would reach a mon-arch's throne It must its crown re-sign;

I sink in life's a-larms When by my-self I stand;
It can-not free-ly move Till Thou hast wrought its chain;
It can-not drive the world Un-til it-self be driven;
It on-ly stands un-bent A-mid the clash-ing strife,

Im-pris-on me with-in Thine arms, And strong shall be my hand.
En-slave it with Thy match-less love, And death-less it shall reign.
Its flag can on-ly be un-furled When Thou shalt breathe from heaven.
When on Thy bos-om it has leant, And found in Thee its life. A-MEN.

Words used by permission of Messrs. McClure Naismith Brodie and Company.
Tune copyright by Novello and Company, Ltd. Used by permission.

## 248

Mary F. Maude, 1847
7. 7. 7. 7.
HORSHAM
English traditional melody

*In rather slow time*

1. Thine for - ev - er! God of love, Hear us from Thy throne a - bove;
2. Thine for - ev - er! O how blest They who find in Thee their rest!
3. Thine for - ev - er! Lord of life, Shield us through our earth - ly strife;
4. Thine for - ev - er! Thou our Guide, All our wants by Thee sup - plied,

Thine for - ev - er may we be Here and in e - ter - ni - ty!
Sav-iour, Guard-ian, heaven-ly Friend, O de-fend us to the end!
Thou the Life, the Truth, the Way, Guide us to the realms of day!
All our sins by Thee for-given, Led by Thee from earth to heaven! A-MEN.

Words used by permission of Miss Mary E. Maude.
Tune from "Songs of Praise." Used by permission of the Oxford University Press.

## 249

Rev. Isaac Watts, 1707; alt.
C. M.
MARTYRDOM
Hugh Wilson (1766–1824)

*In rather slow time*

1. A - las! and did my Sav - iour bleed, And did my Sov - ereign die!
2. Was it for sins that I have done He suf - fered on the tree?
3. Well might the sun in dark - ness hide, And shut his glo - ries in,
4. Thus might I hide my blush - ing face While His dear cross ap - pears;
5. But drops of grief can ne'er re - pay The debt of love I owe;

Would He de - vote that sa - cred head For sin - ners such as I!
A - maz - ing pit - y! Grace un-known! And love be - yond de - gree!
When He, the might - y Mak - er, died For man the crea-ture's sin.
Dis - solve my heart in thank-ful -ness, And melt mine eyes to tears.
Here, Lord, I give my - self a - way; 'Tis all that I can do. A-MEN.

From a sonnet by
Archbishop Richard Chevenix Trench
Arranged by Rev. William Pierson Merrill   10. 10. 10. 10.

ALL SAINTS
E. T. Davies

*With quiet confidence and joy*

1. Lord, what a change with - in us one short hour
2. We kneel, and all a - round us seems to lower;
3. Why should we ev - er weak or heart - less be,

Spent in Thy pres - ence will pre - vail to make;
We rise, and all, the dis - tant and the near,
Why are we ev - er o - ver - borne with care,

What heav - y bur - dens from our bos - oms take,
Stands forth in sun - ny out - line, brave and clear;
Anx - ious, or trou - bled, when with us is prayer,

What parch - ed grounds re - fresh as with a shower!
We kneel, how weak; we rise, how full of power!
And joy and strength and cour - age are with Thee! A - MEN.

Tune from "A Students' Hymnal." Used by permission of Mr. E. T. Davies.

# 251

Rev. John S. B. Monsell, 1862      S. M.      ST. ANDREW
Joseph Barnby, 1866

*In moderate time*

1. Sweet is Thy mer - cy, Lord; Be - fore Thy mer - cy seat
2. Wher - e'er Thy Name is blest, Wher - e'er Thy peo - ple meet,
3. Light Thou my wea - ry way, Lead Thou my wan-dering feet,
4. Thus shall the heaven - ly host Hear all my songs re - peat

My soul, a - dor-ing, pleads Thy word And owns Thy mer - cy sweet.
There I de - light in Thee to rest, And find Thy mer - cy sweet.
That while I stay on earth I may Still find Thy mer - cy sweet.
To Fa - ther, Son, and Ho - ly Ghost, My joy, Thy mer - cy sweet. A - MEN.

# 252

Eliza Fanny Morris (1821–1874)      7. 7. 7. 5.      CAPETOWN
Friedrich Filitz, 1847

*In moderate time*

1. God of pit - y, God of grace, When we hum - bly seek Thy face,
2. When Thy love our hearts shall fill, And we long to do Thy will,
3. Should we wan - der from Thy fold, And our love to Thee grow cold,
4. Should the hand of sor - row press, Earth - ly care and want dis - tress,
5. And, what-e'er our cry may be, When we lift our hearts to Thee,

Bend from heaven, Thy dwell-ing place; Hear, for - give, and save.
Turn - ing to Thy ho - ly hill, Lord, ac - cept and save.
With a pit - ying eye be - hold; Lord, for - give, and save.
May our souls Thy peace pos - sess; Je - sus, hear and save.
From our bur - den set us free; Hear, for - give, and save. A-MEN.

# 253

Rev. Louis F. Benson, 1926 · S. M. · SWABIA · Johann M. Spiess, 1745

*In moderate time*

1. I name Thy hal-lowed Name, I bring Thee a new day;
2. Thy King-dom come to me, And build with-in my heart
3. Thy will be done by me In lit-tle things, close by,
4. Give me my bread to-day, E-nough to keep me strong,
5. If an-y tempt me, lead To pur-er air a-bove;

Lord, keep my life from sin and shame, And teach me how to pray.
A shrine for me, a throne for Thee, A tem-ple set a-part.
That so my home on earth may be More like Thy heaven on high.
E-nough to share; and help me pray For those who do me wrong.
Thy power is gen-tle in our need, Thy glo-ry is Thy love. A-MEN.

Words copyright, 1927, by the Presbyterian Board of Christian Education.

# 254

Bishop George W. Doane, 1824 · C. M. · ST. JAMES · Raphael Courteville, d. 1772

*In moderate time*

1. Thou art the Way: to Thee a-lone From sin and death we flee;
2. Thou art the Truth: Thy word a-lone True wis-dom can im-part;
3. Thou art the Life: the rend-ing tomb Pro-claims Thy con-quering arm,
4. Thou art the Way, the Truth, the Life: Grant us that Way to know,

And he who would the Fa-ther seek Must seek Him, Lord, by Thee.
Thou on-ly canst in-form the mind And pu-ri-fy the heart.
And those who put their trust in Thee Nor death nor hell shall harm.
That Truth to keep, that Life to win, Whose joys e-ter-nal flow. A-MEN.

# 255

## The Life in Christ

James Montgomery, 1834

6. 5. 6. 5. D.
(FIRST TUNE)

ST. MARY MAGDALENE
Rev. John B. Dykes (1823–1876)

*In moderate time*

1. In the hour of tri - al, Je - sus, plead for me;
2. With its witch - ing pleas - ures Would this vain world charm,
3. When in dust and ash - es To the grave I sink,

Lest by base de - ni - al I de - part from Thee:
Or its sor - did treas - ures Spread to work me harm,
While heaven's glo - ry flash - es O'er the shelv - ing brink,

When Thou seest me wa - ver, With a look re - call,
Bring to my re - mem - brance Sad Geth - sem - a - ne,
On Thy truth re - ly - ing Through that mor - tal strife,

Nor for fear or fa - vor Suf - fer me to fall.
Or, in dark - er sem - blance, Cross-crowned Cal-va - ry.
Lord, re - ceive me, dy - ing, To e - ter - nal life. A-MEN.

**255**

James Montgomery, 1834

6. 5. 6. 5. D.
(SECOND TUNE)

PENITENCE (LANE)
Spencer Lane, 1879

*In moderate time*

1. In the hour of tri - al, Je - sus, plead for me;
2. With its witch - ing pleas - ures Would this vain world charm,
3. When in dust and ash - es To the grave I sink,

Lest by base de - ni - al I de - part from Thee:
Or its sor - did treas - ures Spread to work me harm,
While heaven's glo - ry flash - es O'er the shelv - ing brink,

When Thou seest me wa - ver, With a look re - call,
Bring to my re - mem - brance Sad Geth - sem - a - ne,
On Thy truth re - ly - ing Through that mor - tal strife,

Nor for fear or fa - vor Suf - fer me to fall.
Or, in dark - er sem - blance, Cross-crowned Cal - va - ry.
Lord, re - ceive me, dy - ing, To e - ter - nal life. A-MEN.

# The Life in Christ

Rev. Samuel Johnson, 1846      11. 10. 11. 10.      HENLEY
Lowell Mason, 1854

*In moderate time*

1. Fa - ther, in Thy mys - te - rious pres - ence kneel - ing,
2. Lord, we have wan - dered forth through doubt and sor - row,
3. Now, Fa - ther, now in Thy dear pres - ence kneel - ing,

Fain would our souls feel all Thy kin - dling love;
And Thou hast made each step an on - ward one;
Our spir - its yearn to feel Thy kin - dling love;

For we are weak, and need some deep re - veal - ing
And we will ev - er trust each un - known mor - row;
Now make us strong; we need Thy deep re - veal - ing

Of trust and strength and calm - ness from a - bove.
Thou wilt sus - tain us till its work is done.
Of trust and strength and calm - ness from a - bove. A-MEN.

**257**

Joseph Scriven (1820–1886)

*Moderately fast*

8. 7. 8. 7. D.

WHAT A FRIEND
C. Crozat Converse, 1868

1. What a Friend we have in Je - sus, All our sins and griefs to bear!
2. Have we tri - als and temp-ta - tions? Is there trou-ble an - y-where?
3. Are we weak and heav - y - la - den, Cum-bered with a load of care?

What a priv - i - lege to car - ry Ev - ery-thing to God in prayer!
We should nev - er be dis-cour - aged: Take it to the Lord in prayer!
Pre - cious Sav-iour, still our Ref - uge— Take it to the Lord in prayer!

O what peace we of - ten for - feit, O what need-less pain we bear,
Can we find a friend so faith - ful, Who will all our sor-rows share?
Do thy friends de-spise, for-sake thee? Take it to the Lord in prayer!

All be-cause we do not car - ry Ev - ery-thing to God in prayer!
Je - sus knows our ev - ery weak-ness— Take it to the Lord in prayer!
In His arms He'll take and shield thee, Thou wilt find a sol - ace there. A-MEN.

Henry Montague Butler (1833-1918)    10. 10. 10. 10.    Walter Greatorex (1877- )

WOODLANDS

*With exultation and majesty. May be sung in unison*

1. "Lift up your hearts!" We lift them, Lord, to Thee;
2. A - bove the lev - el of the for - mer years,
3. Lift ev - ery gift that Thou Thy - self hast given;
4. Then, as the trump - et call, in aft - er years,

Here at Thy feet none oth - er may we see;
The mire of sin, the weight of guilt - y fears,
Low lies the best till lift - ed up to heaven:
"Lift up your hearts!" rings peal - ing in our ears,

"Lift up your hearts!" E'en so, with one ac - cord,
The mist of doubt, the blight of love's de - cay,
Low lie the bound - ing heart, the teem - ing brain,
Still shall those hearts re - spond, with full ac - cord

We lift them up, we lift them to the Lord.
O Lord of Light, lift all our hearts to - day!
Till, sent from God, they mount to God a - gain.
"We lift them up, we lift them to the Lord!" A-MEN.

Words from "A Students' Hymnal" (Hymns of the Kingdom).
Used by permission of Mr. E. M. Butler and the Oxford University Press.
Tune used by permission of Mr. W. Greatorex

# 259 Aspiration
C. M.

William Cowper, 1772

DALEHURST
Arthur Cottman, 1874

1. O for a clos-er walk with God, A calm and heaven-ly frame,
2. Re-turn, O ho-ly Dove, re-turn, Sweet mes-sen-ger of rest!
3. The dear-est i-dol I have known, What-e'er that i-dol be,
4. So shall my walk be close with God, Calm and se-rene my frame;

A light to shine up-on the road That leads me to the Lamb!
I hate the sins that made Thee mourn And drove Thee from my breast.
Help me to tear it from Thy throne, And wor-ship on-ly Thee.
So pur-er light shall mark the road That leads me to the Lamb. A-MEN.

# 260
C. M.

Rev. Charles Wesley (1707–1788)

MARTYRDOM
Hugh Wilson (1766–1824)

*Moderately slow and dignified*

1. O for a heart to praise my God! A heart from sin set free;
2. A heart re-signed, sub-mis-sive, meek, My great Re-deem-er's throne,
3. A hum-ble, low-ly, con-trite heart, Be-liev-ing, true, and clean,
4. A heart in ev-ery thought re-newed, And full of love di-vine,
5. Thy na-ture, gra-cious Lord, im-part; Come quick-ly from a-bove;

A heart that al-ways feels Thy blood, So free-ly shed for me;
Where on-ly Christ is heard to speak, Where Je-sus reigns a-lone;
Which neith-er life nor death can part From Him that dwells with-in;
Per-fect and right and pure and good, A cop-y, Lord, of Thine!
Write Thy new Name up-on my heart, Thy new, best Name of Love. A-MEN.

# The Life in Christ

Sarah F. Adams, 1841     6. 4. 6. 4. 6. 6. 6. 4.     BETHANY    Lowell Mason, 1856

*In moderate time*

1. Near - er, my God, to Thee, Near - er to Thee!
2. Though like the wan - der - er, The sun gone down,
3. There let the way ap - pear Steps un - to heaven:
4. Then, with my wak - ing thoughts Bright with Thy praise,
5. Or if on joy - ful wing Cleav - ing the sky,

E'en though it be a cross That rais - eth me;
Dark - ness be o - ver me, My rest a stone;
All that Thou send - est me In mer - cy given:
Out of my ston - y griefs Beth - el I'll raise;
Sun, moon, and stars for - got, Up - ward I fly,

Still all my song shall be, Near - er, my God, to Thee,
Yet in my dreams I'd be Near - er, my God, to Thee,
An - gels to beck - on me Near - er, my God, to Thee,
So by my woes to be Near - er, my God, to Thee,
Still all my song shall be, Near - er, my God, to Thee,

Near - er, my God, to Thee, Near - er to Thee! A-MEN.

William Henry Burleigh, 1868  10. 10. 10. 10.  Samuel Sebastian Wesley (1810–1876)

ELLINGHAM

*In moderate time*

1. Lead us, O Fa - ther, in the paths of peace:
2. Lead us, O Fa - ther, in the paths of truth:
3. Lead us, O Fa - ther, in the paths of right:
4. Lead us, O Fa - ther, to Thy heaven - ly rest,

With - out Thy guid - ing hand we go a - stray,
Un - helped by Thee, in er - ror's maze we grope,
Blind - ly we stum - ble when we walk a - lone,
How - ev - er rough and steep the path - way be,

And doubts ap - pall, and sor - rows still in - crease;
While pas - sion stains and fol - ly dims our youth,
In - volved in shad - ows of a dark - ening night;
Through joy or sor - row, as Thou deem - est best,

Lead us through Christ, the true and liv - ing Way.
And age comes on un - cheered by faith or hope.
On - ly with Thee we jour - ney safe - ly on.
Un - til our lives are per - fect - ed in Thee. A-MEN.

# 263 The Life in Christ

Anna B. Warner, 1852  II. 10. 11. 10.  HENLEY
Lowell Mason, 1854

*In moderate time*

1. We would see Je - sus; for the shad - ows length - en
2. We would see Je - sus, the great Rock Foun - da - tion
3. We would see Je - sus: sense is all too blind - ing,
4. We would see Je - sus: this is all we're need - ing;

A - cross this lit - tle land - scape of our life;
Where - on our feet were set by sov - ereign grace:
And heaven ap - pears too dim, too far a - way;
Strength, joy, and will - ing - ness come with the sight;

We would see Je - sus, our weak faith to strength - en
Not life nor death, with all their ag - i - ta - tion,
We would see Thee, to gain a sweet re - mind - ing
We would see Je - sus, dy - ing, ris - en, plead - ing;

For the last wea - ri - ness, the fi - nal strife.
Can thence re - move us, if we see His face.
That Thou hast prom - ised our great debt to pay.
Then wel - come day, and fare - well mor - tal night. A - MEN.

# 264

## Aspiration

Rev. Robert Seagrave, 1742
Stanza 3, alt.

7. 6. 7. 6. 7. 7. 7. 6

AMSTERDAM
James Nares (1715–1783)
"The Foundery Collection," 1742

*With spirit*

1. Rise, my soul, and stretch thy wings, Thy bet-ter por-tion trace;
2. Riv-ers to the o-cean run, Nor stay in all their course;
3. Cease, my soul, then, cease to mourn, Press on-ward to the prize;

Rise from tran-si-to-ry things Toward heaven, thy des-tined place.
Fire as-cend-ing seeks the sun; Both speed them to their source:
Soon the Sav-iour will re-turn Tri-um-phant in the skies:

Sun and moon and stars de-cay, Time shall soon this earth re-move;
So my soul, de-rived from God, Longs to view His glo-rious face,
Yet a sea-son, and we know Hap-py en-trance will be given,

Rise, my soul, and haste a-way To seats pre-pared a-bove.
For-ward tends to His a-bode, To rest in His em-brace.
All our sor-rows left be-low, And earth ex-changed for heaven. A-MEN.

# The Life in Christ

Rev. George Duffield, 1858

7. 6. 7. 6. D.
(FIRST TUNE)

WEBB
George J. Webb, 1837

*In moderate rhythm*

1. Stand up, stand up for Je - sus, Ye sol - diers of the cross;
2. Stand up, stand up for Je - sus, The trump - et call o - bey;
3. Stand up, stand up for Je - sus, Stand in His strength a - lone;
4. Stand up, stand up for Je - sus, The strife will not be long;

Lift high His roy - al ban - ner, It must not suf - fer loss:
Forth to the might - y con - flict, In this His glo - rious day:
The arm of flesh will fail you, Ye dare not trust your own:
This day the noise of bat - tle, The next the vic - tor's song:

From vic - tory un - to vic - tory His ar - my He shall lead,
Ye that are men now serve Him A - gainst un - num - bered foes;
Put on the gos - pel ar - mor, Each piece put on with prayer;
To Him that o - ver - com - eth A crown of life shall be;

Till ev - ery foe is van - quished, And Christ is Lord in - deed.
Let cour - age rise with dan - ger, And strength to strength op-pose.
Where du - ty calls. or dan - ger, Be nev - er want-ing there.
He with the King of Glo - ry Shall reign e - ter - nal - ly. A-MEN.

# Loyalty and Courage

Rev. George Duffield, 1858

7. 6. 7. 6. D.
(SECOND TUNE)

MILES ANIMOSUS
Geoffrey Turton Shaw

*Unison. With vigor*

1. Stand up, stand up for Je - sus, Ye sol - diers of the cross;
2. Stand up, stand up for Je - sus, The trump - et call o - bey;
3. Stand up, stand up for Je - sus, Stand in His strength a - lone;
4. Stand up, stand up for Je - sus, The strife will not be long;

Lift high His roy - al ban - ner, It must not suf - fer loss:
Forth to the might - y con - flict, In this His glo - rious day:
The arm of flesh will fail you, Ye dare not trust your own:
This day the noise of bat - tle, The next the vic - tor's song:

From vic - tory un - to vic - tory His ar - my He shall lead,
Ye that are men now serve Him A - gainst un - num - bered foes;
Put on the gos - pel ar - mor, Each piece put on with prayer;
To him that o - ver - com - eth, A crown of life shall be;

Till ev - ery foe is van - quished, And Christ is Lord in - deed.
Let cour - age rise with dan - ger, And strength to strength op - pose.
Where du - ty calls, or dan - ger, Be nev - er want - ing there.
He with the King of Glo - ry Shall reign e - ter - nal - ly. A - MEN.

Tune copyright by Geoffrey Shaw.

# The Life in Christ

Rev. Martin Luther, 1529
Trans. by Rev. Frederick H. Hedge, 1853

8. 7. 8. 7. 6. 6. 6. 6. 7.

EIN' FESTE BURG
Rev. Martin Luther, 1529

*May be sung in unison. In majestic style*

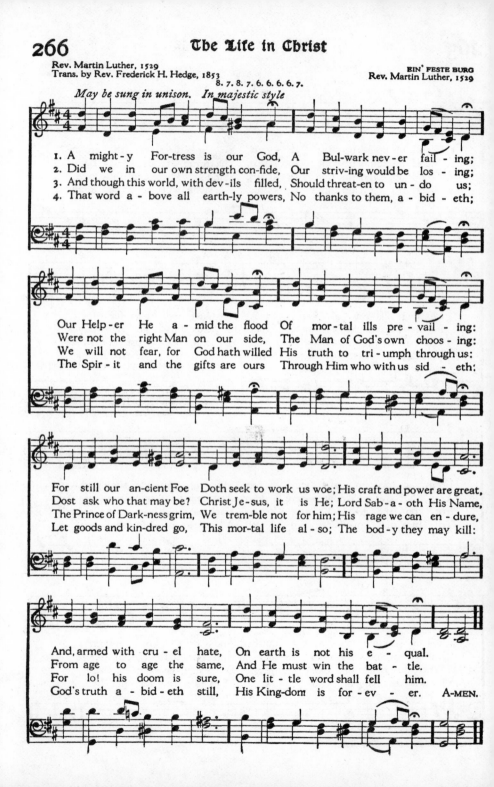

1. A might-y For-tress is our God, A Bul-wark nev-er fail - ing;
2. Did we in our own strength con-fide, Our striv-ing would be los - ing;
3. And though this world, with dev-ils filled, Should threat-en to un - do us;
4. That word a - bove all earth-ly powers, No thanks to them, a - bid - eth;

Our Help-er He a-mid the flood Of mor-tal ills pre - vail - ing:
Were not the right Man on our side, The Man of God's own choos - ing:
We will not fear, for God hath willed His truth to tri - umph through us:
The Spir - it and the gifts are ours Through Him who with us sid - eth:

For still our an-cient Foe Doth seek to work us woe; His craft and power are great,
Dost ask who that may be? Christ Je-sus, it is He; Lord Sab-a-oth His Name,
The Prince of Dark-ness grim, We trem-ble not for him; His rage we can en - dure,
Let goods and kin-dred go, This mor-tal life al - so; The bod-y they may kill:

And, armed with cru - el hate, On earth is not his e - qual.
From age to age the same, And He must win the bat - tle.
For lo! his doom is sure, One lit - tle word shall fell him.
God's truth a - bid - eth still, His King-dom is for - ev - er. A-MEN.

# Loyalty and Courage

Rev. Frederick W. Faber, 1849
Stanzas 2, 3, alt.

ST. CATHERINE
Henri F. Hemy, 1865
Alt. by James G. Walton, 1871

8. 8. 8. 8. 8. 8.

*With dignity and conviction*

1. Faith of our fa - thers! liv - ing still In spite of dun - geon, fire, and sword, O how our hearts beat high with joy When-e'er we hear that glo - rious word: Faith of our fa - thers, ho - ly faith! We will be true to thee till death.

2. Faith of our fa - thers! God's great power Shall win all na - tions un - to thee; And through the truth that comes from God Man - kind shall then be tru - ly free: Faith of our fa - thers, ho - ly faith! We will be true to thee till death.

3. Faith of our fa - thers! we will love Both friend and foe in all our strife, And preach thee, too, as love knows how By kind - ly words and vir - tuous life: Faith of our fa - thers, ho - ly faith! We will be true to thee till death. A - MEN.

# 268 The Life in Christ

Rev. John E. Bode, 1868

7. 6. 7. 6. D.
(FIRST TUNE)

DAY OF REST
James W. Elliott, 1875

*In moderate time*

1. O Je - sus, I have prom - ised To serve Thee to the end;
2. O let me feel Thee near me! The world is ev - er near;
3. O let me hear Thee speak - ing In ac - cents clear and still,
4. O Je - sus, Thou hast prom - ised To all who fol - low Thee

Be Thou for - ev - er near me, My Mas - ter and my Friend:
I see the sights that daz - zle, The tempt - ing sounds I hear;
A - bove the storms of pas - sion, The mur - murs of self - will!
That where Thou art in glo - ry There shall Thy serv - ant be;

I shall not fear the bat - tle If Thou art by my side,
My foes are ev - er near me, A - round me and with - in;
O speak to re - as - sure me, To has - ten or con - trol!
And, Je - sus, I have prom - ised To serve Thee to the end;

*Unison*          *Harmony*

Nor wan - der from the path - way If Thou wilt be my Guide.
But, Je - sus, draw Thou near - er, And shield my soul from sin.
O speak, and make me lis - ten, Thou Guard - ian of my soul!
O give me grace to fol - low, My Mas - ter and my Friend! A - MEN.

Tune used by permission of Novello and Company, Ltd.

# Loyalty and Courage

Rev. John E. Bode, 1868

7. 6. 7. 6. D.
(SECOND TUNE)

ANGEL'S STORY
Arthur H. Mann, 1883

*In moderate time*

1. O Je - sus, I have prom - ised To serve Thee to the end;
2. O let me feel Thee near me! The world is ev - er near;
3. O let me hear Thee speak - ing In ac - cents clear and still,
4. O Je - sus, Thou hast prom - ised To all who fol - low Thee

Be Thou for - ev - er near me, My Mas - ter and my Friend:
I see the sights that daz - zle, The tempt - ing sounds I hear;
A - bove the storms of pas - sion, The mur - murs of self - will!
That where Thou art in glo - ry There shall Thy serv - ant be;

I shall not fear the bat - tle If Thou art by my side,
My foes are ev - er near me, A - round me and with - in;
O speak to re - as - sure me, To has - ten or con - trol!
And, Je - sus, I have prom - ised To serve Thee to the end;

Nor wan - der from the path - way If Thou wilt be my Guide.
But, Je - sus, draw Thou near - er, And shield my soul from sin.
O speak, and make me lis - ten, Thou Guard - ian of my soul!
O give me grace to fol - low, My Mas - ter and my Friend! A - MEN.

Music used by permission of E. R. Goodliffe.

# 269

Rev. Charles Wesley, 1749      S. M.      SOLDIERS OF CHRIST
Rev. William P. Merrill, 1895

*In martial rhythm*

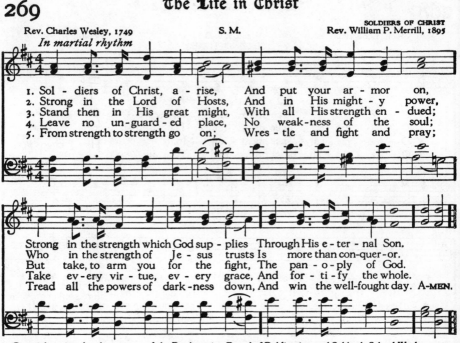

1. Sol - diers of Christ, a - rise, And put your ar - mor on,
2. Strong in the Lord of Hosts, And in His might - y power,
3. Stand then in His great might, With all His strength en - dued;
4. Leave no un - guard - ed place, No weak-ness of the soul;
5. From strength to strength go on; Wres - tle and fight and pray;

Strong in the strength which God sup - plies Through His e - ter - nal Son.
Who in the strength of Je - sus trusts Is more than con-quer-or.
But take, to arm you for the fight, The pan - o - ply of God.
Take ev - ery vir - tue, ev - ery grace, And for - ti - fy the whole.
Tread all the powers of dark-ness down, And win the well-fought day. A-MEN.

Copyright, 1895, by the trustees of the Presbyterian Board of Publication and Sabbath-School Work.

# 270

Rev. John S. B. Monsell, 1863      PENTECOST
L. M.      Rev. William Boyd, 1868
(FIRST TUNE)

*With marked rhythm*

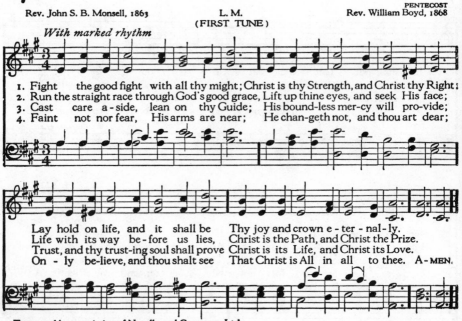

1. Fight the good fight with all thy might; Christ is thy Strength, and Christ thy Right;
2. Run the straight race through God's good grace, Lift up thine eyes, and seek His face;
3. Cast care a - side, lean on thy Guide; His bound-less mer-cy will pro-vide;
4. Faint not nor fear, His arms are near; He chan-geth not, and thou art dear;

Lay hold on life, and it shall be Thy joy and crown e - ter - nal-ly.
Life with its way be - fore us lies, Christ is the Path, and Christ the Prize.
Trust, and thy trust-ing soul shall prove Christ is its Life, and Christ its Love.
On - ly be-lieve, and thou shalt see That Christ is All in all to thee. A-MEN.

Tune used by permission of Novello and Company, Ltd.

# 270  Loyalty and Courage

Rev. John S. B. Monsell, 1863

COURAGE
Horatio W. Parker, 1903

L. M. with Refrain
(SECOND TUNE)

*In martial rhythm*

1. Fight the good fight with all thy might; Christ is thy
2. Run the straight race through God's good grace, Lift up thine
3. Cast care a-side, lean on thy Guide; His bound-less
4. Faint not nor fear, His arms are near; He chan-geth

Strength, and Christ thy Right: Lay hold on life, and it shall be
eyes, and seek His face; Life with its way be-fore us lies,
mer-cy will pro-vide; Trust, and thy trust-ing soul shall prove
not, and thou art dear; On-ly be-lieve, and thou shalt see

Thy joy and crown e-ter-nal-ly; Lay hold on life, and
Christ is the Path, and Christ the Prize; Life with its way be-
Christ is its Life, and Christ its Love; Trust, and thy trust-ing
That Christ is All in all to thee; On-ly be-lieve, and

it shall be Thy joy and crown e-ter-nal-ly.
fore us lies, Christ is the Path, and Christ the Prize.
soul shall prove Christ is its Life, and Christ its Love.
thou shalt see That Christ is All in all to thee. A-MEN.

Tune copyright, 1903. Used by permission of Mrs. Horatio Parker.

# The Life in Christ

Bishop Reginald Heber, 1827

C. M. D.
(FIRST TUNE)

ALL SAINTS NEW
Henry S. Cutler, 1872

*In martial rhythm*

1. The Son of God goes forth to war, A king-ly crown to gain;
2. The mar-tyr first, whose ea-gle eye Could pierce be-yond the grave,
3. A glo-rious band, the cho-sen few On whom the Spir-it came,
4. A no-ble ar-my, men and boys, The ma-tron and the maid,

His blood-red ban-ner streams a-far: Who fol-lows in His train?
Who saw his Mas-ter in the sky, And called on Him to save:
Twelve val-iant saints, their hope they knew, And mocked the cross and flame:
A-round the Sav-iour's throne re-joice, In robes of light ar-rayed:

Who best can drink his cup of woe, Tri-um-phant o-ver pain,
Like Him, with par-don on his tongue In midst of mor-tal pain,
They met the ty-rant's bran-dished steel, The li-on's gor-y mane;
They climbed the steep as-cent of heaven Through per-il, toil, and pain:

Who pa-tient bears his cross be-low, He fol-lows in His train.
He prayed for them that did the wrong: Who fol-lows in His train?
They bowed their necks the death to feel: Who fol-lows in their train?
O God, to us may grace be given To fol-low in their train! A-MEN.

# Loyalty and Courage

Bishop Reginald Heber, 1827

C. M. D.
(SECOND TUNE)

CRUSADER
Samuel B. Whitney, 1889

*In martial rhythm*

1. The Son of God goes forth to war, A king-ly crown to gain;
2. The mar-tyr first, whose ea-gle eye Could pierce be-yond the grave,
3. A glo-rious band, the cho-sen few On whom the Spir-it came,
4. A no-ble ar-my, men and boys, The ma-tron and the maid,

His blood-red ban-ner streams a-far: Who fol-lows in His train?
Who saw his Mas-ter in the sky, And called on Him to save:
Twelve val-iant saints, their hope they knew, And mocked the cross and flame;
A-round the Sav-iour's throne re-joice, In robes of light ar-rayed:

The Son of God,* goes forth to war,*

He (Who) fol-lows in His (their) train.*

Who best can drink his cup of woe, Tri-um-phant o-ver pain,
Like Him, with par-don on His tongue In midst of mor-tal pain,
They met the ty-rant's bran-dished steel, The li-on's gor-y mane;
They climbed the steep as-cent of heaven Through per-il, toil, and pain:

He (Who) fol-lows in His (their) train.*

Who pa-tient bears his cross be-low, He fol-lows in His train.
He prayed for them that did the wrong: Who fol-lows in His train?
They bowed their necks the death to feel: Who fol-lows in their train?
O God, to us may grace be given To fol-low in their train! A-MEN.

*These words are to be repeated in every stanza.

# The Life in Christ

Frances Ridley Havergal, 1877　　　6. 5. 6. 5. 12l.　　　ARMAGEDDON
John Goss, 1871

*In stately rhythm*

1. Who is on the Lord's side? Who will serve the King?
   Who will be His help-ers, Oth-er lives to bring? Who will leave the
   world's side? Who will face the foe? Who is on the Lord's side?
   Who for Him will go? By Thy call of mer - cy, By Thy grace di - vine,
   We are on the Lord's side, Sav - iour, we are Thine.

2. Not for weight of glo - ry, Not for crown and palm,
   En - ter we the ar - my, Raise the war - rior psalm; But for Love that
   claim - eth Lives for whom He died: He whom Je - sus nam - eth
   Must be on His side. By Thy love con-strain-ing, By Thy grace di - vine,
   We are on the Lord's side, Sav - iour, we are Thine.

3. Fierce may be the con - flict, Strong may be the foe,
   But the King's own ar - my None can o - ver-throw: Round His stand - ard
   ran - ging, Vic - tory is se - cure; For His truth un-chan - ging
   Makes the tri - umph sure. Joy - ful - ly en - list - ing By Thy grace di - vine,
   We are on the Lord's side, Sav - iour, we are Thine. A-MEN.

# 273 Loyalty and Courage

George T. Coster, 1900

6. 6. 6. 6. 8. 8.

ARTHUR'S SEAT
John Goss, 1874

*In march rhythm*

1. March on, O soul, with strength! Like those strong men of old
2. The sons of fa-thers we By whom our faith is taught
3. March on, O soul, with strength, As strong the bat-tle rolls!
4. Not long the con-flict: soon The ho-ly war shall cease,

Who 'gainst en-thron-ed wrong Stood con-fi-dent and bold;
To fear no ill, to fight The ho-ly fight they fought:
'Gainst lies and lusts and wrongs, Let cour-age rule our souls:
Faith's war-fare end-ed, won The home of end-less peace!

Who, thrust in prison or cast to flame,
He-ro-ic war-riors, ne'er from Christ
In keen-est strife, Lord, may we stand,
Look up! the vic-tor's crown at length!

Still made their glo-ry in Thy Name.
By an-y lure or guile en-ticed.
Up-held and strength-ened by Thy hand.
March on, O soul, march on, with strength! A-MEN.

By permission of Vernon B. Coster.

Rev. Henry F. Lyte, 1824      8. 7. 8. 7. D.      CRUCIFER
Henry Smart, 1867

*In moderate time*

1. Je - sus, I my cross have tak - en, All to leave, and fol - low Thee;
2. Man may trou - ble and dis - tress me, 'T will but drive me to Thy breast;
3. Take, my soul, thy full sal - va - tion, Rise o'er sin and fear and care;
4. Haste, then, on from grace to glo - ry, Armed by faith and winged by prayer;

Des - ti - tute, de - spised, for - sak - en, Thou from hence my All shalt be:
Life with tri - als hard may press me, Heaven will bring me sweet - er rest;
Joy to find in ev - ery sta - tion Some - thing still to do or bear;
Heaven's e - ter - nal day's be - fore thee: God's own hand shall guide thee there.

Per - ish ev - ery fond am - bi - tion, All I've sought, or hoped, or known;
O 't is not in grief to harm me While Thy love is left to me;
Think what Spir - it dwells with - in thee, What a Fa - ther's smile is thine,
Soon shall close thy earth - ly mis - sion; Swift shall pass thy pil - grim days;

Yet how rich is my con - di - tion: God and heaven are still my own.
O 't were not in joy to charm me, Were that joy un - mixed with Thee.
What a Sav - iour died to win thee: Child of heaven, shouldst thou re - pine?
Hope soon change to glad fru - i - tion, Faith to sight, and prayer to praise. A - MEN.

# 275 Loyalty and Courage

St. Andrew of Crete (660–732)
Trans. by Rev. John M. Neale, 1862
Alt. in "The Parish Hymn Book," 1863        6. 5. 6. 5. D.

ST. ANDREW OF CRETE
Rev. John B. Dykes, 1868

*In moderate time*

1. Chris-tian, dost thou see them    On the ho-ly ground,
2. Chris-tian, dost thou feel them,    How they work with-in,
3. Chris-tian, dost thou hear them,    How they speak thee fair?
4. "Well I know thy trou-ble,    O My serv-ant true,

How the powers of dark-ness Rage thy steps a-round?
Striv-ing, tempt-ing, lur-ing, Goad-ing in-to sin?
"Al-ways fast and vig-il? Al-ways watch and prayer?"
Thou art ver-y wea-ry— I was wea-ry too;

Chris-tian, up and smite them, Count-ing gain but loss,
Chris-tian, nev-er trem-ble; Nev-er be down-cast;
Chris-tian, an-swer bold-ly, "While I breathe I pray!"
But that toil shall make thee Some day all Mine own,

In the strength that com-eth By the ho-ly cross.
Gird thee for the bat-tle; Thou shalt win at last.
Peace shall fol-low bat-tle, Night shall end in day.
And the end of sor-row Shall be near My throne." A-MEN.

John Bunyan (1628–1688); alt.     6. 5. 6. 5. 6. 6. 6. 5.     **MONKS GATE**
                                            (FIRST TUNE)     English traditional melody

*With spirit and dignity*

1. He who would val - iant be 'Gainst all dis - as - ter,
2. Who so be - set him round With dis - mal sto - ries,
3. Since, Lord, Thou dost de - fend Us with Thy Spir - it,

Let him in con - stan - cy Fol - low the Mas - ter.
Do but them - selves con - found— His strength the more is.
We know we at the end Shall life in - her - it.

There's no dis - cour - age - ment Shall make him once re - lent
No foes shall stay his might; Though he with gi - ants fight,
Then, fan - cies, flee a - way! I'll fear not what men say,

His first a - vowed in - tent To be a pil - grim.
He will make good his right To be a pil - grim.
I'll la - bor night and day To be a pil - grim. A-MEN.

From "The Riverdale Hymn Book." Used by permission of the publishers, Fleming H. Revell Company.
Tune from "The English Hymnal." Used by permission of the Oxford University Press.

**276**

John Bunyan (1628–1688); alt.  6. 5. 6. 5. 6. 6. 6. 5. (SECOND TUNE)  ST. DUNSTAN'S
Rev. Charles Winfred Douglas, 1917

*In stately rhythm*

1. He who would val - iant be 'Gainst all dis - as - ter,
2. Who so be - set him round With dis - mal sto - ries,
3. Since, Lord, Thou dost de - fend Us with Thy Spir - it,

Let him in con - stan - cy Fol - low the Mas - ter.
Do but them - selves con - found— His strength the more is.
We know we at the end Shall life in - her - it.

There's no dis - cour - age - ment Shall make him once re - lent
No foes shall stay his might; Though he with gi - ants fight,
Then, fan - cies, flee a - way! I'll fear not what men say,

His first a - vowed in - tent To be a pil - grim.
He will make good his right To be a pil - grim.
I'll la - bor night and day To be a pil - grim. A - MEN.

Copyright, 1918, by Canon Winfred Douglas. Used by permission.

# The Life in Christ

Rev. Walter J. Mathams     6. 4. 6. 4. 10. 10.     SURSUM CORDA
George Lomas (1834–1884)

*In moderate time*

1. Christ of the Up-ward Way, My Guide di - vine,
   Where Thou hast set Thy feet May I place mine;
   And move and march wher - ev - er Thou hast trod,
   Keep - ing face for - ward up the hill of God.

2. Give me the heart to hear Thy voice and will,
   That with - out fault or fear I may ful - fill
   Thy pur - pose with a glad and ho - ly zest,
   Like one who would not bring less than his best.

3. Give me the good stout arm To shield the right,
   And wield Thy sword of truth With all my might,
   That, in the war - fare I must wage for Thee,
   More than a vic - tor I may ev - er be.

4. Christ of the Up-ward Way, My Guide di - vine,
   Where Thou hast set Thy feet May I place mine;
   And when Thy last call comes se - rene and clear,
   Calm may my an - swer be, "Lord, I am here." A-MEN.

Music copyright.  Words used by permission.

**278**

Rev. Philip Doddridge, 1755      C. M.      George F. Handel, 1728   CHRISTMAS

*With spirit*

1. A - wake, my soul, stretch ev-ery nerve, And press with vig-or on; A heaven-ly race de-
2. A cloud of wit-ness-es a - round Hold thee in full sur-vey: For-get the steps al-
3. 'Tis God's all-an-i-mat-ing voice That calls thee from on high; 'Tis His own hand pre-
4. Blest Sav-iour, in-tro-duced by Thee, Have I my race be-gun; And, crowned with vic-to-ry,

mands thy zeal, And an im-mor-tal crown, And an im-mor-tal crown.
read - y trod, And on-ward urge thy way, And on - ward urge thy way.
sents the prize To thine as-pir-ing eye, To thine as-pir-ing eye.
at Thy feet I'll lay my hon-ors down, I'll lay my hon-ors down. A-MEN.

**279**

DENNIS

Rev. Philip Doddridge, 1755      S. M.      Arr. from Hans G. Nägeli, by
Lowell Mason, 1845

*With a spirit of joy. In moderate time*

1. How gen - tle God's com-mands, How kind His pre - cepts are!
2. Be - neath His watch-ful eye His saints se - cure-ly dwell;
3. Why should this anx - ious load Press down your wea - ry mind?
4. His good - ness stands ap-proved, Down to the pres - ent day;

Come, cast your bur - dens on the Lord, And trust His con-stant care.
That hand which bears all na - ture up Shall guide His chil-dren well.
Haste to your heaven-ly Fa - ther's throne, And sweet re - fresh-ment find.
I'll drop my bur - den at His feet, And bear a song a-way. A-MEN.

# The Life in Christ

Rev. Benjamin Schmolck, c. 1704
Trans. by Jane Laurie Borthwick, 1854    6. 6. 6. 6. D.

JEWETT
Carl Maria von Weber
Arr. by Joseph P. Holbrook, 1862

*In moderate time*

1. My Je - sus, as Thou wilt! O may Thy will be mine!
2. My Je - sus, as Thou wilt! Though seen through many a tear,
3. My Je - sus, as Thou wilt! All shall be well for me;

In - to Thy hand of love I would my all re - sign.
Let not my star of hope Grow dim or dis - ap - pear.
Each chan - ging fu - ture scene I glad - ly trust with Thee.

Through sor - row or through joy, Con - duct me as Thine own;
Since Thou on earth hast wept, And sor - rowed oft a - lone,
Straight to my home a - bove I trav - el calm - ly on,

And help me still to say, "My Lord, Thy will be done."
If I must weep with Thee, My Lord, Thy will be done.
And sing, in life or death, "My Lord, Thy will be done." A-MEN.

# 281 Trust

Katharina von Schlegel, born 1697
Trans. by Jane Laurie Borthwick (1813–1897)

FINLANDIA
Jean Sibelius
Arr. for this book, 1932

10. 10. 10. 10. 10. 10.

*May be sung in unison*
*In moderate time and flowing rhythm*

1. Be still, my soul: the Lord is on thy side; Bear patient-
2. Be still, my soul: thy God doth un-der-take To guide the
3. Be still, my soul: the hour is has-tening on When we shall

ly the cross of grief or pain; Leave to thy God to or-der and pro-vide;
fu-ture as He has the past. Thy hope, thy con-fi-dence let noth-ing shake;
be for-ev-er with the Lord, When dis-ap-point-ment, grief, and fear are gone,

In ev-ery change He faith-ful will re-main. Be still, my soul: thy
All now mys-te-rious shall be bright at last. Be still, my soul: the
Sor-row for-got, love's pur-est joys re-stored. Be still, my soul: when

best, thy heaven-ly Friend Through thorn-y ways leads to a joy-ful end.
waves and winds still know His voice who ruled them while He dwelt be-low.
change and tears are past, All safe and bless-ed we shall meet at last. A-MEN.

# The Life in Christ

John G. Whittier, 1867
C. M. D.

PENTATONE
Henry Walford Davies

*In moderate time*

1. I bow my fore-head to the dust, I veil mine eyes for shame,
2. I know not what the fu-ture hath Of mar-vel or sur-prise,
3. I know not where His is-lands lift Their frond-ed palms in air;

And urge, in trem-bling self - dis-trust, A prayer with-out a claim.
As - sured a - lone that life and death His mer-cy un-der - lies.
I on - ly know I can - not drift Be - yond His love and care.

No of - fering of mine own I have, No works my faith to prove;
And so be - side the si - lent sea I wait the muf-fled oar:
And Thou, O Lord, by whom are seen Thy crea - tures as they be,

I can but give the gifts He gave, And plead His love for love.
No harm from Him can come to me On o - cean or on shore.
For - give me if too close I lean My hu-man heart on Thee. A-MEN.

Tune from "A Students' Hymnal" (Hymns of the Kingdom). Used by permission of the Oxford University Press.

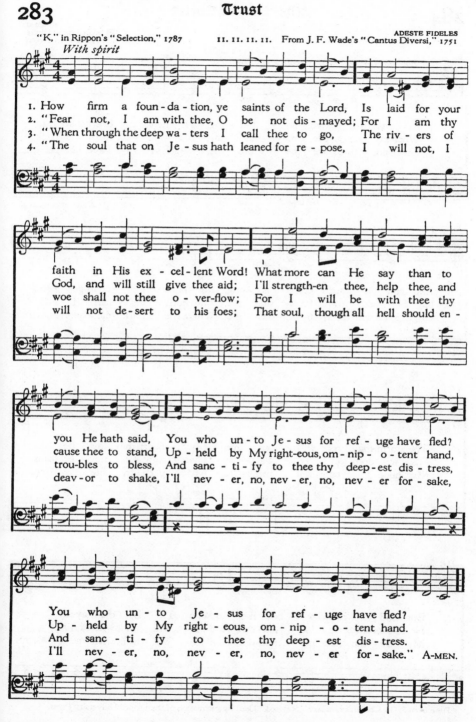

ADESTE FIDELES

"K," in Rippon's "Selection," 1787    11. 11. 11. 11.    From J. F. Wade's "Cantus Diversi," 1751

*With spirit*

1. How firm a foun-da-tion, ye saints of the Lord, Is laid for your
2. "Fear not, I am with thee, O be not dis-mayed; For I am thy
3. "When through the deep wa-ters I call thee to go, The riv-ers of
4. "The soul that on Je-sus hath leaned for re-pose, I will not, I

faith in His ex-cel-lent Word! What more can He say than to
God, and will still give thee aid; I'll strength-en thee, help thee, and
woe shall not thee o-ver-flow; For I will be with thee thy
will not de-sert to his foes; That soul, though all hell should en-

you He hath said, You who un-to Je-sus for ref-uge have fled?
cause thee to stand, Up-held by My right-eous, om-nip-o-tent hand,
trou-bles to bless, And sanc-ti-fy to thee thy deep-est dis-tress,
deav-or to shake, I'll nev-er, no, nev-er, no, nev-er for-sake,

You who un-to Je-sus for ref-uge have fled?
Up-held by My right-eous, om-nip-o-tent hand.
And sanc-ti-fy to thee thy deep-est dis-tress.
I'll nev-er, no, nev-er, no, nev-er for-sake." A-MEN.

# The Life in Christ

Anna Laetitia Waring (1820–1910)

NYLAND
Finnish hymn melody
Harmonized by David Evans

7. 6. 7. 6. D.
(FIRST TUNE)

*Not too slowly, with flowing rhythm*

1. In heaven-ly love a - bid - ing, No change my heart shall fear;
2. Wher-ev - er He may guide me, No want shall turn me back;
3. Green pas - tures are be - fore me, Which yet I have not seen;

And safe is such con - fid - ing, For noth - ing chan-ges here.
My Shep-herd is be - side me, And noth - ing can I lack.
Bright skies will soon be o'er me, Where the dark clouds have been.

The storm may roar with - out me, My heart may low be laid;
His wis-dom ev - er wak - eth, His sight is nev - er dim;
My hope I can - not meas-ure, My path to life is free;

But God is round a - bout me, And can I be dis-mayed?
He knows the way He tak - eth, And I will walk with Him.
My Sav - iour has my treas-ure, And He will walk with me. A-MEN.

Tune from "The Church Hymnary." Revised. Used by permission of the Oxford University Press.

# Trust

Anna Laetitia Waring (1820–1910)

7. 6. 7. 6. D.
(SECOND TUNE)

**BENTLEY**
John Hullah, 1867

*In moderate time, with flowing rhythm*

1. In heaven-ly love a - bid - ing, No change my heart shall fear;
2. Wher - ev - er He may guide me, No want shall turn me back;
3. Green pas - tures are be - fore me, Which yet I have not seen;

And safe is such con - fid - ing, For noth - ing chan - ges here.
My Shep - herd is be - side me, And noth - ing can I lack.
Bright skies will soon be o'er me, Where the dark clouds have been.

The storm may roar with - out me, My heart may low be laid;
His wis - dom ev - er wak - eth, His sight is nev - er dim;
My hope I can - not meas - ure, My path to life is free;

But God is round a - bout me, And can I be dis-mayed?
He knows the way He tak - eth, And I will walk with Him.
My Sav - iour has my treas - ure, And He will walk with me. A-MEN.

# The Life in Christ

Rev. Ray Palmer, 1830      6. 6. 4. 6. 6. 6. 4.      OLIVE7   Lowell Mason, 1832

*In moderate time*

1. My faith looks up to Thee, Thou Lamb of Cal - va - ry, Sav - iour di - vine: Now hear me while I pray, Take all my guilt a - way, O let me from this day Be whol - ly Thine!

2. May Thy rich grace im - part Strength to my faint - ing heart, My zeal in - spire; As Thou hast died for me, O may my love to Thee Pure, warm, and change - less be, A liv - ing fire!

3. While life's dark maze I tread, And griefs a - round me spread, Be Thou my Guide; Bid dark - ness turn to day, Wipe sor - row's tears a - way, Nor let me ev - er stray From Thee a - side.

4. When ends life's tran - sient dream, When death's cold, sul - len stream Shall o'er me roll, Blest Sav - iour, then, in love, Fear and dis - trust re - move; O bear me safe a - bove, A ran - somed soul! A-MEN.

# 286 Trust

Rev. Edward Hopper, 1871     7. 7. 7. 7. 7. 7.     John E. Gould, 1871

PILOT

*In moderate time*

1. Je - sus, Sav - iour, pi - lot me  O - ver
2. As  a  moth - er  stills  her  child,  Thou  canst
3. When  at  last  I  near  the  shore,  And  the

life's  tem - pes - tuous  sea;  Un - known waves be - fore  me  roll,
hush  the  o - cean  wild;  Bois-terous waves  o - bey Thy  will
fear - ful  break - ers  roar  'Twixt me and  the peace - ful  rest,

Hid - ing  rock  and  treach - erous  shoal;  Chart  and
When Thou  say'st  to  them, "Be  still!"  Won - drous
Then, while lean  ing  on  Thy  breast,  May  I

com - pass  came from Thee: Je - sus, Sav - iour, pi - lot me.
Sov - ereign of  the  sea,  Je - sus, Sav - iour, pi - lot me.
hear Thee  say  to  me,  "Fear not, I  will  pi - lot thee."  A - MEN.

287

Frances Ridley Havergal, 1874

8. 5. 8. 3.

BULLINGER
Rev. Ethelbert W. Bullinger, 1874

*In rather slow time*

1. I am trust - ing Thee, Lord Je - sus, Trust - ing on - ly Thee;
2. I am trust - ing Thee to guide me; Thou a - lone shalt lead,
3. I am trust - ing Thee for pow - er: Thine can nev - er fail;
4. I am trust - ing Thee, Lord Je - sus; Nev - er let me fall;

Trust-ing Thee for full sal - va - tion, Great and free.
Ev - ery day and hour sup-ply - ing All my need.
Words which Thou Thy-self shalt give me Must pre - vail.
I am trust - ing Thee for - ev - er, And for all. A - MEN.

288

Anon. in Rowland Hill's "Psalms and Hymns," 1783
Based on Psalm lv

7. 7. 7. 7.

SAVANNAH
Rev. John Wesley's "Foundery Collection," 1742

*In moderate time*

1. Cast thy bur - den on the Lord, On - ly lean up - on His word;
2. He sus-tains thee by His hand, He en - a - bles thee to stand;
3. Hu - man coun - sels come to naught; That shall stand which God hath wrought;
4. Heaven and earth may pass a - way, God's free grace shall not de - cay;
5. Je - sus, Guard-ian of Thy flock, Be Thy-self our con-stant Rock;

Thou wilt soon have cause to bless His e - ter - nal faith-ful-ness.
Those whom Je - sus once hath loved From His grace are nev - er moved.
His com - pas - sion, love, and power Are the same for - ev - er-more.
He hath prom-ised to ful - fill All the pleas - ure of His will.
Make us, by Thy power-ful hand, Strong as Zi - on's moun-tain stand. A-MEN

# Trust

Cardinal John H. Newman, 1833     10. 4. 10. 4. 10. 10.     LUX BENIGNA
Rev. John B. Dykes, 1865

*In moderate time*

1. Lead, kind-ly Light, a-mid th'en-cir-cling gloom, Lead Thou me on;
2. I was not ev-er thus, nor prayed that Thou Shouldst lead me on;
3. So long Thy power hath blest me, sure it still Will lead me on,

The night is dark, and I am far from home; Lead Thou me on:
I loved to choose and see my path; but now Lead Thou me on.
O'er moor and fen, o'er crag and tor-rent, till The night is gone;

Keep Thou my feet; I do not ask to see
I loved the gar-ish day, and, spite of fears,
And with the morn those an-gel fa-ces smile,

The dis-tant scene—one step e-nough for me.
Pride ruled my will: re-mem-ber not past years.
Which I have loved long since, and lost a-while. A-MEN.

# The Life in Christ

Rev. John J. Moment

O QUANTA QUALIA
From "Méthode du Plain Chant," by
François de la Feillée, 1808

11. 11. 11. 11. Dactylic

*May be sung in unison. In moderate time, with flowing rhythm*

1. God of com-pas-sion, in mer - cy be-friend us;
2. Wan-dering and lost, Thou hast sought us and found us,
3. How shall we stray, with Thy hand to di-rect us,

Giv - er of grace for our needs all - a - vail - ing,
Stilled our rude hearts with Thy word of con - sol - ing;
Thou who the stars in their cours - es art guid - ing?

Wis - dom and strength for each day do Thou send us,
Wrap now Thy peace, like a man - tle, a - round us,
What shall we fear, with Thy power to pro - tect us,

Pa - tience un - tir - ing and cour - age un - fail - ing.
Guard - ing our thoughts and our pas - sions con - troll - ing.
We who walk forth in Thy great - ness con - fid - ing? A-MEN.

# 291 Trust

Samuel Rodigast, 1676
Trans. by Catherine Winkworth, 1863    8. 7. 8. 7. 4. 4. 8. 8.

WAS GOTT THUT DAS IST WOHLGETHAN
"Weimar Gesangbuch," 1681
Severus Gastorius, fl. 1675

*In well-defined rhythm*

1. What-e'er my God or-dains is right; His ho-ly will a-bid-eth;
2. What-e'er my God or-dains is right; He nev-er will de-ceive me;
3. What-e'er my God or-dains is right; Here shall my stand be tak-en;

I will be still, what-e'er He doth, And fol-low where He guid-eth.
He leads me by the prop-er path; I know He will not leave me,
Though sor-row, need, or death be mine, Yet am I not for-sak-en;

He is my God; Though dark my road, He holds me that I
And take, con-tent, What He hath sent; His hand can turn my
My Fa-ther's care Is round me there; He holds me that I

shall not fall; Where-fore to Him I leave it all.
griefs a-way, And pa-tient-ly I wait His day.
shall not fall, And so to Him I leave it all. A-MEN.

Psalm xci
James Montgomery, 1822

8. 7. 8. 7. D.

AUTUMN
Arr. from "Psaumes Octante Trois," Geneva, 1551

*Moderately fast*

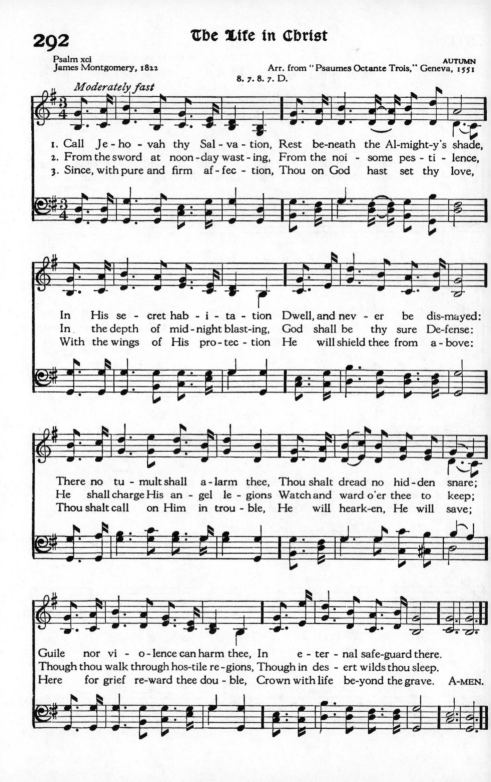

1. Call Je - ho - vah thy Sal - va - tion, Rest be-neath the Al-might-y's shade,
2. From the sword at noon-day wast-ing, From the noi - some pes - ti - lence,
3. Since, with pure and firm af - fec - tion, Thou on God hast set thy love,

In His se - cret hab - i - ta - tion Dwell, and nev - er be dis-mayed:
In the depth of mid-night blast-ing, God shall be thy sure De-fense:
With the wings of His pro-tec - tion He will shield thee from a - bove:

There no tu - mult shall a - larm thee, Thou shalt dread no hid-den snare;
He shall charge His an - gel le - gions Watch and ward o'er thee to keep;
Thou shalt call on Him in trou - ble, He will heark-en, He will save;

Guile nor vi - o - lence can harm thee, In e - ter - nal safe-guard there.
Though thou walk through hos-tile re - gions, Though in des - ert wilds thou sleep.
Here for grief re-ward thee dou - ble, Crown with life be-yond the grave. A-MEN.

# 293      Comfort

Thomas Moore (1779-1852)
and Thomas Hastings (1784-1872)     11. 10. 11. 10.     CONSOLATION
Samuel Webbe (1740-1816)

*Moderately fast*

1. Come, ye dis-con-so-'late, wher-e'er ye lan-guish,
2. Joy of the des-o-late, Light of the stray-ing,
3. Here see the Bread of Life; see wa-ters flow-ing

Come to the mer-cy seat, fer-vent-ly kneel;
Hope of the pen-i-tent, fade-less and pure!
Forth from the throne of God, pure from a-bove:

Here bring your wound-ed hearts, here tell your an-guish:
Here speaks the Com-fort-er, ten-der-ly say-ing,
Come to the feast of love; come, ev-er know-ing

Earth has no sor-rows that heaven can-not heal.
"Earth has no sor-rows that heaven can-not cure."
Earth has no sor-rows but heaven can re-move. A-MEN.

**294**

Rev. Paul Gerhardt, 1656
Trans. by Rev. John Wesley, 1739

S. M.

ST. BRIDE
Samuel Howard (1710–1782)

*Moderately slow, with well-defined rhythm*

1. Give to the winds thy fears; Hope and be un - dis - mayed;
2. Through waves, and clouds, and storms, He gen - tly clears thy way;
3. Leave to His sov - ereign sway To choose and to com - mand;
4. Far, far a - bove thy thought His coun - sel shall ap - pear,

God hears thy sighs and counts thy tears, God shall lift up thy head.
Wait thou His time; so shall this night Soon end in joy - ous day.
So shalt thou, won - dering, own His way, How wise, how strong His hand!
When ful - ly He the work hath wrought That caused thy need - less fear. A-MEN.

Tune from "The Church Hymnary," Revised. Used by permission of the Oxford University Press.

**295**

Jane Crewdson (1809–1863)

C. M.

WIGTOWN
"Scottish Psalter," 1635

*Moderately slow*

1. There is no sor - row, Lord, too light To bring in prayer to Thee;
2. Thou, who hast trod the thorn-y road, Wilt share each small dis - tress;
3. There is no se - cret sigh we breathe But meets Thine ear di - vine;
4. Life's ills with - out, sin's strife with - in, The heart would o - ver - flow,

There is no anx-ious care too slight To wake Thy sym - pa - thy.
The love which bore the great-er load Will not re - fuse the less.
And ev - ery cross grows light be - neath The shad-ow, Lord, of Thine.
But for that love which died for sin, That love which wept with woe. A-MEN.

# 296 Comfort

William Cowper, 1779 · 7. 6. 7. 6. D. · BENTLEY · John Hullah, 1867

*In moderate time*

1. Some - times a light sur - pris - es The Chris - tian while he sings;
2. In ho - ly con - tem - pla - tion We sweet - ly then pur - sue
3. It can bring with it noth - ing But He will bear us through;
4. Though vine nor fig tree nei - ther Their wont - ed fruit shall bear,

It is the Lord, who ris - es With heal - ing in His wings:
The theme of God's sal - va - tion, And find it ev - er new;
Who gives the lil - ies cloth - ing Will clothe His peo - ple, too:
Though all the field should with - er, Nor flocks nor herds be there;

When com - forts are de - clin - ing, He grants the soul a - gain
Set free from pres - ent sor - row, We cheer - ful - ly can say,
Be - neath the spread-ing heav - ens No crea - ture but is fed;
Yet God the same a - bid - ing, His praise shall tune my voice,

A sea - son of clear shin - ing, To cheer it af - ter rain.
Let the un-known to - mor - row Bring with it what it may.
And He who feeds the ra - vens Will give His chil - dren bread.
For while in Him con - fid - ing I can - not but re - joice. A-MEN.

# The Life in Christ

Rev. Edward H. Plumptre, 1865     S. M. with Refrain     MARION<br>Arthur H. Messiter, 1885

*Joyfully*

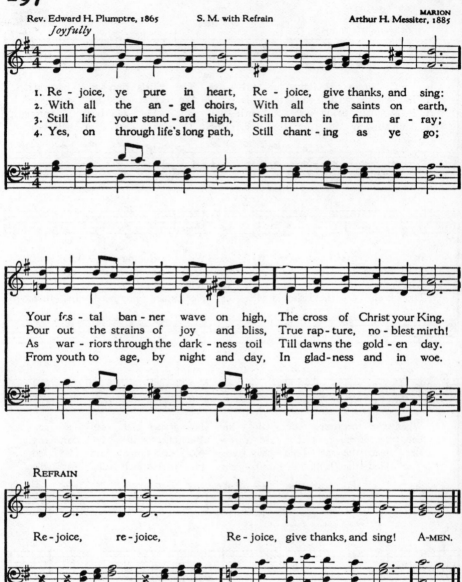

1. Re - joice, ye pure in heart, Re - joice, give thanks, and sing:
2. With all the an - gel choirs, With all the saints on earth,
3. Still lift your stand - ard high, Still march in firm ar - ray;
4. Yes, on through life's long path, Still chant - ing as ye go;

Your fes - tal ban - ner wave on high, The cross of Christ your King.
Pour out the strains of joy and bliss, True rap - ture, no - blest mirth!
As war - riors through the dark - ness toil Till dawns the gold - en day,
From youth to age, by night and day, In glad - ness and in woe.

REFRAIN

Re - joice, re - joice, Re - joice, give thanks, and sing! A-MEN.

Re - joice, re - joice,

5. Then on, ye pure in heart,
Rejoice, give thanks, and sing;
Your festal banner wave on high,
The cross of Christ your King.

**298**     JOY

Charitie Lees de Chenez     7. 6. 7. 6. D.     GOSTERWOOD<br>English traditional melody

*May be sung in unison. In moderate time, with dignity*

1. The King of Glo-ry stand-eth Be-side the heart of sin;
2. At times, with sud-den glo-ry, He speaks, and all is done;
3. O Christ, Thy love is might-y; Long-suf-fering is Thy grace;

His might-y voice com-mand-eth The ra-ging waves with-in;
With-out one stroke of bat-tle The vic-to-ry is won,
And glo-rious is the splen-dor That beam-eth from Thy face.

The floods of deep-est an-guish Roll back-ward at His will,
While we, with joy be-hold-ing, Can scarce be-lieve it true
Our hearts up-leap in glad-ness When we be-hold that love,

As o'er the storm a-ris-eth His man-date, "Peace, be still."
That e'en our king-ly Je-sus, Can form such hearts a-new.
As we go sing-ing on-ward, To dwell with Thee a-bove. A-MEN.

Tune from "Songs of Praise." Used by permission of the Oxford University Press.

# 299

## The Life in Christ

Rev. Paul Gerhardt, 1656
Trans. by Catherine Winkworth, 1855

S. M.
(FIRST TUNE)

SELMA

Adapted by R. A. Smith (1780–1829)
From a traditional melody of the Isle of Arran

*Moderately slow*

1. Since Je-sus is my Friend, And I to Him be-long,
2. He whis-pers in my breast Sweet words of ho-ly cheer;
3. My heart for glad-ness springs; It can-not more be sad;
4. The Sun that lights mine eyes Is Christ, the Lord I love;

It mat-ters not what foes in-tend, How-ev-er fierce and strong.
How they who seek in God their rest Shall ev-er find Him near.
For ver-y joy it laughs and sings, Sees naught but sun-shine glad.
I sing for joy of that which lies Stored up for me a-bove. A-MEN.

Tune from "Songs of Praise." Used by permission of the Oxford University Press.

# 299

Rev. Paul Gerhardt, 1656
Trans. by Catherine Winkworth, 1855

S. M.
(SECOND TUNE)

GREENWOOD

Joseph E. Sweetser, 1849

*Moderately slow*

1. Since Je-sus is my Friend, And I to Him be-long,
2. He whis-pers in my breast Sweet words of ho-ly cheer;
3. My heart for glad-ness springs; It can-not more be sad;
4. The Sun that lights mine eyes Is Christ, the Lord I love;

It mat-ters not what foes in-tend, How-ev-er fierce and strong.
How they who seek in God their rest Shall ev-er find Him near.
For ver-y joy it laughs and sings, Sees naught but sun-shine glad.
I sing for joy of that which lies Stored up for me a-bove. A-MEN.

Anna Laetitia Waring (1820–1910)      C. M. D.      PENTATONE
Henry Walford Davies

*In moderate time.   Serenely*

1. My heart is rest-ing, O my God, I will give thanks and sing;
2. I have a her-it-age of joy, That yet I must not see;
3. My heart is rest-ing, O my God, My heart is in Thy care;

My heart is at the se-cret source Of ev-ery pre-cious thing.
But the hand that bled to make it mine Is keep-ing it for me.
I hear the voice of joy and health Re-sound-ing ev-ery-where.

I thirst for springs of heaven-ly life, And here all day they rise;
And a new song is in my mouth, To long-loved mu-sic set:
"Thou art my por-tion, saith my soul," Ten thou-sand voi-ces say,

I seek the treas-ure of Thy love, And close at hand it lies.
"Glo-ry to Thee for all the grace I have not tast-ed yet."
And the mu-sic of their glad A-men Will nev-er die a-way. A-MEN.

Tune from "A Students' Hymnal" (Hymns of the Kingdom). Used by permission of the Oxford University Press.

Bishop Edward H. Bickersteth, 1875

10. 10.

PAX TECUM
Alt. from George T. Caldbeck, by
Charles J. Vincent, 1877

*In rather slow time*

1. Peace, per - fect peace, in
this dark world of sin? The blood of
Je - sus whis - pers peace with - in.

2. Peace, per - fect peace, by
throng - ing du - ties pressed? To do the
will of Je - sus, this is rest.

3. Peace, per - fect peace, with
sor - rows sur - ging round? On Je - sus'
bos - om naught but calm is found.

4. Peace, per - fect peace, with
loved ones far a - way? In Je - sus'
keep - ing we are safe and they. A - MEN.

5. Peace, perfect peace, our future all unknown?
   Jesus we know, and He is on the throne.

6. Peace, perfect peace, death shadowing us and ours?
   Jesus has vanquished death and all its powers.

7. It is enough: earth's struggles soon shall cease,
   And Jesus call us to heaven's perfect peace.

# 302

## Peace

John Greenleaf Whittier (1807–1892)     8. 6. 8. 8. 6.     Frederick Charles Maker (1844–1927)

**REST**

*In moderate time*

1. Dear Lord and Fa - ther of man-kind, For - give our fool - ish ways;
2. In sim - ple trust like theirs who heard, Be - side the Syr - ian sea,
3. O Sab - bath rest by Gal - i - lee! O calm of hills a - bove,
4. Drop Thy still dews of qui - et - ness, Till all our striv - ings cease;

Re - clothe us in our right - ful mind, In pur - er lives Thy
The gra - cious call - ing of the Lord, Let us, like them, with -
Where Je - sus knelt to share with Thee The si - lence of e -
Take from our souls the strain and stress, And let our or - dered

serv - ice find, In deep - er rev - erence, praise.
out a word Rise up and fol - low Thee.
ter - ni - ty, In - ter - pret - ed by love!
lives con - fess The beau - ty of Thy peace. A - MEN.

5. Breathe through the pulses of desire
   Thy coolness and Thy balm;
   Let sense be dumb, let flesh retire;
   Speak through the earthquake, wind, **and fire,**
   O still, small voice of **calm!**

Copyright, by permission of the Psalms and Hymns Trust.

# 303 The Life in Christ

Rev. Stopford A. Brooke, 1881     10. 4. 10. 4. 10. 10.     LUX BEATA
Albert L. Peace, 1885

*Serenely, but not too slowly*

1. Im - mor - tal Love, with - in whose right - eous will
2. The days are gone when far and wide my will
3. What - e'er of pain Thy lov - ing hand al - lot,
4. So may I, far a - way, when eve - ning falls

Is al - ways peace, O pit - y me, storm-tossed on waves of ill;
Drove me a - stray; And now I fain would climb the ar - duous hill,
I glad - ly bear; On - ly, O Lord, let peace be not for - got,
On life and love, Ar - rive at last the ho - ly, hap - py halls,

Let pas - sion cease; Come down in power with - in my heart to reign,
That nar - row way Which leads through mist and rocks to Thine a - bode;
Nor yet Thy care, Free - dom from storms and wild de - sires with - in,
With Thee a - bove— Wound-ed, yet healed; sin - lad - en, yet for - given;

For I am weak, and strug - gle has been vain.
Toil - ing for man, and Thee, Al - might - y God.
Peace from the fierce op - pres - sion of my sin.
And sure Thy good - ness is my on - ly heaven. A-MEN.

Words used by permission of Miss Honor Brooke.
Tune used by permission of W. Paxton and Co., Ltd.

# Peace

James Edmeston, 1821      8. 7. 8. 7. 8. 7.     "Essay on the Church Plain Chant," 1782

CORINTH

*In march rhythm*

1. Lead us, heaven-ly Fa - ther, lead us    O'er the world's tem -
2. Sav - iour, breathe for - give - ness o'er us,    All our weak - ness
3. Spir - it of our God, de - scend - ing,    Fill our hearts with

pes - tuous sea;   Guard us, guide us, keep us, feed us,
Thou dost know;   Thou didst tread this earth be - fore us,
heaven - ly joy,   Love with ev - ery pas - sion blend - ing,

For we have no help but Thee;   Yet pos - sess - ing
Thou didst feel its keen - est woe;   Lone and drear - y,
Pleas - ure that can nev - er cloy;   Thus pro - vid - ed,

ev - ery bless - ing,   If our God our Fa - ther be.
faint and wea - ry,   Through the des - ert Thou didst go.
par - doned, guid - ed,   Noth - ing can our peace de - stroy. A-MEN.

Adelaide Anne Procter (1825-1864)    10. 4. 10. 4.    SUBMISSION
Albert Lister Peace (1844-1912)

*In moderate time*

1. I do not ask, O Lord, that life may be A pleas-ant road;
2. For one thing on-ly, Lord, dear Lord, I plead: Lead me a-right,
3. I do not ask, O Lord, that Thou shouldst shed Full ra-diance here;
4. Joy is like rest-less day; but peace di-vine Like qui-et night;

I do not ask that Thou wouldst take from me Aught of its load.
Though strength should fal-ter, and though heart should bleed, Through peace to light.
Give but a ray of peace, that I may tread With-out a fear.
Lead me, O Lord, till per-fect day shall shine Through peace to light. A-MEN.

306    Love and Communion

Charlotte Elliott, 1834    8. 8. 8. 6.    FLEMMING
Friedrich F. Flemming, 1810

*Moderately slow*

1. O Ho-ly Sav-iour, Friend un-seen, The faint, the weak on Thee may lean,
2. Blest with this fel-low-ship di-vine, Take what Thou wilt, I'll ne'er re-pine;
3. Though faith and hope may long be tried, I ask not, need not aught be-side;
4. Blest is my lot, what-e'er be-fall; What can dis-turb me, who ap-pall,

Help me, throughout life's vary-ing scene, By faith to cling to Thee.
E'en as the branch-es to the vine, My soul would cling to Thee.
How safe, how calm, how sat-is-fied, The souls that cling to Thee!
While as my Strength, my Rock, my All, Sav-iour, I cling to Thee? A-MEN.

# Love and Communion

Rev. George Matheson, 1882      8. 8. 8. 8. 6.      ST. MARGARET
Albert L. Peace, 1885

*Moderately slow. With exaltation*

1. O Love that wilt not let me go,
2. O Light that fol-lowest all my way,
3. O Joy that seek-est me through pain,
4. O Cross that lift-est up my head,

I rest my wea-ry soul in Thee;
I yield my flick-ering torch to Thee;
I can-not close my heart to Thee;
I dare not ask to fly from Thee;

I give Thee back the life I owe,
My heart re-stores its bor-rowed ray,
I trace the rain-bow through the rain,
I lay in dust life's glo-ry dead,

That in Thine o-cean depths its flow May rich-er, full-er be.
That in Thy sun-shine's blaze its day May bright-er, fair-er be.
And feel the prom-ise is not vain That morn shall tear-less be.
And from the ground there blos-soms red Life that shall end-less be. A-MEN.

Tune used by permission of Novello and Company, Ltd.

# The Life in Christ

Rev. Charles Wesley, 1747  8. 7. 8. 7. D.  (FIRST TUNE)  BEECHER  John Zundel, 1870

*In moderate time*

1. Love di - vine, all loves ex - cel - ling, Joy of heaven, to earth come down,
2. Breathe, O breathe Thy lov - ing Spir - it In - to ev - ery trou - bled breast!
3. Come, Al - might - y to de - liv - er, Let us all Thy life re - ceive;
4. Fin - ish, then, Thy new cre - a - tion; Pure and spot - less let us be;

Fix in us Thy hum - ble dwell-ing, All Thy faith - ful mer - cies crown!
Let us all in Thee in - her - it, Let us find the prom - ised rest;
Sud - den - ly re - turn, and nev - er, Nev - er more Thy tem - ples leave.
Let us see Thy great sal - va - tion Per - fect - ly re - stored in Thee;

Je - sus, Thou art all com - pas - sion, Pure, un - bound - ed love Thou art;
Take a - way the love of sin - ning; Al - pha and O - me - ga be;
Thee we would be al - ways bless-ing, Serve Thee as Thy hosts a - bove;
Changed from glo - ry in - to glo - ry, Till in heaven we take our place,

Vis - it us with Thy sal - va - tion, En - ter ev - ery trem - bling heart.
End of faith, as its Be - gin - ning, Set our hearts at lib - er - ty.
Pray, and praise Thee with-out ceas - ing, Glo - ry in Thy per - fect love.
Till we cast our crowns be - fore Thee, Lost in won-der, love, and praise. A-MEN.

Rev. Charles Wesley, 1747

8. 7. 8. 7. D.
(SECOND TUNE)

LOVE DIVINE (LE JEUNE)
George Le Jeune, 1887

*In moderate time*

1. Love di-vine, all loves ex-cel-ling, Joy of heaven, to earth come down,
2. Breathe, O breathe Thy lov-ing Spir-it In-to ev-ery trou-bled breast!
3. Come, Al-might-y to de-liv-er, Let us all Thy life re-ceive;
4. Fin-ish, then, Thy new cre-a-tion; Pure and spot-less let us be:

Fix in us Thy hum-ble dwell-ing, All Thy faith-ful mer-cies crown!
Let us all in Thee in-her-it, Let us find the prom-ised rest;
Sud-den-ly re-turn, and nev-er, Nev-er-more Thy tem-ples leave.
Let us see Thy great sal-va-tion Per-fect-ly re-stored in Thee;

Je-sus, Thou art all com-pas-sion, Pure, un-bound-ed love Thou art;
Take a-way the love of sin-ning; Al-pha and O-me-ga be;
Thee we would be al-ways bless-ing, Serve Thee as Thy hosts a-bove;
Changed from glo-ry in-to glo-ry, Till in heaven we take our place,

Vis-it us with Thy sal-va-tion, En-ter ev-ery trem-bling heart.
End of faith, as its Be-gin-ning, Set our hearts at lib-er-ty.
Pray, and praise Thee, with-out ceas-ing, Glo-ry in Thy per-fect love.
Till we cast our crowns be-fore Thee, Lost in won-der, love, and praise. A-MEN.

# The Life in Christ

## 309

Latin, 11th century
Trans. by Rev. Edward Caswall, 1849

C. M.

ST. AGNES
Rev. John B. Dykes, 1866

*In moderate time*

1. Je - sus, the ver - y thought of Thee With sweet-ness fills my breast;
2. Nor voice can sing, nor heart can frame, Nor can the mem - ory find
3. O Hope of ev - ery con - trite heart, O Joy of all the meek,
4. But what to those who find? Ah, this Nor tongue nor pen can show:
5. Je - sus, our on - ly Joy be Thou, As Thou our Prize wilt be;

But sweet-er far Thy face to see, And in Thy pres - ence rest.
A sweet-er sound than Thy blest Name, O Sav-iour of man - kind!
To those who fall, how kind Thou art! How good to those who seek!
The love of Je - sus, what it is None but His loved ones know.
Je - sus, be Thou our Glo - ry now, And through e - ter - ni - ty. A - MEN.

## 310

Rev. John Newton, 1779
Stanza 5, line 1, alt.

C. M.

ST. PETER
Alexander R. Reinagle, 1836

*In moderate time. In a spirit of joy*

1. How sweet the Name of Je - sus sounds In a be - liev - er's ear!
2. It makes the wound-ed spir - it whole, And calms the trou - bled breast;
3. Dear Name! the Rock on which I build, My Shield and Hid - ing Place,
4. Je - sus, my Shep-herd, Broth - er, Friend, My Proph-et, Priest, and King,
5. Weak is the ef - fort of my heart, And cold my warm-est thought;

It soothes his sor-rows, heals his wounds, And drives a - way his fear.
'Tis man - na to the hun-gry soul, And to the wea - ry rest.
My nev - er - fail - ing Treas-ury, filled With bound-less stores of grace;
My Lord, my Life, my Way, my End, Ac - cept the praise I bring.
But when I see Thee as Thou art, I'll praise Thee as I ought. A - MEN.

Frances Ridley Havergal, 1873     7. 6. 7. 6. D.     JESU DILECTISSIME
Robert H. McCartney (1844–1895)

*In moderate time*

1. I could not do with-out Thee, O Sav-iour of the lost,
2. I could not do with-out Thee; I can-not stand a-lone,
3. I could not do with-out Thee; No oth-er friend can read
4. I could not do with-out Thee, For years are fleet-ing fast,

Whose pre-cious blood re-deemed me At such tre-men-dous cost;
I have no strength or good-ness, No wis-dom of my own;
The spir-it's strange deep long-ings, In-ter-pret-ing its need;
And soon in sol-emn lone-ness The riv-er must be passed;

Thy right-eous-ness, Thy par-don, Thy pre-cious blood, must be
But Thou, be-lov-ed Sav-iour, Art All in all to me,
No hu-man heart could en-ter Each dim re-cess of mine,
But Thou wilt nev-er leave me, And though the waves roll high,

My on-ly hope and com-fort, My glo-ry and my plea.
And weak-ness will be pow-er, If lean-ing hard on Thee.
And soothe, and hush, and calm it, O bless-ed Lord, but Thine.
I know Thou wilt be near me, And whis-per, "It is I." A-MEN.

# 312 The Life in Christ

Rev. Johann C. Schwedler (1672–1730)
Trans. by Rev. Benjamin H. Kennedy, 1863

HENDON
Rev. H. A. César Malan, 1827

7. 7. 7. 7. 7.

*With exaltation*

1. Ask ye what great thing I know
2. Who de - feats my fier - cest foes?
3. Who is life in life to me?
4. This is that great thing I know;

That de - lights and stirs me so? What the high re -
Who con - soles my sad - dest woes? Who re - vives my
Who the death of death will be? Who will place me
This de - lights and stirs me so: Faith in Him who

ward I win? Whose the name I glo - ry in?
faint - ing heart, Heal - ing all its hid - den smart?
on His right, With the count - less hosts of light?
died to save, Him who tri - umphed o'er the grave,

Je - sus Christ, the Cru - ci - fied.
Je - sus Christ, the Cru - ci - fied.
Je - sus Christ, the Cru - ci - fied.
Je - sus Christ, the Cru - ci - fied.  A - MEN.

# 313 Love and Communion

From a 17th century Latin version of a
Spanish sonnet ascribed to Francis Xavier
Trans. by Rev. Edward Caswall, 1849

C. M.

SOLOMON
George Frederick Handel (1685-1759)

*In moderate time*

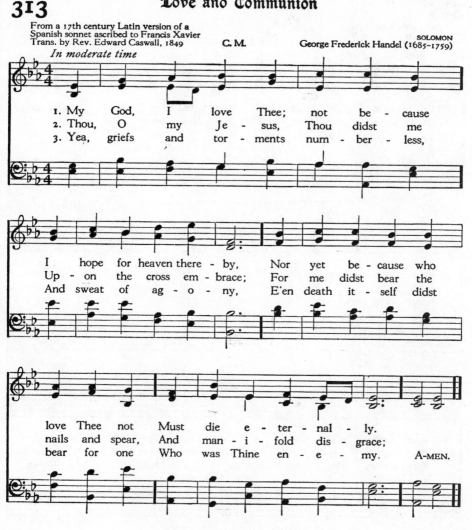

1. My God, I love Thee; not be-cause
   I hope for heaven there-by, Nor yet be-cause who
   love Thee not Must die e-ter-nal-ly.

2. Thou, O my Je-sus, Thou didst me
   Up-on the cross em-brace; For me didst bear the
   nails and spear, And man-i-fold dis-grace;

3. Yea, griefs and tor-ments num-ber-less,
   And sweat of ag-o-ny, E'en death it-self didst
   bear for one Who was Thine en-e-my. A-MEN.

4. Then why, O blessèd Jesus Christ,
   Should I not love Thee well?
   Not for the hope of winning heaven,
   Or of escaping hell;

5. Not with the hope of gaining aught,
   Not seeking a reward;
   But as Thyself hast lovèd me,
   O ever-loving Lord!

6. E'en so I love Thee, and will love,
   And in Thy praise will sing;
   Solely because Thou art my God,
   And my Eternal King.

# The Life in Christ

314

Rev. Paul Gerhardt, 1653
Trans. by Rev. John Wesley, 1739
Altered and revised, 1931

8. 8. 8. 8. 8. 8.

STELLA
Old English melody

*Moderately fast*

1. Je - sus, Thy bound - less love to me No thought can
2. O grant that noth - ing in my soul May dwell, but
3. O Love, how gra - cious is Thy way! All fear be

reach, no tongue de - clare; O knit my thank - ful heart to Thee,
Thy pure love a - lone; O may Thy love pos - sess me whole,
fore Thy pres - ence flies; Care, an - guish, sor - row, melt a - way,

And reign with - out a ri - val there! Thine whol - ly,
My joy, my treas - ure, and my crown! All cold - ness
Wher - e'er Thy heal - ing beams a - rise. O Je - sus,

Thine a - lone, I'd live, My - self to Thee en - tire - ly give.
from my heart re - move; May ev - ery act, word, thought, be love.
noth - ing may I see, Noth - ing de - sire, or seek, but Thee. A-MEN.

# 315 Love and Communion

Elizabeth Prentiss (1818–1878)  6. 4. 6. 4. 6. 6. 4.  William Howard Doane (1832–1916)

MORE LOVE TO THEE

*In moderate time*

1. More love to Thee, O Christ, More love to Thee!
2. Once earth-ly joy I craved, Sought peace and rest;
3. Then shall my lat-est breath Whis-per Thy praise;

Hear Thou the prayer I make On bend-ed knee;
Now Thee a-lone I seek; Give what is best:
This be the part-ing cry My heart shall raise;

This is my ear-nest plea, More love, O Christ, to Thee,
This all my prayer shall be, More love, O Christ, to Thee,
This still its prayer shall be, More love, O Christ, to Thee,

More love to Thee, More love to Thee!
More love to Thee, More love to Thee!
More love to Thee, More love to Thee! A-MEN.

# 316

## The Life in Christ

Rev. Ralph Wardlaw, 1817　　　　7. 7. 7. 7. 7.　　　　HENDON
Rev. H. A. César Malan, 1827

*Joyously*

1. Christ, of all my hopes the Ground, Christ, the Spring of all my joy, Still in Thee may
2. Let Thy love my heart in-flame; Keep Thy fear be-fore my sight; Be Thy praise my
3. Foun-tain of o'er-flow-ing grace, Free-ly from Thy full-ness give; Till I close my
4. Firm-ly trust-ing in Thy blood, Noth-ing shall my heart con-found; Safe-ly I shall
5. Thus, O thus, an en-trance give To the land of cloud-less sky; Hav-ing known it

I be found, Still for Thee my powers em-ploy, Still for Thee my powers em-ploy.
high-est aim; Be Thy smile my chief de-light, Be Thy smile my chief de-light.
earth-ly race, May I prove it Christ to live, May I prove it Christ to live.
pass the flood, Safe-ly reach Em-man-uel's ground, Safe-ly reach Em-man-uel's ground.
Christ to live, Let me know it gain to die, Let me know it gain to die. A-MEN.

# 317

## The Inner Life

Psalm xlii　　　　SPOHR
Tate and Brady's "New Version," 1696　　　C. M.　　　Louis Spohr, 1835

*In moderate time*

1. As pants the hart for cool-ing streams When heat-ed in the chase,
2. For Thee, my God, the liv-ing God, My thirst-y soul doth pine;
3. Why rest-less, why cast down, my soul? Trust God; and He'll em-ploy
4. Why rest-less, why cast down, my soul? Hope still; and thou shalt sing

So longs my soul, O God, for Thee, And Thy re-fresh-ing grace.
O when shall I be-hold Thy face, Thou Maj-es-ty di-vine!
His aid for thee, and change these sighs To thank-ful hymns of joy.
The praise of Him who is thy God, Thy health's e-ter-nal Spring. A-MEN.

John Bull, 1839

7. 7. 7. 7. D.

WEIMAR

Melody by Melchior Vulpius (1560–1616)
Adapted by Johann Sebastian Bach

*Moderately slow*

1. Let my life be hid in Thee, Life of life and Light of light! Love's il - lim - it - a - ble sea! Depth of peace, of power the height! Let my life be hid in Thee From vex - a - tion and an - noy; Calm in Thy tran - quil - li - ty, All my mourn - ing turned to joy.

2. Let my life be hid in Thee When a - larms are gath - ering round, Cov - ered with Thy pan - o - ply, Safe with - in Thy ho - ly ground. Let my life be hid in Thee, In the world and yet a - bove; Hid in Thine e - ter - ni - ty, In the o - cean of Thy love. A - MEN.

# The Life in Christ

Rev. Ray Palmer, 1858

C. M.
(FIRST TUNE)

SAWLEY
James Walch, 1860

1. Je - sus, these eyes have nev - er seen That ra - diant form of Thine;
2. I see Thee not, I hear Thee not, Yet art Thou oft with me;
3. Yet though I have not seen, and still Must rest in faith a - lone;
4. When death these mor - tal eyes shall seal, And still this throb-bing heart,

The veil of sense hangs dark be-tween Thy bless-ed face and mine.
And earth hath ne'er so dear a spot As where I meet with Thee.
I love Thee, dear - est Lord, and will, Un - seen, but not un-known.
The rend-ing veil shall Thee re - veal, All - glo-rious as Thou art. A-MEN.

319

Rev. Ray Palmer, 1858

C. M.
(SECOND TUNE)

OSBORNE
Henry Carey (1692–1743)

1. Je - sus, these eyes have nev - er seen That ra - diant form of Thine;
2. I see Thee not, I hear Thee not, Yet art Thou oft with me;
3. Yet though I have not seen, and still Must rest in faith a - lone;
4. When death these mor - tal eyes shall seal, And still this throb-bing heart,

The veil of sense hangs dark be-tween Thy bless-ed face and mine.
And earth hath ne'er so dear a spot As where I meet with Thee.
I love Thee, dear-est Lord, and will, Un - seen, but not un - known.
The rend-ing veil shall Thee re - veal, All - glo - rious as Thou art. A-MEN.

From "The Enlarged Songs of Praise." Used by permission of the Oxford University Press.

The Inner Life

Eliza Scudder, 1871          10. 10. 10. 10.          FFIGYSBREN
Welsh hymn melody

*In moderate time, devotionally*

1. Thou Life with-in my life, than self more near,
2. Be-low all depths Thy sav-ing mer-cy lies,
3. Take part with me a-gainst these doubts that rise
4. How shall I call Thee who art al-ways here?

Thou veil-ed Pres-ence in-fin-ite-ly clear,
Through thick-est gloom I see Thy light a-rise;
And seek to throne Thee far in dis-tant skies;
How shall I praise Thee who art still most dear?

From all il-lu-sive shows of sense I flee,
A-bove the high-est heavens Thou art not found
Take part with me a-gainst this self that found
What may I give Thee save what Thou hast given,

To find my cen-ter and my rest in Thee.
More sure-ly than with-in this earth-ly round.
As-sume the bur-den of these sins and cares.
And whom but Thee have I in earth or heaven? A-MEN.

Tune from "Songs of Praise." Used by permission of the Oxford University Press.

FRANKFORT
Rev. Philipp Nicolai, 1599
Harmonized by Johann Sebastian Bach (1685–1750)

Rev. Philipp Nicolai (1556–1608)

8. 8. 7. 8. 8. 7. 4. 8. 4. 8.

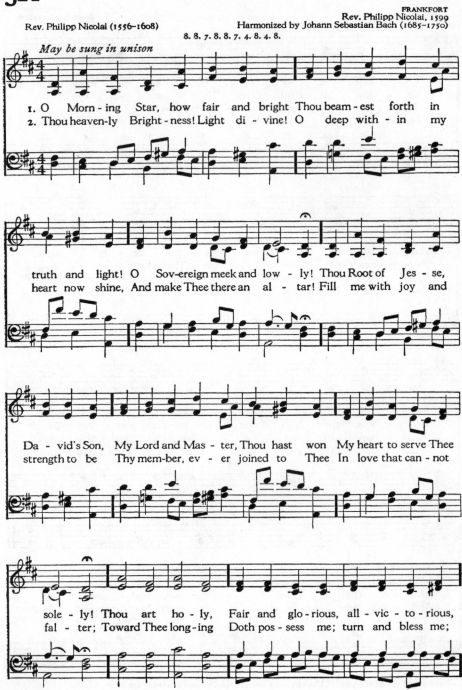

*May be sung in unison*

1. O Morn-ing Star, how fair and bright Thou beam-est forth in
2. Thou heaven-ly Bright-ness! Light di-vine! O deep with-in my

truth and light! O Sov-ereign meek and low-ly! Thou Root of Jes-se,
heart now shine, And make Thee there an al-tar! Fill me with joy and

Da-vid's Son, My Lord and Mas-ter, Thou hast won My heart to serve Thee
strength to be Thy mem-ber, ev-er joined to Thee In love that can-not

sole-ly! Thou art ho-ly, Fair and glo-rious, all-vic-to-rious,
fal-ter; Toward Thee long-ing Doth pos-sess me; turn and bless me;

Rich in bless - ing, Rule and might o'er all pos - sess - ing.
Here in sad - ness Eye and heart long for Thy glad - ness! A-MEN.

## 322

John Oxenham, 1917      C. M.      ST. AGNES
Rev. John B. Dykes, 1866

*In rather slow time*

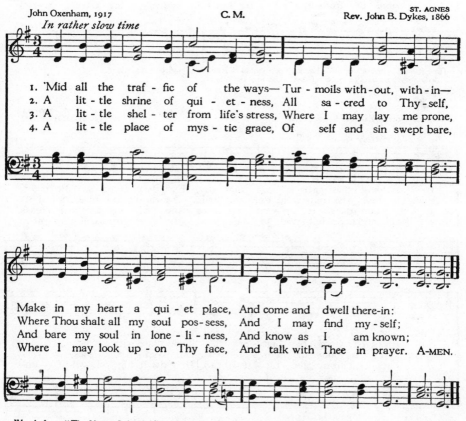

1. 'Mid all the traf - fic of the ways— Tur - moils with-out, with-in—
2. A lit - tle shrine of qui - et - ness, All sa - cred to Thy-self,
3. A lit - tle shel - ter from life's stress, Where I may lay me prone,
4. A lit - tle place of mys - tic grace, Of self and sin swept bare,

Make in my heart a qui - et place, And come and dwell there-in:
Where Thou shalt all my soul pos-sess, And I may find my-self;
And bare my soul in lone - li - ness, And know as I am known;
Where I may look up - on Thy face, And talk with Thee in prayer. A-MEN.

Words from "The Vision Splendid," by John Oxenham. Used by permission of Messrs. Pinker and Morrison.

**323**

Rev. Frederick Lucian Hosmer, 1904

8. 6. 8. 4.
(FIRST TUNE)

KINGTON
Rev. F. Llewellyn Edwards

*Moderately slow*

1. When shad-ows gath-er on our way, Fast deep-ening as the night,
2. A - mid the out-ward toil and strife, The world's dull roar and din,
3. When bur-dens sore up - on us press, And vex - ing cares in-crease,
4. Though fond hopes fail, and joy de - part, And friends should faith-less prove,

Be Thou, O God, the spir-it's stay, Our in - ward Light.
Still speak Thy word of high-er life, Thou Voice with - in.
Spring Thou, a fount of qui - et-ness, Our hid - den Peace.
O save us from the bit - ter heart, In - dwell - ing Love! A-men.

Tune from "Songs of Praise." Used by permission of Rev. F. Llewellyn Edwards.
Words copyright by The Beacon Press. Used by permission.

**323**

Rev. Frederick Lucian Hosmer, 1904

8. 6. 8. 4.
(SECOND TUNE)

ST. CUTHBERT
Rev. John B. Dykes, 1861

*Moderately slow*

1. When shad-ows gath-er on our way, Fast deep-ening as the night,
2. A - mid the out-ward toil and strife, The world's dull roar and din,
3. When bur-dens sore up - on us press, And vex - ing cares in-crease,
4. Though fond hopes fail, and joy de - part, And friends should faith-less prove,

Be Thou, O God, the spir-it's stay, Our in-ward Light.
Still speak Thy word of high-er life, Thou Voice with - in.
Spring Thou, a fount of qui - et - ness, Our hid - den Peace.
O save us from the bit - ter heart, In - dwell-ing Love! A-MEN.

Words copyright by The Beacon Press. Used by permission.

# The Inner Life

**324**

Anon., c. 1904       10. 10. 10. 6.       Rev. Calvin W. Laufer, 1932

KERR

*May be sung in unison.*   *Moderately slow*

1. I sought the Lord, and aft - er - ward I knew
2. Thou didst reach forth Thy hand and mine en - fold;
3. I find, I walk, I love, but O the whole

He moved my soul to seek Him, seek - ing me;
I walked and sank not on the storm - vexed sea;
Of love is but my an - swer, Lord, to Thee!

It was not I that found, O Sav - iour true;
'Twas not so much that I on Thee took hold
For Thou wert long be - fore - hand with my soul;

No, I was found of Thee.
As Thou, dear Lord, on me.
Al - ways Thou lov - edst me. A - MEN.

Music copyright, 1933, by Calvin W. Laufer. Used by permission.

# The Life in Christ

Ancient Irish; trans. by Mary Byrne
Versified by Eleanor Hull

SLANE
Ancient Irish traditional melody
Harmonized by David Evans

10. 10. 10. 10.

*Unison. Moderately slow. With great dignity*

1. Be Thou my Vi - sion, O Lord of my heart;
2. Be Thou my Wis - dom, and Thou my true Word;
3. Rich - es I heed not, nor man's emp - ty praise,
4. High King of heav - en, my vic - to - ry won,

Naught be all else to me, save that Thou art —
I ev - er with Thee and Thou with me, Lord;
Thou mine in - her - it - ance, now and al - ways:
May I reach heav - en's joys, O bright heaven's Sun!

Thou my best thought, by day or by night, . . . .
Thou my great Fa - ther, I Thy true son; . . . .
Thou and Thou on - ly, first in my heart, . . . .
Heart of my own heart, what - ev - er be - fall, . . . .

# The Inner Life

Wak - ing     or     sleep-ing,   Thy   pres - ence my   light.
Thou    in    me    dwell-ing,    and    I    with Thee   one.
High   King   of    heav-en,      my   Treas - ure Thou   art.
Still    be   my    Vi - sion,     O    Rul - er   of    all.    A - MEN.

Tune from "The Church Hymnary," Revised. Used by permission of the Oxford University Press.
Words used by permission of Miss Eleanor Hull.

## 326

ACH GOTT UND HERR
"Neu Leipziger Gesangbuch," 1682
Dora Greenwell (1821–1882)          8. 8. 8. 7.          Arr. by Johann Sebastian Bach (1685–1750)

*Slow and dignified*

1. I   am not skilled to   un-der-stand   What God hath willed, what God hath planned;
2. I   take God at   His word and deed: "Christ died   to   save   me"—this I read;
3. And was there then no oth - er way For   God to take?—I   can-not say;
4. That He should leave His place on high And   come for sin - ful   man   to   die,

I   on - ly know at   His   right hand Stands One who is   my Sav - iour.
And in   my heart I   find   a   need Of   Him to   be   my Sav - iour.
I   on - ly bless Him, day by   day, Who saved me through my Sav - iour.
You count it strange?— so do not   I,   Since I   have known my Sav - iour. A-MEN.

5. And O that He fulfilled may see
   The travail of His soul in me,
   And with His work contented be,
   As I with my dear Saviour!

6. Yea, living, dying, let me bring
   My strength, my solace, from this spring,
   That He who lives to be my King
   Once died to be my Saviour.

# The Life in Christ

**327**

Jean Sophia Pigott, 1876

8. 7. 8. 5. D. with Refrain

RESTING
James Mountain
" Hymns of Consecration and Faith "

*In moderate time and graceful rhythm*

1. Je - sus, I am rest - ing, rest - ing In the joy of what Thou art;
2. O how great Thy lov - ing - kind - ness, Vast - er, broad - er than the sea!
3. Sim - ply trust - ing Thee, Lord Je - sus, I be - hold Thee as Thou art,
4. Ev - er lift Thy face up - on me As I work and wait for Thee;

I am find - ing out the great - ness Of Thy lov - ing heart.
O how mar - vel - ous Thy good - ness Lav - ished all on me!
And Thy love, so pure, so change - less, Sat - is - fies my heart;
Rest - ing 'neath Thy smile, Lord Je - sus, Earth's dark shad - ows flee.

Here I gaze and gaze up - on Thee, As Thy beau - ty fills my soul,
Yes, I rest in Thee, Be - lov - ed, Know what wealth of grace is Thine,
Sat - is - fies its deep - est long - ing, Meets, sup - plies my ev - ery need,
Bright - ness of my Fa - ther's glo - ry, Sun - shine of my Fa - ther's face,

For by Thy trans - form - ing im - age, Thou hast made me whole.
Know Thy cer - tain - ty of prom - ise And have made it mine.
Com - pass - eth me round with bless - ings: Thine is love in - deed.
Let Thy glo - ry e'er shine on me, Fill me with Thy grace.

# The Inner Life

**REFRAIN**

Je - sus, I am rest-ing, rest - ing In the joy of what Thou art;

I am find - ing out the great-ness Of Thy lov - ing heart. A-MEN.

Tune used by permission of Marshall, Morgan, and Scott, Ltd.

## 328

" The Yattendon Hymnal "
Based on Rev. Isaac Watts

SELMA
Traditional melody of the Isle of Arran
Adapted by Robert Archibald Smith (1780–1829)

S. M.

*Moderately slow*

1. My Lord, my Life, my Love, To Thee, to Thee I call;
2. My on - ly sun to cheer The dark - ness where I dwell;
3. For how shall man, Thy child, With-out Thee hap - py be,
4. Re - turn my Love, my Life, Thy grace hath won my heart;

I can - not live if Thou re-move: Thou art my Joy, my All.
The best and on - ly true de-light My song hath found to tell.
Who hath no com-fort nor de-sire In all the world but Thee?
If Thou for - give, if Thou re-turn, I will no more de - part. A-MEN.

# The Life in Christ

HERZLIEBSTER JESU
Early form of melody
Johann Crüger, 1640

Archbishop Johann Olaf Wallin (1779–1839)

11. 11. 11. 5.

*To be sung in unison. Moderately slow*

1. Where is the Friend for whom I'm ev - er
2. When sum - mer winds blow gen - tly, then I
3. O where such beau - ty is it - self re -
4. And yet to hide Him oft a cloud pre -

yearn - ing? My long - ing grows when day to night is
hear Him; Where sing the birds, where rush the streams I'm
veal - ing In all that lives, through all cre - a - tion
vail - eth, My prayer can reach Him, but my vi - sion

turn - ing; And though I find Him not as day re -
near Him. But bet - ter far when in my heart He
steal - ing, What must the source be whence it comes— the
fail - eth; Would I could see His face and heart so

ced - eth My heart still plead - eth.
bless - es Me with ca - ress - es.
Giv - er? Beau - ty for - ev - er.
lov - ing, And cease my rov - ing! A - MEN.

5. My soul, be strong! Hope, pray with self-denial!
The heavenly Friend submits Himself to trial:
So shalt thou find in Him, on Him depending,
Mercy unending.

Jean Ingelow (1820–1897)  10. 10. 10. 6.  Robert Alexander Stewart Macalister

TEMPLE BRYAN

*In moderate time, with feeling*

1. And didst Thou love the race that loved not Thee?
2. O God, O Kins-man loved, but not e - nough;
3. By that one like - ness which is ours and Thine,

And didst Thou take to heaven a hu - man brow? Dost plead with man's voice
O Man, with eyes ma - jes - tic aft - er death, Whose feet have toiled a -
By that one na - ture which doth hold us kin, By that high heaven where,

by the mar - velous sea? Art Thou his kins - man now?
long our path - ways rough, Whose lips drawn hu - man breath:
sin - less, Thou dost shine To draw us sin - ners in; A-MEN.

4. By Thy last silence in the judgment hall,
   By long foreknowledge of the deadly Tree,
   By darkness, by the wormwood and the gall,
   I pray Thee visit me.

5. Come, lest this heart should, cold and cast away,
   Die ere the Guest adored she entertain—
   Lest eyes which never saw Thine earthly day
   Should miss Thy heavenly reign.

Tune copyright, 1927, by the Oxford University Press. Used by permission.

# 331 The Life in Christ

Rev. Johann Christian Schwedler (1672-1730)
Trans. by Rev. G. R. Woodward; alt.

WOLLT IHR WISSEN, WAS MEIN PREIS
"Melodienbuch von Rautenburg," by J. Cammin
7. 7. 7. 7. 4. 7.
Harmonized by G. H. Palmer

*With exultation*

1. What, ye ask me, is my prize? What the se - cret
   to be wise? What the wealth I val - ue most?
   What the name where - in I boast? Je - sus, Je - sus,
   Je - sus Christ, the Cru - ci - fied.

2. Who the ground of my be - lief? Who in song my
   min - strel chief? Who for - giv - eth all my sin?
   Who my suc - cor grace to win? Je - sus, Je - sus,
   Je - sus Christ, the Cru - ci - fied.

3. Who doth com - fort me in woe? Who pro - tect me
   from my foe? Who re - vives my faint - ing soul?
   Who doth heal and make me whole? Je - sus, Je - sus,
   Je - sus Christ, the Cru - ci - fied.

4. Who by death hath con - quered death? Who re - ceives my
   part - ing breath? Who can grant me end - less rest?
   Who en - rolls me 'mid the blest? Je - sus, Je - sus,
   Je - sus Christ, the Cru - ci - fied.

A - MEN.

Words and tune from "Songs of Syon." Used by permission of Rev. George R. Woodward.

# 332 The Inner Life

Annie S. Hawks, 1872
Refrain added by Rev. Robert Lowry   6. 4. 6. 4. with Refrain

NEED

Rev. Robert Lowry, 1872

*In moderate time*

1. I need Thee ev - ery hour, Most gra - cious Lord;
2. I need Thee ev - ery hour; Stay Thou near by;
3. I need Thee ev - ery hour, In joy or pain;
4. I need Thee ev - ery hour; Teach me Thy will,
5. I need Thee ev - ery hour, Most Ho - ly One;

No ten - der voice like Thine Can peace af - ford.
Temp - ta - tions lose their power When Thou art nigh.
Come quick - ly, and a - bide, Or life is vain.
And Thy rich prom - is - es In me ful - fill.
O make me Thine in - deed, Thou bless - ed Son.

**Refrain**

I need Thee, O I need Thee, Ev - ery hour I need Thee!

O bless me now, my Sav - iour — I come to Thee! A - MEN.

Copyright, 1900, by Mary Runyon Lowry. Renewal 1914. Used by permission.

Rev. Samuel J. Stone, 1866     7. 6. 7. 6. D.     AURELIA
Samuel S. Wesley, 1864

*In moderate time, with breadth and dignity*

1. The Church's one Foun-da-tion Is Je-sus Christ her Lord;
2. E-lect from ev-ery na-tion, Yet one o'er all the earth,
3. 'Mid toil and trib-u-la-tion, And tu-mult of her war,
4. Yet she on earth hath un-ion With God the Three in One,

She is His new cre-a-tion By wa-ter and the word:
Her char-ter of sal-va-tion One Lord, one faith, one birth;
She waits the con-sum-ma-tion Of peace for-ev-er-more;
And mys-tic sweet com-mun-ion With those whose rest is won:

From heaven He came and sought her To be His ho-ly Bride;
One ho-ly Name she bless-es, Par-takes one ho-ly food,
Till with the vi-sion glo-rious Her long-ing eyes are blest,
O hap-py ones and ho-ly! Lord, give us grace that we,

With His own blood He bought her, And for her life He died.
And to one hope she press-es, With ev-ery grace en-dued.
And the great Church vic-to-rious Shall be the Church at rest.
Like them, the meek and low-ly, On high may dwell with Thee. A-MEN.

**334**

Bishop A. Cleveland Coxe, 1839      C. M.

ST. ANNE
Probably by William Croft (1678–1727)
"Supplement to the New Version"

*Majestically*

1. O where are kings and em-pires now Of old that went and came?
2. We mark her good-ly bat-tle-ments, And her foun-da-tions strong;
3. For not like king-doms of the world Thy ho-ly Church, O God;
4. Un-shak-en as e-ter-nal hills, Im-mov-a-ble she stands,

But, Lord, Thy Church is pray-ing yet, A thou-sand years the same.
We hear with-in the sol-emn voice Of her un-end-ing song.
Though earth-quake shocks are threat-ening her, And tem-pests are a-broad,
A moun-tain that shall fill the earth, A house not made by hands. A-MEN.

**335**

Rev. Samuel Longfellow, 1864      C. M.

ST. JAMES
Raphael Courteville, d. 1772

*In moderate time*

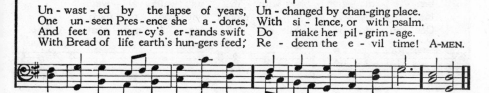

1. One ho-ly Church of God ap-pears Through ev-ery age and race,
2. From old-est time, on far-thest shores, Be-neath the pine or palm,
3. The truth is her pro-phet-ic gift, The soul her sa-cred page;
4. O liv-ing Church, thine er-rand speed, Ful-fill thy task sub-lime;

Un-wast-ed by the lapse of years, Un-changed by chan-ging place.
One un-seen Pres-ence she a-dores, With si-lence, or with psalm.
And feet on mer-cy's er-rands swift Do make her pil-grim-age.
With Bread of life earth's hun-gers feed; Re-deem the e-vil time! A-MEN.

# The Church and the Sacraments

Anon. (Latin, 7th century)
Trans. by Rev. John M. Neale, 1851

8. 7. 8. 7. 8. 7.

REGENT SQUARE
Henry Smart, 1867

*In moderate time, with dignity*

1. Christ is made the sure Foun-da-tion, Christ the Head and Cor-ner Stone, Cho-sen of the Lord and pre-cious, Bind-ing all the Church in one; Ho-ly Zi-on's help for-ev-er, And her con-fi-dence a-lone.

2. To this tem-ple, where we call Thee, Come, O Lord of hosts, to-day: With Thy wont-ed lov-ing-kind-ness Hear Thy peo-ple as they pray; And Thy full-est ben-e-dic-tion Shed with-in its walls al-way.

3. Here vouch-safe to all Thy serv-ants What they ask of Thee to gain, What they gain from Thee for-ev-er With the bless-ed to re-tain, And here-aft-er in Thy glo-ry Ev-er-more with Thee to reign.

4. Laud and hon-or to the Fa-ther, Laud and hon-or to the Son, Laud and hon-or to the Spir-it, Ev-er Three and ev-er One, One in might, and One in glo-ry, While un-end-ing a-ges run! A-MEN.

# The Church

**337**

Psalm cxxxvii
Rev. Timothy Dwight, 1800

S. M.

ST. THOMAS
"Williams' Psalmody," 1770

*Joyously*

1. I love Thy King-dom, Lord, The house of Thine a-bode,
2. I love Thy Church, O God: Her walls be-fore Thee stand,
3. For her my tears shall fall, For her my prayers as-cend;
4. Be-yond my high-est joy I prize her heaven-ly ways,
5. Sure as Thy truth shall last, To Zi-on shall be given

The Church our blest Re-deem-er saved With His own pre-cious blood.
Dear as the ap-ple of Thine eye, And grav-en on Thy hand.
To her my cares and toils be given, Till toils and cares shall end.
Her sweet com-mun-ion, sol-emn vows, Her hymns of love and praise.
The bright-est glo-ries earth can yield, And bright-er bliss of heaven. A-MEN.

**338**

Rev. Samuel Johnson, 1860

C. M.

MIRFIELD
Arthur Cottman, 1872

*Not too fast*

1. Cit-y of God, how broad and far Out-spread thy walls sub-lime!
2. How pure-ly hath thy speech come down From man's pri-me-val youth;
3. How gleam thy watch fires through the night With nev-er-faint-ing ray!
4. In vain the sur-ge's an-gry shock, In vain the drift-ing sands:

The true thy char-tered free-men are Of ev-ery age and clime.
How grand-ly hath thine em-pire grown Of free-dom, love, and truth!
How rise thy towers, se-rene and bright, To meet the dawn-ing day!
Un-harmed up-on th' e-ter-nal Rock Th' e-ter-nal cit-y stands. A-MEN.

Rev. John Newton, 1779     8. 7. 8. 7. D.     AUSTRIAN HYMN

Franz Joseph Haydn, 1797

*With exultation*

1. Glo - rious things of thee are spo - ken, Zi - on, cit - y of our God;
2. See, the streams of liv - ing wa - ters, Spring-ing from e - ter - nal Love,
3. Round each hab - i - ta - tion hov-ering, See the cloud and fire ap - pear

He whose word can - not be bro - ken Formed thee for His own a - bode:
Well sup - ply thy sons and daugh-ters, And all fear of want re - move:
For a glo - ry and a cov-ering, Show - ing that the Lord is near:

On the Rock of A - ges found - ed, What can shake thy sure re-pose?
Who can faint, while such a riv - er Ev - er flows their thirst to as-suage;
Thus de - riv - ing from their ban - ner Light by night and shade by day,

With sal-va-tion's walls sur-round-ed, Thou mayst smile at all thy foes.
Grace, which, like the Lord the Giv - er, Nev - er fails from age to age?
Safe they feed up - on the man - na Which He gives them when they pray. A-MEN.

## 340

Adapted from Rev. Isaac Watts (1674–1748)
As in "Scottish Paraphrases," 1781　　C. M.

IRISH
Melody from "A Collection of Hymns
and Sacred Poems," Dublin, 1749

*Moderately fast; with exultation*

1. How glo-rious Zi - on's courts ap-pear, The cit - y of our God!
2. Its walls, de - fend - ed by His grace, No power shall e'er o'er-throw,
3. Lift up the ev - er - last - ing gates, The doors wide o - pen fling!
4. Trust in the Lord, for - ev - er trust, And ban - ish all your fears;

His throne He hath es-tab - lished here, Here fixed His loved a - bode.
Sal - va - tion is its bul - wark sure A - gainst th' as-sail-ing foe.
En - ter, ye na-tions, who o - bey The stat - utes of our King!
Strength in the Lord Je - ho - vah dwells E - ter - nal as His years. A-MEN.

## 341

Christian Fellowship

John Oxenham, 1908　　C. M.

ST. PETER
Alexander R. Reinagle, 1836

*In moderate time*

1. In Christ there is no East or West, In Him no South or North;
2. In Him shall true hearts ev - ery-where Their high com - mun - ion find;
3. Join hands, then, broth-ers of the faith, What - e'er your race may be.
4. In Christ now meet both East and West, In Him meet South and North;

But one great fel - low-ship of love Through-out the whole wide earth.
His serv - ice is the gold - en cord Close bind - ing all man - kind.
Who serves my Fa - ther as a son Is sure - ly kin to me.
All Christ-ly souls are one in Him Through-out the whole wide earth. A-MEN.

Words from "Bees in Amber." Used by permission of the American Tract Society, holders of the copyright.

Thomas H. Gill, 1868     8. 7. 8. 7. 8. 8. 7.

NUN FREUT EUCH
Melody by Rev. Martin Luther in
"Geistliche Lieder," Wittenberg, 1535

*Moderately fast*

1. We come un - to our fa - thers' God, Their Rock is our sal - va - tion;
2. Their joy un - to the Lord we bring, Their song to us de - scend - eth;
3. Ye saints to come, take up the strain, The same sweet theme en - deav - or;

Th' e - ter - nal arms, their dear a - bode, We make our hab - i - ta - tion.
The Spir - it who in them did sing To us His mu - sic lend - eth:
Un - bro - ken be the gold - en chain! Keep on the song for - ev - er!

We bring Thee, Lord, the praise they brought, We seek Thee as Thy
His song in them, in us, is one; We raise it high, we
Safe in the same dear dwell - ing place, Rich with the same e -

saints have sought In ev - ery gen - e - ra - tion.
send it on— The song that nev - er end - eth.
ter - nal grace, Bless the same bound - less Giv - er. A - MEN.

# 343

Rev. John Fawcett, 1782    S. M.    BOYLSTON
Lowell Mason, 1832

*In moderate time*

1. Blest be the tie that binds Our hearts in Chris - tian love:
2. Be - fore our Fa - ther's throne We pour our ar - dent prayers;
3. We share our mu - tual woes, Our mu - tual bur - dens bear,
4. From sor - row, toil, and pain, And sin, we shall be free;

The fel - low - ship of kin - dred minds Is like to that a - bove.
Our fears, our hopes, our aims, are one, Our com - forts and our cares.
And of - ten for each oth - er flows The sym - pa - thiz - ing tear.
And per - fect love and friend - ship reign Through all e - ter - ni - ty. A-MEN.

# 344

Composite based on
John Greenleaf Whittier (1807-1892)    8. 8. 8.    O MENSCH SIEH
Bohemian Brethren's "Gesangbuch," 1566

*Rather slowly*

1. For - give, O Lord, our sev - ering ways, The ri - val
2. Thy grace im - part; in time to be Shall one great
3. White flowers of love its walls shall climb, Soft bells of
4. A sweet - er song shall then be heard, Con - fess - ing,
5. That song shall swell from shore to shore, One hope, one

al - tars that we raise, The wran - gling tongues that mar Thy praise.
tem - ple rise to Thee— One Church for all hu - man - i - ty.
peace shall ring its chime, Its days shall all be ho - ly time.
in a world's ac - cord, The in - ward Christ, the liv - ing Word.
faith, one love re - store The seam - less robe that Je - sus wore. A-MEN.

Bernhardt S. Ingemann, 1825
Trans. by Rev. Sabine Baring-Gould, 1867, 1875

ST. ASAPH
William S. Bambridge, 1872

8. 7. 8. 7. D.

*With exultation*

1. Through the night of doubt and sor - row On - ward goes the pil - grim band,
2. One the light of God's own pres - ence O'er His ran - somed peo - ple shed,
3. One the strain that lips of thou - sands Lift as from the heart of one,
4. On - ward, there - fore, pil - grim broth - ers, On - ward, with the cross our aid;

Sing - ing songs of ex - pec - ta - tion, March - ing to the prom - ised land:
Chas - ing far the gloom and ter - ror, Bright-ening all the path we tread;
One the con - flict, one the per - il, One the march in God be - gun;
Bear its shame, and fight its bat - tle, Till we rest be - neath its shade;

Clear be - fore us through the dark - ness Gleams and burns the guid - ing light;
One the ob - ject of our jour - ney, One the faith which nev - er tires,
One the glad - ness of re - joi - cing On the far e - ter - nal shore,
Soon shall come the great a - wak - ing, Soon the rend - ing of the tomb,

Broth - er clasps the hand of broth - er, Step-ping fear - less through the night.
One the ear - nest look-ing for - ward, One the hope our God in - spires;
Where the One Al - might - y Fa - ther Reigns in love for - ev - er-more.
Then the scat-tering of all shad-ows And the end of toil and gloom. A-MEN.

Words used by permission of A. W. Ridley and Company.

# 346

## Christian Fellowship

Alexander Pope, 1712
Stanza 3, line 4, alt.

10. 10. 10. 10.

RUSSIAN HYMN
Alexis T. Lwoff, 1833

*With majesty*

1. Rise, crowned with light, im-pe-rial Sa-lem, rise!
2. See a long race thy spa-cious courts a-dorn:
3. The seas shall waste, the skies in smoke de-cay,

Ex-alt thy tow-ering head and lift thine eyes!
See fu-ture sons, and daugh-ters yet un-born,
Rocks fall to dust, and moun-tains melt a-way;

See heaven its spar-kling por-tals wide dis-play,
In crowd-ing ranks on ev-ery side a-rise,
But fixed His word, His sav-ing power re-mains;

And break up-on thee in a flood of day!
De-mand-ing life, im-pa-tient for the skies.
Thy realm shall last, thy own Mes-si-ah reigns! A-MEN.

# 347

Rev. John Cennick, 1742      7. 7. 7. 7.      PLEYEL'S HYMN

Arr. from Ignaz J. Pleyel, 1790

*With spirit*

1. Chil - dren of the heaven-ly King, As ye jour - ney, sweet-ly sing;
2. We are travel - ing home to God In the way the fa - thers trod;
3. Fear not, breth - ren; joy - ful stand On the bor - ders of your land.
4. Lord, o - be - dient - ly we go, Glad-ly leav - ing all be - low;

Sing your Sav - iour's wor - thy praise, Glo - rious in His works and ways.
They are hap - py now, and we Soon their hap - pi - ness shall see.
Je - sus Christ, your Fa - ther's Son, Bids you un - dis-mayed go on.
On - ly Thou our Lead - er be, And we still will fol - low Thee. A-MEN.

# 348

Baptism

Rev. William A. Muhlenberg, 1826      8. 7. 8. 7.      BROCKLESBURY

Charlotte A. Barnard, 1868

*In moderate time*

1. Sav - iour, who Thy flock art feed - ing With the shep-herd's kind-est care,
2. Now, these lit - tle ones re - ceiv - ing, Fold them in Thy gra-cious arm;
3. Nev - er, from Thy pas - ture rov - ing, Let them wan-der far a - way;
4. Then, with - in Thy fold e - ter - nal, Let them find a rest-ing place,

All the fee - ble gen - tly lead-ing, While the lambs Thy bos - om share;
There, we know, Thy word be - liev-ing, On - ly there se - cure from harm.
Let Thy ten - der-ness, so lov-ing, Keep them through life's dan-gerous way.
Feed in pas-tures ev - er ver-nal, Drink the riv - ers of Thy grace. A-MEN.

**349**

Bishop Reginald Heber, 1812    C. M.    Isaac B. Woodbury, 1842
SILOAM

*In moderate time, with graceful rhythm*

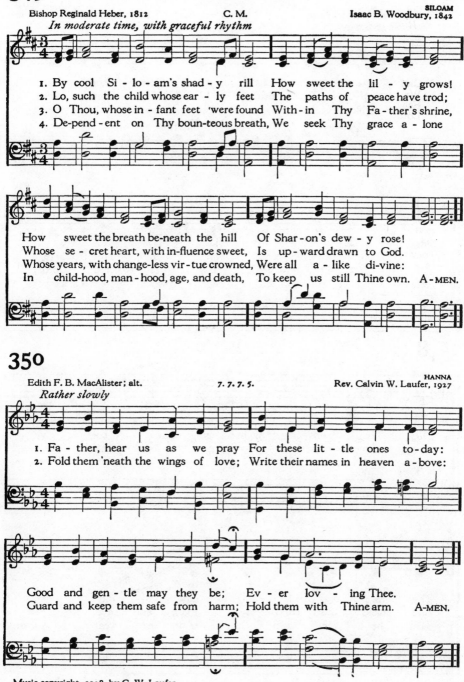

1. By cool Si - lo - am's shad - y rill    How    sweet the    lil - y grows!
2. Lo, such the child whose ear - ly feet    The    paths of    peace have trod;
3. O Thou, whose in - fant feet 'were found    With - in    Thy    Fa - ther's shrine,
4. De - pend - ent on Thy boun - teous breath, We    seek Thy    grace a - lone

How    sweet the breath be-neath the hill    Of Shar - on's dew - y rose!
Whose se - cret heart, with in-fluence sweet,    Is up - ward drawn to God.
Whose years, with change-less vir - tue crowned, Were all    a - like    di - vine:
In    child-hood, man - hood, age, and death, To keep    us    still Thine own.    A-MEN.

**350**

Edith F. B. MacAlister; alt.    7. 7. 7. 5.    Rev. Calvin W. Laufer, 1927
HANNA

*Rather slowly*

1. Fa - ther, hear us    as    we pray For these lit - tle    ones    to-day:
2. Fold them 'neath the wings of    love; Write their names in heaven a - bove:

Good and gen - tle may they    be;    Ev - er lov - ing Thee.
Guard and keep them safe from    harm; Hold them with    Thine arm.    A-MEN.

Music copyright, 1928, by C. W. Laufer.

Heinrich von Laufenberg, d. c. 1458
Trans. by Catherine Winkworth      L. M.      VOM HIMMEL HOCH
"Geistliche Lieder," Leipzig, 1539

*In moderate time*

1. Lord Jesus Christ, our Lord most dear,
As Thou wast once an infant here,
So give this child of Thine, we pray,
Thy grace and blessing day by day.

2. As in Thy heavenly Kingdom, Lord,
All things obey Thy sacred word,
Do Thou Thy mighty succor give,
And shield this child by morn and eve.

3. Their watch let angels round him keep
Wher-e'er he be, awake, asleep;
Thy holy cross now let him bear,
That he Thy crown with saints may wear. A-MEN.

# 352 The Lord's Supper

Rev. Horatius Bonar, 1855

10. 10. 10. 10.

MORECAMBE
Frederick C. Atkinson, 1870

*Rather slowly, with deep reverence*

1. Here, O my Lord, I see Thee face to face;
Here would I touch and han - dle things un - seen,
Here grasp with firm - er hand e - ter - nal grace,
And all my wea - ri - ness up - on Thee lean.

2. Here would I feed up - on the bread of God,
Here drink with Thee the roy - al wine of heaven;
Here would I lay a - side each earth - ly load,
Here taste a - fresh the calm of sin for - given.

3. This is the hour of ban - quet and of song;
This is the heaven - ly ta - ble spread for me:
Here let me feast, and, feast - ing, still pro - long
The brief, bright hour of fel - low - ship with Thee.

4. I have no help but Thine, nor do I need
An - oth - er arm save Thine to lean up - on:
It is e - nough, my Lord, e - nough in - deed;
My strength is in Thy might, Thy might a - lone.

A-MEN.

# 353

## The Church and the Sacraments

Bishop Reginald Heber, 1827      9. 8. 9. 8.      EUCHARISTIC HYMN
Rev. John S. B. Hodges, 1869

*Rather slowly*

1. Bread of the world in mer - cy bro-ken, Wine of the soul in mer - cy shed;
2. Look on the heart by sor - row bro-ken, Look on the tears by sin - ners shed;

By whom the words of life were spo-ken, And in whose death our sins are dead:
And be Thy feast to us the to-ken That by Thy grace our souls are fed. A-MEN.

# 354

Anon. (Latin, 11th century)
Trans. and arr. by Rev. Ray Palmer, 1858      L. M.      QUEBEC
Henry Baker, 1862

*In moderate time*

1. Je - sus, Thou Joy of lov - ing hearts, Thou Fount of life, Thou Light of men,
2. Thy truth un-changed hath ev - er stood; Thou sav - est those that on Thee call;
3. We taste Thee, O Thou liv - ing Bread, And long to feast up - on Thee still;
4. Our rest-less spir - its yearn for Thee, Wher-e'er our change-ful lot is cast,
5. O Je - sus, ev - er with us stay, Make all our mo-ments calm and bright;

From the best bliss that earth im-parts We turn un - filled to Thee a - gain.
To them that seek Thee Thou art good, To them that find Thee All in all.
We drink of Thee, the Foun-tain-head, And thirst our souls from Thee to fill.
Glad when Thy gra-cious smile we see, Blest when our faith can hold Thee fast.
Chase the dark night of sin a - way, Shed o'er the world Thy ho - ly light. A-MEN.

# The Lord's Supper

Rev. William Bright, 1874

10. 10. 10. 10. 10. 10.

UNDE ET MEMORES
William H. Monk, 1875

*In moderate time*

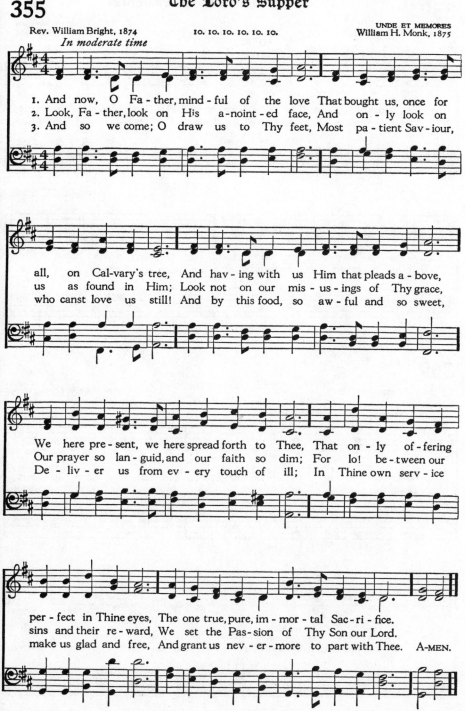

1. And now, O Fa-ther, mind-ful of the love That bought us, once for all, on Cal-vary's tree, And hav-ing with us Him that pleads a-bove, We here pre-sent, we here spread forth to Thee, That on-ly of-fering per-fect in Thine eyes, The one true, pure, im-mor-tal Sac-ri-fice.

2. Look, Fa-ther, look on His a-noint-ed face, And on-ly look on us as found in Him; Look not on our mis-us-ings of Thy grace, Our prayer so lan-guid, and our faith so dim; For lo! be-tween our sins and their re-ward, We set the Pas-sion of Thy Son our Lord.

3. And so we come; O draw us to Thy feet, Most pa-tient Sav-iour, who canst love us still! And by this food, so aw-ful and so sweet, De-liv-er us from ev-ery touch of ill; In Thine own serv-ice make us glad and free, And grant us nev-er-more to part with Thee. A-MEN.

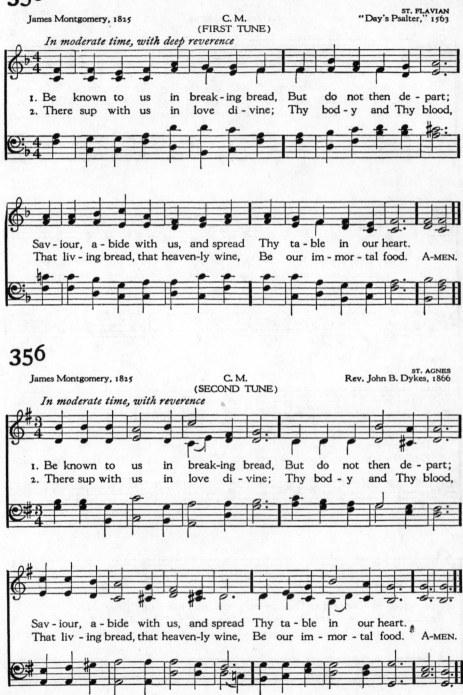

James Montgomery, 1825

C. M.
(FIRST TUNE)

ST. FLAVIAN
"Day's Psalter," 1563

*In moderate time, with deep reverence*

1. Be known to us in break-ing bread, But do not then de - part;
2. There sup with us in love di - vine; Thy bod - y and Thy blood,

Sav - iour, a - bide with us, and spread Thy ta - ble in our heart.
That liv - ing bread, that heaven-ly wine, Be our im - mor - tal food. A-MEN.

James Montgomery, 1825

C. M.
(SECOND TUNE)

ST. AGNES
Rev. John B. Dykes, 1866

*In moderate time, with reverence*

1. Be known to us in break-ing bread, But do not then de - part;
2. There sup with us in love di - vine; Thy bod - y and Thy blood,

Sav - iour, a - bide with us, and spread Thy ta - ble in our heart.
That liv - ing bread, that heaven-ly wine, Be our im - mor - tal food. A-MEN.

**357**

Anon.
Trans. by Rev. Philip Schaff, 1869

7. 7. 6. 7. 7. 6.

BREAD OF LIFE (WARREN)
Samuel P. Warren

*Not too fast; with feeling*

1. O Bread of life from heav - en, To saints and an - gels
2. O fount of grace re - deem - ing, O riv - er ev - er
3. Je - sus, this feast re - ceiv - ing, Thy word of truth be -

giv - en, O Man - na from a - bove!
stream - ing From Je - sus' ho - ly side!
liev - ing, We Thee un - seen a - dore!

The souls that hun - ger, feed Thou, The hearts that seek Thee,
Come Thou, Thy - self be - stow - ing On thirst - ing souls, and
Grant, when the veil is rend - ed, That we, to heaven as -

lead Thou, With Thy sweet, ten - der love.
flow - ing Till all are sat - is - fied.
cend - ed, May see Thee ev - er - more. A-MEN.

# 358

James Montgomery, 1825      C. M.      DALEHURST<br>
Arthur Cottman, 1874

*Rather slowly*

1. Ac - cord - ing to Thy gra - cious word, In meek hu - mil - i - ty,
2. Thy bod - y, bro - ken for my sake, My bread from heaven shall be;
3. When to the cross I turn mine eyes, And rest on Cal - va - ry,
4. Re - mem - ber Thee, and all Thy pains, And all Thy love to me:
5. And when these fail - ing lips grow dumb, And mind and mem - ory flee,

This will I do, my dy - ing Lord, I will re - mem - ber Thee.
Thy tes - ta - men - tal cup I take, And thus re - mem - ber Thee.
O Lamb of God, my Sac - ri - fice, I must re - mem - ber Thee;
Yea, while a breath, a pulse re - mains Will I re - mem - ber Thee.
When Thou shalt in Thy King-dom come, Je - sus, re - mem - ber me. A-MEN.

# 359

Rev. Louis F. Benson, 1924      8. 7. 8. 7.      AGAPE<br>
Rev. C. J. Dickinson (1822–1883)

*Rather slowly*

1. For the bread, which Thou hast bro - ken; For the wine, which Thou hast poured;
2. By this pledge that Thou dost love us, By Thy gift of peace re - stored,
3. With our saint - ed ones in glo - ry Seat - ed at our Fa - ther's board,
4. In Thy serv - ice, Lord, de - fend us, In our hearts keep watch and ward,

For the words, which Thou hast spo - ken; Now we give Thee thanks, O Lord.
By Thy call to heaven a - bove us, Hal-low all our lives, O Lord.
May the Church that wait - eth for Thee Keep love's tie un - bro - ken, Lord.
In the world where Thou dost send us Let Thy King-dom come, O Lord. A-MEN.

Words used by permission of Mrs. Robert F. Jefferys.

Rev. John Morison (1749-1798)
As in "Scottish Paraphrases," 1781     L. M.     ROCKINGHAM OLD
Edward Miller, 1790

*Moderately slow*

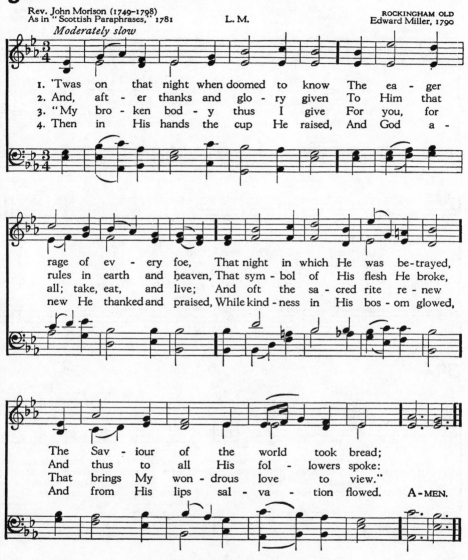

1. 'Twas on that night when doomed to know The ea - ger
2. And, aft - er thanks and glo - ry given To Him that
3. "My bro - ken bod - y thus I give For you, for
4. Then in His hands the cup He raised, And God a -

rage of ev - ery foe, That night in which He was be-trayed,
rules in earth and heaven, That sym - bol of His flesh He broke,
all; take, eat, and live; And oft the sa - cred rite re - new
new He thanked and praised, While kind - ness in His bos - om glowed,

The Sav - iour of the world took bread;
And thus to all His fol - lowers spoke:
That brings My won - drous love to view."
And from His lips sal - va - tion flowed. A - MEN.

5. "My blood I thus pour forth," He cries,
    "To cleanse the soul in sin that lies;
    In this the covenant is sealed,
    And heaven's eternal grace revealed.

6. "With love to man this cup is fraught;
    Let all partake the sacred draught;
    Through latest ages let it pour,
    In memory of My dying hour."

Rev. Robert H. Baynes, 1864     7. 7. 7.     MELFORD "M. B. F.," 1886

*Rather slowly*

1. Je - sus, to Thy ta - ble led, Now let ev - ery
2. While in pen - i - tence we kneel, Thy sweet pres - ence
3. While on Thy dear cross we gaze, Mourn-ing o'er our
4. When we taste the mys - tic wine, Of Thine out - poured
5. From the bonds of sin re - lease, Cold and wav - ering

heart be fed With the true and liv - ing Bread.
let us feel, All Thy won - drous love re - veal.
sin - ful ways, Turn our sad - ness in - to praise.
blood the sign, Fill our hearts with love di - vine.
faith in - crease; Lamb of God, grant us Thy peace. A - MEN.

# 362

Rev. Aaron R. Wolfe, 1858     S. M.     SCHUMANN Mason and Webb's "Cantica Laudis," Boston, 1850

*Not too fast; with solemnity*

1. A part - ing hymn we sing A - round Thy ta - ble, Lord;
2. Here have we seen Thy face, And felt Thy pres - ence here;
3. The pur - chase of Thy blood, By sin no lon - ger led,
4. In self - for - get - ting love Be our com - mun - ion shown,

A - gain our grate - ful trib - ute bring, Our sol - emn vows re - cord.
So may the sa - vor of Thy grace In word and life ap - pear.
The path our dear Re - deem - er trod May we re - joi - cing tread.
Un - til we join the Church a - bove, And know as we are known. A - MEN.

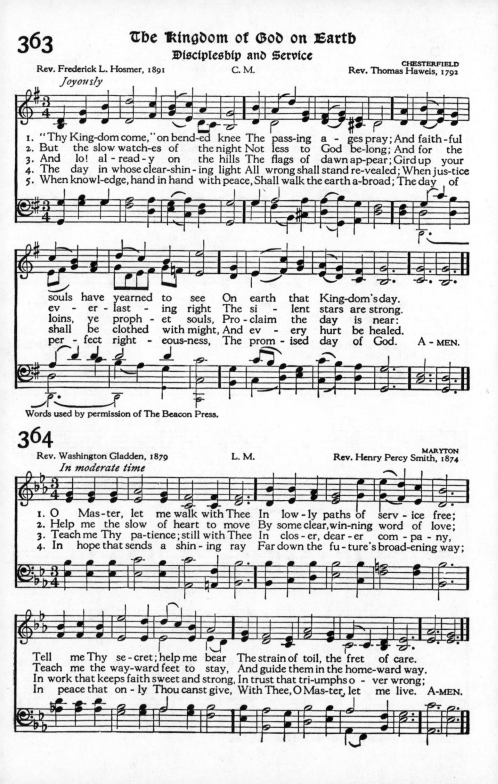

# 363
## The Kingdom of God on Earth
### Discipleship and Service

Rev. Frederick L. Hosmer, 1891       C. M.      CHESTERFIELD
Rev. Thomas Haweis, 1792

*Joyously*

1. "Thy King-dom come," on bend-ed knee The pass-ing a - ges pray; And faith-ful
2. But the slow watch-es of the night Not less to God be-long; And for the
3. And lo! al - read - y on the hills The flags of dawn ap-pear; Gird up your
4. The day in whose clear-shin-ing light All wrong shall stand re-vealed; When jus-tice
5. When knowl-edge, hand in hand with peace, Shall walk the earth a-broad; The day of

souls have yearned to see On earth that King-dom's day.
ev - er - last - ing right The si - lent stars are strong.
loins, ye proph - et souls, Pro - claim the day is near:
shall be clothed with might, And ev - ery hurt be healed.
per - fect right - eous-ness, The prom - ised day of God. A - MEN.

Words used by permission of The Beacon Press.

# 364

Rev. Washington Gladden, 1879      L. M.      MARYTON
Rev. Henry Percy Smith, 1874

*In moderate time*

1. O Mas-ter, let me walk with Thee In low-ly paths of serv-ice free;
2. Help me the slow of heart to move By some clear, win-ning word of love;
3. Teach me Thy pa-tience; still with Thee In clos - er, dear - er com - pa - ny,
4. In hope that sends a shin - ing ray Far down the fu-ture's broad-ening way;

Tell me Thy se - cret; help me bear The strain of toil, the fret of care.
Teach me the way-ward feet to stay, And guide them in the home-ward way.
In work that keeps faith sweet and strong, In trust that tri-umphs o - ver wrong;
In peace that on - ly Thou canst give, With Thee, O Mas-ter, let me live. A-MEN.

# The Kingdom of God on Earth

Rev. Sabine Baring–Gould, 1865      6. 5. 6. 5. D. with Refrain      ST. GERTRUDE
Arthur S. Sullivan, 1871

*With martial rhythm*

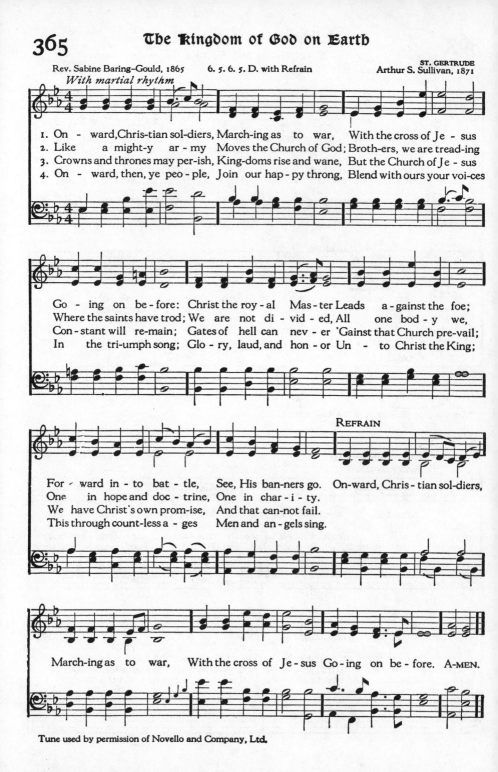

1. On - ward, Chris-tian sol-diers, March-ing as to war, With the cross of Je - sus
2. Like a might-y ar - my Moves the Church of God; Broth-ers, we are tread-ing
3. Crowns and thrones may per-ish, King-doms rise and wane, But the Church of Je - sus
4. On - ward, then, ye peo - ple, Join our hap - py throng, Blend with ours your voi-ces

Go - ing on be - fore: Christ the roy - al Mas - ter Leads a - gainst the foe;
Where the saints have trod; We are not di - vid - ed, All one bod - y we,
Con - stant will re - main; Gates of hell can nev - er 'Gainst that Church pre-vail;
In the tri-umph song; Glo - ry, laud, and hon - or Un - to Christ the King;

**REFRAIN**

For - ward in - to bat - tle, See, His ban-ners go. On-ward, Chris - tian sol-diers,
One in hope and doc - trine, One in char - i - ty.
We have Christ's own prom-ise, And that can-not fail.
This through count-less a - ges Men and an - gels sing.

March-ing as to war, With the cross of Je - sus Go-ing on be - fore. A-MEN.

Tune used by permission of Novello and Company, Ltd.

Tune used by permission of Dr. T. Tertius Noble.

# 367 The Kingdom of God on Earth

Rev. Calvin W. Laufer, 1919  10. 10. 10. 10.  Rev. Calvin W. Laufer, 1919  FIELD

*In moderate time*

1. We thank Thee, Lord, Thy paths of serv - ice lead
2. We've sought and found Thee in the se - cret place
3. We've felt Thy touch in sor - row's dark - ened way
4. We've seen Thy glo - ry like a man - tle spread

To bla - zoned heights and down the slopes of need;
And mar - veled at the ra - diance of Thy face;
A - bound with love and sol - ace for the day;
O'er hill and dale in saf - fron flame and red;

They reach Thy throne, en - com - pass land and sea,
But of - ten in some far - off Gal - i - lee
And, 'neath the bur - dens there, Thy sov - reign - ty
But in the eyes of men, re - deemed and free,

And he who jour - neys in them walks with Thee.
Be - held Thee fair - er yet while serv - ing Thee.
Has held our hearts en - thralled while serv - ing Thee.
A splen - dor great - er yet while serv - ing Thee. A - MEN.

Copyright, 1919, by Calvin W. Laufer.

Rev. Shepherd Knapp, 1907      11. 10. 11. 10.      WELWYN
Alfred Scott-Gatty (1847-1918)

*With marked rhythm. May be sung in unison*

1. Lord God of Hosts, whose pur - pose, nev - er swerv - ing,
2. Strong Son of God, whose work was His that sent Thee,
3. O Prince of Peace, Thou bring - er of good ti - dings,
4. Lord God, whose grace has called us to Thy serv - ice,

Leads toward the day of Je - sus Christ Thy Son,
One with the Fa - ther, thought and deed and word,
Teach us to speak Thy word of hope and cheer—
How good Thy thoughts toward us, how great their sum!

Grant us to march a - mong Thy faith - ful le - gions,
One make us all, true com - rades in Thy serv - ice,
Rest for the soul, and strength for all man's striv - ing,
We work with Thee, we go where Thou wilt lead us,

Armed with Thy cour - age, till the world is won.
And make us one in Thee with God the Lord.
Light for the path of life, and God brought near.
Un - til in all the earth Thy King - dom come. A-MEN.

Tune used by permission of The Very Reverend the Abbot of Downside.
Words copyright, 1907, by Rev. Shepherd Knapp. Used by permission.

Rev. Henry Alford, 1871
Stanzas 2, 3, alt.

6. 5. 6. 5. 12l.

FORWARD
Henry Smart, 1872

*With spirit*

1. "For-ward!" be our watch-word, Steps and voi-ces joined; Seek the things be-fore us,
2. Far  o'er yon ho - ri - zon  Rise the cit - y towers,  Where our God a-bid - eth;
3. To  th' e-ter - nal Fa -ther  Loud-est an-thems raise, To the Son, and Spir - it,

Not  a  look be - hind: Burns the fi - ery pil - lar  At our ar-my's head;
That fair home is  ours: Flash the streets with jas - per,  Shine the gates with gold;
Ech - o  songs of praise, To  the Lord of  glo - ry,  Bless-ed Three in One,

Who shall dream of shrink-ing, By  our Cap-tain led? For-ward through the des - ert,
Flows the glad-dening riv - er, Shed-ding joys un - told. Thith-er,  on-ward thith-er,
Be  by men and  an - gels End-less hon - or done. Weak are earth - ly prais - es,

Through the toil and fight; Jor-dan flows be-fore  us,  Zi - on beams with light.
In  the Spir-it's might; Pil-grims to your coun - try,  For-ward in - to light!
Dull  the songs of night: For-ward in - to  tri - umph, For-ward in - to  light! A-MEN.

# 370

## Discipleship and Service

Rev. Marion Franklin Ham, 1912      10. 10. 10. 10.      Horatio W. Parker, 1894

PRO PATRIA

*In march rhythm*

1. O Lord of life, Thy King - dom is at hand,
2. Lo! in our hearts shines forth the morn - ing star,
3. Now gleams at last up - on our wait - ing eyes
4. For - ward a - gain we move at Thy com - mand,

Blest reign of love and lib - er - ty and light;
Shed - ding its lus - ter on our dark - ened way;
The glo - ry of the King - dom that shall be;
The flam - ing pil - lar lead - ing on a - new;

Time long fore - told by seers of ev - ery land;
And we be - hold, as pil - grims from a - far,
When truth in con - quering gran - deur shall a - rise,
One in the faith of all Thy proph - et band,

The cher - ished dream of watch - ers through the night.
The ho - ly dawn - ing of Thy per - fect day.
And man shall rule the world with eq - ui - ty.
On - ward we press to make the vi - sion true. A - MEN.

Words from "Hymn and Tune Book." Copyright by The Beacon Press. Used by permission.
Tune used by permission of Mrs. Horatio W. Parker.

# The Kingdom of God on Earth

LLANGLOFFAN
Welsh hymn melody

Rev. Ernest W. Shurtleff, 1888     7. 6. 7. 6. D.     D. Evans' "Hymnau a Thonau," 1865

*In moderate time, with martial rhythm*

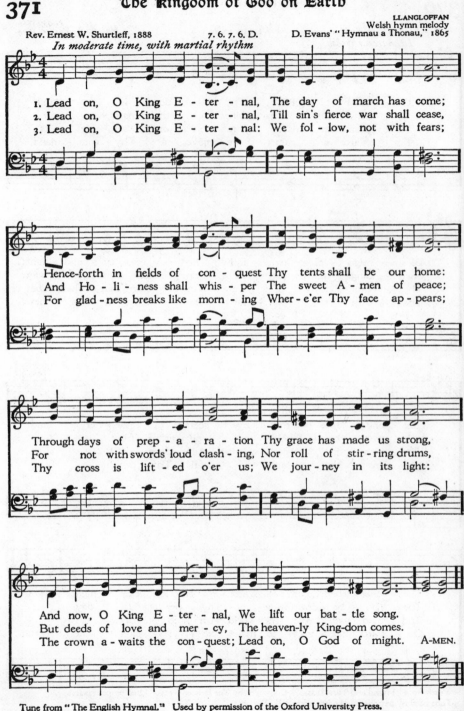

1. Lead on, O King E - ter - nal, The day of march has come;
2. Lead on, O King E - ter - nal, Till sin's fierce war shall cease,
3. Lead on, O King E - ter - nal: We fol - low, not with fears;

Hence-forth in fields of con - quest Thy tents shall be our home:
And Ho - li - ness shall whis - per The sweet A - men of peace;
For glad - ness breaks like morn - ing Wher - e'er Thy face ap - pears;

Through days of prep - a - ra - tion Thy grace has made us strong,
For not with swords' loud clash - ing, Nor roll of stir - ring drums,
Thy cross is lift - ed o'er us; We jour - ney in its light:

And now, O King E - ter - nal, We lift our bat - tle song.
But deeds of love and mer - cy, The heaven-ly King-dom comes.
The crown a - waits the con - quest; Lead on, O God of might. A-MEN.

Tune from "The English Hymnal." Used by permission of the Oxford University Press.

# Discipleship and Service

Bishop Edward H. Bickersteth, 1848     7. 6. 7. 6. D.     **LANCASHIRE**
                                                    Henry Smart, 1836

*With marked rhythm*

1. O broth-ers, lift your voi-ces, Tri-um-phant songs to raise;
2. O Chris-tian broth-ers, glo-rious Shall be the con-flict's close;
3. Not un-to us, Lord Je-sus: To Thee all praise be due,
4. Great God of our sal-va-tion, Thy pres-ence we a-dore;

Till heaven on high re-joi-ces, And earth is filled with praise:
The cross hath been vic-to-rious, And shall be o'er its foes:
Whose blood-bought mer-cy frees us, Has freed our breth-ren too.
Praise, glo-ry, ad-o-ra-tion Be Thine for-ev-er-more;

Ten thou-sand hearts are bound-ing With ho-ly hopes and free;
Faith is our bat-tle to-ken; Our Lead-er all con-trols;
Not un-to us: in glo-ry The an-gels catch the strain,
Still on in con-flict press-ing On Thee Thy peo-ple call,

The gos-pel trump is sound-ing, The trump of Ju-bi-lee.
Our tro-phies, fet-ters bro-ken; Our cap-tives, ran-somed souls.
And cast their crowns be-fore Thee Ex-ult-ing-ly a-gain.
Thee King of kings con-fess-ing, Thee crown-ing Lord of all. A-MEN.

# The Kingdom of God on Earth

James Russell Lowell, 1845
Stanza 3, line 2, alt.

8. 7. 8. 7. D.

TON-Y-BOTEL
Welsh hymn melody

*In unison, with great breadth*

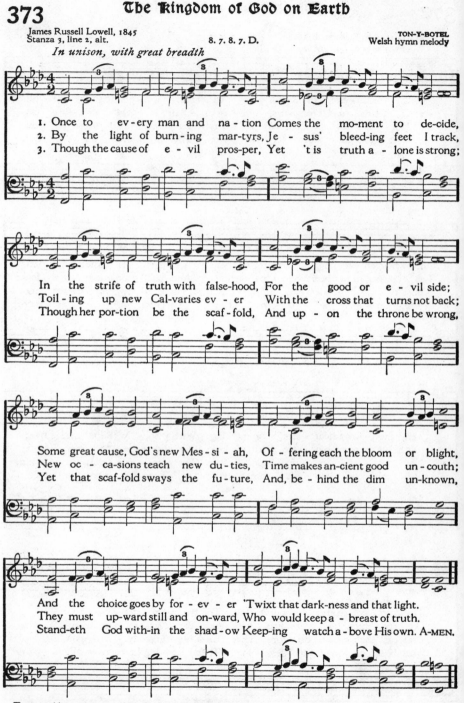

1. Once to ev-ery man and na-tion Comes the mo-ment to de-cide,
2. By the light of burn-ing mar-tyrs, Je - sus' bleed-ing feet I track,
3. Though the cause of e - vil pros-per, Yet 't is truth a - lone is strong;

In the strife of truth with false-hood, For the good or e - vil side;
Toil - ing up new Cal-varies ev - er With the cross that turns not back;
Though her por-tion be the scaf - fold, And up - on the throne be wrong,

Some great cause, God's new Mes - si - ah, Of - fering each the bloom or blight,
New oc - ca-sions teach new du - ties, Time makes an-cient good un - couth;
Yet that scaf-fold sways the fu - ture, And, be - hind the dim un-known,

And the choice goes by for - ev - er 'Twixt that dark-ness and that light.
They must up-ward still and on-ward, Who would keep a - breast of truth.
Stand-eth God with-in the shad - ow Keep-ing watch a - bove His own. A-MEN.

Tune used by permission of W. Gwenlyn Evans and Sons.

**374**

Bishop Arthur Cleveland Coxe, 1840; alt.     8. 7. 8. 7. D.

BLAENHAFREN
Traditional Welsh melody

*In unison, with great breadth*

1. We are liv-ing, we are dwell-ing In a grand and aw-ful time,
2. Will ye play, then? will ye dal-ly Far be-hind the bat-tle line?
3. Sworn to yield, to wa-ver, nev-er; Con-se-crat-ed, born a-gain;

In an age on a-ges tell-ing; To be liv-ing is sub-lime.
Up! it is Je-ho-vah's ral-ly; God's own arm hath need of thine.
Sworn to be Christ's sol-diers ev-er, O for Christ at least be men!

Hark! the wak-ing up of na-tions, Hosts ad-van-cing to the fray;
Worlds are char-ging, heaven be-hold-ing; Thou hast but an hour to fight;
O let all the soul with-in you For the truth's sake go a-broad!

Hark! what sound-eth is cre-a-tion's Groan-ing for the lat-ter day.
Now, the bla-zoned cross un-fold-ing, On, right on-ward for the right!
Strike! let ev-ery nerve and sin-ew Tell on a-ges, tell for God. A-MEN.

## 375 The Kingdom of God on Earth

Ebenezer Elliott, 1850     7. 6. 7. 6. 8. 8. 8. 5.     COMMONWEALTH
Josiah Booth, 1888

*In moderate time*

1. When wilt Thou save the peo - ple? O God of mer - cy, when?
2. Shall crime bring crime for - ev - er, Strength aid - ing still the strong?
3. When wilt Thou save the peo - ple? O God of mer - cy, when?

Not kings and lords, but na - tions! Not thrones and crowns, but men!
Is it Thy will, O Fa - ther, That man shall toil for wrong?
The peo - ple, Lord, the peo - ple, Not thrones and crowns, but men!

Flowers of Thy heart, O God, are they; Let them not pass, like weeds, a - way,
"No," say Thy moun-tains; "No," Thy skies; Man's cloud-ed sun shall bright-ly rise,
God save the peo - ple; Thine they are, Thy chil-dren, as Thine an - gels fair;

Their her - it - age a sun - less day. God save the peo - ple!
And songs as - cend, in - stead of sighs. God save the peo - ple!
From vice, op - pres-sion, and de - spair, God save the peo - ple! A-MEN.

Tune used by permission of Clifford Booth.

**376**

Rev. Horatius Bonar, 1843                    L. M.                    Rev. William Boyd, 1868

PENTECOST

*With spirit*

1. Go, la-bor on: spend, and be spent, Thy joy to do the Fa-ther's will:
2. Go, la-bor on; 'tis not for nought; Thy earth-ly loss is heaven-ly gain:
3. Go la-bor on while it is day: The world's dark night is hasten-ing on;
4. Toil on, faint not, keep watch and pray, Be wise the err-ing soul to win;

It is the way the Mas-ter went; Should not the serv-ant tread it still?
Men heed thee, love thee, praise thee not; The Mas-ter prais-es: what are men?
Speed, speed thy work, cast sloth a-way; It is not thus that souls are won.
Go forth in-to the world's high-way, Com-pel the wan-derer to come in.   A-MEN.

Tune used by permission of Novello and Company, Ltd.

**377**

Psalm lxxii. Rev. Isaac Watts, 1719                    L. M.                    John Hatton, d. 1793

DUKE STREET

*With exultation*

1. Je - sus shall reign wher-e'er the sun Does his suc-ces-sive jour-neys run;
2. For Him shall end-less prayer be made, And prais-es throng to crown His head;
3. Peo-ple and realms of ev-ery tongue Dwell on His love with sweet-est song;
4. Bless-ings a-bound wher-e'er He reigns; The pris-oner leaps to lose his chains,
5. Let ev-ery crea-ture rise and bring Pe - cu-liar hon-ors to our King;

His King-dom stretch from shore to shore, Till moons shall wax and wane no more.
His Name, like sweet per-fume, shall rise With ev-ery morn-ing sac-ri-fice.
And in-fant voi-ces shall pro-claim Their ear-ly bless-ings on His Name.
The wea-ry find e - ter-nal rest, And all the sons of want are blest.
An - gels de-scend with songs a-gain, And earth re-peat the loud A - men! A-MEN.

Rev. Samuel Wolcott, 1869　　　　6. 6. 4. 6. 6. 6. 4.　　TRINITY (ITALIAN HYMN)
Felice de Giardini, 1769

*In moderate time. With spirit*

1. Christ for the world we sing; The world to
2. Christ for the world we sing; The world to
3. Christ for the world we sing; The world to
4. Christ for the world we sing; The world to

Christ we bring With lov - ing zeal; The poor and
Christ we bring With fer - vent prayer; The way - ward
Christ we bring With one ac - cord; With us the
Christ we bring With joy - ful song; The new - born

them that mourn, The faint and o - ver - borne,
and the lost, By rest - less pas - sions tossed,
work to share, With us re - proach to dare,
souls whose days, Re - claimed from er - ror's ways,

Sin - sick and sor - row-worn, Whom Christ doth heal.
Re - deemed at count - less cost From dark de - spair.
With us the cross to bear, For Christ our Lord.
In - spired with hope and praise, To Christ be - long. A - MEN.

Laura S. Copenhaver, 1894
With martial rhythm

10. 10. 10. 10.

NATIONAL HYMN
George William Warren, 1892

*Trumpets, before each stanza*

1. Her-alds of Christ, who bear the King's com-mands,
2. Through des-ert ways, dark fen, and deep mo-rass,
3. Where once the crook-ed trail in dark-ness wound
4. Lord, give us faith and strength the road to build,

Im - mor - tal ti - dings in your mor - tal hands,
Through jun - gles, slug - gish seas, and moun - tain pass,
Let march - ing feet and joy - ous song re - sound,
To see the prom - ise of the day ful - filled,

Pass on and car - ry swift the news ye bring:
Build ye the road, and fal - ter not, nor stay;
Where burn the fu - neral pyres, and cen - sers swing,
When war shall be no more and strife shall cease

Make straight, make straight the high - way of the King.
Pre - pare a - cross the earth the King's high - way.
Make straight, make straight the high - way of the King.
Up - on the high - way of the Prince of Peace. A-MEN.

Words used by permission of Mrs. Horatio W. Parker.

# The Kingdom of God on Earth

Rev. Godfrey Thring, 1873     6. 5. 6. 5. D. with Refrain     VALOUR
Arthur H. Mann, 1889

*In march rhythm*

1. From the east-ern moun-tains, Press-ing on they come, . . .
2. Gath-er in the peo-ple, All who've gone a-stray, . . .
3. On-ward through the dark-ness Of the lone-ly night, . . .

Wise Men in their wis-dom To His hum-ble home;
Throw Thy ra-diance o'er them, Guide them on their way:
Shin-ing still be-fore them With Thy kind-ly light,

Stirred by deep de-vo-tion, Hast-ing from a-far, . . .
Those who nev-er knew Thee, Those who've wan-dered far, . . .
Guide them all, Thy chil-dren, Home-ward from a-far, . . .

Ev-er jour-ney-ing on-ward, Guid-ed by a star. . . .
Lead them by the bright-ness Of Thy guid-ing star. . . .
Young and old to-geth-er, By Thy guid-ing star. . . .

# Missions

**REFRAIN**

Light of light that shin-eth Ere the worlds be-gan, . .

Draw Thou near, and light-en Ev-ery heart of man. A-MEN.

## 381

Rev. Bourne H. Draper, 1803      L. M.      MISSIONARY CHANT
Heinrich Christopher Zeuner, 1832

*With spirit, but broadly*

1. Ye Chris-tian her-alds, go pro-claim Sal-va-tion through Em-man-uel's Name;
2. God shield you with a wall of fire, With flam-ing zeal your breasts in-spire,
3. And when our la-bors all are o'er, Then we shall meet to part no more;

To dis-tant climes the ti-dings bear, And plant the Rose of Shar-on there.
Bid ra-ging winds their fu-ry cease, And hush the tem-pests in-to peace.
Meet with the blood-bought throng to fall, And crown our Je-sus Lord of all. A-MEN.

**382**

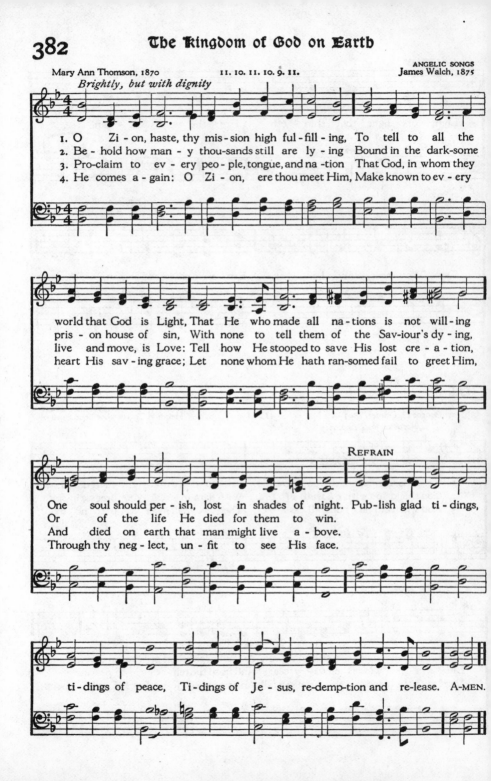

Mary Ann Thomson, 1870     11. 10. 11. 10. 9. 11.     ANGELIC SONGS / James Walch, 1875

*Brightly, but with dignity*

1. O Zi - on, haste, thy mis - sion high ful - fill - ing, To tell to all the
2. Be - hold how man - y thou-sands still are ly - ing Bound in the dark-some
3. Pro-claim to ev - ery peo - ple, tongue, and na - tion That God, in whom they
4. He comes a - gain: O Zi - on, ere thou meet Him, Make known to ev - ery

world that God is Light, That He who made all na - tions is not will - ing
pris - on house of sin, With none to tell them of the Sav-iour's dy - ing,
live and move, is Love: Tell how He stooped to save His lost cre - a - tion,
heart His sav - ing grace; Let none whom He hath ran-somed fail to greet Him,

One soul should per - ish, lost in shades of night. Pub-lish glad ti - dings,
Or of the life He died for them to win.
And died on earth that man might live a - bove.
Through thy neg - lect, un - fit to see His face.

REFRAIN

ti - dings of peace, Ti - dings of Je - sus, re-demp-tion and re-lease. A-MEN.

# 383

Mary C. Gates, 1890

8. 8. 8. 6.
(FIRST TUNE)

ISLEWORTH
Samuel Howard (1710–1782)

*May be sung in unison. Moderately slow*

1. Send Thou, O Lord, to ev - ery place Swift mes - sen - gers be - fore Thy face,
2. Send men whose eyes have seen the King, Men in whose ears His sweet words ring;
3. To bring good news to souls in sin; The bruised and bro - ken hearts to win;
4. Gird each one with the Spir - it's sword, The sword of Thine own death-less Word;

The her-alds of Thy won-drous grace, Where Thou Thy-self wilt come.
Send such Thy lost ones home to bring; Send them where Thou wilt come.
In ev - ery place to bring them in Where Thou Thy-self wilt come.
And make them con-querors, con-quering, Lord, Where Thou Thy-self wilt come. A-MEN.

# 383

Mary C. Gates, 1890

8. 8. 8. 6.
(SECOND TUNE)

ELMHURST
Edwin Drewett, 1887

*In moderate time*

1. Send Thou, O Lord, to ev - ery place Swift mes - sen - gers be - fore Thy face,
2. Send men whose eyes have seen the King, Men in whose ears His sweet words ring;
3. To bring good news to souls in sin; The bruised and bro - ken hearts to win;
4. Gird each one with the Spir - it's sword, The sword of Thine own death-less Word;

The her - alds of Thy won-drous grace, Where Thou Thy-self wilt come.
Send such Thy lost ones home to bring; Send them where Thou wilt come.
In ev - ery place to bring them in Where Thou Thy-self wilt come.
And make them con-querors, con-quering, Lord, Where Thou Thy-self wilt come. A-MEN.

# The Kingdom of God on Earth

Bishop George W. Doane, 1848          L. M.          WALTHAM
J. Baptiste Calkin, 1872

*Moderately fast, with dignity*

1. Fling out the ban - ner! let it float Sky - ward and sea - ward,
2. Fling out the ban - ner! an - gels bend In anx - ious si - lence
3. Fling out the ban - ner! dis - tant lands Shall see from far the
4. Fling out the ban - ner! sin - sick souls That sink and per - ish

high and wide; The sun that lights its shin - ing folds,
o'er the sign, And vain - ly seek to com - pre - hend
glo - rious sight, And na - tions, crowd - ing to be born,
in the strife, Shall touch in faith its ra - diant hem

The Cross on which the Sav - iour died.
The won - der of the Love di - vine.
Bap - tize their spir - its in its light.
And spring im - mor - tal in - to life.          A - MEN.

5. Fling out the banner! let it float
   Skyward and seaward, high and wide,
   Our glory, only in the cross;
   Our only hope, the Crucified!

6. Fling out the banner! wide and high,
   Seaward and skyward, let it shine:
   Nor skill, nor might, nor merit ours;
   We conquer only in that sign.

Tune used by permission of Novello and Company, Ltd.

# 385

## Missions

Bishop Reginald Heber, 1819

7. 6. 7. 6. D.

MISSIONARY HYMN
Lowell Mason, 1823

*Moderately fast*

1. From Green-land's i - cy moun-tains, From In - dia's cor - al strand,
2. Can we, whose souls are light - ed With wis - dom from on high,
3. Waft, waft, ye winds, His sto - ry, And you, ye wa - ters, roll,

Where Af - ric's sun - ny foun - tains Roll down their gold - en sand,
Can we to men be - night - ed The lamp of life de - ny?
Till like a sea of glo - ry It spreads from pole to pole;

From many an an - cient riv - er, From many a palm - y plain,
Sal - va - tion! O sal - va - tion! The joy - ful sound pro - claim,
Till o'er our ran-somed na - ture The Lamb for sin - ners slain,

They call us to de - liv - er Their land from er - ror's chain.
Till each re - mot - est na - tion Has learned Mes - si - ah's Name.
Re - deem - er, King, Cre - a - tor, In bliss re - turns to reign. A-MEN.

Rev. John Ellerton (1826–1893)  11. 10. 11. 10.  DONNE SECOURS
"Genevan Psalter," 1551

*In unison; with moderate time*

1. O Son of God, our Cap-tain of sal-va-tion,
2. Those whom Thy Spir-it's dread vo-ca-tion sev-ers
3. And all true help-ers, pa-tient, kind, and skill-ful,
4. Thus, Lord, Thy bless-ed saints in mem-ory keep-ing,

Thy-self by suf-fering schooled to hu-man grief,
To lead the van-guard of Thy con-quering host;
Who shed Thy light a-cross our dark-ened earth,
Still be Thy Church's watch-word, "Com-fort ye,"

We bless Thee for Thy sons of con-so-la-tion,
Whose toil-some years are spent in brave en-deav-ors
Coun-sel the doubt-ing, and re-strain the will-ful,
Till in our Fa-ther's house shall end all weep-ing,

# Missions

Who fol-low in the steps of Thee their Chief;
To bear Thy sav-ing Name from coast to coast;
Soothe the sick bed, and share the chil-dren's mirth.
And ev-ery want be sat-is-fied in Thee. A-MEN.

Words from "The Church Hymnary," Revised. By permission of the Oxford University Press.

## 387

Margaret E. Sangster (1838–1912)   L. M.   MISSIONARY CHANT
Heinrich Christopher Zeuner, 1832

*Rather slowly*

1. O Christ, for-get not them who stand
2. Thine is the work they strive to do,

Thy van-guard in the dis-tant land. In flood, in
Their foes so man-y, they so few. Be with Thine

flame, in dark, in dread, Sus-tain, we pray, each lift-ed head.
own, Thy loved, who stand, Christ's van-guard, in the storm-swept land. A-MEN.

Words used by permission of Miss Margaret E. Sangster.

# The Kingdom of God on Earth

From Psalm cxvii
Rev. Isaac Watts (1674-1748)

LASST UNS ERFREUEN
"Geistliche Kirchengesäng," Cologne, 1623
8. 8. 4. 4. 8. 8. with Alleluias

*In unison. Jubilantly*

1. From all that dwell be-low the skies   Let   the Cre - a-tor's praise a - rise:
2. In ev-ery land be - gin the song,   To   ev-ery land the strains be-long:
3. E - ter-nal are Thy mer-cies, Lord;   E - ter-nal truth at-tends Thy word:

*Harmony*   *Unison*

Al - le - lu - ia! Al - le - lu - ia!   Let   the Re-deem-er's Name be
Al - le - lu - ia! Al - le - lu - ia!   In   cheer-ful sound all voi - ces
Al - le - lu - ia! Al - le - lu - ia!   Thy praise shall sound from shore to

*Harmony*

sung   Through ev - ery land, in ev - ery tongue.   Al - le - lu - ia! Al - le -
raise   And   fill the world with joy-ful praise.   Al - le - lu - ia! Al - le -
shore,   Till   suns shall rise and set no more.   Al - le - lu - ia! Al - le -

*Unison*   *Harmony*

lu - ia! Al-le-lu - ia! Al-le - lu - ia!   Al-le-lu - ia!
lu - ia! Al-le-lu - ia! Al-le - lu - ia!   Al-le-lu - ia!
lu - ia! Al-le-lu - ia! Al-le - lu - ia!   Al-le-lu - ia!   A-MEN.

Tune from "Songs of Praise." By permission of the Oxford University Press.

**389**

Rev. Samuel F. Smith, 1832  7. 6. 7. 6. D.  WEBB
George J. Webb, 1837

*Jubilantly*

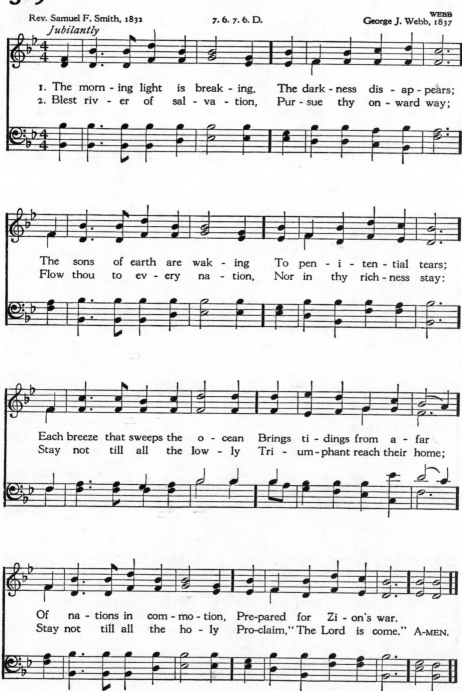

1. The morn - ing light is break - ing, The dark - ness dis - ap - pears;
2. Blest riv - er of sal - va - tion, Pur - sue thy on - ward way;

The sons of earth are wak - ing To pen - i - ten - tial tears;
Flow thou to ev - ery na - tion, Nor in thy rich - ness stay:

Each breeze that sweeps the o - cean Brings ti - dings from a - far
Stay not till all the low - ly Tri - um - phant reach their home;

Of na - tions in com - mo - tion, Pre-pared for Zi - on's war.
Stay not till all the ho - ly Pro-claim, "The Lord is come." A-MEN.

# The Kingdom of God on Earth

Rev. Robert Murray, 1880　　　7. 6. 7. 6. D.　　　LANCASHIRE
Henry Smart, 1836

*Broadly, with exultation*

1. From o-cean un-to o-cean　Our land shall own Thee Lord,
2. O Christ, for Thine own glo-ry,　And for our coun-try's weal,
3. Our Sav-iour King, de-fend us,　And guide where we should go;

And, filled with true de-vo-tion,　O-bey Thy sov-ereign word.
We hum-bly plead be-fore Thee,　Thy-self in us re-veal;
Forth with Thy mes-sage send us,　Thy love and light to show;

Our prai-ries and our moun-tains,　For-est and fer-tile field,
And may we know, Lord Je-sus,　The touch of Thy dear hand;
Till, fired with true de-vo-tion,　En-kin-dled by Thy word,

Our riv-ers, lakes, and foun-tains,　To Thee shall trib-ute yield.
And, healed of our dis-eas-es,　The Temp-ter's power with-stand.
From o-cean un-to o-cean　Our land shall own Thee Lord. A-MEN.

**391**

Thomas Hastings, 1832   11. 10. 11. 10.   WESLEY
Lowell Mason, 1833

*In stately rhythm*

1. Hail to the bright-ness of Zi-on's glad morn-ing!
2. Hail to the bright-ness of Zi-on's glad morn-ing,
3. Lo, in the des-ert rich flow-ers are spring-ing,
4. See, from all lands, from the isles of the o-cean,

Joy to the lands that in dark-ness have lain!
Long by the proph-ets of Is-rael fore-told!
Streams ev-er co-pious are glid-ing a-long;
Praise to the Sav-iour as-cend-ing on high;

Hushed be the ac-cents of sor-row and mourn-ing;
Hail to the mil-lions from bond-age re-turn-ing!
Loud from the moun-tain tops ech-oes are ring-ing,
Fall-en the en-gines of war and com-mo-tion,

Zi-on in tri-umph be-gins her mild reign.
Gen-tiles and Jews the blest vi-sion be-hold.
Wastes rise in ver-dure, and min-gle in song.
Shouts of sal-va-tion are rend-ing the sky.   A-MEN.

Rev. John Marriott, c. 1813     6. 6. 4. 6. 6. 6. 4.     Rev. John B. Dykes, 1875

*With dignity and breadth*

1. Thou, whose al - might - y word Cha - os and
2. Thou, who didst come to bring On Thy re -
3. Spir - it of truth and love, Life - giv - ing,
4. Ho - ly and bless - ed Three, Glo - ri - ous

dark - ness heard, And took their flight, Hear us, we
deem - ing wing Heal - ing and sight, Health to the
ho - ly Dove, Speed forth Thy flight; Move o'er the
Trin - i - ty, Wis - dom, Love, Might! Bound - less as

hum - bly pray; And, where the gos - pel's day
sick in mind, Sight to the in - ly blind,
wa - ters' face, Bear - ing the lamp of grace,
o - cean's tide Roll - ing in full - est pride,

Sheds not its glo - rious ray, Let there be light!
O now to all man - kind Let there be light!
And in earth's dark - est place Let there be light!
Through the world far and wide Let there be light! A - MEN.

# 393

Somerset Corry Lowry, 1855      8. 7. 8. 7. D.      IN BABILONE
Dutch traditional melody

*In moderate time. With dignity*

1. Son of God, e - ter - nal Sav-iour, Source of life and truth and grace,
2. As Thou, Lord, hast lived for oth-ers, So may we for oth - ers live;
3. Come, O Christ, and reign a - mong us, King of love and Prince of peace;
4. See the Christ-like host ad - van-cing, High and low - ly, great and small,

Son of Man, whose birth in - car-nate Hal - lows all our hu - man race;
Free - ly have Thy gifts been grant-ed, Free - ly may Thy serv-ants give.
Hush the storm of strife and pas-sion, Bid its cru - el dis - cords cease.
Linked in bonds of com - mon serv - ice For the com - mon Lord of all.

Thou, our Head, who, throned in glo - ry, For Thine own dost ev - er plead,
Thine the gold and Thine the sil - ver, Thine the wealth of land and sea,
Ah, the past is dark be-hind us, Strewn with wrecks and stained with blood!
Thou who pray-edst, Thou who will - est That Thy peo - ple should be one,

Fill us with Thy love and pit - y, Heal our wrongs, and help our need.
We but stew-ards of Thy boun-ty, Held in sol - emn trust for Thee.
But be - fore us gleams the vi - sion Of the com - ing broth-er-hood.
Grant, O grant our hope's fru - i - tion: Here on earth Thy will be done. A-MEN.

Tune used by permission of Professor Julius Rontgen.
Words used by permission of the Hon. Mrs. Lowry.

**394**

SCHUMANN
Mason and Webb's "Cantica
Laudis," Boston, 1850

Bishop W. Walsham How, 1864      S. M.

*In moderate time*

1. We give Thee but Thine own, What-e'er the gift may be:
2. May we Thy boun-ties thus As stew-ards true re-ceive,
3. To com-fort and to bless, To find a balm for woe,
4. The cap-tive to re-lease, To God the lost to bring,
5. And we be-lieve Thy word, Though dim our faith may be:

All that we have is Thine a-lone, A trust, O Lord, from Thee.
And glad-ly, as Thou bless-est us, To Thee our first fruits give.
To tend the lone and fa-ther-less, Is an-gels' work be-low.
To teach the way of life and peace— It is a Christ-like thing.
What-e'er for Thine we do, O Lord, We do it un-to Thee. A-MEN.

**395**

ST. HELEN'S

Harriet Osgood Munger, 1894      8. 5. 8. 3.      Robert Prescott Stewart (1825–1894)

*In moderate time*

1. O my Fa-ther, I would know Thee And Thy ho-ly will;
2. I would turn my high-est pow-ers In-to serv-ice sweet;
3. As the bird who scorns earth's sad-ness, Mount-ing on the wing,
4. Shar-ing thus the Mas-ter's spir-it, Fol-lowing where He trod,

From Thy fount my thirst-y spir-it Dai-ly fill.
For all min-is-try to oth-ers Make me meet.
Would my soul, her fret o'er-com-ing, Rise and sing.
I would rise through joy-ous serv-ice Un-to God. A-MEN.

Tune used by permission of The Society for Promoting Christian Knowledge.

# Stewardship

Rev. Sylvanus D. Phelps, 1862     6. 4. 6. 4. 6. 6. 6. 4.     SOMETHING FOR JESUS
Rev. Robert Lowry, 1872

*In moderate time*

1. Sav - iour! Thy dy - ing love Thou gav - est me,
2. At the blest mer - cy seat, Plead - ing for me,
3. Give me a faith - ful heart, Guid - ed by Thee,
4. All that I am and have— Thy gifts so free—

Nor should I aught with - hold, Dear Lord, from Thee:
My fee - ble faith looks up, Je - sus, to Thee;
That each de - part - ing day Hence - forth may see
In joy, in grief, through life, Dear Lord, for Thee;

In love my soul would bow, My heart ful - fill its vow,
Help me the cross to bear, Thy won - drous love de - clare,
Some work of love be - gun, Some deed of kind - ness done,
And when Thy face I see, My ran - somed soul shall be,

Some of - fering bring Thee now, Some - thing for Thee.
Some song to raise, or prayer, Some - thing for Thee.
Some wan - derer sought and won, Some - thing for Thee.
Through all e - ter - ni - ty, Of - fered for Thee. A-MEN.

Copyright property of Mary Runyon Lowry. Used by permission.

Rev. Robert Davis, 1908        8. 4. 8. 4. 8. 8.    Melody in "Hirschberg Gesangbuch," 1741 O JESU

*Meditatively, yet not too slowly*

1. I thank Thee, Lord, for strength of arm
2. I thank Thee, Lord, for snug - thatched roof
3. I thank Thee, Lord, for lav - ish love

To win my bread, And that, be - yond my need, is meat
In cold and storm, And that, be - yond my need, is room
On me be - stowed, E - nough to share with love - less folk

For friend un - fed: I thank Thee much for
For friend for - lorn: I thank Thee much for
To ease their load: Thy love to me I

bread to live; I thank Thee more for bread to give.
place to rest, But more for shel - ter for my guest.
ill could spare, Yet dear - er is Thy love I share. A-MEN.

Words used by permission of Rev. Robert Davis.

# 398

Bishop Christopher Wordsworth, 1863
Revised, 1872

8. 8. 8. 4.

ALMSGIVING
Rev. John B. Dykes, 1865

*Joyfully*

1. O Lord of heaven and earth and sea, To Thee all praise and glo-ry be;
2. Thou didst not spare Thine on - ly Son, But gavest Him for a world un-done,
3. We lose what on our-selves we spend; We have as treas - ure with-out end
4. To Thee, from whom we all de - rive—Our life, our gifts, our power to give;

How shall we show our love to Thee, Who giv - est all?
And free - ly with that bless - ed One Thou giv - est all.
What-ev - er, Lord, to Thee we lend, Who giv - est all.
O may we ev - er with Thee live, Who giv - est all! A-MEN.

# 399

Frances R. Havergal, 1872

L. M.

CANONBURY
Robert Schumann, 1839

*In moderate time*

1. Lord, speak to me, that I may speak In liv - ing ech - oes of Thy tone;
2. O lead me, Lord, that I may lead The wan-dering and the wa-vering feet;
3. O teach me, Lord, that I may teach The pre-cious things Thou dost im-part;
4. O fill me with Thy full - ness, Lord, Un - til my ver - y heart o'er-flow
5. O use me, Lord, use e - ven me, Just as Thou wilt, and when, and where;

As Thou hast sought, so let me seek Thy err - ing chil-dren lost and lone.
O feed me, Lord, that I may feed Thy hun-gering ones with man-na sweet!
And wing my words, that they may reach The hid-den depths of many a heart.
In kin-dling thought and glow-ing word, Thy love to tell, Thy praise to show.
Un - til Thy bless - ed face I see, Thy rest, Thy joy, Thy glo - ry share. A-MEN.

# The Kingdom of God on Earth
## Brotherhood

GREENLAND
Arr. from J. Michael Haydn
Rev. Louis F. Benson, 1910          7. 6. 7. 6. D.          In B. Jacob's "National Psalmody," 1819

*Not too slow*

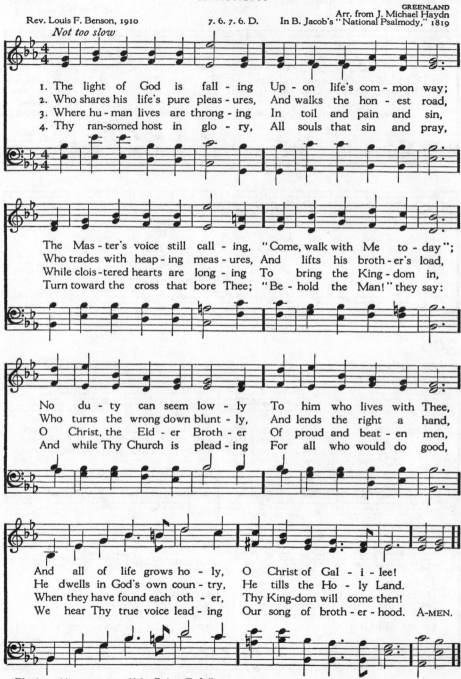

1. The light of God is fall-ing Up-on life's com-mon way;
2. Who shares his life's pure pleas-ures, And walks the hon-est road,
3. Where hu-man lives are throng-ing In toil and pain and sin,
4. Thy ran-somed host in glo-ry, All souls that sin and pray,

The Mas-ter's voice still call-ing, "Come, walk with Me to-day";
Who trades with heap-ing meas-ures, And lifts his broth-er's load,
While clois-tered hearts are long-ing To bring the King-dom in,
Turn toward the cross that bore Thee; "Be-hold the Man!" they say:

No du-ty can seem low-ly To him who lives with Thee,
Who turns the wrong down blunt-ly, And lends the right a hand,
O Christ, the Eld-er Broth-er Of proud and beat-en men,
And while Thy Church is plead-ing For all who would do good,

And all of life grows ho-ly, O Christ of Gal-i-lee!
He dwells in God's own coun-try, He tills the Ho-ly Land.
When they have found each oth-er, Thy King-dom will come then!
We hear Thy true voice lead-ing Our song of broth-er-hood. A-MEN.

Words used by permission of Mrs. Robert F. Jefferys.

# 401

## Brotherhood

Rev. William Pierson Merrill, 1911     S. M.     FESTAL SONG
William H. Walter, 1894

*With spirit*

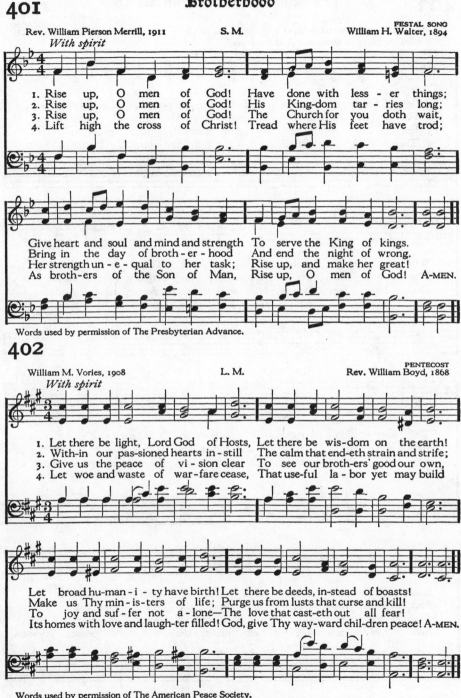

1. Rise up, O men of God! Have done with less - er things;
2. Rise up, O men of God! His King-dom tar - ries long;
3. Rise up, O men of God! The Church for you doth wait,
4. Lift high the cross of Christ! Tread where His feet have trod;

Give heart and soul and mind and strength To serve the King of kings.
Bring in the day of broth - er - hood And end the night of wrong.
Her strength un - e - qual to her task; Rise up, and make her great!
As broth-ers of the Son of Man, Rise up, O men of God! A-MEN.

Words used by permission of The Presbyterian Advance.

# 402

William M. Vories, 1908     L. M.     PENTECOST
Rev. William Boyd, 1868

*With spirit*

1. Let there be light, Lord God of Hosts, Let there be wis-dom on the earth!
2. With-in our pas-sioned hearts in - still The calm that end-eth strain and strife;
3. Give us the peace of vi - sion clear To see our broth-ers' good our own,
4. Let woe and waste of war-fare cease, That use-ful la - bor yet may build

Let broad hu-man - i - ty have birth! Let there be deeds, in-stead of boasts!
Make us Thy min - is - ters of life; Purge us from lusts that curse and kill!
To joy and suf - fer not a - lone—The love that cast-eth out all fear!
Its homes with love and laugh-ter filled! God, give Thy way-ward chil-dren peace! A-MEN.

Words used by permission of The American Peace Society.
Tune used by permission of Novello and Company, Ltd.

# The Kingdom of God on Earth

John Greenleaf Whittier (1807–1892)    11. 10. 11. 10.    Alfred Scott-Gatty (1847–1918)

WELWYN

*May be sung in unison. Not too slowly*

1. O broth - er man, fold to thy heart thy broth - er;
2. For he whom Je - sus loved has tru - ly spo - ken:
3. Fol - low with rev - erent steps the great ex - am - ple
4. Then shall all shack - les fall; the storm - y clan - gor

Where pit - y dwells, the peace of God is there;
The ho - lier wor - ship which He deigns to bless
Of Him whose ho - ly work was do - ing good;
Of wild war mu - sic o'er the earth shall cease;

To wor - ship right - ly is to love each oth - er,
Re - stores the lost, and binds the spir - it bro - ken,
So shall the wide earth seem our Fa - ther's tem - ple,
Love shall tread out the bale - ful fire of an - ger,

Each smile a hymn, each kind - ly deed a prayer.
And feeds the wid - ow and the fa - ther - less.
Each lov - ing life a psalm of grat - i - tude.
And in its ash - es plant the tree of peace. A - MEN.

Tune used by permission of The Very Reverend the Abbot of Downside.

# 404

Rev. John Johns, 1837      S. M.      GARDEN CITY
Horatio W. Parker, 1890

*In moderate time*

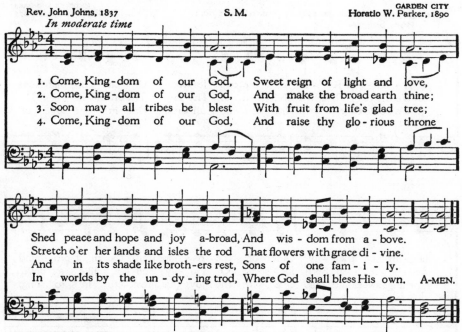

1. Come, King-dom of our God, Sweet reign of light and love,
2. Come, King-dom of our God, And make the broad earth thine;
3. Soon may all tribes be blest With fruit from life's glad tree;
4. Come, King-dom of our God, And raise thy glo-rious throne

Shed peace and hope and joy a-broad, And wis - dom from a - bove.
Stretch o'er her lands and isles the rod That flowers with grace di - vine.
And in its shade like broth-ers rest, Sons of one fam - i - ly.
In worlds by the un - dy - ing trod, Where God shall bless His own. A-MEN.

Tune used by permission of Mrs. Horatio W. Parker.

# 405

Rev. John Howard Masterman      L. M.      T. Williams' "Psalmodia Evangelica," 1789    TRURO

*In moderate time*

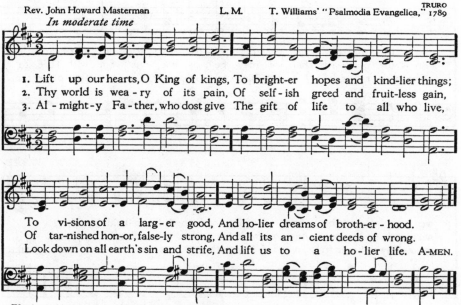

1. Lift up our hearts, O King of kings, To bright-er hopes and kind-lier things;
2. Thy world is wea - ry of its pain, Of self - ish greed and fruit-less gain,
3. Al - might-y Fa - ther, who dost give The gift of life to all who live,

To vi-sions of a larg - er good, And ho-lier dreams of broth-er - hood.
Of tar-nished hon-or, false-ly strong, And all its an - cient deeds of wrong.
Look down on all earth's sin and strife, And lift us to a ho-lier life. A-MEN.

Words used by permission of Rev. John Howard Masterman.

Rev. John W. Chadwick, 1864          10. 10. 10. 10. 10. 10.          UNDE ET MEMORES
William H. Monk, 1875

*With majesty*

1. E - ter - nal Rul - er of the cease-less round Of cir - cling plan - ets
2. We are of Thee, the chil - dren of Thy love, The broth-ers of Thy
3. We would be one in ha - tred of all wrong, One in our love of

sing - ing on their way; Guide of the na - tions from the night pro-found
well - be - lov - ed Son; De - scend, O Ho - ly Spir - it, like a dove
all things sweet and fair, One with the joy that break-eth in - to song,

In - to the glo - ry of the per - fect day: Rule in our hearts, that
In - to our hearts, that we may be as one; As one with Thee, to
One with the grief that trem - bles in - to prayer, One in the power that

we may ev - er be Guid - ed and strength-ened and up-held by Thee.
whom we ev - er tend; As one with Him, our Broth - er and our Friend.
makes Thy chil-dren free To fol - low truth, and thus to fol - low Thee. A-MEN.

# 407

## Brotherhood

Rev. Edwin P. Parker, 1888     6. 4. 6. 4. 6. 6. 4.     LOVE'S OFFERING
Rev. Edwin P. Parker, 1888

*In moderate time*

1. Mas - ter, no of - fer - ing, Cost - ly and sweet,
2. Dai - ly our lives would show Weak - ness made strong,
3. Some word of hope for hearts Bur - dened with fears,
4. Thus in Thy serv - ice, Lord, Till e - ven - tide

May we, like Mag - da - lene, Lay at Thy feet;
Toil - some and gloom - y ways Bright - ened with song;
Some balm of peace for eyes Blind - ed with tears,
Clos - es the day of life, May we a - bide!

Yet may love's in - cense rise, Sweet - er than sac - ri - fice,
Some deeds of kind - ness done, Some souls by pa - tience won,
Some dews of mer - cy shed, Some way - ward foot - steps led,
And when earth's la - bors cease, Bid us de - part in peace,

Dear Lord, to Thee, Dear Lord, to Thee.
Dear Lord, to Thee, Dear Lord, to Thee.
Dear Lord, to Thee, Dear Lord, to Thee.
Dear Lord, to Thee, Dear Lord, to Thee. A - MEN.

# 408 The Kingdom of God on Earth
## The City

Rev. William George Tarrant, 1895
Stanza 3, alt.

7. 6. 8. 6. D.

PATMOS
Henry J. Storer, 1891

1. The fa - thers built this cit - y In a - ges long a - go,
2. Yet still the cit - y stand - eth, A hive of toil - ing men,
3. Let all the peo - ple praise Thee, Give all Thy sav - ing health,

And, bus - y in its bus - y streets, They hur - ried to and fro;
And moth - er's love makes hap - py home For chil - dren now as then;
Or vain the la - borer's strong right arm And vain the mer - chant's wealth;

The chil - dren played a - round them And sang the songs of yore,
O God of a - ges, help us Such cit - i - zens to be
Send forth Thy light to stab - lish The glo - ry of the Word,

Till, one by one, they fell a - sleep, To work and play no more.
That chil - dren's chil - dren here may sing The songs of lib - er - ty!
Un - til this cit - y is be - come The cit - y of the Lord! A-MEN.

Words used by permission of The Beacon Press.

# The City

Rev. W. Russell Bowie, 1909     8. 6. 8. 6. 8. 6.     MORWELLHAM   Charles Steggall (1826–1905)

*With exultation*

1. O Ho - ly Cit - y seen of John,
2. O shame to us who rest con - tent
3. Give us, O God, the strength to build
4. Al - read - y in the mind of God

Where Christ, the Lamb, doth reign, With - in whose four-square walls shall come
While lust and greed for gain In street and shop and ten - e - ment
The Cit - y that hath stood Too long a dream, whose laws are love,
That Cit - y ris - eth fair; Lo, how its splen - dor chal - len - ges

No night, nor need, nor pain, And where the tears are
Wring gold from hu - man pain, And bit - ter lips in
Whose ways are broth - er - hood, And where the sun that
The souls that great - ly dare, Yea, bids us seize the

wiped from eyes That shall not weep a - gain!
blind de - spair Cry, "Christ hath died in vain"!
shin - eth is God's grace for hu - man good.
whole of life And build its glo - ry there! A - MEN.

NOTE: One stanza of the hymn as originally written has been omitted.
Used by permission of Rev. W. Russell Bowie.
Words Copyright, 1910, by A. S. Barnes and Company. Used by permission.

Rev. Frank Mason North, 1903     L. M.     William Gardiner's "Sacred Melodies," 1815

GERMANY

*In moderate time*

1. Where cross the crowd - ed ways of life, Where sound the
2. In haunts of wretch - ed - ness and need, On shad - owed
3. From ten - der child - hood's help - less - ness, From wom - an's
4. The cup of wa - ter given for Thee Still holds the

cries of race and clan, A - bove the noise of self - ish strife,
thresh-olds dark with fears, From paths where hide the lures of greed,
grief, man's bur - dened toil, From fam-ished souls, from sor - row's stress,
fresh - ness of Thy grace; Yet long these mul - ti - tudes to see

We hear Thy voice, O Son of Man.
We catch the vi - sion of Thy tears.
Thy heart has nev - er known re - coil.
The sweet com - pas - sion of Thy face.     A - MEN.

5. O Master, from the mountain side,
   Make haste to heal these hearts of pain;
   Among these restless throngs abide,
   O tread the city's streets again,

6. Till sons of men shall learn Thy love,
   And follow where Thy feet have trod;
   Till glorious from Thy heaven above
   Shall come the City of our God.

# The Nation

Katharine Lee Bates, 1904        C. M. D.        MATERNA
Samuel A. Ward, 1882

*In moderate time*

1. O beau - ti - ful for spa - cious skies, For am - ber waves of grain,
2. O beau - ti - ful for pil - grim feet, Whose stern, im - pas-sioned stress
3. O beau - ti - ful for glo - rious tale Of lib - er - at - ing strife,
4. O beau - ti - ful for pa - triot dream That sees, be - yond the years,

For pur - ple moun-tain maj - es - ties A - bove the fruit - ed plain!
A thor - ough - fare for free - dom beat A - cross the wil - der - ness!
When val - iant - ly for man's a - vail Men lav - ished pre - cious life!
Thine al - a - bas - ter cit - ies gleam, Un-dimmed by hu - man tears!

A - mer - i - ca! A - mer - i - ca! God shed His grace on thee,
A - mer - i - ca! A - mer - i - ca! God mend thine ev - ery flaw,
A - mer - i - ca! A - mer - i - ca! May God thy gold re - fine,
A - mer - i - ca! A - mer - i - ca! God shed His grace on thee,

And crown thy good with broth - er-hood From sea to shin - ing sea!
Con-firm thy soul in self - con-trol, Thy lib - er - ty in law!
Till all suc - cess be no - ble-ness And ev - ery gain di - vine!
And crown thy good with broth - er-hood From sea to shin - ing sea! A - MEN.

Words used by permission of Mrs. George S. Burgess.

# The Kingdom of God on Earth

Rev. Samuel F. Smith, 1832          6. 6. 4. 6. 6. 6. 4.          AMERICA
"Thesaurus Musicus," 1740

1. My coun-try, 'tis of thee, Sweet land of
2. My na-tive coun-try, thee, Land of the
3. Let mu-sic swell the breeze, And ring from
4. Our fa-thers' God, to Thee, Au-thor of

lib-er-ty, Of thee I sing; Land where my
no-ble free, Thy name I love; I love thy
all the trees Sweet free-dom's song: Let mor-tal
lib-er-ty, To Thee we sing: Long may our

fa-thers died, Land of the pil-grims' pride,
rocks and rills, Thy woods and tem-pled hills;
tongues a-wake; Let all that breathe par-take;
land be bright With free-dom's ho-ly light;

From ev-ery moun-tain side Let free-dom ring.
My heart with rap-ture thrills Like that a-bove.
Let rocks their si-lence break, The sound pro-long.
Pro-tect us by Thy might, Great God, our King. A-MEN.

# 413
## The Nation

Stanzas 1 and 2, Siegfried A. Mahlmann, 1815
Stanza 3, William E. Hickson, 1836      6. 6. 4. 6. 6. 6. 4.

DORT

Lowell Mason, 1832

*With martial rhythm*

1. God bless our na-tive land; Firm may she ev-er stand Through storm and night: When the wild tem-pests rave, Rul-er of wind and wave, Do Thou our coun-try save By Thy great might.

2. For her our prayers shall rise To God a-bove the skies; On Him we wait; Thou who art ev-er nigh, Guard-ing with watch-ful eye, To Thee a-loud we cry, God save the State!

3. Not for this land a-lone, But be God's mer-cies shown From shore to shore; And may the na-tions see That men should broth-ers be, And form one fam-i-ly The wide world o'er. A-MEN.

# The Kingdom of God on Earth

Rev. Daniel C. Roberts, 1876      10. 10. 10. 10.      NATIONAL HYMN
George William Warren, 1892

*In martial rhythm*

*Trumpets, before
each stanza*

1. God of our fa - thers, whose al - might - y hand
2. Thy love di - vine hath led us in the past;
3. From war's a-larms, from dead - ly pes - ti - lence,
4. Re - fresh Thy peo - ple on their toil-some way,

Leads forth in beau - ty all the star - ry band
In this free land by Thee our lot is cast;
Be Thy strong arm our ev - er sure de - fense;
Lead us from night to nev - er - end - ing day;

Of shin - ing worlds in splen - dor through the skies,
Be Thou our Rul - er, Guard - ian, Guide, and Stay;
Thy true re - li - gion in our hearts in - crease,
Fill all our lives with love and grace di - vine,

Our grate - ful songs be - fore Thy throne a - rise.
Thy word our law, Thy paths our cho - sen way.
Thy boun - teous good - ness nour - ish us in peace.
And glo - ry, laud, and praise be ev - er Thine. A-MEN.

**415**

Rev. Henry van Dyke, 1912

C. M. D.

AMERICA BEFRIEND
Rev. William Pierson Merrill, 1912

*With spirit*

1. O    Lord our God, Thy might-y hand  Hath made our coun-try free;
2. The strength of  ev-ery state in-crease  In    un-ion's gold-en chain;
3. O    suf-fer  not her feet  to stray;  But  guide her  un-taught might,
4. Through all the  wait-ing land pro-claim  Thy  gos-pel  of good will;

From all  her broad and hap-py land  May wor-ship rise  to Thee.
Her thou-sand cit-ies  fill  with peace,  Her  mil-lion fields with grain.
That she  may walk  in  peace-ful day,  And  lead the world in  light.
And may  the  joy  of  Je-sus' Name  In  ev-ery bos-om thrill.

Ful-fill  the prom-ise  of  her youth,  Her  lib-er-ty  de-fend;
The vir-tues of  her  min-gled blood  In   one new peo-ple blend;
Bring down the proud, lift  up   the  poor,  Un-e-qual ways a-mend;
O'er hill  and vale, from  sea  to  sea,  Thy  ho-ly reign ex-tend;

By law and or-der, love and truth,  A-mer-i-ca,  A-mer-i-ca  be-friend!
By u-ni-ty and broth-er-hood,  A-mer-i-ca,  A-mer-i-ca  be-friend!
By jus-tice, na-tion-wide and sure,  A-mer-i-ca,  A-mer-i-ca  be-friend!
By faith and hope and char-i-ty,  A-mer-i-ca,  A-mer-i-ca  be-friend! A-MEN.

Tune used by permission of Rev. William P. Merrill.

Rev. William Pierson Merrill, 1911     8. 7. 8. 7. D.     HYFRYDOL
Rowland Hugh Prichard (1811–1887)

*With dignity and nobility*

1. Not a - lone for might - y em - pire, Stretch-ing far o'er land and sea;
2. Not for bat - tle - ship and for - tress, Not for con - quests of the sword;
3. For the ar - mies of the faith - ful, Souls that passed and left no name;
4. God of jus - tice, save the peo - ple From the clash of race and creed,

Not a - lone for boun - teous har - vests, Lift we up our hearts to Thee.
But for con-quests of the spir - it, Give we thanks to Thee, O Lord;
For the glo - ry that il - lu - mines Pa - triot lives of death-less fame;
From the strife of class and fac - tion: Make our na - tion free in-deed.

Stand-ing in the liv - ing pres - ent, Mem - o - ry and hope be - tween,
For the price-less gift of free - dom, For the home, the church, the school;
For our proph-ets and a - pos - tles, Loy - al to the liv - ing Word;
Keep her faith in sim - ple man-hood Strong as when her life be - gan,

Lord, we would with deep thanks-giv - ing Praise Thee most for things un-seen.
For the o - pen door to man - hood In a land the peo-ple rule.
For all he - roes of the Spir - it, Give we thanks to Thee, O Lord.
Till it find its full fru - i - tion In the broth-er-hood of man. A-MEN.

Tune from "The English Hymnal." Used by permission of the Oxford University Press.

Rev. Henry Scott Holland (1847–1918)   8. 7. 8. 7. 8. 7.   RHUDDLAN
Welsh traditional melody

*May be sung in unison. Majestically*

1. Judge  e - ter - nal, throned in splen - dor,  Lord  of  lords and
2. Still  the  wea - ry  folk  are  pin - ing  For  the  hour that
3. Crown,  O  God, Thine own  en - deav - or:  Cleave our  dark - ness

King  of  kings,  With Thy liv - ing  fire  of  judg - ment
brings  re - lease;  And  the  cit - y's  crowd - ed  clan - gor
with Thy  sword;  Feed  the  faint  and  hun - gry  peo - ples

Purge  this  realm  of  bit - ter  things: Sol - ace  all  its
Cries  a - loud  for  sin  to  cease; And  the  home - steads
With  the  rich - ness  of  Thy  Word; Cleanse the  bod - y

wide  do - min - ion  With  the  heal - ing  of  Thy wings.
and  the  wood - lands  Plead  in  si - lence  for  their peace.
of  this  na - tion  Through the  glo - ry  of  the  Lord.  A-MEN.

From "Songs of Praise." By permission of the Oxford University Press.

Rev. Robert Freeman, 1927      8. 8. 8. 10. 8. 8.      MARCUS WHITMAN
Rev. William Pierson Merrill, 1927

*In march rhythm*

1. Brav - ing the wilds all un - ex - plored, Dream-ers of dreams and
2. Fair knights of jus - tice and of good, They gave to e - vil
3. Guards of the sa - cred al - tar flame, Bring - ers of learn - ing
4. Theirs was the Pres - ence ev - er sure, Theirs was the all - a -

pi - o - neers, Wield - ing the sick - le, goad, and sword,
bat - tle gage; Bear - ing their souls in rec - ti - tude,
and of faith, They lu - mined life in the bless - ed Name,
bound - ing grace, Theirs was the pas - sion ev - er pure

They marched with the sun to the last fron - tiers — God of the val - iant,
They left a good - ly her - it - age — God of the right - eous,
And hope they flared in the day of death — God of the faith - ful,
To hon - or the Lord in all their ways — God of the Christ-like,

grant that we, Their sons, do fol - low val - iant - ly!
grant that we, Their sons, do fol - low right-eous - ly!
grant that we, Their sons, do fol - low faith - ful - ly!
grant that we Do fol - low, fol - low worth - i - ly! A-MEN.

Copyright, 1928, Board of National Missions of the Presbyterian Church, U. S. A.

# The Nation

Gilbert K. Chesterton  
7. 6. 7. 6. D.

**LLANGLOFFAN**  
Welsh hymn melody  
D. Evans' "Hymnau a Thonau," 1865

*With breadth and earnestness*

1. O God of earth and al - tar, Bow down and hear our cry;
2. From all that ter - ror teach - es, From lies of tongue and pen;
3. Tie in a liv - ing teth - er The priest and prince and thrall;

Our earth - ly rul - ers fal - ter, Our peo - ple drift and die;
From all the eas - y speech - es That com - fort cru - el men;
Bind all our lives to - geth - er, Smite us and save us all;

The walls of gold en - tomb us, The swords of scorn di - vide;
From sale and prof - a - na - tion Of hon - or and the sword;
In ire and ex - ul - ta - tion A - flame with faith, and free,

Take not Thy thun - der from us, But take a - way our pride.
From sleep and from dam - na - tion, De - liv - er us, good Lord!
Lift up a liv - ing na - tion, A sin - gle sword to Thee. A-MEN.

Words and tune from "The English Hymnal." By permission of the Oxford University Press.

# The Kingdom of God on Earth

Henry F. Chorley, 1842
Rev. John Ellerton, 1870; alt.

11. 10. 11. 9.

RUSSIAN HYMN
Alexis Lwoff, 1833

*Majestically*

1. God the Om - nip - o - tent! King, who or - dain - est
2. God the All - mer - ci - ful! earth hath for - sak - en
3. God the All - right-eous One! man hath de - fied Thee;
4. God the All - wise! by the fire of Thy chas - tening
5. So shall Thy peo - ple, with thank - ful de - vo - tion,

Thun - der Thy clar - ion, the light - ning Thy sword;
Thy ways all - ho - ly, and slight - ed Thy word;
Yet to e - ter - ni - ty stand - eth Thy word;
Earth shall to free - dom and truth be re - stored;
Praise Him who saved them from per - il and sword,

Show forth Thy pit - y on high where Thou reign - est;
Let not Thy wrath in its ter - rors a - wak - en;
False - hood and wrong shall not tar - ry be - side Thee;
Through the thick dark - ness Thy King - dom is has - tening;
Sing - ing in cho - rus from o - cean to o - cean

Give to us peace in our time, O Lord.
Give to us peace in our time, O Lord.
Give to us peace in our time, O Lord.
Thou wilt give peace in Thy time, O Lord.
Peace to the na - tions, and praise to the Lord. A-MEN.

Words from "The Church Hymnary," Revised. By permission of the Oxford University Press.

**421**

Rev. Henry W. Baker (1821–1877)     L. M.     George Frederick Handel (1685–1759)

CANNONS

(FIRST TUNE)

*In moderate time. With marked rhythm*

1. O God of love, O King of peace, Make wars through-out the world to cease;
2. Re - mem-ber, Lord, Thy works of old, The won-ders that our fa - thers told;
3. Whom shall we trust but Thee, O Lord? Where rest but on Thy faith-ful word?
4. Where saints and an - gels dwell a - bove, All hearts are knit in ho - ly love;

The wrath of sin - ful man re-strain: Give peace, O God, give peace a-gain!
Re - mem-ber not our sin's dark stain: Give peace, O God, give peace a-gain!
None ev - er called on Thee in vain: Give peace, O God, give peace a-gain!
O bind us in that heaven-ly chain: Give peace, O God, give peace a-gain! A-MEN.

**421**

Rev. Henry W. Baker (1821–1877)     L. M.     Henry Baker, 1862

QUEBEC

(SECOND TUNE)

*In moderate time*

1. O God of love, O King of peace, Make wars through-out the world to cease;
2. Re - mem-ber, Lord, Thy works of old, The won-ders that our fa - thers told;
3. Whom shall we trust but Thee, O Lord? Where rest but on Thy faith-ful word?
4. Where saints and an - gels dwell a - bove, All hearts are knit in ho - ly love;

The wrath of sin - ful man re-strain: Give peace, O God, give peace a-gain!
Re - mem-ber not our sin's dark stain: Give peace, O God, give peace a-gain!
None ev - er called on Thee in vain: Give peace, O God, give peace a-gain!
O bind us in that heaven-ly chain: Give peace, O God, give peace a-gain! A-MEN.

Rev. John S. B. Monsell, 1863          7. 6. 7. 6. D.          MEIRIONYDD
                                                              Welsh hymn melody

*In moderate time. With dignity*

1. Light of the world, we hail Thee, Flush-ing the east-ern skies;
2. Light of the world, Thy beau - ty Steals in - to ev - ery heart,
3. Light of the world, il - lu - mine This dark-ened land of Thine,

Nev - er shall dark - ness veil Thee A - gain from hu - man eyes;
And glo - ri - fies with du - ty Life's poor - est, hum-blest part;
Till ev - ery-thing that's hu - man Be filled with what's di - vine;

Too long, a - las, with-hold - en, Now spread from shore to shore;
Thou rob - est in Thy splen - dor The sim - ple ways of men,
Till ev - ery tongue and na - tion, From sin's do - min - ion free,

Thy light, so glad and gold - en, Shall set on earth no more.
And help-est them to ren - der Light back to Thee a - gain.
Rise in the new cre - a - tion Which springs from love and Thee. A-MEN.

Tune used by permission of Dr. Basil Harwood.

John Addington Symonds (1840–1893)

L. M.
(FIRST TUNE)

Robert G. McCutchan, 1930

DEPAUW

*With well-defined rhythm*

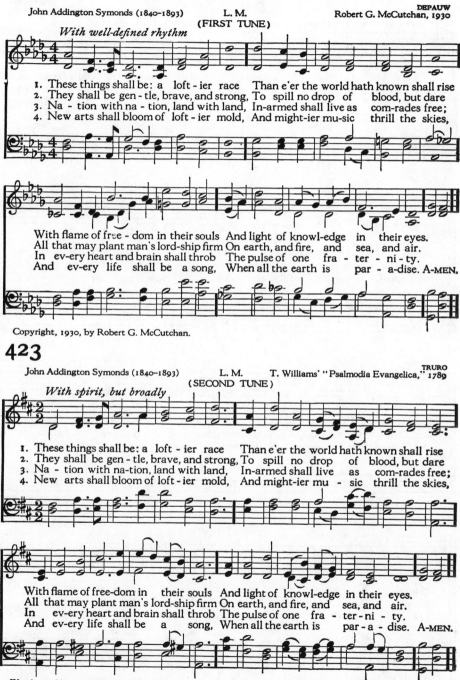

1. These things shall be: a loft-ier race Than e'er the world hath known shall rise
2. They shall be gen-tle, brave, and strong, To spill no drop of blood, but dare
3. Na-tion with na-tion, land with land, In-armed shall live as com-rades free;
4. New arts shall bloom of loft-ier mold, And might-ier mu-sic thrill the skies,

With flame of free-dom in their souls And light of knowl-edge in their eyes.
All that may plant man's lord-ship firm On earth, and fire, and sea, and air.
In ev-ery heart and brain shall throb The pulse of one fra-ter-ni-ty.
And ev-ery life shall be a song, When all the earth is par-a-dise. A-MEN.

Copyright, 1930, by Robert G. McCutchan.

## 423

John Addington Symonds (1840–1893)

L. M.   T. Williams' "Psalmodia Evangelica," 1789
(SECOND TUNE)

TRURO

*With spirit, but broadly*

1. These things shall be: a loft-ier race Than e'er the world hath known shall rise
2. They shall be gen-tle, brave, and strong, To spill no drop of blood, but dare
3. Na-tion with na-tion, land with land, In-armed shall live as com-rades free;
4. New arts shall bloom of loft-ier mold, And might-ier mu-sic thrill the skies,

With flame of free-dom in their souls And light of knowl-edge in their eyes.
All that may plant man's lord-ship firm On earth, and fire, and sea, and air.
In ev-ery heart and brain shall throb The pulse of one fra-ter-ni-ty.
And ev-ery life shall be a song, When all the earth is par-a-dise. A-MEN.

Words used by permission of John Murray.

Clifford Bax                    10. 10. 10. 10. 10.          Melody in "Genevan Psalter," 1551
                                                                                    OLD 124TH

*May be sung in unison. With spirit, but broadly*

1. Turn back, O man, for-swear thy fool-ish ways. Old now is
2. Earth might be fair and all men glad and wise. Age aft-er
3. Earth shall be fair, and all her peo-ple one: Nor till that

earth, and none may count her days, Yet thou, her child, whose
age their trag-ic em-pires rise, Built while they dream, and
hour shall God's whole will be done. Now, ev-en now, once

head is crowned with flame, Still wilt not hear thine in-ner God pro-
in that dream-ing weep: Would man but wake from out his haunt-ed
more from earth to sky, Peals forth in joy man's old, un-daunt-ed

claim— "Turn back, O man, for-swear thy fool-ish ways."
sleep, Earth might be fair and all men glad and wise.
cry— "Earth shall be fair, and all her folk be one!" A-MEN.

Words used by permission of A. D. Peters.

Rev. Frederick L. Hosmer, 1905     6. 6. 6. 6.     ST. CECILIA
Rev. Leighton G. Hayne, 1863

*With spirit*

1. Thy King-dom come, O Lord, Wide-cir-cling as the sun;
2. One in the bond of peace, The serv-ice glad and free
3. Speed, speed the longed-for time Fore-told by rap-tured seers—
4. Till rise at last, to span Its firm foun-da-tions broad,

Ful-fill of old Thy word And make the na-tions one:
Of truth and right-eous-ness, Of love and eq-ui-ty.
The proph-e-cy sub-lime, The hope of all the years—
The com-mon-wealth of man, The cit-y of our God. A-MEN.

Words used by permission of The Beacon Press.

426

Bishop Christopher Wordsworth, 1871     8. 8. 8. 4.     ALMSGIVING
Rev. John B. Dykes, 1865

*In moderate time*

1. Fa-ther of all, from land and sea The na-tions sing, "Thine, Lord, are we;
2. O Son of God, whose love so free For men did make Thee Man to be,
3. Join high with low, join young with old, In love that nev-er wax-es cold;
4. O Spir-it blest, who from a-bove Cam'st gen-tly glid-ing like a dove,

Count-less in num-ber, but in Thee May we be one."
U-nit-ed to our God in Thee May we be one.
Un-der one Shep-herd, in one fold, Make us all one.
Calm all our strife, give faith and love; O make us one! A-MEN.

# 427 The Life Everlasting

Rev. Henry Alford, 1867      7. 6. 8. 6. D.      ALFORD    Rev. John B. Dykes, 1875

*In moderate time; with exultation*

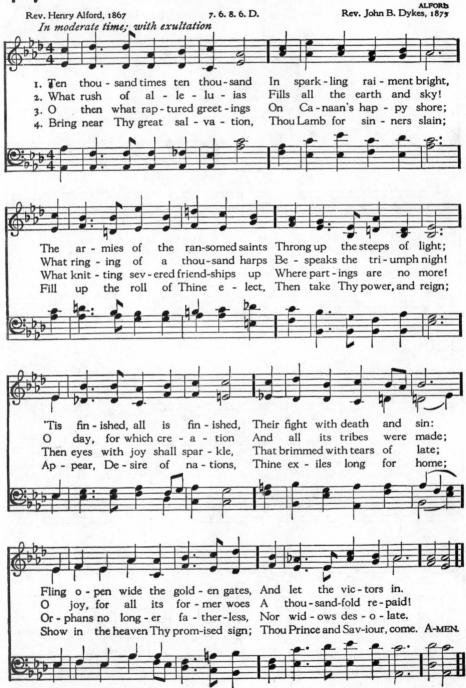

1. Ten thou - sand times ten thou-sand   In spark - ling rai - ment bright,
2. What rush of al - le - lu - ias   Fills all the earth and sky!
3. O then what rap - tured greet-ings   On Ca - naan's hap - py shore;
4. Bring near Thy great sal - va - tion,   Thou Lamb for sin - ners slain;

The ar - mies of the ran-somed saints Throng up the steeps of light;
What ring - ing of a thou-sand harps Be - speaks the tri - umph nigh!
What knit - ting sev - ered friend-ships up Where part-ings are no more!
Fill up the roll of Thine e - lect, Then take Thy power, and reign;

'Tis fin - ished, all is fin - ished, Their fight with death and sin:
O day, for which cre - a - tion And all its tribes were made;
Then eyes with joy shall spar - kle, That brimmed with tears of late;
Ap - pear, De - sire of na - tions, Thine ex - iles long for home;

Fling o - pen wide the gold - en gates, And let the vic - tors in.
O joy, for all its for - mer woes A thou-sand-fold re - paid!
Or - phans no long - er fa - ther-less, Nor wid - ows des - o - late.
Show in the heaven Thy prom-ised sign; Thou Prince and Sav-iour, come. A-MEN.

# 428 The Life Everlasting

Rev. Horatius Bonar, 1866          8. 8. 7. 8. 8. 7.          BONAR
John Baptiste Calkin, 1867

*Joyfully*

1. Up - ward where the stars are burn - ing, Si - lent, si - lent
2. Where the Lamb on high is seat - ed, By ten thou - sand
3. Bless - ing, hon - or, with - out meas - ure, Heaven-ly rich - es,

in their turn - ing Round the nev - er - chan - ging pole;
voi - ces greet - ed, Lord of lords, and King of kings.
earth - ly treas - ure, Lay we at His bless - ed feet:

Up - ward where the sky is bright - est, Up - ward where the
Son of Man, they crown, they crown Him, Son of God, they
Poor the praise that now we ren - der, Loud shall be our

blue is light - est, Lift I now my long - ing soul.
own, they own Him; With His Name the pal - ace rings.
voi - ces yon - der, When be - fore His throne we meet. A-MEN.

# The Life Everlasting

**429**

Bishop William Walsham How, 1864    10. 10. 10. 4.    SARUM
(FIRST TUNE)    Joseph Barnby, 1869

*In moderate time; with exultation*

1. For all the saints who from their la - bors rest, Who Thee by
faith be - fore the world con - fessed, Thy Name, O Je - sus,
be for - ev - er blest. Al - le - lu - ia! Al - le - lu - ia!

2. Thou wast their Rock, their For - tress, and their Might; Thou, Lord, their
Cap - tain in the well - fought fight; Thou, in the dark - ness
drear, their one true Light. Al - le - lu - ia! Al - le - lu - ia!

3. O may Thy sol - diers, faith - ful, true, and bold, Fight as the
saints who no - bly fought of old, And win with them the
vic - tor's crown of gold. Al - le - lu - ia! Al - le - lu - ia!

4. O blest com - mun - ion, fel - low - ship di - vine! We fee - bly
strug - gle, they in glo - ry shine; Yet all are one in
Thee, for all are Thine. Al - le - lu - ia! Al - le - lu - ia! A-MEN.

5. And when the fight is fierce, the warfare long,
Steals on the ear the distant triumph song,
And hearts are brave again, and arms are strong. Alleluia! Alleluia!

6. From earth's wide bounds, from ocean's farthest coast,
Through gates of pearl streams in the countless host,
Singing to Father, Son, and Holy Ghost, Alleluia! Alleluia!

# 429

## The Life Everlasting

Bishop William Walsham How, 1864     10. 10. 10. 4.     SINE NOMINE
                                     (SECOND TUNE)       R. Vaughan Williams, 1906

*Voices in unison. In moderate time*

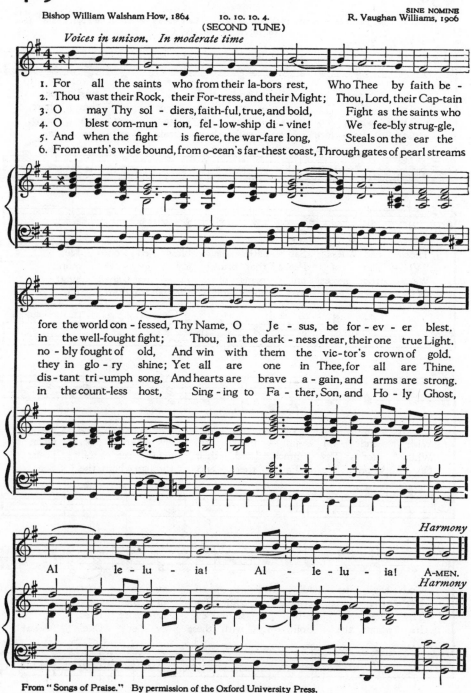

1. For all the saints who from their la-bors rest, Who Thee by faith be-
2. Thou wast their Rock, their For-tress, and their Might; Thou, Lord, their Cap-tain
3. O may Thy sol - diers, faith-ful, true, and bold, Fight as the saints who
4. O blest com-mun - ion, fel - low-ship di - vine! We fee-bly strug-gle,
5. And when the fight is fierce, the war-fare long, Steals on the ear the
6. From earth's wide bound, from o-cean's far-thest coast, Through gates of pearl streams

fore the world con - fessed, Thy Name, O Je - sus, be for - ev - er blest.
in the well-fought fight; Thou, in the dark - ness drear, their one true Light.
no - bly fought of old, And win with them the vic-tor's crown of gold.
they in glo - ry shine; Yet all are one in Thee, for all are Thine.
dis-tant tri-umph song, And hearts are brave a - gain, and arms are strong.
in the count-less host, Sing-ing to Fa - ther, Son, and Ho - ly Ghost,

*Harmony*

Al le - lu - ia! Al - le - lu - ia! A-MEN.

*Harmony*

From "Songs of Praise." By permission of the Oxford University Press.

# 430 The Life Everlasting

Pierre Abélard (1079–1142)
Trans. by Rev. John Mason Neale, 1854; alt.

O QUANTA QUALIA
La Feillée's "Méthode du Plain Chant," 1808

10. 10. 10. 10. Dactylic

*With exultation*

1. O what their joy and their glo - ry must be,
2. Tru - ly Je - ru - sa - lem name we that shore,
3. There, where no trou - bles dis - trac - tion can bring,
4. Low be - fore Him with our prais - es we fall,

Those end - less Sab - baths the bless - ed ones see;
"Vi - sion of Peace," that brings joy ev - er - more;
We the sweet an - thems of Zi - on shall sing;
Of whom, and in whom, and through whom are all;

Crown for the val - iant, to wea - ry ones rest;
Wish and ful - fill - ment can sev - ered be ne'er,
While for Thy grace, Lord, their voi - ces of praise
Of whom, the Fa - ther; and through whom, the Son;

God shall be All, and in all ev - er blest.
Nor the thing prayed for come short of the prayer.
Thy bless - ed peo - ple shall ev - er - more raise.
In whom, the Spir - it, with these ev - er One. A-MEN.

# The Life Everlasting

Rev. Frederick W. Faber, 1854 · 11. 10. 11. 10. 9. 11. · PILGRIMS (SMART)
Henry Smart, 1868

*In moderate time*

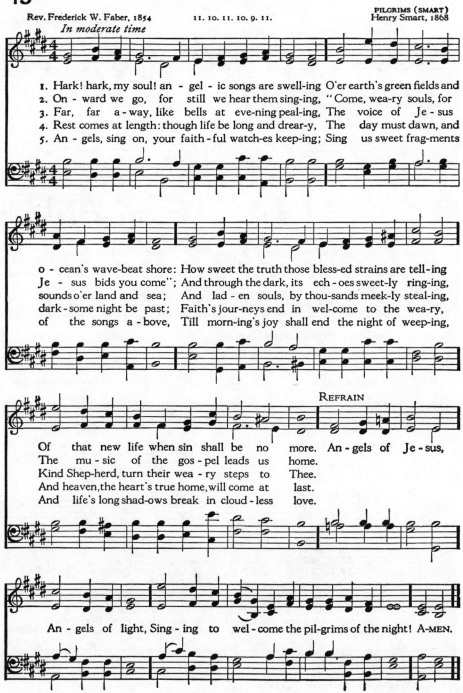

1. Hark! hark, my soul! an - gel - ic songs are swell-ing O'er earth's green fields and
2. On - ward we go, for still we hear them sing-ing, "Come, wea-ry souls, for
3. Far, far a - way, like bells at eve-ning peal-ing, The voice of Je - sus
4. Rest comes at length: though life be long and drear-y, The day must dawn, and
5. An - gels, sing on, your faith - ful watch-es keep-ing; Sing us sweet frag-ments

o - cean's wave-beat shore: How sweet the truth those bless-ed strains are tell-ing
Je - sus bids you come"; And through the dark, its ech - oes sweet-ly ring-ing,
sounds o'er land and sea; And lad - en souls, by thou-sands meek-ly steal-ing,
dark - some night be past; Faith's jour-neys end in wel-come to the wea-ry,
of the songs a - bove, Till morn-ing's joy shall end the night of weep-ing,

REFRAIN

Of that new life when sin shall be no more. An - gels of Je - sus,
The mu - sic of the gos - pel leads us home.
Kind Shep-herd, turn their wea - ry steps to Thee.
And heaven, the heart's true home, will come at last.
And life's long shad-ows break in cloud - less love.

An - gels of light, Sing - ing to wel - come the pil-grims of the night! A-MEN.

# 432

## The Life Everlasting

Based on Rev. 22:1
Christina G. Rossetti, 1893

9. 8. 10. 5.

ACHNASHEEN
Charles H. Lloyd, 1903

*In rather slow time, with flowing rhythm*

1. We know not a voice of that riv - er, If vo - cal or si - lent it be,
2. More deep than the seas is that riv - er, More full than their man - i - fold tides,
3. O good - ly the banks of that riv - er, O good - ly the fruits that they bear,
4. For lo! on each bank of that riv - er, The tree that is life - giv-ing grows,

Where for-ev - er and ev - er and ev - er It flows to no sea.
Where for-ev - er and ev - er and ev - er It flows and a - bides.
Where for-ev - er and ev - er and ev - er It flows and is fair.
Where for-ev - er and ev - er and ev - er The pure riv - er flows. A-MEN.

Words used by permission of The MacMillan Company.

# 433

Rev. Louis F. Benson, 1923

C. M.

VITTEL WOODS
Bradley Keeler, 1924

*In moderate time*

1. O Love that lights the east - ern sky And shrouds the eve - ning rest,
2. O life, con - tent be-neath the blue! Or, if God will, the gray,
3. O death that sails so close to shore At twi - light! From my gate
4. What lies be - yond the aft - er - glow? To life's new dawn how far?

From out whose hand the swal-lows fly, With - in whose heart they nest!
Then tran - quil yet, till light breaks through To melt the mist a - way!
I scan the dark-ening sea once more, And for its mes - sage wait.
As if an an - swer, spo - ken low, Love lights the eve - ning star. A-MEN.

Used by permission of Mrs. Robert F. Jefferys.

RUTHERFORD
Chrétien Urhan, 1834
Anne Ross Cousin, 1857     7. 6. 7. 6. 7. 6. 7. 5.     Arr. by Edward F. Rimbault, 1867

*In moderate time*

1. The sands of time are sink - ing, The dawn of heav - en breaks;
2. O Christ, He is the foun - tain, The deep, sweet well of love!
3. With mer - cy and with judg - ment My web of time He wove,

The sum - mer morn I've sighed for, The fair, sweet morn, a - wakes;
The streams on earth I've tast - ed More deep I'll drink a - bove:
And aye the dews of sor - row Were lus - tered by His love.

Dark, dark hath been the mid - night, But day - spring is at hand,
There to an o - cean full - ness His mer - cy doth ex - pand,
I'll bless the hand that guid - ed, I'll bless the heart that planned,

And glo - ry, glo - ry dwell - eth In Im - man - uel's land.
And glo - ry, glo - ry dwell - eth In Im - man - uel's land.
When throned where glo - ry dwell - eth In Im - man - uel's land. A-MEN.

# 435
## The Life Everlasting

Bernard of Cluny, 12th century
Trans. by Rev. John M. Neale, 1851

7. 6. 7. 6. D.
(FIRST TUNE)

EWING
Alexander Ewing, 1853

*Jubilantly*

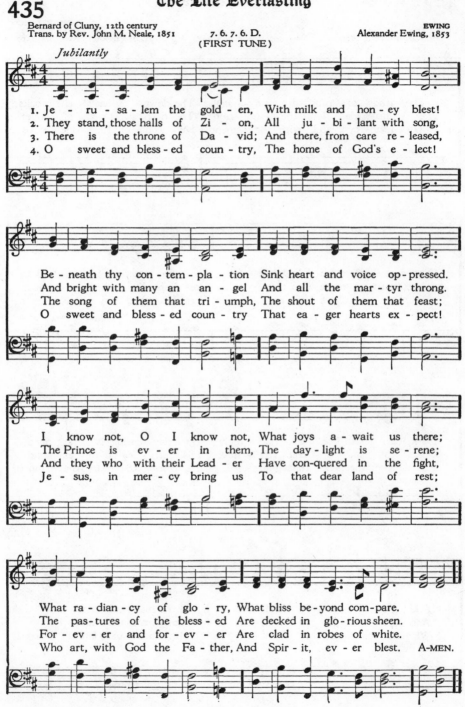

1. Je - ru - sa - lem the gold - en, With milk and hon - ey blest!
2. They stand, those halls of Zi - on, All ju - bi - lant with song,
3. There is the throne of Da - vid; And there, from care re - leased,
4. O sweet and bless - ed coun - try, The home of God's e - lect!

Be - neath thy con - tem - pla - tion Sink heart and voice op - pressed.
And bright with many an an - gel And all the mar - tyr throng.
The song of them that tri - umph, The shout of them that feast;
O sweet and bless - ed coun - try That ea - ger hearts ex - pect!

I know not, O I know not, What joys a - wait us there;
The Prince is ev - er in them, The day - light is se - rene;
And they who with their Lead - er Have con-quered in the fight,
Je - sus, in mer - cy bring us To that dear land of rest;

What ra - dian - cy of glo - ry, What bliss be - yond com - pare.
The pas - tures of the bless - ed Are decked in glo - rious sheen.
For - ev - er and for - ev - er Are clad in robes of white.
Who art, with God the Fa - ther, And Spir - it, ev - er blest. A-MEN.

# The Life Everlasting

Bernard of Cluny, 12th century
Trans. by Rev. John M. Neale, 1851

URBS BEATA
George F. Le Jeune, 1887

7. 6. 7. 6. D. with Refrain
(SECOND TUNE)

*Jubilantly*

1. Je - ru - sa - lem the gold - en, With milk and hon-ey blest! Be-neath thy con-tem-
2. They stand, those halls of Zi - on, All ju-bi-lant with song, And bright with many an
3. There is the throne of Da - vid; And there, from care re-leased, The song of them that
4. O sweet and bless-ed coun-try, The home of God's e - lect! O sweet and bless-ed

pla - tion Sink heart and voice op-pressed. I know not, O I know not,
an - gel And all the mar - tyr throng. The Prince is ev - er in them,
tri - umph, The shout of them that feast; And they who with their Lead - er
coun - try That ea - ger hearts ex - pect! Je - sus, in mer - cy bring us

What joys a-wait us there; What ra-dian-cy of glo-ry, What bliss be-yond com-pare.
The day-light is se-rene; The pas-tures of the bless-ed Are decked in glo-rious sheen.
Have con-quered in the fight, For - ev - er and for-ev - er Are clad in robes of white.
To that dear land of rest; Who art, with God the Fa-ther, And Spir-it, ev - er blest.

REFRAIN

Je - ru - - - - - - - - sa - lem the gold - en!

Je - ru - sa - lem the gold - en, With milk and hon - ey blest!

Be-neath thy con - tem - pla - tion Sink heart and voice op-pressed. A-MEN.

"F. B. P.," 16th century          C. M. D.          MATERNA
Samuel A. Ward, 1882

*Joyfully*

1. O moth - er dear, Je - ru - sa - lem, When shall I come to thee?
2. Thy gar - dens and thy good - ly walks Con - tin - ual - ly are green,
3. Those trees for - ev - er - more bear fruit, And ev - er - more do spring;

When shall my sor - rows have an end? Thy joys when shall I see?
Where grow such sweet and pleas - ant flowers As no - where else are seen.
There ev - er - more the an - gels are, And ev - er - more do sing.

O hap - py har - bor of the saints! O sweet and pleas - ant soil!
Right through the streets, with sil - ver sound, The liv - ing wa - ters flow,
Je - ru - sa - lem, my hap - py home, Would God I were in thee!

In thee no sor - row may be found, No grief, no care, no toil.
And on the banks, on ei - ther side, The trees of life do grow.
Would God my woes were at an end, Thy joys that I might see! A-MEN.

# The Life Everlasting

Rev. Godfrey Thring, 1886      7. 6. 8. 6. D.     PATMOS   Henry J. Storer. 1891

*With exultation*

1. I heard a sound of voi - ces  A - round the great white throne,
2. From ev - ery clime and kin - dred,  And na - tions from a - far,
3. O Lamb of God who reign - est,  Thou Bright and Morn - ing Star,

With harp - ers harp - ing on their harps  To Him who sat there - on;
As ser - ried ranks re - turn - ing home  In tri - umph from a war,
Whose glo - ry light - ens that new earth  Which now we see from far;

"Sal - va - tion, glo - ry, hon - or,"  I heard the song a - rise,
I heard the saints up - rais - ing,  The myr - iad hosts a - mong,
O wor - thy Judge E - ter - nal,  When Thou dost bid us come,

As through the courts of heaven it rolled  In won-drous har - mo - nies.
In praise of Him who died, and lives,  Their one glad tri - umph song.
Then o - pen wide the gates of pearl,  And call Thy serv - ants home. A-MEN.

# 438 The Life Everlasting

Alfred Tennyson, 1889

Irregular

CROSSING THE BAR
Joseph Barnby, 1893

*Rather slow*

STANZA I

Sun-set and eve-ning star, And one clear call for me! And may there be no moan-ing

STANZA 2

of the bar When I put out to sea, But such a tide as mov-ing seems a-sleep,

Too full for sound and foam, When that which drew from out the bound-less deep

*rall.*

STANZA 3

Turns a - gain home. Twi-light and eve - ning bell, And aft - er

home. Twi - - - light and eve - ning bell,

that the dark! And may there be no sad - ness of fare-well When I em-bark;

# The Life Everlasting

Tune used by permission of Novello and Company, Ltd.

STANZA 4     *cre - - scen - - - - do    rit.*

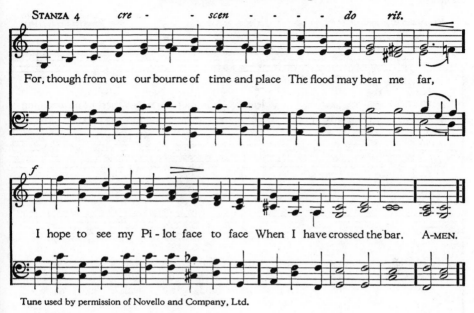

For, though from out our bourne of time and place The flood may bear me far,

I hope to see my Pi - lot face to face When I have crossed the bar. A-MEN.

## 439

Christina G. Rossetti (1830–1894)      8. 6.      ULTIMA
Rev. James Moffatt

*Moderately slow*

1. Soon - er or lat - er: yet   at last   The Jor - dan must be past.
3. When mys - te - ries shall be   re - vealed, All se - crets be un - sealed:

2. Soon - er or lat - er: yet   one   day We   all must pass that way.
4. Je - sus, most mer - ci - ful   of   men, Show mer - cy on us then;
5. Lord God of mer - cy and of   men, Show mer - cy on us then. A - MEN.

From "The Church Hymnary," Revised. Used by permission.
Copyright, 1927, by the Oxford University Press.

Rev. John Ellerton, 1871      7. 7. 7. 7. 8. 8.      REQUIESCAT
Rev. John B. Dykes, 1875

*Rather slow*

1. Now the la - borer's task is o'er; Now the bat - tle
2. There the tears of earth are dried; There its hid - den
3. "Earth to earth, and dust to dust"; Calm - ly now the

day is past; Now up - on the far - ther shore
things are clear; There the work of life is tried
words we say; Left be - hind, we wait in trust,

Lands the voy - a - ger at last. Fa - ther, in Thy gra - cious
By a just - er Judge than here. Fa - ther, in Thy gra - cious
For the res - ur - rec - tion day. Fa - ther, in Thy gra - cious

keep - ing Leave we now Thy serv - ant sleep - ing.
keep - ing Leave we now Thy serv - ant sleep - ing.
keep - ing Leave we now Thy serv - ant sleep - ing. A-MEN.

Rev. William George Tarrant, 1888     7. 6. 7. 6. D.     TOURS
Berthold Tours, 1872

*Joyfully*

1. With hap-py voi-ces sing-ing, Thy chil-dren, Lord, ap-pear;
2. For though no eye be-holds Thee, No hand Thy touch may feel,

Their joy-ous prais-es bring-ing In an-thems sweet and clear.
Thy u-ni-verse un-folds Thee, Thy star-ry heavens re-veal;

For skies of gold-en splen-dor, For az-ure roll-ing sea,
The earth and all its glo-ry, Our homes and all we love,

For blos-soms sweet and ten-der, O Lord, we wor-ship Thee.
Tell forth the won-drous sto-ry Of One who reigns a-bove. A-MEN.

Words used by permission of The Beacon Press.
Tune used by permission of Novello and Company, Ltd.

Jemima Luke, 1841

Irregular
(FIRST TUNE)

EAST HORNDON
English traditional melody

_Unison. In moderate time_

1. I think when I read that sweet sto - ry of old,
2. I wish that His hands had been placed on my head,
3. Yet still to His foot - stool in prayer I may go,
4. I long for the joy of that glo - ri - ous time,

When Je - sus was here a - mong men,
That His arm had been thrown a - round me,
And ask for a share in His love;
The sweet - est and bright - est and best,

How He called lit - tle chil - dren as lambs to His fold,
And that I might have seen His kind look when He said,
And if I now ear - nest - ly seek Him be - low,
When the dear lit - tle chil - dren of ev - er - y clime

I should like to have been with them then.
"Let the lit - tle ones come un - to Me."
I shall see Him and hear Him a - bove.
All shall crowd to His arms and be blest. A - MEN.

Tune from "Songs of Praise." Used by permission of the Oxford University Press.

SWEET STORY
A Greek folk song

Jemima Luke, 1841      Irregular      Arr. by William B. Bradbury, 1859
(SECOND TUNE)

*In moderate time*

1. I think when I read that sweet sto - ry of old,
2. I wish that His hands had been placed on my head,
3. Yet still to His foot - stool in prayer I may go,
4. I long for the joy of that glo - ri - ous time,

When Je - sus was here a - mong men,
That His arm had been thrown a - round me,
And ask for a share in His love;
The sweet - est and bright - est and best,

How He called lit - tle chil - dren as lambs to His fold,
And that I might have seen His kind look when He said,
And if I now ear - nest - ly seek Him be - low,
When the dear lit - tle chil - dren of ev - er - y clime

I should like to have been with them then.
"Let the lit - tle ones come un - to Me."
I shall see Him and hear Him a - bove.
All shall crowd to His arms and be blest.    A-MEN.

Katherine Hankey, 1866; refrain added

7. 6. 7. 6. D. with Refrain

I LOVE TO TELL THE STORY
William G. Fischer, 1869

*Joyously*

1. I love to tell the sto - ry Of un - seen things a - bove,
2. I love to tell the sto - ry; For those who know it best

Of Je - sus and His glo - ry, Of Je - sus and His love. I love to tell the
Seem hun - ger - ing and thirst - ing To hear it, like the rest. And when, in scenes of

sto - ry, Be - cause I know it's true; It sat - is - fies my long - ings
glo - ry, I sing the new, new song, 'T will be the old, old sto - ry

**Refrain**

As noth - ing else could do. I love to tell the sto - ry, 'T will be my theme in
That I have loved so long.

glo - ry To tell the old, old sto - ry Of Je - sus and His love. A-men.

**444**

CHILDHOOD
"A Students' Hymnal,"
University of Wales, 1923

Rev. Stopford Augustus Brooke (1832–1916)  8. 8. 8. 6.

*In moderate time*

1. It fell up-on a sum-mer day, When Je-sus walked in Gal-i-lee,
2. He took them in His arms, and laid His hands on each re-mem-bered head;
3. "For-bid them not; un-less ye bear The child-like heart your hearts with-in,
4. O Fa-ther, grant this child-like heart, That I may come to Christ, and feel

The moth-ers from a vil-lage brought Their chil-dren to His knee.
"Suf-fer these lit-tle ones to come To Me," He gen-tly said.
Un-to My King-dom ye may come, But may not en-ter in."
His hands on me in bless-ing laid, Love-giv-ing, strong to heal. A-MEN.

From "A Students' Hymnal." By permission of the Oxford University Press.
Words used by permission of Miss Honor Brooke.

**445**

LYNE
"Magdalen Chapel Hymns," c. 1760

Rev. John Page Hopps (1834–1912)    7. 7. 7. 7.

*In moderate time*

1. Fa-ther, lead me day by day, Ev-er in Thine own sweet way;
2. When in dan-ger, make me brave, Make me know that Thou canst save;
3. When I'm tempt-ed to do wrong, Make me stead-fast, wise, and strong;
4. When my heart is full of glee, Help me to re-mem-ber Thee,
5. May I do the good I know, Be Thy lov-ing child be-low,

Teach me to be pure and true; Show me what I ought to do.
Keep me safe by Thy dear side; Let me in Thy love a-bide.
And when all a-lone I stand, Shield me with Thy might-y hand.
Hap-py most of all to know That my Fa-ther loves me so.
Then at last go home to Thee, Ev-er-more Thy child to be. A-MEN.

Words copyrighted. By permission of the National Sunday School Union of Great Britain. Two stanzas omitted.

William Medlen Hutchings (1827–1876)  Irregular  Robert Newton Quaile, 1911  ATHLONE

*In moderate time*

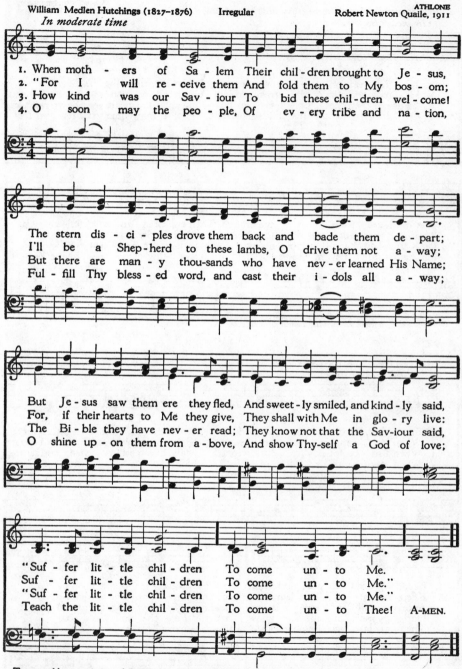

1. When moth - ers of Sa - lem Their chil - dren brought to Je - sus,
2. "For I will re - ceive them And fold them to My bos - om;
3. How kind was our Sav - iour To bid these chil - dren wel - come!
4. O soon may the peo - ple, Of ev - ery tribe and na - tion,

The stern dis - ci - ples drove them back and bade them de - part;
I'll be a Shep - herd to these lambs, O drive them not a - way;
But there are man - y thou-sands who have nev - er learned His Name;
Ful - fill Thy bless - ed word, and cast their i - dols all a - way;

But Je - sus saw them ere they fled, And sweet - ly smiled, and kind - ly said,
For, if their hearts to Me they give, They shall with Me in glo - ry live:
The Bi - ble they have nev - er read; They know not that the Sav-iour said,
O shine up - on them from a - bove, And show Thy-self a God of love;

"Suf - fer lit - tle chil - dren To come un - to Me.
Suf - fer lit - tle chil - dren To come un - to Me."
"Suf - fer lit - tle chil - dren To come un - to Me."
Teach the lit - tle chil - dren To come un - to Thee! A-MEN.

Tune used by permission of the Wesleyan Methodist Sunday School Department, London.

Emily Huntington Miller (1833–1913)       7. 6. 7. 6. D.       GOSTERWOOD
English traditional melody

*In the style of a carol*

1. I love to hear the sto - ry Which an - gel voi - ces tell,
2. I'm glad my bless - ed Sav - iour Was once a child like me,
3. To tell His love and mer - cy My sweet - est songs I'll raise;

How once the King of Glo - ry Came down on earth to dwell.
To show how pure and ho - ly His lit - tle ones might be;
And though I can - not see Him, I know He hears my praise;

I am both weak and sin - ful, But this I sure - ly know,
And if I try to fol - low His foot - steps here be - low,
For He Him - self has prom - ised That e - ven I may go

The Lord came down to save me, Be - cause He loved me so.
He nev - er will for - sake me, Be - cause He loves me so.
To sing a - mong His an - gels, Be - cause He loves me so. A-MEN.

Tune from "Songs of Praise." By permission of the Oxford University Press.

Christina G. Rossetti (1830–1894)     Irregular     MAY SONG
Traditional English carol

*Unison. In the style of a carol*

1. The shep-herds had an an - gel, The Wise Men had a star,
2. Those shep-herds, through the lone - ly night, Sat watch-ing by their sheep,
3. Lord Je - sus is my Guard - ian, So I can noth-ing lack;
4. Lord, bring me near - er day by day, Till I my voice u - nite,

But what have I, a lit - tle child,
Un - til they saw the heaven-ly host
The lambs lie in His bos - - om
And sing my "Glo - ry, glo - - ry,"

To guide me home from far, Where glad stars sing to -
Who neith - er tire nor sleep, All sing - ing "Glo - ry,
A - long life's dan - gerous track: The will - ful lambs that
With an - gels clad in white, All "Glo - ry, glo - ry,"

geth - er, And sing - ing an - gels are?
glo - ry" In fes - ti - val they keep.
go a - stray He, bleed - ing, fetch - es back.
given to Thee, Through all the heaven - ly height. A - MEN.

449

Mary Lundie Duncan (1814–1840)  8. 7. 8. 7. (FIRST TUNE)  DIJON
Old German melody

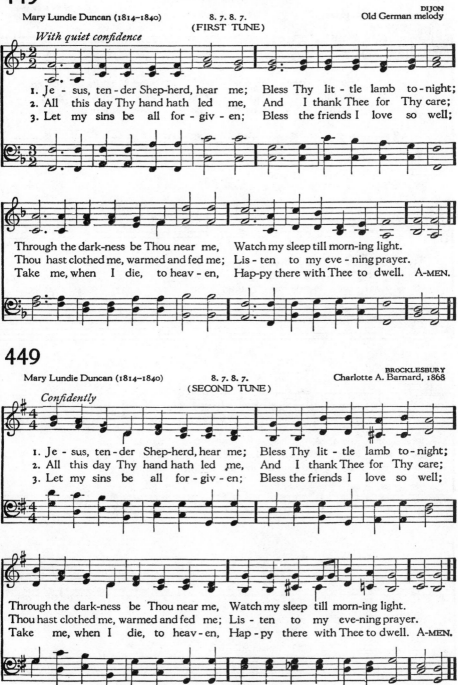

*With quiet confidence*

1. Je - sus, ten - der Shep-herd, hear me; Bless Thy lit - tle lamb to - night;
2. All this day Thy hand hath led me, And I thank Thee for Thy care;
3. Let my sins be all for - giv - en; Bless the friends I love so well;

Through the dark-ness be Thou near me, Watch my sleep till morn-ing light.
Thou hast clothed me, warmed and fed me; Lis - ten to my eve - ning prayer.
Take me, when I die, to heav - en, Hap-py there with Thee to dwell. A-MEN.

449

Mary Lundie Duncan (1814–1840)  8. 7. 8. 7. (SECOND TUNE)  BROCKLESBURY
Charlotte A. Barnard, 1868

*Confidently*

1. Je - sus, ten - der Shep-herd, hear me; Bless Thy lit - tle lamb to - night;
2. All this day Thy hand hath led me, And I thank Thee for Thy care;
3. Let my sins be all for - giv - en; Bless the friends I love so well;

Through the dark-ness be Thou near me, Watch my sleep till morn-ing light.
Thou hast clothed me, warmed and fed me; Lis - ten to my eve-ning prayer.
Take me, when I die, to heav - en, Hap - py there with Thee to dwell. A-MEN.

Anne H. Shepherd, 1836     C. M. with Refrain     CHILDREN'S PRAISES
Henry E. Matthews, c. 1853

*Joyously*

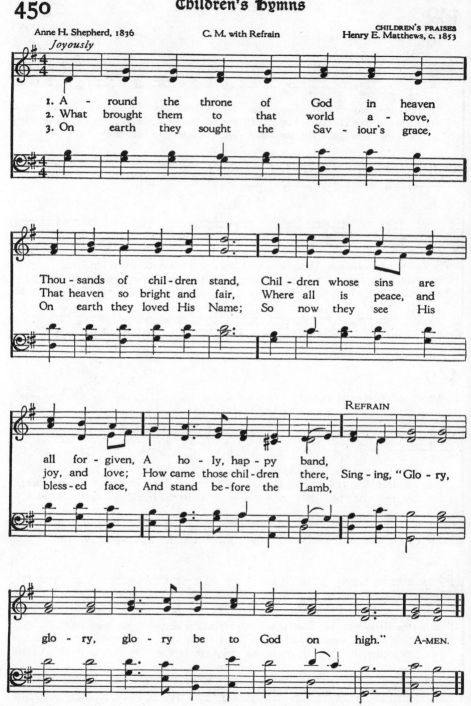

1. A - round the throne of God in heaven
2. What brought them to that world a - bove,
3. On earth they sought the Sav - iour's grace,

Thou - sands of chil - dren stand, Chil - dren whose sins are
That heaven so bright and fair, Where all is peace, and
On earth they loved His Name; So now they see His

all for - given, A ho - ly, hap - py band,
joy, and love; How came those chil - dren there,
bless - ed face, And stand be - fore the Lamb,

REFRAIN

Sing - ing, "Glo - ry,

glo - ry, glo - ry be to God on high." A-MEN.

**451**

Thomas Carlyle (1795–1881)   6. 5. 6. 5. Irregular

*To be sung in unison.   Not too fast*

1. So here hath been dawning Another blue day: Think, wilt thou let it  Slip use-less a-way?
2. Be - hold it   a-fore-time No eye ev - er did: So   soon it for - ev - er From all eyes is hid.

Out of    e-ter-ni-ty This new day is born; In-to  e - ter-ni-ty, At night, will re-turn.
Here hath been dawning Another blue day: Think, wilt thou let it Slip useless a-way? A-MEN.

Tune from " The Enlarged Songs of Praise."  By permission of the Oxford University Press.
Copyright, 1925, by R. Vaughan Williams.

**452**

Jane E. Leeson, 1842   7. 7. 7. 7.

*In moderate time*

1. Sav - iour, teach me,  day  by  day,  Love's sweet les - son,  to   o - bey;
2. With  a  child's glad  heart of  love,  At  Thy  bid - ding  may  I move,
3. Teach me  thus  Thy  steps to  trace,  Strong to  fol - low  in  Thy grace,
4. Love  in  lov - ing  finds em- ploy,  In   o - be-dience  all  her joy;

Sweet-er  les - son  can - not  be,   Lov-ing  Him who first loved me.
Prompt to serve and  fol - low Thee,   Lov-ing  Him who first loved me.
Learn-ing how  to  love from Thee,   Lov-ing  Him who first loved me.
Ev - er  new that joy  will  be,   Lov-ing  Him who first loved me. A-MEN.

TEMPUS ADEST FLORIDUM
A spring carol, c. 14th century
Arr. by Ernest MacMillan

Joseph Simpson Cook

7. 6. 7. 6. D.

*In the style of a carol*

1. Gen - tle Ma - ry laid her Child Low - ly in a man - ger;
2. An - gels sang a - bout His birth, Wise Men sought and found Him;
3. Gen - tle Ma - ry laid her Child Low - ly in a man - ger;

There He lay, the Un - de - filed, To the world a stran - ger.
Heav - en's star shone bright - ly forth Glo - ry all a - round Him.
He is still the Un - de - filed, But no more a stran - ger.

Such a Babe in such a place, Can He be the Sav - iour?
Shep - herds saw the won - drous sight, Heard the an - gels sing - ing;
Son of God of hum - ble birth, Beau - ti - ful the sto - ry;

Ask the saved of all the race Who have found His fa - vor.
All the plains were lit that night, All the hills were ring - ing.
Praise His Name in all the earth, Hail! the King of Glo - ry! A-MEN.

Tune used by permission of Dr. Ernest MacMillan.

Cecil F. Alexander, 1848      8. 7. 8. 7. 8. 8.      Henry J. Gauntlett, 1849

IRBY

*In the style of a carol*

1. Once in roy - al Da - vid's cit - y Stood a low - ly
2. He came down to earth from heav - en Who is God and
3. Je - sus is our child - hood's pat - tern, Day by day like
4. And our eyes at last shall see Him, Through His own re -

cat - tle shed, Where a moth - er laid her Ba - by
Lord of all, And His shel - ter was a sta - ble,
us He grew; He was lit - tle, weak, and help - less,
deem - ing love; For that Child so dear and gen - tle

In a man - ger for His bed: Ma - ry was that
And His cra - dle was a stall: With the poor, and
Tears and smiles like us He knew: And He feel - eth
Is our Lord in heaven a - bove, And He leads His

moth - er mild, Je - sus Christ, her lit - tle Child.
mean, and low - ly, Lived on earth our Sav - iour ho - ly.
for our sad - ness, And He shar - eth in our glad-ness.
chil - dren on To the place where He is gone. A - MEN.

Rev. Francis Pott, 1861     8. 5. 8. 5. 8. 4. 3.     ANGEL VOICES
Arthur S. Sullivan, 1872

*Joyfully*

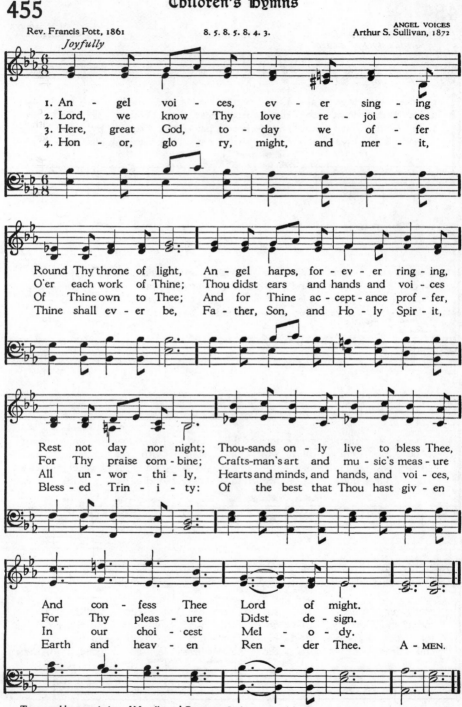

1. An - gel voi - ces, ev - er sing - ing
2. Lord, we know Thy love re - joi - ces
3. Here, great God, to - day we of - fer
4. Hon - or, glo - ry, might, and mer - it,

Round Thy throne of light, An - gel harps, for - ev - er ring - ing,
O'er each work of Thine; Thou didst ears and hands and voi - ces,
Of Thine own to Thee; And for Thine ac - cept - ance prof - fer,
Thine shall ev - er be, Fa - ther, Son, and Ho - ly Spir - it,

Rest not day nor night; Thou-sands on - ly live to bless Thee,
For Thy praise com - bine; Crafts-man's art and mu - sic's meas - ure
All un - wor - thi - ly, Hearts and minds, and hands, and voi - ces,
Bless - ed Trin - i - ty: Of the best that Thou hast giv - en

And con - fess Thee Lord of might.
For Thy pleas - ure Didst de - sign.
In our choi - cest Mel - o - dy.
Earth and heav - en Ren - der Thee. A - MEN.

Tune used by permission of Novello and Company, Ltd.

Frances R. Havergal, 1871     6. 5. 6. 5. D. with Refrain     **HERMAS**
Frances R. Havergal, 1871

*In jubilant style*

1. Gold - en harps are sound-ing, An - gel voi - ces ring, Pearl-y gates are o-pened,
2. He who came to save us, He who bled and died, Now is crowned with glo-ry
3. Pray - ing for His chil-dren In that bless-ed place, Call-ing them to glo-ry,

O - pened for the King: Christ, the King of Glo - ry, Je - sus, King of Love,
At His Fa-ther's side; Nev - er more to suf - fer, Nev - er more to die,
Send-ing them His grace; His bright home pre - par - ing, Faith-ful ones, for you;

**REFRAIN**

Is gone up in tri-umph To His throne a - bove. All His work is end - ed,
Je - sus, King of Glo - ry, Is gone up on high.
Je - sus ev - er liv - eth, Ev - er lov - eth too.

Joy - ful - ly we sing; Je - sus hath as - cend-ed: Glo - ry to our King! A-MEN.

# 457

Rev. Thomas J. Potter, 1860
Recast in Morrell and How's "Psalms and Hymns," 1867
and S. P. C. K., "Psalms and Hymns," 1869

6. 5. 6. 5. 12l.

ST. THERESA
Arthur S. Sullivan, 1874

*In unison.  With spirit*

1. Bright-ly gleams our ban-ner, Point-ing to the sky,   Wav-ing on Christ's sol-diers
2. Je - sus, Lord and Mas-ter, At Thy sa-cred feet,   Here, with hearts re-joi-cing,
3. Pat - tern of our child-hood, Once Thy-self a child,   Make our child-hood ho-ly,

To their home on high.   March-ing through the des-ert, Glad-ly thus we pray,
See Thy chil-dren meet.   Of - ten have we left Thee, Of - ten gone a-stray;
Pure, and meek, and mild.   In   the   hour   of   dan - ger   Whith-er can we flee,

REFRAIN

Still with hearts u-nit-ed, Sing-ing on our way.   Bright-ly gleams our ban-ner,
Keep us, might-y Sav-iour, In   the nar-row way.
Save to Thee, dear Sav-iour. On - ly un - to Thee?

Point-ing to the   sky,   Wav-ing on Christ's sol-diers To their home on high. A-MEN.

Tune used by permission of Novello and Company, Ltd.

Anon., in "Hymns for the Young," 1832    8. 7. 8. 7. 8. 7.

SICILIAN MARINERS
Arr. from a Sicilian melody

*In the style of a carol*

1. Sav - iour, like a Shep - herd lead us, Much we need Thy
2. Thou hast prom - ised to re - ceive us, Poor and sin - ful
3. Ear - ly let us seek Thy fa - vor; Ear - ly let us

ten - der care; In Thy pleas - ant pas - tures feed us,
though we be; Thou hast mer - cy to re - lieve us,
do Thy will; Bless - ed Lord and on - ly Sav - iour,

For our use Thy folds pre - pare: Bless - ed Je - sus!
Grace to cleanse, and power to free: Bless - ed Je - sus!
With Thy love our bos - oms fill: Bless - ed Je - sus!

Bless - ed Je - sus! Thou hast bought us, Thine we are.
Bless - ed Je - sus! Let us ear - ly turn to Thee.
Bless - ed Je - sus! Thou hast loved us; love us still. A-MEN.

Rev. Martin Rinkart, c. 1636
Trans. by Catherine Winkworth, 1858    6. 7. 6. 7. 6. 6. 6. 6.

NUN DANKET
Johann Crüger, 1648

*In majestic style*

1. Now thank we all our God  With  heart and hands and voi - ces,
2. O  may this boun - teous God  Through all  our  life be near  us,
3. All  praise and thanks to  God  The  Fa - ther now be giv - en,

Who won-drous things hath done,  In  whom His world re - joi - ces;
With ev - er joy - ful hearts  And  bless-ed  peace to  cheer  us;
The Son, and Him who reigns  With  Them in high - est  heav - en,

Who,  from  our moth - ers'  arms,  Hath  blessed us  on  our  way
And  keep  us  in  His  grace,  And  guide us when per - plexed,
The  one  e - ter - nal  God,  Whom earth and heaven a - dore;

With  count-less gifts  of  love,  And  still  is  ours  to - day.
And  free  us  from  all  ills  In  this  world and  the  next.
For  thus  it  was,  is  now,  And  shall  be  ev - er - more.  A-MEN.

Rev. Henry Alford, 1844      7. 7. 7. 7. D.      ST. GEORGE'S, WINDSOR
George J. Elvey, 1859

*In a spirit of joy*

1. Come, ye thank-ful peo-ple, come, Raise the song of har-vest home:
2. All the world is God's own field, Fruit un-to His praise to yield;
3. For the Lord our God shall come, And shall take His har-vest home;
4. E-ven so, Lord, quick-ly come To Thy fi-nal har-vest home;

All is safe-ly gath-ered in, Ere the win-ter storms be-gin;
Wheat and tares to-geth-er sown, Un-to joy or sor-row grown:
From His field shall in that day All of-fen-ses purge a-way;
Gath-er Thou Thy peo-ple in, Free from sor-row, free from sin;

God, our Mak-er, doth pro-vide For our wants to be sup-plied:
First the blade, and then the ear, Then the full corn shall ap-pear:
Give His an-gels charge at last In the fire the tares to cast,
There, for-ev-er pu-ri-fied, In Thy pres-ence to a-bide:

Come to God's own tem-ple, come, Raise the song of har-vest home.
Lord of har-vest, grant that we Whole-some grain and pure may be.
But the fruit-ful ears to store In His gar-ner ev-er-more.
Come, with all Thine an-gels, come, Raise the glo-rious har-vest home. A-MEN.

**KREMSER**
Old Netherlands melody in
"The Collection," by Adrianus Valerius, 1625

Julia Bulkley Cady Cory

12. 11. 12. 11.

*May be sung in unison. Majestically*

1. We praise Thee, O God, our Re-deem-er, Cre-a-tor,
2. We wor-ship Thee, God of our fa-thers, we bless Thee;
3. With voi-ces u-nit-ed our prais-es we of-fer,

In grate-ful de-vo-tion our trib-ute we bring.
Through life's storm and tem-pest our Guide hast Thou been.
To Thee, great Je-ho-vah, glad an-thems we raise.

We lay it be-fore Thee, we kneel and a-dore Thee,
When per-ils o'er-take us, es-cape Thou wilt make us,
Thy strong arm will guide us, our God is be-side us,

We bless Thy ho-ly Name, glad prais-es we sing.
And with Thy help, O Lord, our bat-tles we win.
To Thee, our great Re-deem-er, for-ev-er be praise. A-MEN.

Words used by permission.

Rev. Leonard Bacon, 1833  L. M.  DUKE STREET
John Hatton, d. 1793

*With dignity*

1. O God, be-neath Thy guid - ing hand Our ex-iled fa-thers crossed the sea;
2. Thou heard'st, well pleased, the song, the prayer: Thy bless-ing came; and still its power
3. Laws, free-dom, truth, and faith in God Came with those ex-iles o'er the waves;
4. And here Thy Name, O God of love, Their chil-dren's chil-dren shall a-dore,

And when they trod the win - try strand, With prayer and psalm they worshiped Thee.
Shall on-ward, through all a - ges, bear The mem-ory of that ho - ly hour.
And, where their pil-grim feet have trod, The God they trust-ed guards their graves.
Till these e - ter - nal hills re - move, And spring a-dorns the earth no more. A-MEN.

**463**

Psalm cxxxvi. Based on John Milton's version, 1623
Rev. Henry Williams Baker (1821-1877)  7. 7. 7. 7.  MONKLAND
Arr. by John B. Wilkes, 1861

*In jubilant style*

1. Praise, O praise our God and King; Hymns of ad - o - ra - tion sing;
2. Praise Him that He made the sun Day by day his course to run;
3. Praise Him that He gave the rain To ma - ture the swell - ing grain;
4. He hath bid the fruit - ful field Crops of pre - cious in - crease yield;
5. Glo - ry to our boun - teous King! Glo - ry let cre - a - tion sing,

For His mer-cies still en-dure, Ev - er faith-ful, ev - er sure.
For His mer-cies still en-dure, Ev - er faith-ful, ev - er sure.
For His mer-cies still en-dure, Ev - er faith-ful, ev - er sure.
For His mer-cies still en-dure, Ev - er faith-ful, ev - er sure.
Glo - ry to the Fa - ther, Son, And blest Spir - it, Three in One! A-MEN.

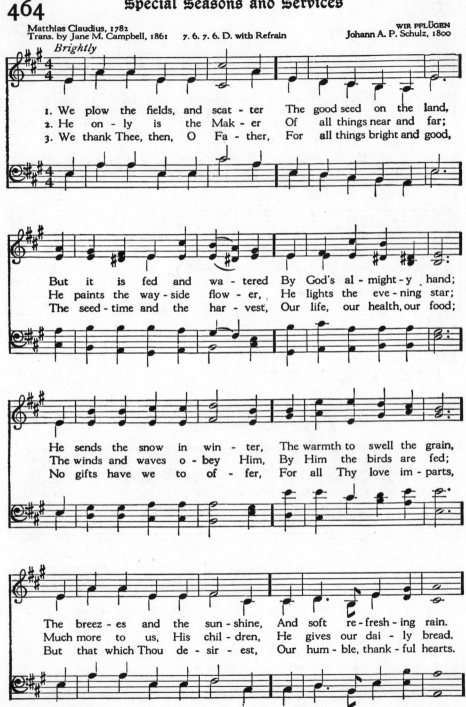

Matthias Claudius, 1782
Trans. by Jane M. Campbell, 1861    7. 6. 7. 6. D. with Refrain

WIR PFLÜGEN
Johann A. P. Schulz, 1800

*Brightly*

1. We plow the fields, and scat-ter The good seed on the land,
2. He on-ly is the Mak-er Of all things near and far;
3. We thank Thee, then, O Fa-ther, For all things bright and good,

But it is fed and wa-tered By God's al-might-y hand;
He paints the way-side flow-er, He lights the eve-ning star;
The seed-time and the har-vest, Our life, our health, our food;

He sends the snow in win-ter, The warmth to swell the grain,
The winds and waves o-bey Him, By Him the birds are fed;
No gifts have we to of-fer, For all Thy love im-parts,

The breez-es and the sun-shine, And soft re-fresh-ing rain.
Much more to us, His chil-dren, He gives our dai-ly bread.
But that which Thou de-sir-est, Our hum-ble, thank-ful hearts.

**REFRAIN**

All good gifts a - round us Are sent from heaven a - bove;

Then thank the Lord, O thank the Lord For all His love. A-MEN.

## 465

RATISBON
Old German melody

Psalm lxvii. Rev. Henry F. Lyte, 1834    7. 7. 7. 7. 7. 7.    Arr. in J. G. Werner's "Choralbuch," 1815

*Not too slow*

1. God of mer - cy, God of grace, Show the bright-ness of Thy face;
2. Let the peo - ple praise Thee, Lord; Be by all that live a - dored.
3. Let the peo - ple praise Thee, Lord; Earth shall then her fruits af - ford;

Shine up - on us, Sav - iour, shine, Fill Thy Church with light di - vine:
Let the na - tions shout and sing Glo - ry to their Sav - iour King;
God to man His bless - ing give, Man to God de - vot - ed live;

And Thy sav - ing health ex - tend Un - to earth's re - mot - est end.
At Thy feet their trib - ute pay, And Thy ho - ly will o - bey.
All be - low, and all a - bove, One in joy, and light, and love. A-MEN.

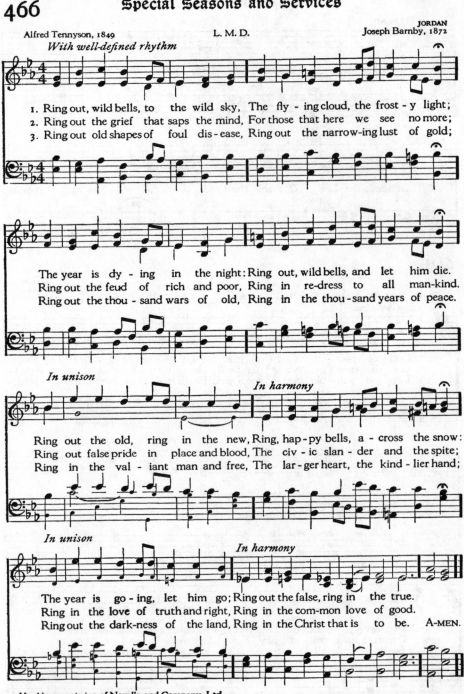

Alfred Tennyson, 1849     L. M. D.     JORDAN  
Joseph Barnby, 1872

*With well-defined rhythm*

1. Ring out, wild bells, to the wild sky, The fly - ing cloud, the frost - y light;
2. Ring out the grief that saps the mind, For those that here we see no more;
3. Ring out old shapes of foul dis - ease, Ring out the narrow-ing lust of gold;

The year is dy - ing in the night: Ring out, wild bells, and let him die.
Ring out the feud of rich and poor, Ring in re-dress to all man-kind.
Ring out the thou - sand wars of old, Ring in the thou-sand years of peace.

*In unison*     *In harmony*

Ring out the old, ring in the new, Ring, hap-py bells, a - cross the snow:
Ring out false pride in place and blood, The civ - ic slan - der and the spite;
Ring in the val - iant man and free, The lar - ger heart, the kind - lier hand;

*In unison*     *In harmony*

The year is go - ing, let him go; Ring out the false, ring in the true.
Ring in the love of truth and right, Ring in the com-mon love of good.
Ring out the dark-ness of the land, Ring in the Christ that is to be. A-MEN.

Used by permission of Novello and Company, Ltd.

# The New Year

Frances Ridley Havergal (1836–1879); alt. 13. 13. 13. 14.

HOYTE (ST. COLUMBA)
W. Stevenson Hoyte, 1889

*Joyously*

1. From glo - ry un - to glo - ry! Be this our joy - ous song,
2. The full - ness of His bless - ing en - com - pass - eth our way;
3. O let our ad - o - ra - tion for all that He hath done
4. Now on - ward, ev - er on - ward, from strength to strength we go,

As on the King's own high - way we brave - ly march a - long.
The full - ness of His prom - is - es crowns ev - ery bright-ening day;
Peal out be - yond the stars of God, while voice and life are one;
While grace for grace a - bun-dant - ly shall from His full - ness flow,

From glo - ry un - to glo - ry! O word of stir - ring cheer,
The full - ness of His glo - ry is beam - ing from a - bove,
And let our con - se - cra - tion be real and deep and true,
To glo - ry's full fru - i - tion, from glo - ry's fore - taste here,

As dawns the sol - emn bright-ness of an - oth - er glad New Year!
While more and more we learn to know the full - ness of His love.
O e - ven now our hearts shall bow and joy - ful vows re - new.
Un - til His ver - y pres-ence crown our hap - pi - est New Year. A-MEN.

THE NEW YEAR
Frances Ridley Havergal, 1873     6. 5. 6. 5. 12l.     Arthur H. Mann, 1885

*In marching rhythm*

1. Stand-ing at the por-tal Of the open-ing year, Words of com-fort
2. For the year be-fore us, O what rich sup-plies! For the poor and
3. He will nev-er fail us, He will not for-sake; His e-ter-nal

meet us, Hush-ing ev-ery fear; Spo-ken through the si-lence
need-y Liv-ing streams shall rise; For the sad and sin-ful
cove-nant He will nev-er break; Rest-ing on His prom-ise,

By our Fa-ther's voice; Ten-der, strong, and faith-ful,
Shall His grace a-bound; For the faint and fee-ble
What have we to fear? God is all-suf-fi-cient

*REFRAIN*

Mak-ing us re-joice. On-ward, then, and fear not, Chil-dren of the
Per-fect strength be found.
For the com-ing year.

day; For His word shall nev-er, Nev-er pass a-way. A-MEN.

Frances Whitmarsh Wile, 1912      C. M. D.      FOREST GREEN
English traditional melody

*In moderate time; brightly*

1. All beau - ti - ful the march of days, As sea - sons come and go;
2. O'er white ex - pans - es spar-kling pure The ra - diant morns un-fold;
3. O Thou from whose un - fath-omed law The year in beau - ty flows,

The Hand that shaped the rose hath wrought The crys - tal of the snow;
The sol - emn splen - dors of the night Burn bright-er through the cold;
Thy-self the vi - sion pass-ing by In crys - tal and in rose,

Hath sent the hoar - y frost of heaven, The flow - ing wa - ters sealed,
Life mounts in ev - ery throb-bing vein, Love deep - ens round the hearth,
Day un - to day doth ut - ter speech, And night to night pro-claim,

And laid a si - lent love-li - ness On hill and wood and field.
And clear - er sounds the an - gel hymn, "Good will to men on earth."
In ev - er - chan - ging words of light, The won - der of Thy Name. A-MEN.

Tune from "The English Hymnal." Used by permission of the Oxford University Press.
Words used by permission of The Beacon Press.

# 472 Laying of a Corner Stone

Latin, 7th or 8th century
Trans. by Rev. John Chandler, 1837          6. 6. 6. 6. 8. 8.          R. Huntington Woodman, 1895
*In moderate time*                                                    UNITY

1. Christ is our Cor-ner Stone, On Him a-lone we build;
2. O then with hymns of praise These hal-lowed courts shall ring;
3. Here, gra-cious God, do Thou For-ev-er-more draw nigh;
4. Here may we gain from heaven The grace which we im-plore;

With His true saints a-lone The courts of
Our voi-ces we will raise The Three in
Ac-cept each faith-ful vow, And mark each
And may that grace, once given, Be with us

heaven are filled; On His great love our hopes we place
One to sing; And thus pro-claim in joy-ful song,
sup-pliant sigh; In co-pious shower on all who pray,
ev-er-more, Un-til that day when all the blest

Of pres-ent grace and joys a-bove.
Both loud and long, that glo-rious Name.
Each ho-ly day, Thy bless-ings pour.
To end-less rest are called a-way.          A-MEN.

Copyright, 1895, by the trustees of the Presbyterian Board of Publication and Sabbath-School Work.

**473**

Rev. Frederic William Goadby, 1879
Stanza 2, line 1, alt.

7. 6. 7. 6. D.

DAY OF REST
James W. Elliott, 1875

*In moderate time*

1. O Thou, whose hand has brought us Un - to this joy - ful day,
2. For this Thy house we praise Thee, Reared by Thine own com - mand,
3. And oft as here we gath - er, And hearts in wor - ship blend,

Ac - cept our glad thanks-giv - ing, And lis - ten as we pray;
For ev - ery gen - erous bos - om, And ev - ery will - ing hand;
May truth re - veal its pow - er, And fer - vent prayer as - cend;

And may our prep - a - ra - tion For this day's serv - ice be
And now with - in Thy tem - ple Thy glo - ry let us see,
Here may the bus - y toil - er Rise to the things a - bove,

*Unison*          *Harmony*

With one ac - cord to of - fer Our-selves, O Lord, to Thee.
For all its strength and beau - ty Are noth - ing with - out Thee.
The young, the old, be strength-ened, And all men learn Thy love. A-MEN.

Tune used by permission of Novello and Company, Ltd.

**474**

Rev. Samuel F. Smith, 1894     L. M.     MENDON
German melody
Arr. by Samuel Dyer, 1828

*In moderate time*

1. Found-ed on Thee, our on - ly Lord, On Thee, the ev - er - last - ing Rock,
2. For Thee our wait - ing spir - its yearn, For Thee this house of praise we rear;
3. Come, with Thy Spir - it and Thy power, The Con-queror, once the Cru - ci - fied;
4. Ac - cept the work our hands have wrought; Ac-cept, O God, this earth-ly shrine;

Thy Church shall stand as stands Thy word, Nor fear the storm, nor dread the shock.
To Thee with long-ing hearts we turn; Come, fix Thy glo-rious pres-ence here.
Our God, our Strength, our King, our Tower, Here plant Thy throne, and here a-bide.
Be Thou our Rock, our Life, our Thought, And we, as liv - ing tem-ples, Thine. A-MEN.

**475**

John Greenleaf Whittier (1807–1891)     L. M.     HERR JESU CHRIST
" Pensum Sacrum," Görlitz, 1648
Arr. by Johann Sebastian Bach (1685–1750)

*With dignity*

1. All things are Thine; no gift have we, Lord of all gifts, to of - fer Thee;
2. Thy will was in the build-ers' thought; Thy hand un-seen a-midst us wrought;
3. In weak-ness and in want we call On Thee for whom the heavens are small;
4. O Fa - ther, deign these walls to bless; Fill with Thy love their emp-ti-ness;

And hence with grate-ful hearts to - day, Thine own be-fore Thy feet we lay.
Through mor-tal mo-tive, scheme and plan, Thy wise e - ter - nal pur-pose ran.
Thy glo - ry is Thy chil-dren's good, Thy joy Thy ten-der Fa-ther-hood.
And let their door a gate-way be To lead us from our-selves to Thee. A-MEN.

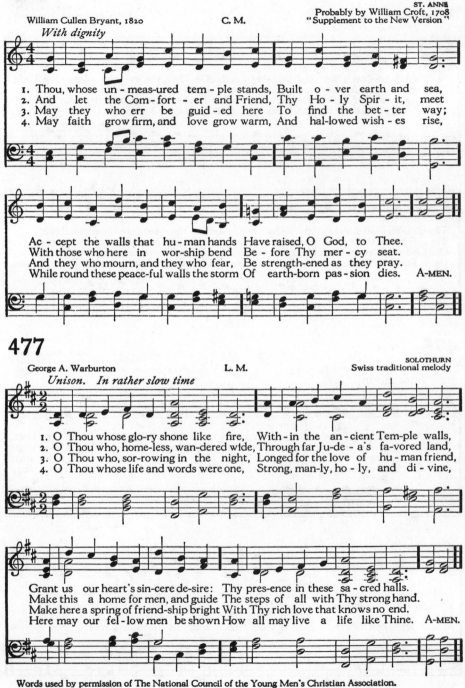

**476**

ST. ANNE
Probably by William Croft, 1708
"Supplement to the New Version"

William Cullen Bryant, 1820                    C. M.

*With dignity*

1. Thou, whose un-meas-ured tem-ple stands, Built o-ver earth and sea,
2. And let the Com-fort-er and Friend, Thy Ho-ly Spir-it, meet
3. May they who err be guid-ed here To find the bet-ter way;
4. May faith grow firm, and love grow warm, And hal-lowed wish-es rise,

Ac-cept the walls that hu-man hands Have raised, O God, to Thee.
With those who here in wor-ship bend Be-fore Thy mer-cy seat.
And they who mourn, and they who fear, Be strength-ened as they pray.
While round these peace-ful walls the storm Of earth-born pas-sion dies. A-MEN.

**477**

SOLOTHURN
Swiss traditional melody

George A. Warburton                    L. M.

*Unison. In rather slow time*

1. O Thou whose glo-ry shone like fire, With-in the an-cient Tem-ple walls,
2. O Thou who, home-less, wan-dered wide, Through far Ju-de-a's fa-vored land,
3. O Thou who, sor-row-ing in the night, Longed for the love of hu-man friend,
4. O Thou whose life and words were one, Strong, man-ly, ho-ly, and di-vine,

Grant us our heart's sin-cere de-sire: Thy pres-ence in these sa-cred halls.
Make this a home for men, and guide The steps of all with Thy strong hand.
Make here a spring of friend-ship bright With Thy rich love that knows no end.
Here may our fel-low men be shown How all may live a life like Thine. A-MEN.

Words used by permission of The National Council of the Young Men's Christian Association.

# 478

## Dedication of an Organ

Rev. Henry Ware, Jr., 1822
Stanza 3, alt.

C. M. D.

BETHLEHEM
Rev. Gottfried W. Fink, 1842

*With a spirit of joy*

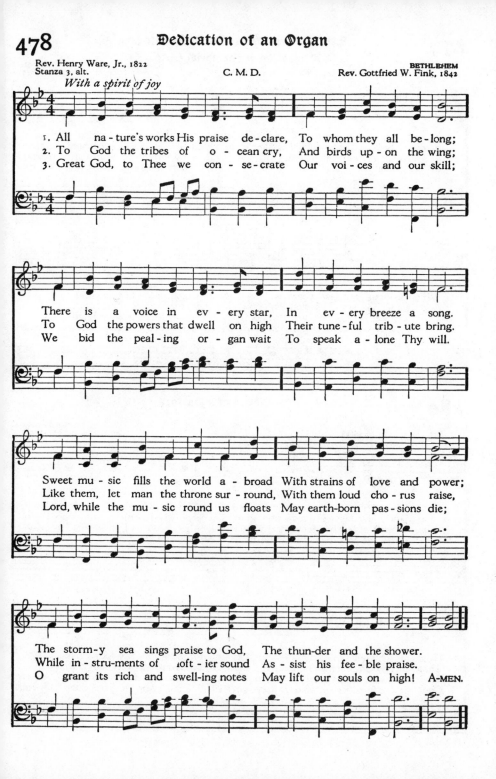

1. All     na - ture's works His praise de - clare,     To  whom they  all  be - long;
2. To     God  the  tribes  of    o - cean cry,     And  birds  up - on  the  wing;
3. Great God,  to  Thee  we  con - se - crate     Our  voi - ces  and  our skill;

There  is   a  voice in   ev - ery star,     In   ev - ery breeze  a   song.
To     God   the powers that dwell  on high     Their tune - ful   trib - ute bring.
We     bid   the peal - ing   or - gan wait     To  speak  a - lone Thy will.

Sweet mu - sic  fills the world a - broad With strains of   love  and  power;
Like them,  let  man the throne sur - round, With them loud  cho - rus  raise,
Lord, while the  mu - sic round us  floats May earth-born  pas - sions die;

The storm - y  sea  sings praise to God,     The thun - der  and the shower.
While  in - stru - ments of  loft - ier sound  As - sist his  fee - ble praise.
O    grant its  rich and  swell-ing notes  May lift our  souls on  high!  A-MEN.

**479**

**Dedication of Memorial Gifts**

From Psalm lxxviii.   Rev. Isaac Watts, 1719   C. M.

DUNDEE
"Scottish Psalter," 1615

*In moderate time*

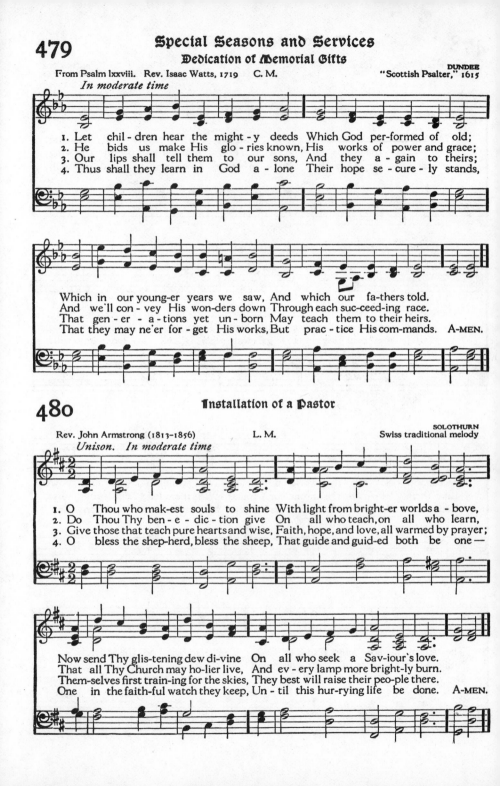

1. Let   chil-dren hear the might-y deeds Which God per-formed of   old;
2. He   bids   us make His   glo - ries known, His   works of   power and grace;
3. Our   lips shall   tell them   to   our sons, And   they   a - gain   to theirs;
4. Thus shall they learn in   God   a - lone   Their hope se - cure-ly stands,

Which in   our young-er years we saw, And   which our   fa-thers told.
And   we'll con - vey His won-ders down Through each suc-ceed-ing race.
That gen - er - a - tions yet un-born May   teach them to their heirs.
That they may ne'er for - get His works, But   prac - tice His com-mands. A-MEN.

**480**

**Installation of a Pastor**

Rev. John Armstrong (1813–1856)   L. M.

SOLOTHURN
Swiss traditional melody

*Unison. In moderate time*

1. O   Thou who mak-est souls to shine With light from bright-er worlds a - bove,
2. Do   Thou Thy ben - e - dic - tion give On   all who teach, on   all   who learn,
3. Give those that teach pure hearts and wise, Faith, hope, and love, all warmed by prayer;
4. O   bless the shep-herd, bless the sheep, That guide and guid-ed both be   one—

Now send Thy glis-tening dew di-vine On   all who seek a   Sav-iour's love.
That all Thy Church may ho-lier live, And ev - ery lamp more bright-ly burn.
Them-selves first train-ing for the skies, They best will raise their peo-ple there.
One   in the faith-ful watch they keep, Un - til this hur-rying life   be done. A-MEN.

# Installation of a Pastor

Rev. Denis Wortman, 1884      10. 10. 10. 10.

TOULON
Derived from Old 124th,
"Genevan Psalter," 1551

*With dignity*

1. God of the proph - ets! Bless the proph - ets' sons;
2. A - noint them proph - ets! Make their ears at - tent
3. A - noint them priests! Strong in - ter - ces - sors they
4. Make them a - pos - tles! Her - alds of Thy cross,

E - li - jah's man - tle o'er E - li - sha cast;
To Thy di - vin - est speech; their hearts a - wake
For par - don, and for char - i - ty and peace!
Forth may they go to tell all realms Thy grace;

Each age its sol - emn task may claim but once;
To hu - man need; their lips make el - o - quent
O that with them might pass the world, a - stray,
In - spired of Thee, may they count all but loss,

Make each one no - bler, strong - er than the last.
To gird the right and ev - ery e - vil break.
In - to the dear Christ's life of sac - ri - fice!
And stand at last with joy be - fore Thy face. A-MEN.

Edward Osler, 1836
Based on Rev. Charles Wesley, 1749    8. 8. 6. 8. 8. 6.

MAGDALEN COLLEGE
William Hayes (1706-1777)

*In moderate time*

1. Lord of the Church, we hum - bly pray For those who
2. Help them to preach the truth of God, Re - demp - tion
3. So may they live to Thee a - lone, Then hear the

guide us in Thy way, And speak Thy ho - ly Word;
through the Sav - iour's blood; Nor let the Spir - it cease
wel - come word, "Well done!" And take their crown a - bove;

With love di - vine their hearts in - spire, And touch their
On all the Church His gifts to shower: To them, a
En - ter in - to their Mas - ter's joy, And all e -

lips with hal - lowed fire, And need - ful grace af - ford.
Mes - sen - ger of power, To us, of life and peace.
ter - ni - ty em - ploy In praise and bliss and love. A-MEN.

William E. Evans
*With spirit*

6. 6. 4. 6. 6. 6. 4.

TRINITY (ITALIAN HYMN)
Felice de Giardini, 1769

1. Come, O Thou God of grace, Dwell in this ho - ly place, E'en now de - scend! This tem - ple, reared to Thee, O may it ev - er be Filled with Thy maj - es - ty, Till time shall end!

2. Be in each song of praise Which here Thy peo - ple raise With hearts a - flame! Let ev - ery an - them rise Like in - cense to the skies, A joy - ful sac - ri - fice, To Thy blest Name!

3. Speak, O e - ter - nal Lord, Out of Thy liv - ing Word, O give suc - cess! Do Thou the truth im - part Un - to each wait - ing heart; Source of all strength Thou art, Thy gos - pel bless!

4. To the great One in Three Glo - ry and prais - es be In love now given! Glad songs to Thee we sing, Glad hearts to Thee we bring, Till we our God and King Shall praise in heaven! A - MEN.

# Special Seasons and Services
## Marriage

Dorothy Blomfield Gurney, 1883      11. 10. 11. 10.      PERFECT LOVE
Joseph Barnby, 1889

*In moderate time*

1. O per - fect Love, all hu - man thought tran - scend - ing,
2. O per - fect Life, be Thou their full as - sur - ance
3. Grant them the joy which bright - ens earth - ly sor - row;

Low - ly we kneel in prayer be - fore Thy throne,
Of ten - der char - i - ty and stead - fast faith,
Grant them the peace which calms all earth - ly strife,

That theirs may be the love which knows no end - ing,
Of pa - tient hope, and qui - et, brave en - dur - ance,
And to life's day the glo - rious un - known mor - row

Whom Thou for - ev - er - more dost join in one.
With child - like trust that fears nor pain nor death.
That dawns up - on e - ter - nal love and life. A-MEN.

Tune used by permission of Novello and Company, Ltd.

Rev. John S. B. Monsell, 1866     7. 6. 7. 6. D.     BLAIRGOWRIE
Rev. John B. Dykes, 1872

*In moderate time*

1. O Love di - vine and gold - en, Mys - te - rious depth and height,
2. O Love di - vine and ten - der, That through our homes dost move,
3. God bless these hands u - nit - ed; God bless these hearts made one!

To Thee the world be - hold - en Looks up for life and light;
Veiled in the sof - tened splen - dor Of ho - ly house - hold love,
Un - sev - ered and un - blight - ed May they through life go on,

O Love di - vine and gen - tle, The Bless - er and the Blest,
A throne with-out Thy bless - ing Were la - bor with - out rest,
Here in earth's home pre - par - ing For the bright home a - bove,

Be - neath Thy care pa - ren - tal The world lies down in rest.
And cot - ta - ges pos - sess - ing Thy bless - ed - ness are blest.
And there for - ev - er shar - ing Its joy where God is Love. A-MEN.

Rev. Washington Gladden, 1897     C. M. D.     FOREST GREEN
English traditional melody

*In moderate time; brightly*

1. Be - hold a Sow - er! from a - far He go - eth forth with might;
2. O Lord of life, to Thee we lift Our hearts in praise for those,
3. Shine forth, O Light, that we may see, With hearts all un - a - fraid,
4. Light up Thy Word; the fet - tered page From kill - ing bond - age free:

The roll - ing years His fur - rows are, His seed, the grow - ing light;
Thy proph-ets, who have shown Thy gift Of grace that ev - er grows,
The mean-ing and the mys - ter - y Of things that Thou hast made:
Light up our way; lead forth this age In love's large lib - er - ty.

For all the just His word is sown, It spring-eth up al - way;
Of truth that spreads from shore to shore, Of wis-dom's wid - ening ray,
Shine forth, and let the dark - ling past, Be - neath Thy beam grow bright;
O Light of light! with - in us dwell, Through us Thy ra - diance pour,

The ten - der blade is hope's young dawn, The har - vest, love's new day.
Of light that shin - eth more and more Un - to Thy per - fect day.
Shine forth, and touch the fu - ture vast With Thine un-trou - bled light.
That word and life Thy truths may tell, And praise Thee ev - er - more. A-MEN.

Tune from "The English Hymnal." Used by permission of the Oxford University Press.
Words used by permission of The Beacon Press.

**487**

F. R. L. von Canitz, 1700
Trans. by Rev. Henry J. Buckoll, 1841     8. 4. 7. 8. 4. 7.

COLUMBIA COLLEGE
George William Warren, 1886

*Unison*

1. Come, my soul, thou must be wak - ing; Now is break - ing
2. Thou, too, hail the light re - turn - ing; Read - y burn - ing
3. Pray that He may pros - per ev - er Each en - deav - or,
4. On - ly God's free gifts a - buse not, Light re - fuse not,

O'er the earth an - oth - er day: Come to
Be the in - cense of thy powers; For the
When thine aim is good and true; But that
But His Spir - it's voice o - bey; Thou with

Him who made this splen - dor; See thou ren - der
night is safe - ly end - ed, God hath tend - ed
He may ev - er thwart thee, And con - vert thee,
Him shalt dwell, be - hold - ing Light en - fold - ing

All thy fee - ble powers can pay.
With His care thy help - less hours.
When thou e - vil wouldst pur - sue.
All things in un - cloud - ed day.     A - MEN.

Music copyright by Harper & Brothers. Used by permission.

Rev. Maltbie D. Babcock, 1901     2. 10. 10. 10.     Arr. from Orlando Gibbons (1583–1625)

SONG 24

*With dignity. May be sung in unison*

1. Be strong! We are not here to play, to dream, to drift; We have hard work to do and loads to lift; Shun not the strug - gle: face it, 'tis God's gift.

2. Be strong! Say not the days are e - vil— who's to blame? And fold the hands and ac - qui - esce— O shame! Stand up, speak out, and brave - ly, in God's Name.

3. Be strong! It mat - ters not how deep in - trenched the wrong, How hard the bat - tle goes, the day, how long; Faint not, fight on! To - mor - row comes the song. A - MEN.

Words from "Thoughts for Every-Day Living." Copyright, 1901, by Charles Scribner's Sons.

# 489

Henry Cary Shuttleworth (1850–1900)    8. 8. 8.

ST. LO
Old Breton melody, as in
" School Worship," 1926

*Moderately fast*

1. Fa - ther of men, in whom are one
2. Man lives not for him - self a - lone,
3. We, friends and com - rades on life's way,
4. O Christ, our El - der Broth - er, who

All hu - man - kind be - neath Thy sun,
In oth - ers' good he finds his own;
Gath - er with - in these walls to pray:
By serv - ing man God's will didst do,

Stab - lish our work in Thee be - gun.
Life's worth in fel - low - ship is known.
Bless Thou our fel - low - ship to - day.
Help us to serve our breth - ren, too.    A - MEN.

5. In all our work, in all our play,
   Be with us, Lord, our Friend, our Stay;
   Lead onward to the perfect day.

6. Then may we know, earth's lesson o'er,
   With comrades missed or gone before,
   Heaven's fellowship forevermore.

**Words reprinted by permission of " The Church Monthly," England.**

Rev. Louis F. Benson, 1894　　　C. M.　　　ST. MAGNUS
Jeremiah Clark (1670–1707)

*In moderate time*

1. O Thou whose feet have climbed life's hill, And trod the path of youth,
2. The call is Thine: be Thou the Way, And give us men, to guide;
3. Who learn of Thee the truth shall find, Who fol - low, gain the goal;
4. A - wake the pur - pose high which strives, And, fall - ing, stands a - gain;
5. Thy life the bond of fel - low - ship, Thy love the law that rules,

Our Sav-iour and our Broth-er still, Now lead us in - to truth.
Let wis-dom broad-en with the day, Let hu - man faith a - bide.
With rev-erence crown the ear-nest mind, And speak with-in the soul.
Con-firm the will of ea - ger lives To quit them-selves like men:
Thy Name, pro-claimed by ev - ery lip, The Mas-ter of our schools. A-MEN.

Words used by permission of Mrs. Robert F. Jefferys.

491　　　Memorial Days
ACH GOTT UND HERR
Melody in "Neu Leipziger Gesangbuch," 1682
Rev. William G. Tarrant (1853–1928)　　　8. 7. 8. 7.　　　Arr. by Johann Sebastian Bach

*With dignity*

1. Now praise we great and fa - mous men, The fa - thers, named in sto - ry;
2. Praise we the wise and brave and strong, Who graced their gen - er - a - tion;
3. Praise we the great of heart and mind, The sing-ers sweet-ly gift - ed,
4. Praise we the peace-ful men of skill Who build-ed homes of beau - ty,
5. So praise we great and fa - mous men, The fa - thers, named in sto - ry;

And praise the Lord who now as then Re - veals in man His glo - ry.
Who helped the right, and fought the wrong, And made our folk a na - tion.
Whose mu - sic like a might-y wind The souls of men up - lift - ed.
And, rich in art, made rich-er still The broth-er - hood of du - ty.
And praise the Lord who now as then · Re - veals in man His glo - ry. A-MEN.

Words used by permission of Mrs. William G. Tarrant.

William Whiting, 1860     8. 8. 8. 8. 8. 8.     MELITA   Rev. John B. Dykes, 1861

*With dignity*

1. E - ter - nal Fa - ther, strong to save, Whose arm doth bind the
2. O Sav - iour, whose al - might - y word The winds and waves sub -
3. O sa - cred Spir - it, who didst brood Up - on the cha - os
4. O Trin - i - ty of love and power, Our breth - ren shield in

rest - less wave, Who bidd'st the might - y o - cean deep
mis - sive heard, Who walk - edst on the foam - ing deep
dark and rude, Who bad'st its an - gry tu - mult cease,
dan - ger's hour; From rock and tem - pest, fire and foe,

Its own ap - point - ed lim - its keep: O hear us when we
And calm a - mid its rage didst sleep: O hear us when we
And gav - est light and life and peace: O hear us when we
Pro - tect them wher - so - e'er they go; And ev - er let there

cry to Thee For those in per - il on the sea.
cry to Thee For those in per - il on the sea.
cry to Thee For those in per - il on the sea.
rise to Thee Glad hymns of praise from land and sea. A-MEN.

## 493 Orisons

Ida F. Leyda, 1922       8. 3. 8. 3.       CELESTIAL VOICES<br/>R. F. Lloyd

*Quietly, and with reverence*

1. In the ear - ly morn - ing Dark shad - ows stay
2. When the day is end - ed Stars shin - ing bright
3. Fa - ther, now we thank Thee, For morn - ing light,

Till the sun - beams bring us God's gift of day.
Bring to tir - ed chil - dren God's gift of night.
For our days of glad - ness, For rest of night. A-MEN.

Words from "Carols." Used by permission of The Leyda Publishing Company.
Music copyright. Used by permission of the author's heirs.

## 494

Rev. Allen Eastman Cross       6. 5. 6. 5.       EUDOXIA<br/>Rev. Sabine Baring-Gould (1834-1924)

*With reverence*

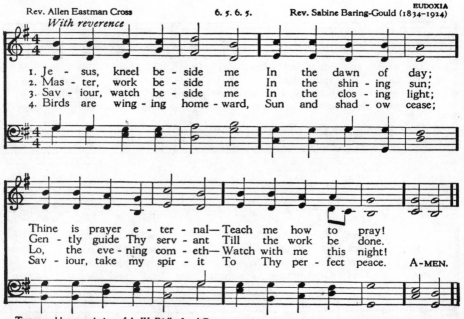

1. Je - sus, kneel be - side me In the dawn of day;
2. Mas - ter, work be - side me In the shin - ing sun;
3. Sav - iour, watch be - side me In the clos - ing light;
4. Birds are wing - ing home - ward, Sun and shad - ow cease;

Thine is prayer e - ter - nal— Teach me how to pray!
Gen - tly guide Thy serv - ant Till the work be done.
Lo, the eve - ning com - eth— Watch with me this night!
Sav - iour, take my spir - it To Thy per - fect peace. A-MEN.

Tune used by permission of A. W. Ridley and Co.
Words used by permission of Rev. Allen Eastman Cross.

# 495

## Orisons

Rev. John Newton, 1779

8. 7. 8. 7.

EVENING PRAYER
John Stainer (1840–1901)

*Unison. In moderate time*

1. May the grace of Christ our Sav-iour   And the Fa-ther's bound-less love,
2. Thus may we a-bide in un-ion   With each oth-er and the Lord,

*Harmony*

With the Ho-ly Spir-it's fa-vor, Rest up-on us from a-bove.
And pos-sess, in sweet com-mun-ion, Joys which earth can-not af-ford.   A-MEN.

Tune used by permission of Novello and Company, Ltd.

# 496

H. R. MacFayden, 1927

L. M.

CWMAFON
Philip James, 1927

*Rather slowly, with feeling*

1. The lone, wild fowl   in loft-y flight, Is still with Thee, nor leaves Thy sight.
2. The ends of   earth are in Thy hand, The sea's dark deep and no man's land.

*f*

*pp   — — frit.*

And I am Thine! I rest in Thee. Great Spir-it, come, and rest in me.
And I am Thine! I rest in Thee. Great Spir-it, come, and rest in me.   A-MEN.

Copyright, 1927, by The Homiletic Review.   Used by permission.

**497**

Harry Lee

L. M.

MY MASTER
Karl P. Harrington, 1927

*In unison. In flowing rhythm*

1. My Mas-ter was so ver-y poor, A man-ger was His cra-dling place;
2. My Mas-ter was so ver-y poor, And with the poor He broke the bread;
3. My Mas-ter was so ver-y poor, They nailed Him na-ked to a cross;

So ver-y rich my Mas-ter was, Kings came from far to gain His grace.
So ver-y rich my Mas-ter was That mul-ti-tudes by Him were fed.
So ver-y rich my Mas-ter was, He gave His all and knew no loss. A-MEN.

Music copyright, 1927, by the Presbyterian Board of Christian Education.

**498**

Rev. Henry Williams Baker (1821–1877)

C. M.

LEICESTER
William Hurst, b. 1849

*Rather slowly, with feeling*

1. I am not wor-thy, ho-ly Lord, That Thou shouldst come to me;
2. I am not wor-thy; cold and bare The lod-ging of my soul;

Speak but the word: one gra-cious word Can set the sin-ner free.
How canst Thou deign to en-ter there? Lord, speak, and make me whole. A-MEN.

Tune used by permission of William Clowes and Sons, Ltd.

# 499

## Orisons

Richard Watson Gilder (1844–1909)   10. 10. 10. 10. 10. 12.

FINLANDIA
Jean Sibelius
Arr. for this book, 1932

*In moderate time and flowing rhythm*

Through love to light! O won-der-ful the way That leads from

dark-ness to the per-fect day; From dark-ness and from

sor-row of the night To morn-ing that comes sing-ing o'er the sea!

Through love } to light! Through light, O God, to Thee,

Who art the Love of love, th'e-ter-nal Light of light! A-MEN.

Words used by permission of Houghton Mifflin Company.

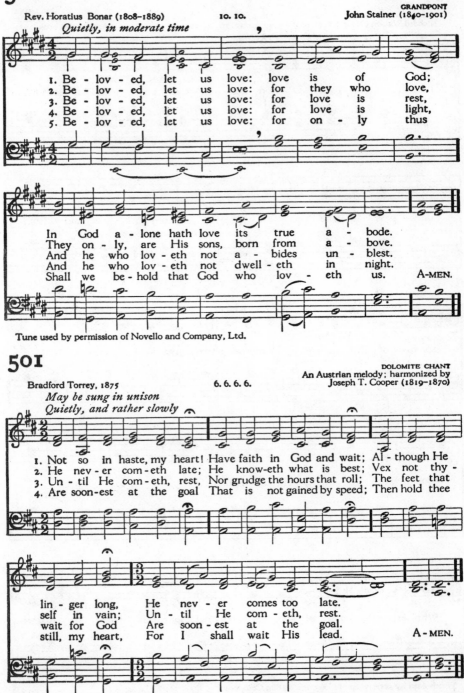

**500**

Rev. Horatius Bonar (1808–1889)  10. 10.  GRANDPONT
John Stainer (1840–1901)

*Quietly, in moderate time*

1. Be - lov - ed, let us love: love is of God;
2. Be - lov - ed, let us love: for they who love,
3. Be - lov - ed, let us love: for love is rest,
4. Be - lov - ed, let us love: for love is light,
5. Be - lov - ed, let us love: for on - ly thus

In God a - lone hath love its true a - bode.
They on - ly, are His sons, born from a - bove.
And he who lov - eth not a - bides un - blest.
And he who lov - eth not dwell - eth in night.
Shall we be - hold that God who lov - eth us. A-MEN.

Tune used by permission of Novello and Company, Ltd.

**501**

DOLOMITE CHANT
An Austrian melody; harmonized by
Joseph T. Cooper (1819–1870)

Bradford Torrey, 1875  6. 6. 6. 6.

*May be sung in unison*
*Quietly, and rather slowly*

1. Not so in haste, my heart! Have faith in God and wait; Al - though He
2. He nev - er com - eth late; He know-eth what is best; Vex not thy -
3. Un - til He com - eth, rest, Nor grudge the hours that roll; The feet that
4. Are soon-est at the goal That is not gained by speed; Then hold thee

lin - ger long, He nev - er comes too late.
self in vain; Un - til He com - eth, rest.
wait for God Are soon - est at the goal.
still, my heart, For I shall wait His lead. A - MEN.

**502**

# Orisons

Rev. William Romanis, 1878     5. 5. 8. 8. 5. 5.     SEELENBRÄUTIGAM
Adam Drese, 1698

*Moderately slow*

1. Round me falls the night. Sav - iour, be my Light;
2. Earth - ly work is done, Earth - ly sounds are none;
3. Dark - ened now each ray O'er the trav - eler's way;

Through the hours in dark - ness shroud - ed
Rest in sleep and si - lence seek - ing,
Let me know that Thou hast found me,

Let me see Thy face un - cloud - ed;
Let me hear Thee soft - ly speak - ing;
Let me feel Thine arms a - round me,

Let Thy glo - ry shine In this heart of mine.
To my spir - it here Whis - per, "I am near."
Sure from ev - ery ill Thou wilt guard me still. A - MEN.

Words used by permission of Dr. W. H. C. Romanis.

# Orisons

## 503

Rev. John Marckant (16th century)
In "Day's Psalter," 1562

C. M.

CHESHIRE TUNE
"Este's Psalter," 1592

*Rather slowly, with feeling*

1. O Lord, turn not a - way Thy face From him that lieth pros-trate,
2. Which gate Thou o - penest wide to those That do la - ment their sin;

La - ment - ing sore his sin - ful life, Be - fore Thy mer - cy gate.
Shut not that gate a - gainst me, Lord, But let me en - ter in. A-MEN.

Words and tune from "Songs of Syon." Used by permission of Rev. George R. Woodward.

## 504

Christina G. Rossetti (1830–1894)

8. 10. 10. 4.

ALL HALLOWS
Frederick Luke Wiseman

*Rather slowly*

1. None oth-er Lamb, none oth-er Name, None oth-er Hope in heaven or earth or sea,
2. My faith burns low, my hope burns low; On-ly my heart's de-sire cries out in me,
3. Lord, Thou art Life, though I be dead; Love's Fire Thou art, how-ev-er cold I be;

None oth - er Hid-ing Place from guilt and shame, None be - side Thee.
By the deep thun-der of its want and woe, Cries out to Thee.
Nor heaven have I, nor place to lay my head, Nor home, but Thee. A-MEN.

Tune used by permission of the Epworth Press.
Words used by permission of The Society for Promoting Christian Knowledge.

# 505

## Orisons

Rev. Paul Gerhardt (1607–1676)
Trans. by Rev. George R. Woodward

NUN RUHEN ALLE WÄLDER (INNSBRUCK)
Heinrich Isaak (c. 1455–1517)
Harmonized by Johann Sebastian Bach (1685–1750)

7. 7. 6. 7. 7. 8.

*May be sung in unison.  Quietly, with flowing rhythm*

1. Now woods and fields are sleep-ing, And dark-ness fast is creep-ing
2.* You al-so, O my dear-est, My friends and kin-dred near-est,

O'er mead-ow, hearth, and hall; But thou, my soul, ere
God rest you safe from harm! His an-gel hosts at-

slum - ber, For bless - ings pass - ing num - ber
tend you, Their gold - en shields de - fend you

Ex - alt the Giv - er of them all.
From night - ly dan - ger and a - larm. A - MEN.

*One or two stanzas may be used as desired, or as befits the occasion.
From "Songs of Syon." Used by permission of Rev. George R. Woodward.

**506**

Trans. based on
Rev. Nicolaus Selnecker (1532–1592)

L. M.

ACH BLEIB BEI UNS
"Geistliche Lieder," Leipzig, 1539
Arr. by Johann Sebastian Bach (1685–1750)

*Meditatively*

1. Lord Je-sus Christ, with us a-bide To cheer our hearts this e - ven-tide,
2. Make us and all Thy peo-ple one To serve Thee whol - ly, Thee a - lone;

Thy word il - lu - mine all our night, O heaven-ly Sun, e - ter-nal Light.
Thy peace on earth may we se - cure, Thy Kingdom stab - lish strong and sure. A-MEN.

**507**

Rev. John Hunter (1848–1917)

L. M.

SOLOTHURN
Swiss traditional melody

*In unison*

1. Dear Mas-ter, in whose life I see All that I would, but fail to be;
2. Though what I dream and what I do In my weak days are al - ways two,

Let Thy clear light for - ev - er shine, To shame and guide this life of mine.
Help me, op-pressed by things un-done, O Thou, whose deeds and dreams were one! A-MEN.

Words used by permission of Canon L. S. Hunter.

FINGAL
Irish traditional melody
Arr. by Leopold L. Dix

John Byrom (1691–1763)      6. 6. 6. 6. D.

*May be sung in unison. In the style of a folk song*

1. My spir - it longs for Thee With - in my trou - bled breast,
2. Un - less it come from Thee, In vain I look a - round;

Though I un - wor - thy be Of so di - vine a Guest.
In all that I can see No rest is to be found.

Of so di - vine a Guest Un - wor - thy though I be,
No rest is to be found But in Thy bless - ed love:

Yet has my heart no rest, Un-less it come from Thee.
O let my wish be crowned, And send it from a - bove! A - - MEN.

Tune used by permission of Mr. Leopold L. Dix.

## Orisons

**509**

Rev. John Ellerton (1826–1893)

9. 8. 9. 8.

SUNSET
George Gilbert Stocks

*In unison; quietly and reverently*

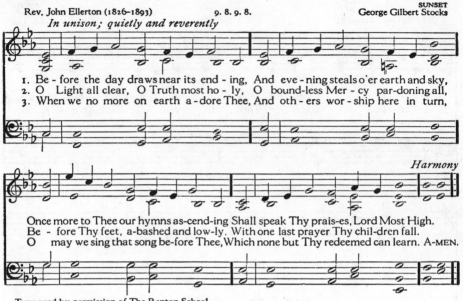

1. Be - fore the day draws near its end - ing, And eve - ning steals o'er earth and sky,
2. O   Light all clear, O Truth most ho - ly, O   bound-less Mer - cy par-doning all,
3. When we no more on earth a - dore Thee, And oth - ers wor - ship here in turn,

*Harmony*

Once more to Thee our hymns as-cend-ing Shall speak Thy prais-es, Lord Most High.
Be - fore Thy feet, a-bashed and low-ly, With one last prayer Thy chil-dren fall.
O   may we sing that song be-fore Thee, Which none but Thy redeemed can learn. A-MEN.

Tune used by permission of The Repton School.

**510**

Rev. Charles Coffin, 1736
Trans. by Rev. John Chandler, 1837

C. M.

ST. COLUMBA (IRISH)
Old Irish hymn melody
From Dr. Petrie's Collection

*With tender feeling*

1. As   now the sun's de - clin - ing rays At   e - ven - tide de - scend;
2. Lord, on   the cross Thine arms were stretched To draw us   to   the   sky;
3. To   God the Fa - ther, God the Son, And God the Ho - ly Ghost,

E'en so   our   years are sink-ing down To their ap-point-ed   end.
O   grant us   then that cross to love, And in those arms to   die.
All   glo - ry   be   from men on earth, And from the an - gel host. A-MEN.

Tune used by permission of Messrs. Stainer and Bell.

# 511

## Orisons

Rev. John Cennick (1718–1755)

8. 3. 3. 6.
(FIRST TUNE)

THANET
Rev. Joseph Jowett (1784–1856)

*Moderately slow*

1. Ere I sleep, for ev - ery fa - vor This day showed
2. O my Lord, what shall I ren - der To Thy Name,
3. Leave me not, but ev - er love me; Let Thy peace

By my God, I will bless my Sav - iour.
Still the same, Gra - cious, good, and ten - der?
Be my bliss, Till Thou hence re - move me. A - MEN.

# 511

Rev. John Cennick (1718–1755)

8. 3. 3. 6.
(SECOND TUNE)

CWMDU
David Emlyn Evans (1843–1913)

*Moderately slow*

1. Ere I sleep, for ev - ery fa - vor This day showed
2. O my Lord, what shall I ren - der To Thy Name,
3. Leave me not, but ev - er love me; Let Thy peace

By my God, I will bless my Sav - iour.
Still the same, Gra - cious, good, and ten - der?
Be my bliss, Till Thou hence re - move me. A - MEN.

Tune used by permission of Mrs. J. W. Jones.

**512**

## Orisons

Jane Crewdson (1809–1863)
*Moderately slow*

8. 8. 8. 6.

GWYNETH
John Price (Beulah)

1. O Sav-iour, I have naught to plead, In earth be-neath or heaven a-bove,
2. The need will soon be past and gone— Ex-ceed-ing great, but quick-ly o'er;

But on-ly my ex-ceed-ing need, And Thy ex-ceed-ing love.
The love un-bought is all Thine own, And lasts for-ev-er-more. A-MEN.

Copyright, 1927, by the Oxford University Press. Used by permission.

**513**

"Paderborn Gesangbuch," 1726
Trans. by Rev. George R. Woodward

L. M.

NU WOL GOTT DAS UNSER GESANG
16th century melody
Harmonized by Rev. George R. Woodward

1. My Je-sus, pierced for love of me, Thank-ful e-nough how can I be?
2. I pray Thee, hith-er come to me; Re-vive me of Thy char-i-ty:
3. As harts, a-thirst up-on the chase, Speed to the wa-ter brooks a-pace,

O bless-ed Sav-iour, if I might Thine ev-er-last-ing love re-quite.
For Thee my spir-it yearn-eth sore; Would I were wor-thy of Thee more!
So long-eth sore mine heart for Thee: O Je-sus, Je-sus, haste to me! A-MEN.

Words and tune used by permission of Rev. George R. Woodward.

# RESPONSES AND ANCIENT HYMNS
# AND CANTICLES

**1**

Rev. Isaac Watts, 1709

L. M.
(FIRST TUNE)

EIN KIND GEBOREN
Old German carol

*With reverence*

1. Come, dear-est Lord, de-scend and dwell  By faith and love  in  ev - ery breast;
2. Come, fill our hearts with in-ward strength; Make our en - lar - ged souls pos-sess

Then    shall we know and taste and feel   The joys that can-not be   ex-pressed.
And learn the height, the breadth, and length Of Thine un-meas-ur - a - ble grace. A-MEN.

**2**

Rev. Isaac Watts, 1709

L. M.
(SECOND TUNE)

FEDERAL STREET
Henry K. Oliver, 1832

*Reverently*

1. Come, dear-est Lord, de - scend and dwell  By  faith and love  in   ev - ery breast;
2. Come, fill our hearts with in-ward strength; Make our  en - lar - ged souls pos-sess

Then  shall we know and taste and  feel    The joys that can-not be   ex-pressed.
And learn the height, the breadth, and length Of Thine un-meas-ur - a - ble  grace. A-MEN.

# Opening Responses: Introits

**3**

Psalm xcv. 6 Edward Shippen Barnes, 1926

O come, let us wor-ship and bow down; Let us kneel be-fore the Lord our Mak-er. A-MEN.

Copyright, 1927, by the Presbyterian Board of Christian Education.

**4**

Petr Iljitch Tschaikowsky (1840–1893)
Arranged by N. Lindsay Norden

O come, let us wor-ship and bow be - fore the Lord. O save us, Son of

God, who from the dead didst rise, O Lord, hear and save us. A - MEN.

Copyrighted by J. Fischer & Bro. Used by permission.

**5**

Rev. Calvin W. Laufer, 1926

The Lord is in His ho - ly tem - ple, Let all the

earth keep si - lence be - fore Him; Keep si - lence be - fore Him.

Copyright, 1927, by Rev. C. W. Laufer. 459

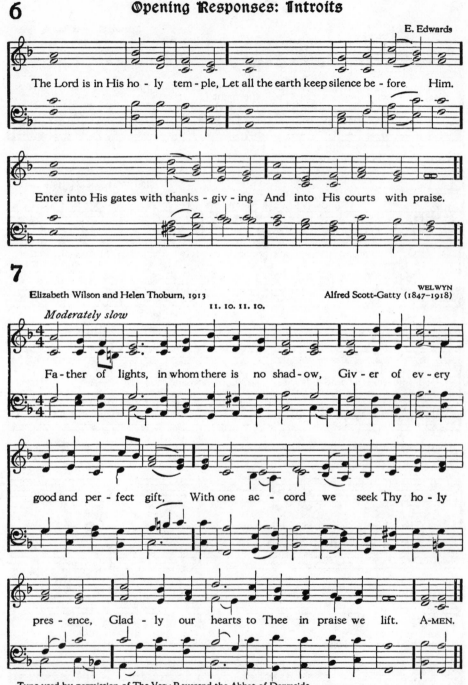

E. Edwards

The Lord is in His ho - ly tem - ple, Let all the earth keep silence be - fore Him.

Enter into His gates with thanks - giv - ing And into His courts with praise.

**7**

Elizabeth Wilson and Helen Thoburn, 1913

11. 10. 11. 10.

WELWYN
Alfred Scott-Gatty (1847–1918)

*Moderately slow*

Fa - ther of lights, in whom there is no shad - ow, Giv - er of ev - ery

good and per - fect gift, With one ac - cord we seek Thy ho - ly

pres - ence, Glad - ly our hearts to Thee in praise we lift. A-MEN.

Tune used by permission of The Very Reverend the Abbot of Downside.
Words used by permission of The National Board of Young Woman's Christian Association.

**8**

"Disciples' Hymn Book"    10. 10. 10. 10.    LANGRAN
James Langran, 1862

1. Fa - ther, the watch-es of the night are o'er; To light and life the
2. Fa - ther, the watch-es of the day are here; More than from those of

soul has risen once more; Bless - ed be Thou, who, through the help-less hours,
night we have to fear; By rude cares trou - bled, by temp-ta-tions pressed,

Hast kept in deep - est peace her slum - bering powers.
Through the day watch - es, Fa - ther, give us rest! A-MEN.

Used by permission of Novello and Company, Ltd.

**9**

Rev. John Mason, 1683; alt.    C. M.    FARRANT
Richard Farrant (c. 1530-1580)

1. Lord, for the mer - cies of the night Our hum - ble thanks we pay,
2. Let this day praise Thee, O Lord God, And so let all our days;

And un - to Thee we ded - i - cate The first fruits of the day.
And O let heaven's e - ter - nal day Be Thine e - ter - nal praise! A-MEN.

461

Rev. John Newton, 1779
C. M.
DALEHURST
Arthur Cottman, 1874

*Rather slow*

1. Ap-proach, my soul, the mer-cy seat Where Je-sus an-swers prayer;
2. Thy prom-ise is my on-ly plea; With this I ven-ture nigh:

There hum-bly fall be-fore His feet, For none can per-ish there.
Thou call-est bur-dened souls to Thee, And such, O Lord, am I. A-men.

**11**

Rev. William Hammond, 1745
7. 7. 7. 7.
HORSHAM
English traditional melody

*With reverence*

1. Lord, we come be-fore Thee now; At Thy feet we hum-bly bow;
2. Lord, on Thee our souls de-pend; In com-pas-sion now de-scend;
3. Send some mes-sage from Thy Word, That may joy and peace af-ford;

O do not our suit dis-dain: Shall we seek Thee, Lord, in vain?
Fill our hearts with Thy rich grace, Tune our lips to sing Thy praise.
Let Thy Spir-it now im-part Full sal-va-tion to each heart. A-men.

Tune from "Songs of Praise." Used by permission of the Oxford University Press.

**12**

William Cowper, 1769      L. M.      SIMEON
S. Stanley (1767–1822)

*Moderately slow*

1. Je - sus, wher-e'er Thy peo - ple meet, There they be-hold Thy mer - cy seat;
2. Here may we prove the power of prayer To strength-en faith and sweet-en care;

Wher-e'er they seek Thee, Thou art found, And ev - ery place is hal-lowed ground.
To teach our faint de - sires to rise, And bring all heaven be-fore our eyes. A-MEN.

**13**

Rev. William Pennefather (1816–1873)      6. 5. 6. 5.      BEMERTON (CASWALL)
Rev. Friedrich Filitz (1804–1876)

*With reverence*

1. Je - sus, stand a - mong us In Thy ris - en power;
2. Breathe the Ho - ly Spir - it In - to ev - ery heart;
3. Thus with quick-ened foot - steps We pur - sue our way,

Let this time of wor - ship Be a hal - lowed hour.
Bid the fears and sor - rows From each soul de - part.
Watch-ing for the dawn - ing Of e - ter - nal day. A-MEN.

Anon.     6. 4. 6. 4. 6. 4. 4. 6.     ST. ISSEY
English traditional melody

*p Rather slow*

May you who en-ter here Draw near to God, Purge your own

hearts of sin Through Christ's shed blood; To aid you on your way

Till shad-ows flee, And Christ you see In His e-ter-nal day.

**17**     **Prayer Responses**

Rev. John Newton, 1779     SAVANNAH
Rev. John Wesley's "Foundery Collection," 1742
7. 7. 7. 7.

*Rather slow*

1. Come, my soul, thy suit pre-pare: Je-sus loves to an-swer prayer;
2. Thou art com-ing to a King, Large pe-ti-tions with Thee bring;

He Him-self has bid thee pray, There-fore will not say thee nay.
For His grace and power are such, None can ev-er ask too much. A-MEN.

Traditional Serbian melody

May the words of my mouth and the med-i -ta - tions of my heart be ac-cept-a -

bie in Thy sight, O Lord, my Strength and my Re - deem - er.

**21**

10. 10. 10. 10.     MORECAMBE
Frederick C. Atkinson, c. 1870

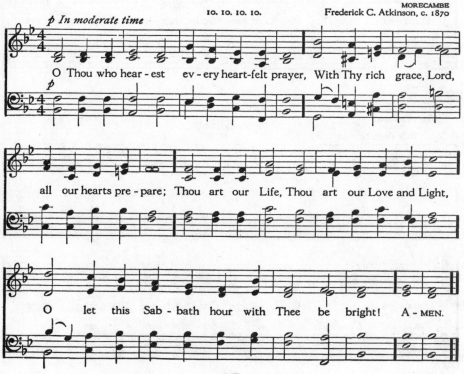

O Thou who hear - est ev - ery heart-felt prayer, With Thy rich grace, Lord,

all our hearts pre -pare; Thou art our Life, Thou art our Love and Light,

O let this Sab - bath hour with Thee be bright! A - MEN.

John Camidge (1735–1803)

O Lord, o-pen Thou our eyes, That we may be-hold won-drous things out of Thy law.

**23**

From Psalm cxix

SELMA
Melody from the Isle of Arran
Adapted by R. A. Smith (1780–1829)

(FIRST TUNE)

*p In moderate time*

Thy word have I hid in my heart, that I might not sin a - gainst Thee.

Bless - ed art Thou, O Lord my God: teach me Thy stat - utes.

**24**

From Psalm cxix

CHESHIRE TUNE
"Este's Psalter," 1592

(SECOND TUNE)

*mp In moderate time*

Thy word have I hid in my heart, that I might not sin a-gainst Thee.

Bless - ed art Thou, O Lord my God: teach me Thy stat - utes.

**25**

*In moderate time*

William Henry Hewlett

Teach me, O Lord, the way of Thy stat - utes, and

I will keep it un - to the end.

Tune used by permission of W. H. Hewlett.

**26** **Offertory Responses**

Ludwig van Beethoven (1770–1827)

All things come of Thee, O Lord; and of Thine own have we giv - en Thee. A-MEN.

**27**

HERR JESU CHRIST
"Pensum Sacrum," Görlitz, 1648

John Greenleaf Whittier (1807–1892)    L. M.    Arr. by Johann Sebastian Bach (1685–1750)

*May be sung in unison*

All things are Thine: no gift have we, Lord of all gifts, to of - fer Thee,

And hence with grate-ful hearts to-day, Thine own be - fore Thy feet we lay.

**28**

Tonus regius
From the Lutheran Service

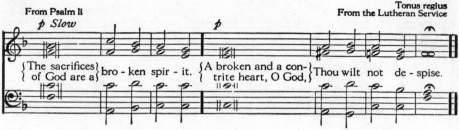

{The sacrifices} bro - ken spir - it. {A broken and a con-} Thou wilt not de - spise.
{of God are a} {trite heart, O God,}

**29**

Rev. Samuel Longfellow, 1886

L. M.
(FIRST TUNE)

DEUS TUORUM MILITUM
Grenoble church melody

*mf Unison. In moderate time*

Bless Thou the gifts our hands have brought; Bless Thou the work our hearts have planned;

Ours is the faith, the will, the thought; The rest, O God, is in Thy hand.

**30**

Rev. Samuel Longfellow, 1886

L. M.
(SECOND TUNE)

LLANGOLLEN (LLEDROD)
Welsh hymn melody

*mf May be sung in unison*

Bless Thou the gifts our hands have brought; Bless Thou the work our hearts have planned;

Ours is the faith, the will, the thought; The rest, O God, is in Thy hand.

**31**

S. M.
(FIRST TUNE)

Bishop W. Walsham How, 1864

WINDERMERE
Arthur Somervell

*mp In moderate time*

We give Thee but Thine own, What-e'er the gift may be:

All that we have is Thine a-lone, A trust, O Lord, from Thee.

Tune from "The Enlarged Songs of Praise." Used by permission of the Oxford University Press and Sir Arthur Somervell.

**32**

S. M.
(SECOND TUNE)

Bishop W. Walsham How, 1864

SELMA
Melody from the Isle of Arran
Adapted by R. A. Smith (1780-1829)

We give Thee but Thine own, What-e'er the gift may be:

All that we have is Thine a-lone, A trust, O Lord, from Thee.

**33**

Jonathan Battishill (1738-1801)

To do good, and to distribute, for-get not; For with such sacrifices God is well pleased.

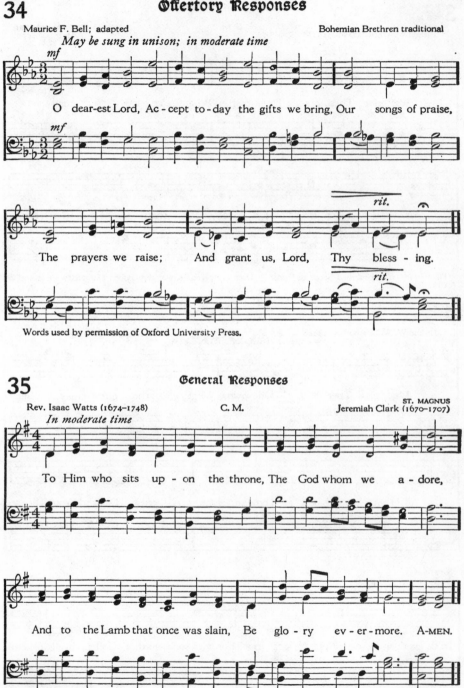

**34**

Maurice F. Bell; adapted

Bohemian Brethren traditional

*May be sung in unison; in moderate time*

O dear-est Lord, Ac-cept to-day the gifts we bring, Our songs of praise,

The prayers we raise; And grant us, Lord, Thy bless-ing.

Words used by permission of Oxford University Press.

**35** General Responses

Rev. Isaac Watts (1674–1748)

C. M.

ST. MAGNUS
Jeremiah Clark (1670–1707)

*In moderate time*

To Him who sits up-on the throne, The God whom we a-dore,

And to the Lamb that once was slain, Be glo-ry ev-er-more. A-MEN.

**36**

Anon.
Trans. by Rev. Philip Schaff, 1869          7. 7. 6. 7. 7. 6.

BREAD OF LIFE (WARREN)
Samuel P. Warren

*Not too fast*

O Bread of life from heav en,

To saints and an-gels giv-en; O Man-na from a-bove!

The souls that hun - ger, feed Thou.

The hearts that seek Thee, lead Thou,

With Thy sweet, ten - der love. A - MEN.

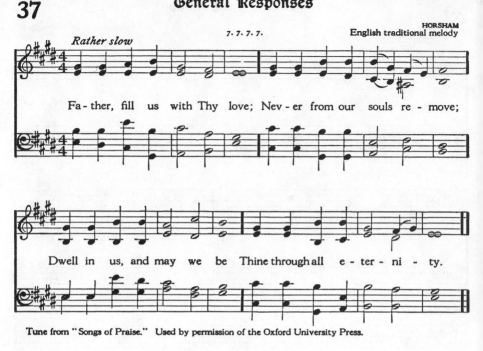

7. 7. 7. 7.

HORSHAM
English traditional melody

*Rather slow*

Fa - ther, fill us with Thy love; Nev - er from our souls re - move;

Dwell in us, and may we be Thine through all e - ter - ni - ty.

Tune from "Songs of Praise." Used by permission of the Oxford University Press.

38

8. 6. 8. 4.

LANDSKRON
"Bohemian Hymnal," 1531

*p Rather slow*

A ho - ly still - ness, breath-ing calm On all the world a - round,

Up - lifts my soul, O God, to Thee, Where rest is found.

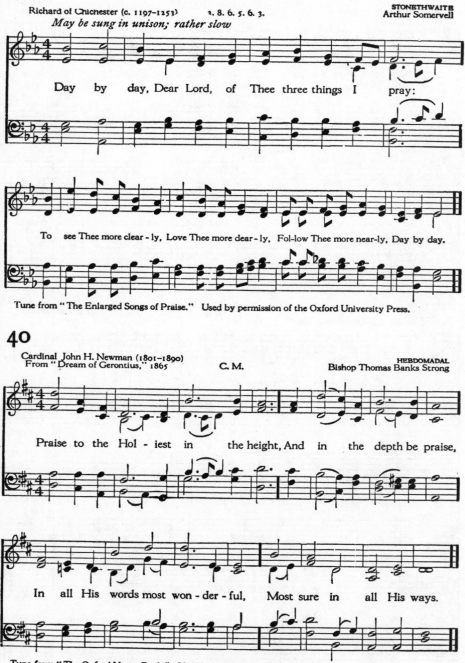

Richard of Chichester (c. 1197-1253)  7. 8. 6. 5. 6. 3.  STONETHWAITE
Arthur Somervell

*May be sung in unison; rather slow*

Day by day, Dear Lord, of Thee three things I pray:

To see Thee more clear-ly, Love Thee more dear-ly, Fol-low Thee more near-ly, Day by day.

Tune from "The Enlarged Songs of Praise." Used by permission of the Oxford University Press.

**40**

Cardinal John H. Newman (1801-1890)
From "Dream of Gerontius," 1865  C. M.  HEBDOMADAL
Bishop Thomas Banks Strong

Praise to the Hol-iest in the height, And in the depth be praise,

In all His words most won-der-ful, Most sure in all His ways.

Tune from "The Oxford Hymn Book." Used by permission of the Oxford University Press.

**41**

Rev. John Newton, 1779      7. 7. 7. 7.      SOLITUDE
Lewis T. Downes, 1851

*Rather slow*

1. Now may He who from the dead Brought the Shep-herd of the sheep,
2. May He teach us to ful - fill What is pleas-ing in His sight;

Je - sus Christ, our King and Head, All our souls in safe-ty keep.
Per-fect us in all His will, And pre - serve us day and night. A-MEN.

**42**

COELITES PLAUDANT
Rouen church melody

II. II. II. 5.

*Unison. In moderate time*

Hon - or and glo - ry, pow - er and sal - va - tion, Be in the

high - est un - to Him who reign - eth Change-less in heav - en

o - ver earth - ly chan - ges, Tri - une, e - ter - nal. A-MEN.

**43**

8. 8. 8. 6.

Rev. George W. Torrance (1836–1907)

TRUST

*In moderate time*

Lord, let us now de-part in peace, Who in Thy Name are gath-ered here;

Dis-close the bright-ness of Thy face, And be for - ev - er near.

Tune used by permission of The Misses Horder.

**44**

Anon.

*Reverently*

12. 12. 12. 12.

BENEDICTION
Henry Barraclough, 1932

Now may the light that shone in Je-sus Christ our Lord, Shine in our hearts and

minds by the in-dwell-ing Word; And may the rad - i - ance which faith and

hope re-store, Be and a-bide with us both now and ev - er-more. A-MEN.

Used by permission of Henry Barraclough.

Rev. Samuel Longfellow, 1864      8. 7. 8. 7. D.      ALLA TRINITA BEATA
From "Laudi Spirituali"

Fa - ther, give Thy ben - e - dic - tion, Give Thy peace be-

fore we part: Still our minds with truth's con - vic - tion,

Calm with trust each anx - ious heart. Let Thy voice with sweet com-mand-ing,

Bid our grief and strug - gles end; Peace which pass - eth

un - der - stand - ing On our wait - ing spir - its send. A-MEN.

# ANCIENT HYMNS AND CANTICLES

# Introduction to Chanting and Plain Song

## Chanting

A chant is not a hymn melody to which a text is fitted, but a series of tones to which the words of a psalm or canticle are recited. Chanting is, therefore, rhythmical reading and the words are of prime importance. They should be sung at a uniform rate of speed throughout, with every syllable clearly enunciated; weak syllables should not be slighted, nor strong syllables unduly prolonged.

## Plain Song

Three ancient hymns have been included in their plain song settings. Plain song is rhythmical speech. The verses are not divided into measures by bar lines; these are used only to indicate the ends of phrases.

No time signature is indicated; the notes themselves represent the relative time values of the syllables. When a syllable extends over more than one note, the stems of the notes are joined.

# Ancient Hymns and Canticles

## O Come, Let Us Sing Unto the Lord

Psalm xcv        VENITE        William Boyce, 1740

1. O come, let us sing ....... unto the Lord: let us heartily rejoice in the..
3. For the Lord is a ........ great .... God: and a great ...............
5. The sea is His,.......... and He made it: and His hands pre -
7. For He is the ........... Lord our God: and we are the people of His
                                                       pasture, and the
10. Glory be to the Father, and to the Son: and ........................

strength of our sal - vation.    2. Let us come before
King a - bove all gods.           His presence with thanks - giving:
pared the dry...... land.    4. In His hand are all
                               the corners of the earth:
sheep of His...... hand.    6. O come, let us wor-
                               ship and fall...... down:
                               8. O worship the Lord in the beauty of holiness:
                               9. For He cometh, for
to the Ho - ly Ghost;   He cometh to judge the earth:
                               11. As it was in the be-
                               ginning, is now, and ev - er shall be:

and show ourselves.................... glad in Him with psalms.
and the strength of the................ hills is His...... also.
and kneel be - - - - fore the Lord our Maker.
let the whole earth .................... stand in awe of Him.
and with righteousness to judge the world,
                            and the peo - ple with His truth.
world without ...................... end.......... A - - men.

47            Richard Goodson      48        Richard Farrant, (c. 1530–1580)

# Ancient Hymns and Canticles

## We Praise Thee, O God

### TE DEUM LAUDAMUS

Verses 1–13

Thomas Attwood (1765–1838)

1. We praise . . . . . . . . . . Thee, O God: we acknowledge Thee to be the Lord.
3. To Thee all angels . . . . cry a - loud, the Heavens, and all the Powers there-in;
5. Holy, . . . . . . . . . . . . . . . : Ho - ly, Holy: Lord . . . . . . . . . . . God of Sab - a - oth;
7. The glorious company of the A - postles: praise . . . . . . . . . . . . . . . . . . . . . . . . . . . . . Thee.
9. The noble . . . . . . . . . . army of Martyrs: praise . . . . . . . . . . . . . . . . . . . . . . . . . . . Thee.
11. The . . . . . . . . . . . . . . . . . Fa - ther of an . . . . . . . . . . . . infi-nite Maj - es - ty;

2. All the earth doth . . . . . . . . . . . wor - ship Thee: the Fa - ther ev - er - lasting.
4. To Thee Cherubim and . . . . . . . Ser - a - phim: con - tin - ual - ly do cry,
6. Heaven and earth are full of the Maj - es - ty: of Thy . . . . glo - ry.
8. The goodly fellowship . . . . . . . . of the Prophets: praise . . . . . . . . . . . . . . . . . . Thee.
10. The holy Church throughout all the world: doth ac-knowl - edge . . . . Thee;
12. Thine a - - - dora-ble, true: and on - ly Son;
13. Also the . . . . . . . . . . . . . . . . . . . . Ho - ly Ghost: the Com - fort - er.

Matthew Camidge (1758–1844)

Verses 14–21

14. Thou art the King of Glory: O . . . . . . . . . . . . . . . . . . . . . . . . . . . . Christ.
16. When Thou tookest upon Thee to de - liv - er man: Thou didst humble Thyself to be born . . . of a Virgin.
18. Thou sittest at the right hand of God: in the . . . . . . . . . . . glo - ry of the Father.
20. We therefore pray Thee, help Thy servants: whom Thou hast redeemèd with Thy pre-cious blood.

15. Thou art the ever-last-ing Son: of............... the Fa - ther.
17. When Thou hadst             Thou didst open
      overcome the  sharpness of death: the Kingdom of Heaven to  all  be-lievers.
19. We believe that  Thou shalt  come: to............ be...... our... Judge.
21. Make them to be
      numbered  with Thy  Saints: in............ glo - ry  ev - er-lasting.

Verses 22–29

Rev. William H. Havergal (1793–1870)

22. O Lord,............ save Thy people: and........ bless Thine her - it - age.
24. Day............... by.... day: we........ mag - ni - fy.... Thee;
26. Vouch - - safe, O  Lord: to keep us this day with - out... sin.
28. O Lord, let Thy mercy be  up - on us: as our...... trust.... is  in  Thee.

23. Gov - - - ern  them: and  lift  them  up  for - ever.
25. And we...... worship Thy  Name: ever,  world with - out...... end.
27. O Lord, have mercy  up - on us: have  mercy  up - on...... us.
29. O Lord, in Thee have  I  trusted: let me  nev - er  be  con - founded.

## O Be Joyful in the Lord

JUBILATE DEO

Psalm c            Rev. Henry Aldrich (1647–1710)

1. O be joyful in the Lord,.......... all ye lands: serve the Lord with gladness, and come before His

3. O go your way into His gates with thanksgiving, and into His courts with praise: be thankful unto Him, and .....

5. Glory be to the Father, and...... to the Son: and ........................

pres - ence with a song. 2. Be ye sure that the Lord He is God; it is He that hath made us, and not we our - selves:

speak good of His Name. 4. For the Lord is gracious, His mercy is ev - er - lasting:

to the Ho - ly Ghost; 6. As it was in the begin- ning, is now, and ev - er shall be:

we are His people, and the.......... sheep of His ........ pasture.

and His truth endureth from gener - ation to gen - er - ation.

world without..................... end.......... A - - men.

**51**       William Byrd (1538–1623)      **52**        Oxford chant

# 53

## Ancient Hymns and Canticles
### Blessèd Be the Lord God

Luke i. 68–79      BENEDICTUS      Joseph Barnby (1838–1896)

1. Blessèd be the Lord.................. God of   Israel:   for He hath visited ....
3. As He spake by the mouth of His..... ho - ly   Prophets:   which have been ......
5. To perform the mercy promised ...... to   our   forefathers: and to re - - -
7. That we being delivered out of the hand of   our   enemies:   might serve..........
9. And thou, child, shalt be called the prophet of   the   Highest:   for thou shalt go before the face of the Lord,
11. Through the tender mercy ........... of   our   God:   whereby the Day-spring from on
13. Glory be to the Father, and.......... to   the   Son:   and ..................

and   re - deemed His   people:   2. And hath raised up a mighty sal - -
since   the   world be - gan;   4. That we should be sav-ed ...............
member His   ho - ly   covenant;   6. To perform the oath which He sware to our fore-
Him   with - out....... fear;   8. In holiness and righteousness be - -
to   pre - pare   His   ways;   10. To give knowledge of salvation ..........
high   hath   visit - ed   us;   12. To give light to them that sit in darkness, and in the
to   the   Ho - ly   Ghost;   14. As it was in the beginning, is now, and ....

va - tion for us:   in the house ......... of   His   serv - ant   David:
from   our   enemies:   and from the........ hand   of   all   that   hate us.
fa - ther Abraham:   that ................ He would   give...... us;
fore........ Him:   all the .............. days...... of   our   life.
unto   His   people:   for the re - - mis - sion   of   their   sins,
shadow of   death:   and to guide our feet into   the   way   of   peace.
ev - er   shall be:   world without........ end....... A - men.

Music used by permission of Novello and Company, Ltd.

# 54

Arr. from Ludwig van Beethoven (1770–1827)

## Ancient Hymns and Canticles

### O All Ye Works of the Lord

BENEDICITE                    T. Tertius Noble, 1918

*Unison*                              *Harmony*

1. O all ye Works of the Lord, bless ye the Lord: praise Him, and magni-fy Him for-ever.

*Unison*                              *Harmony*

2. O ye Angels of the Lord, bless ye the Lord: praise Him, and magni-fy Him for-ever.

| | | | | |
|---|---|---|---|---|
| 3. O ye Heavens,.......... | bless ye the | Lord: | praise Him, and | magni-fy | Him for- | ever. |
| 4. O ye Waters that be a-bove the firmament, | bless ye the | Lord: | praise Him, and | magni-fy | Him for- | ever. |
| 5. O all ye Powers of the Lord, | bless ye the | Lord: | praise Him, and | magni-fy | Him for- | ever. |
| 6. O ye Sun and Moon,.... | bless ye the | Lord: | praise Him, and | magni-fy | Him for- | ever. |
| 7. O ye Stars of Heaven,... | bless ye the | Lord: | praise Him, and | magni-fy | Him for- | ever. |
| 8. O ye Showers and Dew,. | bless ye the | Lord: | praise Him, and | magni-fy | Him for- | ever. |
| 9. O ye Winds of God,..... | bless ye the | Lord: | praise Him, and | magni-fy | Him for- | ever. |
| 10. O ye Fire and Heat,..... | bless ye the | Lord: | praise Him, and | magni-fy | Him for- | ever. |
| 11. O ye Winter and Summer, | bless ye the | Lord: | praise Him, and | magni-fy | Him for- | ever. |
| 12. O ye Dews and Frosts,.. | bless ye the | Lord: | praise Him, and | magni-fy | Him for- | ever. |
| 13. O ye Frost and Cold,.... | bless ye the | Lord: | praise Him, and | magni-fy | Him for- | ever. |
| 14. O ye Ice and Snow,..... | bless ye the | Lord: | praise Him, and | magni-fy | Him for- | ever. |
| 15. O ye Nights and Days,.. | bless ye the | Lord: | praise Him, and | magni-fy | Him for- | ever. |
| 16. O ye Light and Darkness, | bless ye the | Lord: | praise Him, and | magni-fy | Him for- | ever. |
| 17. O ye Lightnings and Clouds, | bless ye the | Lord: | praise Him, and | magni-fy | Him for- | ever. |
| 18. O let the Earth,......... | bless .. the | Lord: | yea, let it praise Him, and | magni-fy | Him for- | ever. |
| 19. O ye Mountains and Hills, | bless ye the | Lord: | praise Him, and | magni-fy | Him for- | ever. |
| 20. O all ye Green Things up-on the earth, | bless ye the | Lord: | praise Him, and | magni-fy | Him for- | ever. |
| 21. O ye Wells,............. | bless ye the | Lord: | praise Him, and | magni-fy | Him for- | ever. |
| 22. O ye Seas and Floods, ... | bless ye the | Lord: | praise Him, and | magni-fy | Him for- | ever. |
| 23. O ye Whales and all that move in the waters, | bless ye the | Lord: | praise Him, and | magni-fy | Him for- | ever. |
| 24. O all ye Fowls of the air, | bless ye the | Lord: | praise Him, and | magni-fy | Him for- | ever. |
| 25. O all ye Beasts and Cattle, | bless ye the | Lord: | praise Him, and | magni-fy | Him for- | ever. |
| 26. O ye Children of Men,... | bless ye the | Lord: | praise Him, and | magni-fy | Him for- | ever. |
| 27. O let Israel,............. | bless .. the | Lord: | praise Him, and | magni-fy | Him for- | ever. |
| 28. O ye Priests of the Lord, | bless ye the | Lord: | praise Him, and | magni-fy | Him for- | ever. |
| 29. O ye Servants of the Lord, | bless ye the | Lord: | praise Him, and | magni-fy | Him for- | ever. |
| 30. O ye Spirits and Souls of the Righteous, | bless ye the | Lord: | praise Him, and | magni-fy | Him for- | ever. |
| 31. O ye holy and humble Men of heart, | bless ye the | Lord: | praise Him, and | magni-fy | Him for- | ever. |
| Glory be to the Father,...... | and to the | Son: | and | to the | Ho - ly | Ghost; |
| As it was in the beginning, is now and | ev | er shall be: | world without | end. | A- | men. |

NOTE: Where more than one choir is singing, the stanzas may be divided among them, all joining in the Gloria.

# 56

## Ancient Hymns and Canticles

### My Soul Doth Magnify the Lord

**MAGNIFICAT**

Luke i. 46–55

Joseph Barnby (1838–1896)

1. My soul doth magni - - fy the Lord, and my spirit hath rejoiced in....
3. For behold from..............hence - forth all generations shall............
6. He hath showed strength..... with His arm; He hath scattered the proud in the imagi-
8. He hath filled the hungry with good.. things; and the rich He hath...........
Glory be to the Father, and.... to the Son, and ........................

God my Sav - iour. 2. For He hath re - - - - -
call me bless - - ed. 4. For He that is mighty hath................
5. And His mercy is on them that.............
na - tion of their hearts. 7. He hath put down the mighty ............
sent.... empty a - way. 9. He remembering His mercy hath holpen His servant
to the Ho - ly Ghost; As it was in the beginning is now and .......

gard - ed the lowliness of His........ hand - maid - en.
magni - fied me; and....................ho - ly is His Name.
fear....... Him throughout all ............gen - er - a - tions.
from their seat, and hath exalted the .......hum - ble and meek.
Is - ra - el; as He promised to our fore-father Abraham and his seed for - ev - er.
ever shall be, world without............end....... A - men.

Music used by permission of Novello and Company, Ltd.

# 57

Thomas Purcell, 1670

# 58

Richard Woodward (1744–1777)

Luke ii. 29

John Blow (1648–1708)

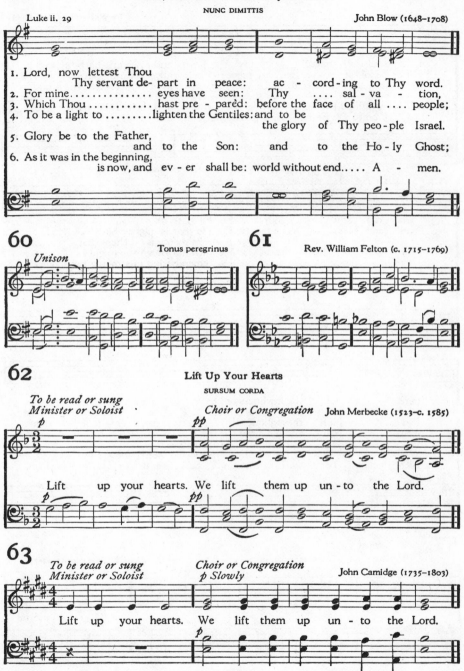

1. Lord, now lettest Thou
   Thy servant de-part in peace: ac - cord-ing to Thy word.
2. For mine............... eyes have seen: Thy .... sal - va - tion,
3. Which Thou ........... hast pre - parèd: before the face of all .... people;
4. To be a light to ........lighten the Gentiles: and to be
   the glory of Thy peo-ple Israel.

5. Glory be to the Father,
   and to the Son: and to the Ho - ly Ghost;
6. As it was in the beginning,
   is now, and ev - er shall be: world without end..... A - men.

**60**

Tonus peregrinus

*Unison*

**61**

Rev. William Felton (c. 1715–1769)

**62**

## Lift Up Your Hearts
**SURSUM CORDA**

*To be read or sung
Minister or Soloist*

*Choir or Congregation*   John Merbecke (1523–c. 1585)

Lift up your hearts. We lift them up un - to the Lord.

**63**

*To be read or sung
Minister or Soloist*

*Choir or Congregation
p Slowly*   John Camidge (1735–1803)

Lift up your hearts. We lift them up un - to the Lord.

**64**

### Lord, Have Mercy Upon Us

KYRIE

From a Lutheran Service of 1528

Lord, have mer-cy up-on us; Christ, have mer-cy up-on us; Lord, have mer-cy up-on us.

**65**

### Lord, Have Mercy Upon Us

KYRIE

John Merbecke (1523–c. 1585)
Arranged by Dr. Healey Willan

Lord, have mer-cy up-on us; Christ, have mer-cy up-on us; Lord, have mer-cy up-on us.

Each of the parts of the threefold Kyrie may be sung three times.
Tune used by permission of Dr. Healey Willan.

**66**

### Lord, Have Mercy Upon Us

KYRIE

From "Serbian Liturgy"
Rev. Sebastian Dabovitch

Lord, have mer - cy up - on us; Christ, have mer - cy up -

on us; Lord, have mer - cy up - on . . . . . . us.

Ancient

*After each Commandment, except the Tenth*

Lord, have mer-cy up-on us, and in-cline our hearts to keep this law.

*After the Tenth Commandment*　　*dim. e rall.*

us, and write all these Thy laws in our hearts, we be - seech Thee.

**68**

George J. Elvey (1816–1893)

*p After each Commandment, except the Tenth*

Lord, have mer-cy, have mer-cy up - on us, and in - cline our hearts to

*After the Tenth Commandment*

keep this law. Lord, have mer-cy, have mer - cy up - on us, and write all

these Thy laws in our hearts, Thy laws in our hearts, we be - seech Thee.

**69**

### Glory to God in the Highest
THE ANGELIC SONG

*Solo, if desired*  CHORUS  From Luther's Service of 1524

Glo-ry to God in the high-est, and on earth peace to men in whom He is well pleas - ed.

*mp*

**70**

### Glory Be to God on High
GLORIA IN EXCELSIS
(Enlarged Form)

Old Scottish chant

1. Glory be to...... God on high: and on earth peace, good will towards men.
2. We praise Thee, we bless Thee, we wor - ship Thee: we glorify Thee, we give thanks to Thee for Thy great glory.

3. O Lord God, .... heaven-ly King: God the......... Fa - ther Al - mighty.
4. O Lord, the only-begotten Son, Je - sus Christ: O Lord God, Lamb of God, Son.... of the Father,

*Slowly*

5. That takest away the .... sins of the world: have mercy up - on us.
6. Thou that takest away the sins of the world: re - ceive our prayer.
7. Thou that sittest at the right hand of God the Fa - ther: have mercy up - on us.

8. For Thou only art.... holy: Thou.............. on - ly art the Lord.
9. Thou only, O Christ, with the Ho - ly Ghost: art most high in the glory of God the Father. A-MEN.

# Ancient Hymns and Canticles

## Holy, Holy, Holy

Thomas Attwood (1765–1838)

Ho - ly, ho - ly, ho - ly, Lord God of Hosts,

heaven and earth are full of the maj - es - ty, the

maj - es - ty of Thy great glo - ry:

Glo - ry be to Thee, Glo - ry be to Thee,

Glo - ry be to Thee, O Lord Most High. A - MEN.

# Ancient Hymns and Canticles

Holy, Holy, Holy

SANCTUS

Peter C. Lutkin (1858–1931)

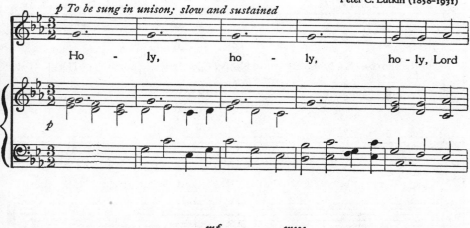

Ho - ly, ho - ly, ho - ly, Lord

God of Hosts, Heaven and earth are full of Thy

glo - ry: Glo - ry be to Thee, O Lord Most High. A - MEN.

Used by permission of The Parish Press, Fort Wayne, Ind.

**73**

Holy, Holy, Holy

SANCTUS

John Merbecke (1523–c. 1585)
Arranged by Dr. Healey Willan

*Unison. In free rhythm*

Ho - ly, ho - ly, ho - ly, Lord God of Hosts, Heaven and earth are full of Thy glo - ry:

Glo - ry be to Thee, O Lord Most High. A - MEN.

Tune used by permission of Dr. Healey Willan.

**74**

Holy, Holy, Holy

SANCTUS

A. S. Cooper

*mf*

*f*

Ho - ly, ho - ly, ho - ly, Lord God of Hosts, Heaven and earth are

*mf*

*ff*

full of Thy glo - ry: Glo - ry be to Thee, O Lord Most High. A - MEN.

*ff*

**75**

O Lamb of God

AGNUS DEI

John Merbecke (1523–c. 1585)
Arranged by Dr. Healey Willan

*p Unison. In free rhythm*

O Lamb of God, that tak-est a - way the sins of the world, have mer - cy up - on us.

*p*

O Lamb of God, that tak-est a-way the sins of the world, have mer-cy up-on us.

*rit.*

O Lamb of God, that tak-est a-way the sins of the world, grant us Thy peace.

Tune used by permission of Dr. Healey Willan.

## 76

### O Christ, Thou Lamb of God

From a Lutheran Service of 1528

*Slow. Unison*

*p*

O Christ, Thou Lamb of God, that tak-est a-way the sins of the

world, have mer-cy up-on us. O Christ, Thou Lamb of God, that

tak-est a-way the sins of the world, grant us Thy peace. A - - - MEN.

## O Lamb of God

AGNUS DEI

Giovanni Pierluigi da Palestrina
(1526-1594)

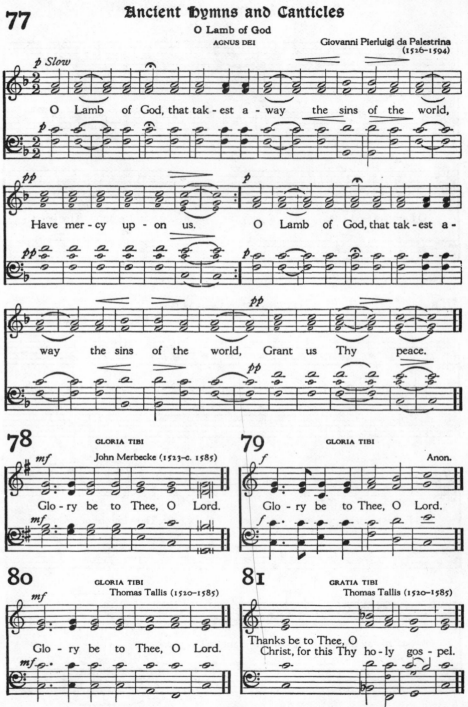

O Lamb of God, that tak-est a - way the sins of the world, Have mer-cy up - on us. O Lamb of God, that tak-est a - way the sins of the world, Grant us Thy peace.

**78** GLORIA TIBI

John Merbecke (1523-c. 1585)

Glo - ry be to Thee, O Lord.

**79** GLORIA TIBI

Anon.

Glo - ry be to Thee, O Lord.

**80** GLORIA TIBI

Thomas Tallis (1520-1585)

Glo - ry be to Thee, O Lord.

**81** GRATIA TIBI

Thomas Tallis (1520-1585)

Thanks be to Thee, O Christ, for this Thy ho - ly gos - pel.

### O Gladsome Light

Greek, 3rd century or earlier
Trans. by Robert Bridges

6. 6. 7. 6. 6. 7.

NUNC DIMITTIS
Louis Bourgeois
"Genevan Psalter," 1549

*With exaltation*

1. O glad-some Light, O Grace Of God the Fa-ther's face,
2. Now, ere day fad-eth quite, We see the eve-ning light,
3. To Thee of right be-longs All praise of ho-ly songs,

Th' e-ter-nal splen-dor wear-ing:
Our wont-ed hymn out-pour-ing:
O Son of God, Life-Giv-er;

Ce-les-tial, ho-ly, blest, Our Sav-iour Je-sus Christ,
Fa-ther of might un-known, Thee, His in-car-nate Son,
Thee, there-fore, O Most High, The world doth glo-ri-fy,

Joy-ful in Thine ap-pear-ing!
And Ho-ly Ghost a-dor-ing.
And shall ex-alt for-ev-er. A-MEN.

Words from "The Yattendon Hymnal." Used by permission of Mrs. Bridges and the Oxford University Press.

## Hail, Gladdening Light

Greek hymn of the 3rd century or earlier
Trans. by Rev. John Keble (1792–1866)          Irregular          John Stainer (1840–1901)

SEBASTE

*In free rhythm*

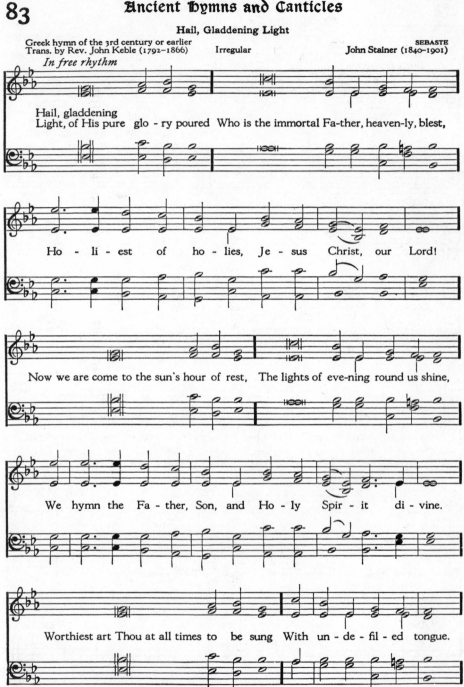

Hail, gladdening
Light, of His pure glo - ry poured Who is the immortal Fa-ther, heaven-ly, blest,

Ho - li - est of ho - lies, Je - sus Christ, our Lord!

Now we are come to the sun's hour of rest, The lights of eve-ning round us shine,

We hymn the Fa - ther, Son, and Ho - ly Spir - it di - vine.

Worthiest art Thou at all times to be sung With un - de - fil - ed tongue.

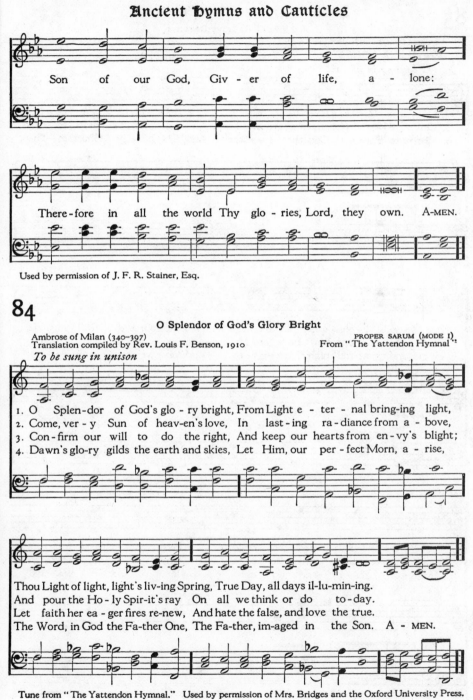

Son of our God, Giv - er of life, a - lone:

There - fore in all the world Thy glo - ries, Lord, they own. A-MEN.

Used by permission of J. F. R. Stainer, Esq.

## 84

### O Splendor of God's Glory Bright

Ambrose of Milan (340–397)
Translation compiled by Rev. Louis F. Benson, 1910

PROPER SARUM (MODE I)
From "The Yattendon Hymnal"

*To be sung in unison*

1. O Splen-dor of God's glo - ry bright, From Light e - ter - nal bring-ing light,
2. Come, ver - y Sun of heav-en's love, In last - ing ra - diance from a - bove,
3. Con-firm our will to do the right, And keep our hearts from en-vy's blight;
4. Dawn's glo-ry gilds the earth and skies, Let Him, our per - fect Morn, a - rise,

Thou Light of light, light's liv-ing Spring, True Day, all days il-lu-min-ing.
And pour the Ho - ly Spir-it's ray On all we think or do to-day.
Let faith her ea - ger fires re-new, And hate the false, and love the true.
The Word, in God the Fa-ther One, The Fa-ther, im-aged in the Son. A - MEN.

Tune from "The Yattendon Hymnal." Used by permission of Mrs. Bridges and the Oxford University Press.

### Of the Father's Love Begotten

Aurelius Clemens Prudentius (348–413)
Trans. by Rev. John Mason Neale, 1854
and Rev. Henry W. Baker, 1859

DIVINUM MYSTERIUM
Twelfth century plain song (Mode V)
Arr. by Rev. Charles Winfred Douglas

*To be sung in unison*

1. Of the Fa-ther's love be - got - ten, Ere the worlds be - gan to be,
2. O ye heights of heaven a - dore Him; An - gel hosts, His prais - es sing;
3. Christ, to Thee with God the Fa - ther, And, O Ho - ly Ghost, to Thee,

He is Al - pha and O - me - ga, He the Source, the End - ing He,
Powers, do - min-ions, bow be - fore Him, And ex - tol our God and King;
Hymn and chant and high thanks-giv - ing And un - wea-ried prais - es be:

Of the things that are, that have . . . been, And that fu - ture
Let no tongue on earth be si - - lent, Ev - ery voice in
Hon - or, glo - ry, and do - min - ion, And e - ter - nal

years shall see, Ev - er - more and ev - er - more!
con - cert ring, Ev - er - more and ev - er - more!
vic - to - ry, Ev - er - more and ev - er - more! A - MEN.

Music used by permission of Rev. Charles Winfred Douglas.

**86** **Father, We Praise Thee**

Gregory the Great (540-604)
Trans. by Rev. Percy Dearmer

PROPER SARUM (MODE VI)
From "The Yattendon Hymnal"

*To be sung in unison*

1. Fa - ther, we praise Thee, now the night is o - ver,
2. Mon - arch of all things, fit us for Thy man - sions;
3. All - ho - ly Fa - ther, Son, and Ho - ly Spir - it,

Ac - tive and watch-ful, stand we all be - fore Thee; Sing-ing, we of - fer
Ban - ish our weak-ness, health and whole-ness send-ing; Bring us to heav - en,
Trin - i - ty bless - ed, send us Thy sal - va - tion; Thine is the glo - ry,

prayer and med - i - ta - tion: Thus we a - dore Thee.
where Thy saints u - nit - ed Joy with - out end - ing.
gleam-ing and re - sound-ing Through all cre - a - tion. A - MEN.

Words from "The Church Hymnary," Revised. Used by permission of the Oxford University Press.
Tune from "The Yattendon Hymnal." Used by permission of Mrs. Bridges and the Oxford University Press.

**93**

Glory Be to the Father

GLORIA PATRI

Second century | Old Scottish chant

Glory be to the Father, and to the Son, and to the Ho - ly Ghost;
As it was in the beginning, is now, and ev - er shall be, world without end..... A - men.

**94**

Doxology

OLD HUNDREDTH (original rhythm)
"Genevan Psalter," arr. by Louis Bourgeois, 1551
English version of last phrase

Bishop Thomas Ken, 1692

L. M.

Praise God from whom all bless - ings flow; Praise Him, all crea-tures here be - low;

Praise Him a - bove, ye heaven-ly host: Praise Fa-ther, Son, and Ho - ly Ghost. A-MEN.

**95**

OLD HUNDREDTH (altered rhythm)
"Genevan Psalter," arr. by Louis Bourgeois, 1551

Bishop Thomas Ken, 1692

L. M.

Praise God from whom all bless-ings flow; Praise Him, all crea-tures here be - low;

Praise Him a - bove, ye heaven-ly host: Praise Fa - ther, Son, and Ho - ly Ghost. A-MEN.

503

# THE PSALTER
## AND
## OTHER RESPONSIVE READINGS

# THE PSALTER
## AND
## OTHER RESPONSIVE READINGS
===

The Selections listed here may be read as appropriate for certain days, occasions or subjects.

### THE CHRISTIAN YEAR

### THE CIVIL YEAR

### CHRISTIAN LIFE AND SERVICE

## SELECTION 1

PSALM 1

BLESSED is the man that walketh not in the counsel of the ungodly,

Nor standeth in the way of sinners, nor sitteth in the seat of the scornful.

But his delight is in the law of the Lord,

And in his law doth he meditate day and night.

And he shall be like a tree planted by the rivers of water,

That bringeth forth his fruit in his season;

His leaf also shall not wither,

And whatsoever he doeth shall prosper.

The ungodly are not so,

But are like the chaff which the wind driveth away.

Therefore the ungodly shall not stand in the judgment,

Nor sinners in the congregation of the righteous.

For the Lord knoweth the way of the righteous,

But the way of the ungodly shall perish.

## SELECTION 2

PSALM 2

WHY do the heathen rage, and the peoples imagine a vain thing?

The kings of the earth set themselves, and the rulers take counsel together, against the Lord, and against his anointed,

Saying, Let us break their bands asunder, and cast away their cords from us.

He that sitteth in the heavens will laugh: the Lord will have them in derision.

Then will he speak unto them in his wrath, and vex them in his sore displeasure.

Yet have I set my king upon my holy hill of Zion.

I will declare the decree: the Lord hath said unto me, Thou art my son; this day have I begotten thee.

Ask of me, and I will give thee the nations for thine inheritance, and the uttermost parts of the earth for thy possession.

Thou shalt break them with a rod of iron;

**Thou shalt dash them in pieces like a potter's vessel.**

Be wise now therefore, O ye kings; be instructed, ye judges of the earth.

**Serve the Lord with fear, and rejoice with trembling.**

Kiss the son, lest he be angry, and ye perish in the way, when his wrath is kindled but a little.

**Blessed are all they that put their trust in him.**


## SELECTION 3

PSALM 4

HEAR me when I call, O God of my righteousness; thou hast set me at large when I was in distress;

**Have mercy upon me, and hear my prayer.**

O ye sons of men, how long will ye turn my glory into shame?

**How long will ye love vanity, and seek after falsehood?**

But know that the Lord hath set apart for himself him that is godly:

**The Lord will hear when I call upon him.**

Stand in awe, and sin not; commune with your own heart upon your bed, and be still.

**Offer the sacrifices of righteousness, and put your trust in the Lord.**

Many there are that say, Who will show us any good? Lord, lift thou up the light of thy countenance upon us.

**Thou hast put gladness in my heart, more than they have in the time that their corn and their wine increased.**

I will both lay me down in peace, and sleep:

**For thou, Lord, alone makest me dwell in safety.**

PSALM 8

O Lord our Lord, how excellent is thy name in all the earth,

**Who hast set thy glory above the heavens!**

Out of the mouth of babes and sucklings hast thou ordained strength because of thine enemies,

**That thou mightest still the enemy and the avenger.**

When I consider thy heavens, the work of thy fingers, the moon
and the stars, which thou hast ordained;

**What is man, that thou art mindful of him? and the son of man,
that thou visitest him?**

For thou hast made him a little lower than the angels, and hast
crowned him with glory and honor.

**Thou madest him to have dominion over the works of thy hands;**

Thou hast put all things under his feet;

**All sheep and oxen, yea, and the beasts of the field;**

The birds of the air, and the fish of the sea, and whatsoever passeth
through the paths of the seas.

**O Lord our Lord, how excellent is thy name in all the earth!**


## SELECTION 4

PSALM 13

HOW long wilt thou forget me, O Lord? for ever?

**How long wilt thou hide thy face from me?**

How long shall I take counsel in my soul, having sorrow in my heart
all the day?

**How long shall mine enemy be exalted over me?**

Consider and hear me, O Lord my God:

**Lighten mine eyes, lest I sleep the sleep of death;**

Lest mine enemy say, I have prevailed against him;

**And those that trouble me rejoice when I am moved.**

But I have trusted in thy mercy; my heart shall rejoice in thy salvation.

**I will sing unto the Lord, because he hath dealt bountifully with
me.**

PSALM 15

Lord, who shall abide in thy tabernacle?

**Who shall dwell in thy holy hill?**

He that walketh uprightly, and worketh righteousness,

**And speaketh the truth in his heart;**

He that slandereth not with his tongue,

**Nor doeth evil to his friend, nor taketh up a reproach against his neighbor;**

In whose eyes a reprobate is despised,

**But who honoreth them that fear the Lord;**

He that sweareth to his own hurt, and changeth not;

**He that putteth not out his money to usury,**

Nor taketh reward against the innocent.

**He that doeth these things shall never be moved.**

## SELECTION 5

PSALM 16

PRESERVE me, O God; for in thee do I put my trust.

**O my soul, thou hast said unto the Lord, Thou art my Lord; I have no good beyond thee.**

As for the saints that are in the earth, they are the excellent, in whom is all my delight.

**Their sorrows shall be multiplied that hasten after another god: their drink offerings of blood will I not offer, nor take their names upon my lips.**

The Lord is the portion of mine inheritance and of my cup:

**Thou maintainest my lot.**

The lines are fallen unto me in pleasant places;

**Yea, I have a goodly heritage.**

I will bless the Lord, who hath given me counsel;

**My heart also instructeth me in the night seasons.**

I have set the Lord always before me;

**Because he is at my right hand, I shall not be moved.**

Therefore my heart is glad, and my glory rejoiceth;

**My flesh also shall dwell in safety.**

For thou wilt not leave my soul in hell;

**Neither wilt thou suffer thine holy one to see corruption.**

Thou wilt show me the path of life: in thy presence is fulness of joy;

**At thy right hand there are pleasures for evermore.**

PSALM 17: 6-8; 15

I have called upon thee, for thou wilt hear me, O God:

Incline thine ear unto me, and hear my speech.

Show thy marvellous lovingkindness, O thou that savest by thy right hand them that take refuge in thee from those that rise up against them.

Keep me as the apple of the eye; hide me under the shadow of thy wings.

As for me, I shall behold thy face in righteousness;

I shall be satisfied, when I awake, with thy likeness.

## SELECTION 6

PSALM 19

THE heavens declare the glory of God;

And the firmament showeth his handywork.

Day unto day uttereth speech,

And night unto night showeth knowledge.

There is no speech nor language; their voice is not heard.

Their line is gone out through all the earth, and their words to the end of the world.

In them hath he set a tabernacle for the sun, which is as a bridegroom coming out of his chamber;

And rejoiceth as a strong man to run his course.

His going forth is from the end of the heavens, and his circuit unto the ends of it:

And there is nothing hid from the heat thereof.

The law of the Lord is perfect, restoring the soul;

The testimony of the Lord is sure, making wise the simple.

The statutes of the Lord are right, rejoicing the heart;

The commandment of the Lord is pure, enlightening the eyes.

The fear of the Lord is clean, enduring for ever;

The judgments of the Lord are true and righteous altogether.

More to be desired are they than gold, yea, than much fine gold;

Sweeter also than honey and the honeycomb.

Moreover by them is thy servant warned;

In keeping them there is great reward.

Who can discern his errors?

Cleanse thou me from hidden faults.

Keep back thy servant also from presumptuous sins;

Let them not have dominion over me:

Then shall I be upright, and I shall be innocent from great transgression.

Let the words of my mouth, and the meditation of my heart, be acceptable in thy sight, O Lord, my rock, and my redeemer.


## SELECTION 7

PSALM 20

THE Lord hear thee in the day of trouble;

The name of the God of Jacob defend thee;

Send thee help from the sanctuary,

And strengthen thee out of Zion;

Remember all thy offerings,

And accept thy burnt sacrifice;

Grant thee thy heart's desire,

And fulfil all thy counsel.

We will triumph in thy salvation, and in the name of our God we will set up our banners;

The Lord fulfil all thy petitions.

Now know I that the Lord saveth his anointed;

He will hear him from his holy heaven with the saving strength of his right hand.

Some trust in chariots, and some in horses;

But we will remember the name of the Lord our God.

They are brought down and fallen: but we are risen and stand upright.

Save, Lord: let the king hear us when we call.

PSALM 23

The Lord is my shepherd; I shall not want.

**He maketh me to lie down in green pastures; he leadeth me beside the still waters.**

He restoreth my soul;

**He leadeth me in the paths of righteousness for his name's sake.**

Yea, though I walk through the valley of the shadow of death, I will fear no evil; for thou art with me;

**Thy rod and thy staff, they comfort me.**

Thou preparest a table before me in the presence of mine enemies;

**Thou anointest my head with oil; my cup runneth over.**

Surely goodness and mercy shall follow me all the days of my life;

**And I shall dwell in the house of the Lord for ever.**


## SELECTION 8

PSALM 24

THE earth is the Lord's, and the fulness thereof; the world, and they that dwell therein.

**For he hath founded it upon the seas, and established it upon the floods.**

Who shall ascend into the hill of the Lord? and who shall stand in his holy place?

**He that hath clean hands, and a pure heart, who hath not lifted up his soul unto vanity, nor sworn deceitfully.**

He shall receive a blessing from the Lord, and righteousness from the God of his salvation.

**This is the generation of them that seek him, that seek thy face, even Jacob.**

Lift up your heads, O ye gates; and be ye lifted up, ye everlasting doors;

**And the King of glory will come in.**

Who is this King of glory?

**The Lord strong and mighty, the Lord mighty in battle.**

Lift up your heads, O ye gates; even lift them up, ye everlasting doors;

And the King of glory will come in.

Who is this King of glory?

The Lord of hosts, he is the King of glory.

## SELECTION 9

PSALM 25

UNTO thee, O Lord, do I lift up my soul.

O my God, I trust in thee;

Let me not be put to shame, let not mine enemies triumph over me.

Yea, let none that wait on thee be ashamed;

Let them be ashamed that transgress without cause.

Show me thy ways, O Lord; teach me thy paths.

Lead me in thy truth, and teach me;

For thou art the God of my salvation; for thee do I wait all the day.

Remember, O Lord, thy tender mercies and thy loving-kindnesses;

For they have been ever of old.

Remember not the sins of my youth, nor my transgressions;

According to thy mercy remember thou me for thy goodness' sake, O Lord.

Good and upright is the Lord:

Therefore will he teach sinners in the way.

The meek will he guide in justice:

And the meek will he teach his way.

All the paths of the Lord are mercy and truth unto such as keep his covenant and his testimonies.

For thy name's sake, O Lord, pardon mine iniquity, for it is great.

What man is he that feareth the Lord?

Him shall he teach in the way that he shall choose.

His soul shall dwell at ease;

And his seed shall inherit the land.

The secret of the Lord is with them that fear him;

And he will show them his covenant.

Mine eyes are ever toward the Lord; for he will pluck my feet out of the net.

**Turn thee unto me, and have mercy upon me; for I am desolate and afflicted.**

The troubles of my heart are enlarged; O bring thou me out of my distresses.

**Look upon mine affliction and my pain; and forgive all my sins.**

Consider mine enemies; for they are many; and they hate me with cruel hatred.

**O keep my soul, and deliver me: let me not be put to shame; for I put my trust in thee.**

Let integrity and uprightness preserve me; for I wait for thee.

**Redeem Israel, O God, out of all his troubles.**

## SELECTION 10

PSALM 27

THE Lord is my light and my salvation; whom shall I fear?

**The Lord is the strength of my life; of whom shall I be afraid?**

When the wicked, even mine enemies and my foes, came upon me to eat up my flesh,

**They stumbled and fell.**

Though a host should encamp against me, my heart shall not fear;

**Though war should rise against me, even then will I be confident.**

One thing have I asked of the Lord, that will I seek after;

**That I may dwell in the house of the Lord all the days of my life, to behold the beauty of the Lord, and to inquire in his temple.**

For in the time of trouble he will hide me in his pavilion;

**In the secret of his tabernacle will he hide me; he will set me up upon a rock.**

And now shall mine head be lifted up above mine enemies round about me;

**Therefore will I offer in his tabernacle sacrifices of joy; I will sing, yea, I will sing praises unto the Lord.**

Hear. O Lord, when I cry with my voice;

Have mercy also upon me, and answer me.

When thou saidst, Seek ye my face;

My heart said unto thee, Thy face, Lord, will I seek.

Hide not thy face from me; put not thy servant away in anger:

Thou hast been my help; leave me not, neither forsake me, O God of my salvation.

When my father and my mother forsake me,

Then the Lord will take me up.

Teach me thy way, O Lord, and lead me in a plain path, because of mine enemies.

Deliver me not over unto the will of mine enemies, for false witnesses are risen up against me, and such as breathe out cruelty.

I had fainted, unless I had believed to see the goodness of the Lord in the land of the living.

Wait on the Lord:

Be of good courage, and he will strengthen thine heart:

Wait, I say, on the Lord.


## SELECTION 11

PSALM 28: 6-9

BLESSED be the Lord, because he hath heard the voice of my supplications.

The Lord is my strength and my shield; my heart trusted in him, and I am helped:

Therefore my heart greatly rejoiceth; and with my song will I praise him.

The Lord is their strength, and he is a stronghold of salvation to his anointed.

Save thy people, and bless thine inheritance;

Be their shepherd also, and bear them up for ever.

PSALM 31: 1-5; 15-16; 19-24

In thee, O Lord, do I put my trust; let me never be put to shame:

Deliver me in thy righteousness.

Bow down thine ear to me; deliver me speedily;

Be thou my strong rock, for a house of defence to save me.

For thou art my rock and my fortress;

Therefore for thy name's sake lead me, and guide me.

Pull me out of the net that they have laid privily for me: for thou art my stronghold.

Into thine hand I commit my spirit: thou hast redeemed me, O God of truth.

My times are in thy hand: deliver me from the hand of mine enemies, and from them that persecute me.

Make thy face to shine upon thy servant: save me for thy mercies' sake.

Oh how great is thy goodness, which thou hast laid up for them that fear thee;

Which thou hast wrought for them that trust in thee, before the sons of men!

Thou wilt hide them in the secret of thy presence from the plottings of man:

Thou wilt keep them secretly in a pavilion from the strife of tongues.

Blessed be the Lord, for he hath showed me his marvellous kindness in a strong city.

For I said in my haste, I am cut off from thine eyes: nevertheless thou heardest the voice of my supplications when I cried unto thee.

O love the Lord, all ye his saints: for the Lord preserveth the faithful, and plentifully rewardeth the proud doer.

Be of good courage, and he will strengthen your heart, all ye that hope in the Lord.

## SELECTION 12

PSALM 32: 1–2; 5–11

BLESSED is he whose transgression is forgiven, whose sin is covered.

Blessed is the man unto whom the Lord imputeth not iniquity, and in whose spirit there is no guile.

I acknowledged my sin unto thee, and mine iniquity did I not hide.

I said, I will confess my transgressions unto the Lord; and thou forgavest the iniquity of my sin.

For this let every one that is godly pray unto thee in a time when thou mayest be found:

Surely in the floods of great waters they will not come nigh unto him.

Thou art my hiding place; thou wilt preserve me from trouble;

Thou wilt compass me about with songs of deliverance.

I will instruct thee and teach thee in the way which thou shalt go; 

I will counsel thee with mine eye upon thee.

Be ye not as the horse, or as the mule, which have no understanding:

Whose mouth must be held in with bit and bridle, else they will not come near unto thee.

Many sorrows shall be to the wicked: but he that trusteth in the Lord, mercy shall compass him about.

Be glad in the Lord, and rejoice, ye righteous: and shout for joy, all ye that are upright in heart.


## SELECTION 13

PSALM 33

REJOICE in the Lord, O ye righteous: praise is comely for the upright.

Praise the Lord with harp: sing unto him with the psaltery and an instrument of ten strings.

Sing unto him a new song; play skillfully with a loud noise.

For the word of the Lord is right; and all his works are done in truth.

He loveth righteousness and justice: the earth is full of the goodness of the Lord.

By the word of the Lord were the heavens made, and all the host of them by the breath of his mouth.

He gathered the waters of the sea together as a heap; he layeth up the deeps in storehouses.

Let all the earth fear the Lord; let all the inhabitants of the world stand in awe of him.

For he spake, and it was done; he commanded, and it stood fast.

**The Lord bringeth the counsel of the nations to nought: he maketh the thoughts of the peoples to be of no effect.**

The counsel of the Lord standeth fast for ever, the thoughts of his heart to all generations.

**Blessed is the nation whose God is the Lord, the people whom he hath chosen for his own inheritance.**

The Lord looketh from heaven; he beholdeth all the sons of men.

**From the place of his habitation he looketh forth upon all the inhabitants of the earth.**

He fashioneth the hearts of them all; he considereth all their works.

**There is no king saved by the multitude of a host; a mighty man is not delivered by much strength.**

A horse is a vain thing for safety; neither shall he deliver any by his great strength.

**Behold, the eye of the Lord is upon them that fear him, upon them that hope in his mercy;**

To deliver their soul from death, and to keep them alive in famine.

**Our soul hath waited for the Lord: he is our help and our shield.**

For our heart shall rejoice in him, because we have trusted in his holy name.

**Let thy mercy, O Lord, be upon us, according as we hope in thee.**


## SELECTION 14

PSALM 34: 1–18

I WILL bless the Lord at all times; his praise shall continually be in my mouth.

**My soul shall make her boast in the Lord; the humble shall hear thereof, and be glad.**

O magnify the Lord with me, and let us exalt his name together.

**I sought the Lord, and he heard me, and delivered me from all my fears.**

They looked unto him, and were lightened; and their faces were not ashamed.

This poor man cried, and the Lord heard him, and saved him out of all his troubles.

The angel of the Lord encampeth round about them that fear him, and delivereth them.

O taste and see that the Lord is good: blessed is the man that trusteth in him.

O fear the Lord, ye his saints; for there is no want to them that fear him.

The young lions do lack, and suffer hunger; but they that seek the Lord shall not want any good thing.

Come, ye children, hearken unto me: I will teach you the fear of the Lord.

What man is he that desireth life, and loveth many days, that he may see good?

Keep thy tongue from evil, and thy lips from speaking guile.

Depart from evil, and do good; seek peace, and pursue it.

The eyes of the Lord are toward the righteous, and his ears are open unto their cry.

The face of the Lord is against them that do evil, to cut off the remembrance of them from the earth.

The righteous cry, and the Lord heareth, and delivereth them out of all their troubles.

The Lord is nigh unto them that are of a broken heart; and saveth such as are of a contrite spirit.

PSALM 36: 5-10

Thy mercy, O Lord, is in the heavens; and thy faithfulness reacheth unto the skies.

Thy righteousness is like the great mountains;

Thy judgments are a great deep: O Lord, thou preservest man and beast.

How excellent is thy lovingkindness, O God! therefore the children of men put their trust under the shadow of thy wings.

They shall be abundantly satisfied with the fatness of thy house;

And thou wilt make them drink of the river of thy pleasure.

For with thee is the fountain of life: in thy light shall we see light.

O continue thy lovingkindness unto them that know thee; and thy righteousness to the upright in heart.

## SELECTION 15

PSALM 37: 1–8; 23–31; 37

FRET not thyself because of evil doers, neither be thou envious against the workers of iniquity.

For they shall soon be cut down like the grass, and wither as the green herb.

Trust in the Lord, and do good; dwell in the land, and feed on his faithfulness.

Delight thyself also in the Lord; and he will give thee the desires of thine heart.

Commit thy way unto the Lord; trust also in him; and he will bring it to pass.

And he will bring forth thy righteousness as the light, and thy justice as the noonday.

Rest in the Lord, and wait patiently for him:

Fret not thyself because of him who prospereth in his way, because of the man who bringeth wicked devices to pass.

Cease from anger, and forsake wrath; fret not thyself, it tendeth only to evildoing.

The steps of a good man are ordered by the Lord; and he delighteth in his way.

Though he fall, he shall not be utterly cast down: for the Lord upholdeth him with his hand.

I have been young, and now am old; yet have I not seen the righteous forsaken, nor his seed begging bread.

He is ever merciful, and lendeth; and his seed is blessed.

Depart from evil, and do good; and dwell for evermore.

For the Lord loveth justice, and forsaketh not his saints;

They are preserved for ever: but the seed of the wicked shall be cut off.

The righteous shall inherit the land, and dwell therein for ever.

The mouth of the righteous speaketh wisdom, and his tongue speaketh justice.

The law of his God is in his heart; none of his steps shall slide.

Mark the perfect man, and behold the upright: for the end of that man is peace.

## SELECTION 16

PSALM 40: 1–13; 16–17

I WAITED patiently for the Lord;

And he inclined unto me, and heard my cry.

He brought me up also out of a horrible pit, out of the miry clay,

And set my feet upon a rock, and established my goings.

And he hath put a new song in my mouth, even praise unto God:

Many shall see it, and fear, and shall trust in the Lord.

Blessed is that man that maketh the Lord his trust,

And respecteth not the proud, nor such as turn aside to lies.

Many, O Lord my God, are thy wonderful works which thou hast done, and thy thoughts which are to us-ward:

They cannot be reckoned up in order unto thee: if I would declare and speak of them, they are more than can be numbered.

Sacrifice and offering thou didst not desire; mine ears hast thou opened:

Burnt offering and sin offering hast thou not required.

Then said I, Lo, I come; in the volume of the book it is written of me:

I delight to do thy will, O my God; yea, thy law is within my heart.

I have preached righteousness in the great congregation;

Lo, I have not refrained my lips, O Lord, thou knowest.

I have not hid thy righteousness within my heart;

I have declared thy faithfulness and thy salvation;

I have not concealed thy lovingkindness and thy truth from the great congregation.

Withhold not thou thy tender mercies from me, O Lord:

Let thy lovingkindness and thy truth continually preserve me.

For innumerable evils have compassed me about: mine iniquities have taken hold upon me, so that I am not able to look up;

They are more than the hairs of mine head; therefore my heart faileth me.

Be pleased, O Lord, to deliver me: O Lord, make haste to help me.

Let all those that seek thee rejoice and be glad in thee;

Let such as love thy salvation say continually, The Lord be magnified.

But I am poor and needy; yet the Lord thinketh upon me:

Thou art my help and my deliverer; make no tarrying, O my God.


## SELECTION 17

PSALM 42: 1–5; 7–11

AS the hart panteth after the water brooks, so panteth my soul after thee, O God.

My soul thirsteth for God, for the living God:

When shall I come and appear before God?

My tears have been my food day and night, while they continually say unto me, Where is thy God?

When I remember these things, I pour out my soul within me: how I went with the throng and led them to the house of God,

With the voice of joy and praise, a multitude keeping holyday.

Why art thou cast down, O my soul? and why art thou disquieted within me?

Hope thou in God: for I shall yet praise him for the help of his countenance.

Deep calleth unto deep at the noise of thy waterfalls:

All thy waves and thy billows are gone over me.

Yet the Lord will command his lovingkindness in the daytime,

And in the night his song shall be with me, and my prayer unto the God of my life.

I will say unto God my rock, Why hast thou forgotten me? why go I mourning because of the oppression of the enemy?

As with a sword in my bones, mine enemies reproach me; while they continually say unto me, Where is thy God?

Why art thou cast down, O my soul? and why art thou disquieted within me?

Hope thou in God: for I shall yet praise him, who is the help of my countenance, and my God.

PSALM 43

Judge me, O God, and plead my cause against an ungodly nation:

O deliver me from the deceitful and unjust man.

For thou art the God of my strength: why dost thou cast me off?

Why go I mourning because of the oppression of the enemy?

O send out thy light and thy truth: let them lead me;

Let them bring me unto thy holy hill and to thy tabernacles.

Then will I go unto the altar of God, unto God my exceeding joy;

Yea, upon the harp will I praise thee, O God my God.

Why art thou cast down, O my soul? and why art thou disquieted within me?

Hope in God: for I shall yet praise him, who is the help of my countenance, and my God.


## SELECTION 18

PSALM 46

GOD is our refuge and strength, a very present help in trouble.

Therefore will we not fear, though the earth be removed, and though the mountains be carried into the midst of the sea;

Though the waters thereof roar and be troubled,

Though the mountains shake with the swelling thereof.

There is a river, the streams whereof make glad the city of God,

The holy place of the tabernacles of the Most High.

God is in the midst of her; she shall not be moved:

God will help her, and that right early.

The nations raged, the kingdoms were moved: he uttered his voice, the earth melted.

**The Lord of hosts is with us; the God of Jacob is our refuge.**

Come, behold the works of the Lord,

**What desolations he hath made in the earth.**

He maketh wars to cease unto the end of the earth;

**He breaketh the bow, and cutteth the spear in sunder; he burneth the chariots in the fire.**

Be still, and know that I am God: I will be exalted among the nations, I will be exalted in the earth.

**The Lord of hosts is with us; the God of Jacob is our refuge.**


## SELECTION 19

PSALM 48: 1–5; 8–14

GREAT is the Lord, and greatly to be praised in the city of our God, in his holy mountain.

**Beautiful for situation, the joy of the whole earth, is mount Zion, on the sides of the north, the city of the great King.**

God is known in her palaces for a refuge.

**For, lo, the kings were assembled, they passed by together.**

They saw it, and so they marvelled; they were amazed, and hasted away.

**As we have heard, so have we seen in the city of the Lord of hosts, in the city of our God:**

God will establish it for ever.

**We have thought of thy lovingkindness, O God, in the midst of thy temple.**

According to thy name, O God, so is thy praise unto the ends of the earth;

**Thy right hand is full of righteousness.**

Let mount Zion rejoice, let the daughters of Judah be glad, because of thy judgments.

**Walk about Zion, and go round about her; number the towers thereof.**

Mark ye well her bulwarks, consider her palaces;

That ye may tell it to the generation following.

For this God is our God for ever and ever;

He will be our guide even unto death.

## SELECTION 20

PSALM 51: 1–17

HAVE mercy upon me, O God, according to thy lovingkindness:

According unto the multitude of thy tender mercies blot out my transgressions.

Wash me thoroughly from mine iniquity, and cleanse me from my sin.

For I acknowledge my transgressions: and my sin is ever before me.

Against thee, thee only have I sinned, and done this evil in thy sight:

That thou mightest be justified when thou speakest, and be clear when thou judgest.

Behold, I was brought forth in iniquity; and in sin did my mother conceive me.

Behold, thou desirest truth in the inward parts; and in the hidden part thou wilt make me to know wisdom.

Purify me with hyssop, and I shall be clean;

Wash me, and I shall be whiter than snow.

Make me to hear joy and gladness; that the bones which thou hast broken may rejoice.

Hide thy face from my sins, and blot out all mine iniquities.

Create in me a clean heart, O God, and renew a right spirit within me.

Cast me not away from thy presence; and take not thy Holy Spirit from me.

Restore unto me the joy of thy salvation; and uphold me with a willing spirit.

Then I will teach transgressors thy ways; and sinners shall be converted unto thee.

Deliver me from bloodguiltiness, O God, thou God of my salvation:

And my tongue shall sing aloud of thy righteousness.

O Lord, open thou my lips;

And my mouth shall show forth thy praise.

For thou desirest not sacrifice; else would I give it:

Thou delightest not in burnt offerings.

The sacrifices of God are a broken spirit;

A broken and a contrite heart, O God, thou wilt not despise.

## SELECTION 21

PSALM 61

HEAR my cry, O God; attend unto my prayer.

From the end of the earth will I cry unto thee, when my heart is overwhelmed:

Lead me to the rock that is higher than I.

For thou hast been a shelter for me, and a strong tower from the enemy.

I will abide in thy tabernacle for ever;

I will trust in the covert of thy wings.

For thou, O God, hast heard my vows: thou hast given me the heritage of those that fear thy name.

Thou wilt prolong the king's life; his years as many generations.

He shall abide before God for ever: O prepare mercy and truth, which may preserve him.

So will I sing praise unto thy name for ever, that I may daily perform my vows.

PSALM 62: 1–2; 5–12

Truly my soul waiteth upon God: from him cometh my salvation.

He only is my rock and my salvation;

He is my defence; I shall not be greatly moved.

My soul, wait thou in silence for God only; for my expectation is from him.

He only is my rock and my salvation:

He is my defence; I shall not be moved.

In God is my salvation and my glory: the rock of my strength, and my refuge, is in God.

Trust in him at all times; ye people, pour out your heart before him; God is a refuge for us.

Surely men of low degree are vanity, and men of high degree are a lie:

To be laid in the balance, they are together lighter than vanity.

Trust not in oppression, and become not vain in robbery:

If riches increase, set not your heart upon them.

God hath spoken once; twice have I heard this; that power belongeth unto God.

Also unto thee, O Lord, belongeth mercy: for thou renderest to every man according to his work.

## SELECTION 22

PSALM 63: 1-8

O GOD, thou art my God; early will I seek thee;

My soul thirsteth for thee, my flesh longeth for thee in a dry and thirsty land, where no water is.

So have I looked upon thee in the sanctuary, to see thy power and thy glory.

Because thy lovingkindness is better than life, my lips shall praise thee.

Thus will I bless thee while I live; I will lift up my hands in thy name.

My soul shall be satisfied as with marrow and fatness;

And my mouth shall praise thee with joyful lips;

When I remember thee upon my bed, and meditate on thee in the night watches.

Because thou hast been my help, therefore in the shadow of thy wings will I rejoice.

My soul followeth hard after thee: thy right hand upholdeth me.

PSALM 65

Praise waiteth for thee, O God, in Zion; and unto thee shall the vow be performed.

O thou that hearest prayer, unto thee shall all flesh come.

Iniquities prevail against me: as for our transgressions, thou wilt purge them away.

Blessed is the man whom thou choosest, and causest to approach unto thee, that he may dwell in thy courts:

We shall be satisfied with the goodness of thy house, even of thy holy temple.

By terrible things in righteousness wilt thou answer us, O God of our salvation;

Who art the confidence of all the ends of the earth, and of them that are afar off upon the sea;

Who by his strength setteth fast the mountains, being girded with power;

Who stilleth the noise of the seas, the noise of their waves, and the tumult of the peoples.

They also that dwell in the uttermost parts are afraid at thy tokens: thou makest the outgoings of the morning and evening to rejoice.

Thou visitest the earth, and waterest it: thou greatly enrichest it with the river of God, which is full of water;

Thou preparest them grain, when thou hast so provided for it.

Thou waterest the ridges thereof abundantly: thou settlest the furrows thereof;

Thou makest it soft with showers: thou blessest the springing thereof.

Thou crownest the year with thy goodness; and thy paths drop fatness.

They drop upon the pastures of the wilderness; and the little hills rejoice on every side.

The pastures are clothed with flocks; the valleys also are covered over with grain;

They shout for joy, they also sing.

## SELECTION 23

PSALM 66: 1–9; 16–20

MAKE a joyful noise unto God, all ye lands.

Sing forth the honor of his name: make his praise glorious.

Say unto God, How terrible art thou in thy works!

Through the greatness of thy power shall thine enemies submit themselves unto thee.

All the earth shall worship thee, and shall sing unto thee; they shall sing to thy name.

**Come and see the works of God: he is terrible in his doing toward the children of men.**

He turned the sea into dry land; they went through the river on foot; there did we rejoice in him.

**He ruleth by his power for ever; his eyes behold the nations; let not the rebellious exalt themselves.**

O bless our God, ye peoples, and make the voice of his praise to be heard;

**Who holdeth our soul in life, and suffereth not our feet to be moved.**

Come and hear, all ye that fear God,

**And I will declare what he hath done for my soul.**

I cried unto him with my mouth, and he was extolled with my tongue.

**If I regard iniquity in my heart, the Lord will not hear me.**

But verily God hath heard me; he hath attended to the voice of my prayer.

**Blessed be God, which hath not turned away my prayer, nor his mercy from me.**

Psalm 67

God be merciful unto us, and bless us; and cause his face to shine upon us;

**That thy way may be known upon earth, thy salvation among all nations.**

Let the peoples praise thee, O God; let all the peoples praise thee.

**O let the nations be glad and sing for joy:**

For thou wilt judge the peoples righteously, and govern the nations upon earth.

**Let the peoples praise thee, O God; let all the peoples praise thee.**

The earth hath yielded her increase; God, even our own God, will bless us.

**God will bless us; and all the ends of the earth shall fear him.**

## SELECTION 24

PSALM 72

GIVE the king thy judgments, O God, and thy righteousness unto the king's son.

**He will judge thy people with righteousness, and thy poor with justice.**

The mountains shall bring peace to the people, and the little hills, by righteousness.

**He will judge the poor of the people,**

He will save the children of the needy, and will break in pieces the oppressor.

**They shall fear thee as long as the sun and moon endure, throughout all generations.**

He will come down like rain upon the mown grass; as showers that water the earth.

**In his days shall the righteous flourish; and abundance of peace so long as the moon endureth.**

He shall have dominion also from sea to sea, and from the River unto the ends of the earth.

**They that dwell in the wilderness shall bow before him; and his enemies shall lick the dust.**

The kings of Tarshish and of the isles shall render tribute;

**The kings of Sheba and Seba shall offer gifts.**

Yea, all kings shall fall down before him; all nations shall serve him.

**For he will deliver the needy when he crieth; the poor also, and him that hath no helper.**

He will spare the poor and needy, and will save the souls of the needy.

**He will redeem their soul from deceit and violence: and precious will their blood be in his sight.**

And he shall live, and to him shall be given of the gold of Sheba:

**Prayer also shall be made for him continually; and daily shall he be praised.**

There shall be an abundance of grain in the earth upon the top of the mountains;

The fruit thereof shall shake like Lebanon; and they of the city shall flourish like grass of the earth.

His name shall endure for ever; his name shall be continued as long as the sun:

And men shall be blessed in him; all nations shall call him blessed.

Blessed be the Lord God, the God of Israel, who only doeth wondrous things.

And blessed be his glorious name for ever: and let the whole earth be filled with his glory. Amen, and Amen.

## SELECTION 25

PSALM 73: 1–26

TRULY God is good to Israel, even to such as are of a clean heart.

But as for me, my feet were almost gone; my steps had well nigh slipped.

For I was envious at the arrogant, when I saw the prosperity of the wicked.

For there are no pangs in their death; but their strength is firm.

They are not in trouble as other men; neither are they plagued like other men.

Therefore pride compasseth them about as a chain; violence covereth them as a garment.

Their eyes stand out with fatness; they have more than heart could wish.

They scoff, and speak wickedly concerning oppression; they speak loftily.

They set their mouth in the heavens, and their tongue walketh through the earth.

Therefore his people return hither; and waters of a full cup are drained by them.

And they say, How doth God know? and is there knowledge in the Most High?

Behold, these are the ungodly, who prosper in the world; they increase in riches.

Verily in vain have I cleansed my heart, and washed my hands in innocency.

**For all the day long have I been plagued, and chastened every morning.**

If I say, I will speak thus; behold, I should offend against the generation of thy children.

**When I thought to know this, it was too painful for me;**

Until I went into the sanctuary of God; then understood I their end.

**Surely thou settest them in slippery places: thou castest them down in destruction.**

How are they brought into desolation in a moment! they are utterly consumed with terrors.

**As a dream when one awaketh, so, O Lord, when thou awakest, thou wilt despise their image.**

Thus my soul was grieved, and I was pricked in my heart.

**So foolish was I, and ignorant; I was as a beast before thee.**

Nevertheless I am continually with thee: thou hast holden me by my right hand.

**Thou wilt guide me with thy counsel, and afterward receive me to glory.**

Whom have I in heaven but thee? and there is none upon earth that I desire besides thee.

**My flesh and my heart faileth; but God is the strength of my heart, and my portion for ever.**


## SELECTION 26

Psalm 77

I CRIED unto God with my voice, even unto God with my voice; and he gave ear unto me.

**In the day of my trouble I sought the Lord:**

My hand was stretched out in the night, and slacked not; my soul refused to be comforted.

**I remembered God, and was troubled: I complained, and my spirit was overwhelmed.**

Thou holdest mine eyes waking: I am so troubled that I cannot speak.

I have considered the days of old, the years of ancient times.

I call to remembrance my song in the night;

I commune with mine own heart; and my spirit maketh diligent search.

Will the Lord cast off for ever? and will he be favorable no more?

Is his mercy clean gone for ever? doth his promise fail for evermore?

Hath God forgotten to be gracious? hath he in anger shut up his tender mercies?

And I said, This is my infirmity: but I will remember the years of the right hand of the Most High.

I will remember the works of the Lord; surely I will remember thy wonders of old.

I will meditate also upon all thy work, and talk of thy doings.

Thy way, O God, is in the sanctuary: who is so great a God as our God?

Thou art the God that doest wonders: thou hast declared thy strength among the peoples.

Thou hast with thine arm redeemed thy people, the sons of Jacob and Joseph.

The waters saw thee, O God, the waters saw thee;

They were afraid; the depths also were troubled.

The clouds poured out water: the skies sent out a sound: thine arrows also went abroad.

The voice of thy thunder was in the heaven;

The lightnings lightened the world; the earth trembled and shook.

Thy way is in the sea, and thy path in the great waters, and thy footsteps were not known.

Thou leddest thy people like a flock by the hand of Moses and Aaron.

## SELECTION 27

PSALM 84

HOW amiable are thy tabernacles, O Lord of hosts!

My soul longeth, yea, even fainteth for the courts of the Lord:

My heart and my flesh cry out for the living God.

**Yea, the sparrow hath found a house, and the swallow a nest for herself, where she may lay her young,**

Even thine altars, O Lord of hosts, my king, and my God.

**Blessed are they that dwell in thy house: they will be still praising thee.**

Blessed is the man whose strength is in thee; in whose heart are the highways to Zion.

**Passing through the valley of Weeping they make it a place of springs;**

Yea, the early rain covereth it with blessings.

**They go from strength to strength; every one of them appeareth before God in Zion.**

O Lord God of hosts, hear my prayer; give ear, O God of Jacob.

**Behold, O God our shield, and look upon the face of thine anointed.**

For a day in thy courts is better than a thousand.

**I had rather be a door-keeper in the house of my God, than to dwell in the tents of wickedness.**

For the Lord God is a sun and shield:

**The Lord will give grace and glory:**

No good thing will he withhold from them that walk uprightly.

**O Lord of hosts, blessed is the man that trusteth in thee.**

## SELECTION 28

PSALM 85

LORD, thou hast been favorable unto thy land;

**Thou hast brought back the captivity of Jacob.**

Thou hast forgiven the iniquity of thy people;

**Thou hast covered all their sins.**

Thou hast taken away all thy wrath;

**Thou hast turned thyself from the fierceness of thine anger.**

Turn us, O God of our salvation,

And cause thine anger toward us to cease.

Wilt thou be angry with us for ever?

Wilt thou draw out thine anger to all generations?

Wilt thou not revive us again: that thy people may rejoice in thee?

Show us thy mercy, O Lord, and grant us thy salvation.

I will hear what God the Lord will speak;

For he will speak peace unto his people, and to his saints; but let them not turn again to folly.

Surely his salvation is nigh them that fear him:

That glory may dwell in our land.

Mercy and truth are met together;

Righteousness and peace have kissed each other.

Truth shall spring out of the earth;

And righteousness shall look down from heaven.

Yea, the Lord will give that which is good;

And our land shall yield her increase.

Righteousness shall go before him;

And shall set us in the way of his steps.

## SELECTION 29

PSALM 86: 1–12; 15–17

BOW down thine ear, O Lord, hear me: for I am poor and needy.

Preserve my soul; for I am holy: O thou my God, save thy servant that trusteth in thee.

Be merciful unto me, O Lord: for I cry unto thee all the day long.

Rejoice the soul of thy servant: for unto thee, O Lord, do I lift up my soul.

For thou, Lord, art good, and ready to forgive;

And plenteous in mercy unto all them that call upon thee.

Give ear, O Lord, unto my prayer; and attend to the voice of my supplications.

In the day of my trouble I will call upon thee: for thou wilt answer me.

Among the gods there is none like unto thee, O Lord;

Neither are there any works like unto thy works.

All nations whom thou hast made shall come and worship before thee, O Lord;

And shall glorify thy name.

For thou art great, and doest wondrous things;

Thou art God alone.

Teach me thy way, O Lord; I will walk in thy truth:

Unite my heart to fear thy name.

I will praise thee, O Lord my God, with all my heart;

And I will glorify thy name for evermore.

Thou, O Lord, art a God full of compassion and gracious,

Longsuffering, and plenteous in mercy and truth.

O turn unto me, and have mercy upon me;

Give thy strength unto thy servant, and save the son of thine handmaid.

Show me a token for good; that they who hate me may see it, and be put to shame:

Because thou, Lord, hast helped me, and comforted me.


## SELECTION 30

Psalm 90

LORD, thou hast been our dwelling place in all generations.

Before the mountains were brought forth, or ever thou hadst formed the earth and the world,

Even from everlasting to everlasting, thou art God.

Thou turnest man to destruction; and sayest, Return, ye children of men.

For a thousand years in thy sight are but as yesterday when it is past, and as a watch in the night.

Thou carriest them away as with a flood; they are as a sleep.

In the morning they are like grass which groweth up.

In the morning it flourisheth, and groweth up; in the evening it is cut down, and withereth.

For we are consumed by thine anger, and by thy wrath are we troubled.

Thou hast set our iniquities before thee, our secret sins in the light of thy countenance.

For all our days are passed away in thy wrath: we spend our years as a tale that is told.

The days of our years are threescore years and ten, and if by reason of strength they be fourscore years;

Yet is their strength labor and sorrow; for it is soon cut off, and we fly away.

Who knoweth the power of thine anger, and thy wrath according to the fear that is due unto thee?

So teach us to number our days, that we may get us an heart of wisdom.

Return, O Lord, how long? and let it repent thee concerning thy servants.

O satisfy us early with thy mercy; that we may rejoice and be glad all our days.

Make us glad according to the days wherein thou hast afflicted us, and the years wherein we have seen evil.

Let thy work appear unto thy servants, and thy glory unto their children.

And let the favor of the Lord our God be upon us;

And establish thou the work of our hands upon us;

Yea, the work of our hands establish thou it.

## SELECTION 31

PSALM 91

HE that dwelleth in the secret place of the Most High shall abide under the shadow of the Almighty.

I will say of the Lord, He is my refuge and my fortress: my God, in him will I trust.

Surely he will deliver thee from the snare of the fowler, and from the noisome pestilence.

He will cover thee with his feathers, and under his wings shalt thou trust;

His truth shall be thy shield and buckler.

Thou shalt not be afraid for the terror by night, nor for the arrow that flieth by day;

For the pestilence that walketh in darkness, nor for the destruction that wasteth at noonday.

A thousand shall fall at thy side, and ten thousand at thy right hand;

But it shall not come nigh thee.

Only with thine eyes shalt thou behold and see the reward of the wicked.

Because thou hast made the Lord, which is my refuge, even the Most High, thy habitation;

There shall no evil befall thee,

Neither shall any plague come nigh thy dwelling.

For he will give his angels charge over thee, to keep thee in all thy ways.

They shall bear thee up in their hands, lest thou dash thy foot against a stone.

Thou shalt tread upon the lion and adder: the young lion and the dragon shalt thou trample under feet.

Because he hath set his love upon me, therefore will I deliver him;

I will set him on high, because he hath known my name.

He shall call upon me, and I will answer him;

I will be with him in trouble;

I will deliver him and honor him.

With long life will I satisfy him, and show him my salvation.

## SELECTION 32

Psalm 95

O COME let us sing unto the Lord: let us make a joyful noise to the rock of our salvation.

Let us come before his presence with thanksgiving, and make a joyful noise unto him with psalms.

For the Lord is a great God and a great King above all gods.

In his hand are the deep places of the earth: the strength of the hills is his also.

The sea is his, and he made it: and his hands formed the dry land.

O come, let us worship and bow down: let us kneel before the Lord our maker.

For he is our God; and we are the people of his pasture, and the sheep of his hand.

To day, oh that ye would hear his voice! Harden not your heart, as in the provocation, and as in the day of temptation in the wilderness;

When your fathers tempted me, proved me, and saw my work.

Forty years long was I grieved with this generation,

And said: It is a people that do err in their heart, and they have not known my ways;

Unto whom I sware in my wrath that they should not enter into my rest.

PSALM 96

O sing unto the Lord a new song: sing unto the Lord, all the earth.

Sing unto the Lord, bless his name; show forth his salvation from day to day.

Declare his glory among the nations, his wonders among all peoples.

For the Lord is great, and greatly to be praised: he is to be feared above all gods.

For all the gods of the nations are idols: but the Lord made the heavens.

Honor and majesty are before him: strength and beauty are in his sanctuary.

Give unto the Lord, O ye kindreds of the people, give unto the Lord glory and strength.

Give unto the Lord the glory due unto his name: bring an offering, and come into his courts.

O worship the Lord in the beauty of holiness: fear before him, all the earth.

Say among the nations that the Lord reigneth;

The world also shall be established that it cannot be moved;

He will judge the people righteously.

Let the heavens rejoice, and let the earth be glad; let the sea roar, and the fulness thereof.

Let the field be joyful, and all that is therein: then shall all the trees of the wood rejoice before the Lord:

For he cometh, for he cometh to judge the earth;

He will judge the world with righteousness, and the peoples with his truth.

## SELECTION 33

PSALM 97: 1-2; 10-12

THE Lord reigneth; let the earth rejoice;

Let the multitude of isles be glad.

Clouds and darkness are round about him;

Righteousness and justice are the foundation of his throne.

Ye that love the Lord, hate evil: he preserveth the souls of his saints;

He delivereth them out of the hand of the wicked.

Light is sown for the righteous, and gladness for the upright in heart.

Rejoice in the Lord, ye righteous; and give thanks at the remembrance of his holiness.

PSALM 98

O sing unto the Lord a new song; for he hath done marvellous things;

His right hand, and his holy arm, hath wrought salvation for him.

The Lord hath made known his salvation;

His righteousness hath he openly showed in the sight of the nations.

He hath remembered his lovingkindness and his faithfulness toward the house of Israel:

All the ends of the earth have seen the salvation of our God.

Make a joyful noise unto the Lord, all the earth;

Make a loud noise, and rejoice, and sing praise.

Sing unto the Lord with the harp; with the harp, and the voice of a psalm.

> With trumpets and sound of cornet make a joyful noise before the Lord, the King.

Let the sea roar, and the fulness thereof; the world, and they that dwell therein.

> Let the floods clap their hands: let the hills be joyful together before the Lord;

For he cometh to judge the earth:

> With righteousness shall he judge the world, and the peoples with equity.

PSALM 100

Make a joyful noise unto the Lord, all ye lands.

> Serve the Lord with gladness: come before his presence with singing.

Know ye that the Lord he is God: it is he that hath made us, and not we ourselves;

> We are his people, and the sheep of his pasture.

Enter into his gates with thanksgiving, and into his courts with praise:

> Be thankful unto him, and bless his name.

For the Lord is good; his mercy is everlasting;

> And his truth endureth to all generations.

## SELECTION 34

PSALM 103

BLESS the Lord, O my soul: and all that is within me, bless his holy name.

> Bless the Lord, O my soul, and forget not all his benefits:

Who forgiveth all thine iniquities; who healeth all thy diseases;

> Who redeemeth thy life from destruction; who crowneth thee with lovingkindness and tender mercies;

Who satisfieth thy mouth with good things; so that thy youth is renewed like the eagle.

**The Lord executeth righteousness and judgment for all that are oppressed.**

He made known his ways unto Moses, his acts unto the children of Israel.

**The Lord is merciful and gracious, slow to anger, and plenteous in mercy.**

He will not always chide: neither will he keep his anger for ever.

**He hath not dealt with us after our sins; nor rewarded us according to our iniquities.**

For as the heaven is high above the earth, so great is his mercy toward them that fear him.

**As far as the east is from the west, so far hath he removed our transgressions from us.**

Like as a father pitieth his children, so the Lord pitieth them that fear him.

**For he knoweth our frame; he remembereth that we are dust.**

As for man, his days are as grass: as a flower of the field, so he flourisheth.

**For the wind passeth over it, and it is gone; and the place thereof shall know it no more.**

But the mercy of the Lord is from everlasting to everlasting upon them that fear him, and his righteousness unto children's children;

**To such as keep his covenant, and to those that remember his commandments to do them.**

The Lord hath established his throne in the heavens; and his kingdom ruleth over all.

**Bless the Lord, ye his angels, that excel in strength, that do his commandments, hearkening unto the voice of his word.**

Bless ye the Lord, all ye his hosts:

**Ye ministers of his, that do his pleasure.**

Bless the Lord, all his works in all places of his dominion:

**Bless the Lord, O my soul.**

## SELECTION 35

PSALM 104: 1–33

BLESS the Lord, O my soul. O Lord my God, thou art very great; thou art clothed with honor and majesty:

**Who coverest thyself with light as with a garment; who stretchest out the heavens like a curtain;**

Who layeth the beams of his chambers in the waters; who maketh the clouds his chariot; who walketh upon the wings of the wind:

**Who maketh winds his messengers; flames of fire his ministers;**

Who laid the foundations of the earth, that it should not be removed for ever.

**Thou coveredst it with the deep as with a garment: the waters stood above the mountains.**

At thy rebuke they fled; at the voice of thy thunder they hasted away (the mountains rose, the valleys sank down) unto the place which thou hadst founded for them.

**Thou hast set a bound that they may not pass over; that they turn not again to cover the earth.**

He sendeth the springs into the valleys; they run among the mountains.

**They give drink to every beast of the field; the wild asses quench their thirst.**

By them the birds of the heavens have their habitation; they sing among the branches.

**He watereth the mountains from his chambers: the earth is filled with the fruit of thy works.**

He causeth the grass to grow for the cattle, and herb for the service of man; that he may bring forth food out of the earth;

**And wine that maketh glad the heart of man, and oil to make his face to shine, and bread which strengtheneth man's heart.**

The trees of the Lord are full of sap; the cedars of Lebanon, which he hath planted;

**Where the birds make their nests; as for the stork, the fir trees are her house.**

The high hills are a refuge for the wild goats; and the rocks for the conies.

**He appointed the moon for seasons; the sun knoweth his going down.**

Thou makest darkness, and it is night; wherein all the beasts of the forest do creep forth.

**The young lions roar after their prey, and seek their food from God.**

The sun ariseth, they get them away, and lay them down in their dens.

**Man goeth forth unto his work and to his labor until the evening.**

O Lord, how manifold are thy works! in wisdom hast thou made them all: the earth is full of thy riches.

**Yonder is the sea, great and wide, wherein are things creeping innumerable, both small and great beasts.**

There go the ships: there is leviathan, whom thou hast made to play therein.

**These wait all upon thee; that thou mayest give them their food in due season.**

That thou givest them they gather: thou openest thine hand, they are filled with good.

**Thou hidest thy face, they are troubled: thou takest away their breath, they die, and return to their dust.**

Thou sendest forth thy spirit, they are created; and thou renewest the face of the earth.

**The glory of the Lord shall endure for ever; the Lord shall rejoice in his works.**

He looketh on the earth, and it trembleth; he toucheth the hills, and they smoke.

**I will sing unto the Lord as long as I live; I will sing praise to my God while I have any being.**

## SELECTION 36

PSALM 107: 1-22

O GIVE thanks unto the Lord, for he is good;

**For his mercy endureth for ever.**

Let the redeemed of the Lord say so, whom he hath redeemed from the hand of the enemy;

**And gathered them out of the lands, from the east, and from the west, from the north, and from the south.**

They wandered in the wilderness in a solitary way; they found no city to dwell in.

**Hungry and thirsty, their soul fainted in them.**

Then they cried unto the Lord in their trouble, and he delivered them out of their distresses.

**And he led them forth by a straight path, that they might go to a city of habitation.**

Oh that men would praise the Lord for his goodness, and for his wonderful works to the children of men!

**For he satisfieth the longing soul, and filleth the hungry soul with goodness.**

Such as sat in darkness and in the shadow of death, being bound in affliction and iron;

**Because they rebelled against the words of God, and contemned the counsel of the Most High.**

Therefore he brought down their heart with labor;

**They fell down, and there was none to help.**

Then they cried unto the Lord in their trouble, and he saved them out of their distresses.

**He brought them out of darkness and the shadow of death, and brake their bands in sunder.**

Oh that men would praise the Lord for his goodness, and for his wonderful works to the children of men!

**For he hath broken the gates of brass, and cut the bars of iron in sunder.**

Fools because of their transgression, and because of their iniquities, are afflicted.

Their soul abhorreth all manner of food; and they draw nea.' unto the gates of death.

Then they cry unto the Lord in their trouble, and he saveth them out of their distresses.

He sendeth his word, and healeth them, and delivereth them from their destructions.

Oh that men would praise the Lord for his goodness, and for his wonderful works to the children of men!

And let them sacrifice the sacrifices of thanksgiving, and declare his works with rejoicing.

## SELECTION 37

PSALM 107: 23–43

THEY that go down to the sea in ships, that do business in great waters;

These see the works of the Lord, and his wonders in the deep.

For he commandeth, and raiseth the stormy wind, which lifteth up the waves thereof.

They mount up to the heaven, they go down again to the depths: their soul is melted because of trouble.

They reel to and fro, and stagger like a drunken man, and are at their wit's end.

Then they cry unto the Lord in their trouble, and he bringeth them out of their distresses.

He maketh the storm a calm, so that the waves thereof are still.

Then are they glad because they are quiet; so he bringeth them unto their desired haven.

Oh that men would praise the Lord for his goodness, and for his wonderful works to the children of men!

Let them exalt him also in the congregation of the people, and praise him in the assembly of the elders.

He turneth rivers into a wilderness, and the watersprings into dry ground;

A fruitful land into barrenness, for the wickedness of them that dwell therein.

He turneth the wilderness into a pool of water, and a dry land into watersprings.

And there he maketh the hungry to dwell, that they may prepare a city for habitation;

And sow the fields, and plant vineyards, and get them fruits of increase.

He blesseth them also, so that they are multiplied greatly; and suffereth not their cattle to decrease.

Again, they are diminished and bowed down through oppression, affliction, and sorrow.

He poureth contempt upon princes, and causeth them to wander in the wilderness, where there is no way.

Yet setteth he the poor on high from affliction, and maketh him families like a flock.

The righteous shall see it, and rejoice; and all iniquity shall stop her mouth.

Whoso is wise will give heed to these things;

And they will consider the lovingkindness of the Lord.

# SELECTION 38

PSALM III: 1–5; 7–10

PRAISE ye the Lord.

I will praise the Lord with my whole heart, in the assembly of the upright, and in the congregation.

The works of the Lord are great, sought out of all them that have pleasure therein.

His work is honorable and glorious: and his righteousness endureth for ever.

He hath made his wonderful works to be remembered;

The Lord is gracious and full of compassion.

He hath given food unto them that fear him;

He will ever be mindful of his covenant.

The works of his hands are truth and justice;

All his commandments are sure.

They stand fast for ever and ever,

**And are done in truth and uprightness.**

He hath sent redemption unto his people;

**He hath commanded his covenant for ever;**

Holy and reverend is his name.

**The fear of the Lord is the beginning of wisdom;**

A good understanding have all they that do his commandments:

**His praise endureth for ever.**

PSALM 113: 1–6

Praise ye the Lord.

**Praise, O ye servants of the Lord, praise the name of the Lord.**

Blessed be the name of the Lord from this time forth and for evermore.

**From the rising of the sun unto the going down of the same the Lord's name is to be praised.**

The Lord is high above all nations,

**And his glory above the heavens.**

Who is like unto the Lord our God, who dwelleth on high,

**Who humbleth himself to behold the things that are in heaven and in the earth!**

## SELECTION 39

PSALM 115: 1–16

NOT unto us, O Lord, not unto us, but unto thy name give glory, for thy mercy, and for thy truth's sake.

**Wherefore should the heathen say, Where is now their God?**

But our God is in the heavens: he hath done whatsoever he hath pleased.

**Their idols are silver and gold, the work of men's hands.**

They have mouths, but they speak not; eyes have they, but they see not;

**They have ears, but they hear not; noses have they, but they smell not;**

They have hands, but they handle not; feet have they, but they walk not; neither speak they through their throat.

They that make them are like unto them; so is every one that trusteth in them.

O Israel, trust thou in the Lord: he is their help and their shield.

O house of Aaron, trust in the Lord: he is their help and their shield.

Ye that fear the Lord, trust in the Lord: he is their help and their shield.

The Lord hath been mindful of us; he will bless us; he will bless the house of Israel.

He will bless the house of Aaron.

He will bless them that fear the Lord, both small and great.

The Lord increase you more and more, you and your children.

Ye are blessed of the Lord, who made heaven and earth.

The heavens, even the heavens, are the Lord's:

But the earth hath he given to the children of men.


## SELECTION 40

Psalm 116: 1–9; 12–19

I LOVE the Lord, because he hath heard my voice and my supplications.

Because he hath inclined his ear unto me, therefore will I call upon him as long as I live.

The sorrows of death compassed me, and the pains of hell gat hold upon me: I found trouble and sorrow.

Then called I upon the name of the Lord; O Lord, I beseech thee, deliver my soul.

Gracious is the Lord, and righteous; yea, our God is merciful.

The Lord preserveth the simple: I was brought low, and he helped me.

Return unto thy rest, O my soul;

For the Lord hath dealt bountifully with thee.

For thou hast delivered my soul from death, mine eyes from tears, and my feet from falling.

I will walk before the Lord in the land of the living.

What shall I render unto the Lord for all his benefits toward me?

I will take the cup of salvation, and call upon the name of the Lord.

I will pay my vows unto the Lord now in the presence of all his people.

Precious in the sight of the Lord is the death of his saints.

O Lord, truly I am thy servant;

I am thy servant, and the son of thine handmaid; thou hast loosed my bonds.

I will offer to thee the sacrifice of thanksgiving, and will call upon the name of the Lord.

I will pay my vows unto the Lord now in the presence of all his people,

In the courts of the Lord's house, in the midst of thee, O Jerusalem.

Praise ye the Lord.

## SELECTION 41

PSALM 118: 1–9; 14–29

O GIVE thanks unto the Lord; for he is good; for his mercy endureth for ever.

Let Israel now say, that his mercy endureth for ever.

Let the house of Aaron now say, that his mercy endureth for ever.

Let them now that fear the Lord say, that his mercy endureth for ever.

I called upon the Lord in distress: the Lord answered me, and set me in a large place.

The Lord is on my side; I will not fear: what can man do unto me?

The Lord taketh my part with them that help me: therefore shall I see my desire upon them that hate me.

It is better to trust in the Lord than to put confidence in man.

It is better to trust in the Lord than to put confidence in princes.

The Lord is my strength and song, and is become my salvation.

The voice of rejoicing and salvation is in the tents of the righteous; the right hand of the Lord doeth valiantly.

**The right hand of the Lord is exalted: the right hand of the Lord doeth valiantly.**

I shall not die, but live, and declare the works of the Lord.

**The Lord hath chastened me sore: but he hath not given me over unto death.**

Open to me the gates of righteousness:

**I will go into them, and I will praise the Lord.**

This is the gate of the Lord, into which the righteous shall enter.

**I will praise thee: for thou hast heard me, and art become my salvation.**

The stone which the builders refused is become the head stone of the corner.

**This is the Lord's doing; it is marvellous in our eyes.**

This is the day which the Lord hath made;

**We will rejoice and be glad in it.**

Save now, we beseech thee, O Lord;

**O Lord, we beseech thee, send now prosperity.**

Blessed be he that cometh in the name of the Lord;

**We have blessed you out of the house of the Lord.**

The Lord is God, and he hath given us light;

**Bind the sacrifice with cords, even unto the horns of the altar.**

Thou art my God, and I will praise thee: thou art my God, I will exalt thee.

**O give thanks unto the Lord; for he is good; for his mercy endureth for ever.**


## SELECTION 42

PSALM 119: 1–24

BLESSED are they that are perfect in the way, who walk in the law of the Lord.

**Blessed are they that keep his testimonies, and that seek him with the whole heart.**

They also do no iniquity: they walk in his ways.

**Thou hast commanded us to keep thy precepts diligently.**

O that my ways were directed to observe thy statutes!

**Then shall I not be ashamed, when I have respect unto all thy commandments.**

I will praise thee with uprightness of heart, when I learn thy righteous judgments.

**I will keep thy statutes: O forsake me not utterly.**

Wherewithal shall a young man cleanse his way? by taking heed thereto according to thy word.

**With my whole heart have I sought thee: O let me not wander from thy commandments.**

Thy word have I hid in mine heart, that I might not sin against thee.

**Blessed art thou, O Lord: teach me thy statutes.**

With my lips have I declared all the ordinances of thy mouth.

**I have rejoiced in the way of thy testimonies, as much as in all riches.**

I will meditate in thy precepts, and have respect unto thy ways.

**I will delight myself in thy statutes: I will not forget thy word.**

Deal bountifully with thy servant, that I may live, and keep thy word.

**Open thou mine eyes, that I may behold wondrous things out of thy law.**

I am a stranger in the earth: hide not thy commandments from me.

**My soul breaketh for the longing that it hath unto thine ordinances at all times.**

Thou hast rebuked the proud that are cursed, that do err from thy commandments.

**Remove from me reproach and contempt; for I have kept thy testimonies.**

Princes also did sit and speak against me; but thy servant did meditate in thy statutes.

**Thy testimonies also are my delight and my counsellors.**

## SELECTION 43

PSALM 119: 33–56

TEACH me, O Lord, the way of thy statutes; and I shall keep it unto the end.

**Give me understanding, and I shall keep thy law; yea, I shall observe it with my whole heart.**

Make me to go in the path of thy commandments; for therein do I delight.

**Incline my heart unto thy testimonies, and not to covetousness.**

Turn away mine eyes from beholding vanity; and quicken thou me in thy way.

**Confirm thy word unto thy servant, who is devoted to thy fear.**

Turn away my reproach which I fear: for thine ordinances are good.

**Behold, I have longed after thy precepts: quicken me in thy righteousness.**

Let thy mercies come also unto me, O Lord, even thy salvation, according to thy word.

**So shall I have an answer for him that reproacheth me: for I trust in thy word.**

And take not the word of truth utterly out of my mouth; for I have hoped in thy ordinances.

**So shall I keep thy law continually for ever and ever.**

And I shall walk at liberty; for I seek thy precepts.

**I will speak of thy testimonies also before kings, and shall not be ashamed.**

And I will delight myself in thy commandments, which I have loved.

**My hands also will I lift up unto thy commandments, which I have loved; and I will meditate in thy statutes.**

Remember the word unto thy servant, upon which thou hast caused me to hope.

**This is my comfort in my affliction: for thy word hath quickened me.**

The proud have had me greatly in derision: yet have I not declined from thy law.

I remembered thine ordinances of old, O Lord, and have comforted myself.

Indignation hath taken hold upon me because of the wicked that forsake thy law.

Thy statutes have been my songs in the house of my pilgrimage.

I have remembered thy name, O Lord, in the night, and have kept thy law.

This I have had, because I have kept thy precepts.

## SELECTION 44

PSALM 119: 89-112

FOR ever, O Lord, thy word is settled in heaven.

Thy faithfulness is unto all generations: thou hast established the earth, and it abideth.

They continue this day according to thine ordinances; for all things are thy servants.

Unless thy law had been my delight, I should then have perished in mine affliction.

I will never forget thy precepts; for with them thou hast quickened me.

I am thine, save me; for I have sought thy precepts.

The wicked have waited for me to destroy me: but I will consider thy testimonies.

I have seen an end of all perfection: but thy commandment is exceeding broad.

O how love I thy law! it is my meditation all the day.

Thou through thy commandments hast made me wiser than mine enemies, for they are ever with me.

I have more understanding than all my teachers, for thy testimonies are my meditation.

I understand more than the aged, because I have kept thy precepts.

I have refrained my feet from every evil way, that I might keep thy word.

I have not departed from thine ordinances; for thou hast taught me.

How sweet are thy words unto my taste! yea, sweeter than honey to my mouth!

Through thy precepts I get understanding: therefore I hate every false way.

Thy word is a lamp unto my feet, and a light unto my path.

I have sworn, and have confirmed it, that I will keep thy righteous judgments.

I am afflicted very much; quicken me, O Lord, according unto thy word.

Accept, I beseech thee, the free-will offerings of my mouth, O Lord, and teach me thine ordinances.

My soul is continually in my hand, yet do I not forget thy law.

The wicked have laid a snare for me, yet I erred not from thy precepts.

Thy testimonies have I taken as an heritage for ever, for they are the rejoicing of my heart.

I have inclined mine heart to perform thy statutes alway, even unto the end.


## SELECTION 45

PSALM 121

I WILL lift up mine eyes unto the hills: from whence shall my help come?

My help cometh from the Lord, who made heaven and earth.

He will not suffer thy foot to be moved: he that keepeth thee will not slumber.

Behold, he that keepeth Israel will neither slumber nor sleep.

The Lord is thy keeper: the Lord is thy shade upon thy right hand.

The sun shall not smite thee by day, nor the moon by night.

The Lord will preserve thee from all evil: he will preserve thy soul.

The Lord will preserve thy going out and thy coming in from this time forth, and even for evermore.

And they that wasted us required of us mirth, saying, Sing us one of the songs of Zion.

w shall we sing the Lord's song in a strange land?

If I forget thee, O Jerusalem, let my right hand forget her cunning.

do not remember thee, let my tongue cleave to the roof of my th;

If I prefer not Jerusalem above my chief joy.

м 138

ill praise thee with my whole heart: before the gods will I sing se unto thee.

I will worship toward thy holy temple, and praise thy name for thy lovingkindness and for thy truth;

thou hast magnified thy word above all thy name.

In the day when I cried thou answeredst me; thou didst encourage me with strength in my soul.

the kings of the earth shall praise thee, O Lord, when they hear words of thy mouth.

Yea, they shall sing of the ways of the Lord: for great is the glory of the Lord.

ugh the Lord is high, yet hath he respect unto the lowly;

But the proud he knoweth afar off.

ugh I walk in the midst of trouble, thou wilt revive me;

Thou wilt stretch forth thine hand against the wrath of mine enemies, and thy right hand will save me;

Lord will perfect that which concerneth me;

Thy mercy, O Lord, endureth for ever: forsake not the works of thine own hands.

## SELECTION 49

м 139: 1–12; 17–18; 23–24

ORD, thou hast searched me, and known me.

Thou knowest my downsitting and mine uprising; thou understandest my thought afar off.

Psalm 122

I was glad when they said unto me, Let us go into the house of the Lord.

Our feet are standing within thy gates, O Jerusalem.

Jerusalem is builded as a city that is compact together:

Whither the tribes go up, the tribes of the Lord,

Unto the testimony of Israel, to give thanks unto the name of the Lord.

For there are set thrones of judgment, the thrones of the house of David.

Pray for the peace of Jerusalem: they shall prosper that love thee.

Peace be within thy walls, and prosperity within thy palaces.

For my brethren and companions' sakes, I will now say, Peace be within thee.

Because of the house of the Lord our God I will seek thy good.

## SELECTION 46

Psalm 123: 1–2

UNTO thee lift I up mine eyes,

O thou that dwellest in the heavens.

Behold, as the eyes of servants look unto the hand of their masters,

And as the eyes of a maiden unto the hand of her mistress;

So our eyes wait upon the Lord our God,

Until that he have mercy upon us.

Psalm 125

They that trust in the Lord shall be as mount Zion,

Which cannot be removed, but abideth for ever.

As the mountains are round about Jerusalem,

So the Lord is round about his people from henceforth even for ever.

For the scepter of wickedness shall not rest upon the lot of the righteous;

Lest the righteous put forth their hands unto iniquity.

Do good, O Lord, unto those that are good,

And to them that are upright in their hearts.

As for such as turn aside unto their crooked ways, the Lord shall lead them forth with the workers of iniquity:

But peace shall be upon Israel.

PSALM 126

When the Lord brought back those that returned to Zion, we were like them that dream.

Then was our mouth filled with laughter, and our tongue with singing:

Then said they among the nations, The Lord hath done great things for them.

The Lord hath done great things for us; whereof we are glad.

Turn again our captivity, O Lord, as the streams in the south.

They that sow in tears shall reap in joy.

He that goeth forth and weepeth, bearing precious seed,

Shall doubtless come again with rejoicing, bringing his sheaves with him.

## SELECTION 47

PSALM 130

OUT of the depths have I cried unto thee, O Lord; Lord, hear my voice;

Let thine ears be attentive to the voice of my supplications.

If thou, Lord, shouldest mark iniquities, O Lord, who shall stand?

But there is forgiveness with thee, that thou mayest be feared.

I wait for the Lord, my soul doth wait,

And in his word do I hope.

My soul waiteth for the Lord more than they that watch for the morning;

Yea, more than they that watch for the morning.

Let Israel hope in the Lord;

For with the Lord there is mercy,

And with him is plenteous redemption.

And he will redeem Israel from all his iniquiti[es]

PSALM 136: 1–9; 23–26

O give thanks unto the Lord; for he is good: for h[is mercy endureth] for ever.

O give thanks unto the God of gods: for his m[ercy endureth for] ever.

O give thanks unto the Lord of lords: for his mercy [endureth for ever:]

To him who alone doeth great wonders: for h[is mercy endureth] for ever:

To him that by wisdom made the heavens: for h[is mercy endureth] for ever:

To him that stretched out the earth above t[he waters: for his] mercy endureth for ever:

To him that made great lights: for his mercy endu[reth for ever:]

The sun to rule by day: for his mercy endure[th for ever:]

The moon and stars to rule by night: for his mercy [endureth for ever:]

Who remembered us in our low estate: for h[is mercy endureth] for ever:

And hath delivered us from our enemies: for h[is mercy endureth] for ever:

Who giveth food to all flesh: for his mercy e[ndureth for ever:]

O give thanks unto the God of heaven:

For his mercy endureth for ever.

## SELECTION 48

PSALM 137: 1–6

BY the rivers of Babylon, there we sat down, yea[, we wept, when we] remembered Zion.

We hanged our harps upon the willows in th[e midst thereof.]

For there they that carried us away captive requ[ired of us a song]

Thou searchest out my path and my lying down, and art acquainted with all my ways.

**For there is not a word in my tongue, but, lo, O Lord, thou knowest it altogether.**

Thou hast beset me behind and before, and laid thine hand upon me.

**Such knowledge is too wonderful for me; it is high, I cannot attain unto it.**

Whither shall I go from thy spirit? or whither shall I flee from thy presence?

**If I ascend up into heaven, thou art there; if I make my bed in hell, behold, thou art there.**

If I take the wings of the morning, and dwell in the uttermost parts of the sea;

**Even there shall thy hand lead me, and thy right hand shall hold me.**

If I say: Surely the darkness shall cover me, and the light about me shall be night;

**Even the darkness hideth not from thee; but the night shineth as the day;**

The darkness and the light are both alike to thee.

**How precious also are thy thoughts unto me, O God! how great is the sum of them!**

If I should count them, they are more in number than the sand:

**When I awake, I am still with thee.**

Search me, O God, and know my heart: try me, and know my thoughts;

**And see if there be any wicked way in me, and lead me in the way everlasting.**

## SELECTION 50

PSALM 141: 1–2

LORD, I have called unto thee: make haste unto me;

**Give ear unto my voice, when I call unto thee.**

Let my prayer be set forth before thee as incense;

**And the lifting up of my hands as the evening sacrifice.**

PSALM 142

I cried unto the Lord with my voice; with my voice unto the Lord did I make my supplication.

**I poured out my complaint before him; I showed before him my trouble.**

When my spirit was overwhelmed within me, then thou knewest my path.

**In the way wherein I walked they have hidden a snare for me.**

Look on my right hand, and see; for there is no man that knoweth me.

**Refuge hath failed me; no man careth for my soul.**

I cried unto thee, O Lord: I said, Thou art my refuge,

**My portion in the land of the living.**

Attend unto my cry; for I am brought very low;

**Deliver me from my persecutors; for they are stronger than I.**

Bring my soul out of prison, that I may praise thy name;

**The righteous shall compass me about; for thou wilt deal bountifully with me.**

PSALM 143: 1–11

Hear my prayer, O Lord, give ear to my supplications;

**In thy faithfulness answer me, and in thy righteousness.**

And enter not into judgment with thy servant;

**For in thy sight shall no man living be justified.**

For the enemy hath persecuted my soul; he hath smitten my life down to the ground;

**He hath made me to dwell in darkness, as those that have been long dead.**

Therefore is my spirit overwhelmed within me;

**My heart within me is desolate.**

I remember the days of old; I meditate on all thy doings;

**I muse on the work of thy hands.**

I stretch forth my hands unto thee;

**My soul thirsteth after thee, as a thirsty land.**

Make haste to answer me, O Lord; my spirit faileth;

**Hide not thy face from me, lest I be like unto them that go down into the pit.**

Cause me to hear thy lovingkindness in the morning; for in thee do I trust;

**Cause me to know the way wherein I should walk; for I lift up my soul unto thee.**

Deliver me, O Lord, from mine enemies: I flee unto thee to hide me.

**Teach me to do thy will; for thou art my God;**

Thy spirit is good; lead me in the land of uprightness.

**Quicken me, O Lord, for thy name's sake: in thy righteousness bring my soul out of trouble.**

## SELECTION 51

PSALM 145

I WILL extol thee my God, O king; and I will bless thy name for ever and ever.

**Every day will I bless thee; and I will praise thy name for ever and ever.**

Great is the Lord, and greatly to be praised; and his greatness is unsearchable.

**One generation shall praise thy works to another, and shall declare thy mighty acts.**

I will speak of the glorious honor of thy majesty, and of thy wondrous works.

**And men shall speak of the might of thy terrible acts; and I will declare thy greatness.**

They shall utter the memory of thy great goodness, and shall sing of thy righteousness.

**The Lord is gracious, and full of compassion; slow to anger, and of great mercy.**

The Lord is good to all; and his tender mercies are over all his works.

**All thy works shall praise thee, O Lord; and thy saints shall bless thee.**

They shall speak of the glory of thy kingdom, and talk of thy power;

**To make known to the sons of men his mighty acts, and the glorious majesty of his kingdom.**

Thy kingdom is an everlasting kingdom, and thy dominion endureth throughout all generations.

**The Lord upholdeth all that fall, and raiseth up all those that are bowed down.**

The eyes of all wait upon thee; and thou givest them their food in due season.

**Thou openest thine hand, and satisfiest the desire of every living thing.**

The Lord is righteous in all his ways, and gracious in all his works.

**The Lord is nigh unto all them that call upon him, to all that call upon him in truth.**

He will fulfil the desire of them that fear him; he also will hear their cry, and will save them.

**The Lord preserveth all them that love him; but all the wicked will he destroy.**

My mouth shall speak the praise of the Lord;

**And let all flesh bless his holy name for ever and ever.**

## SELECTION 52

PSALM 147: 1–9; 11–20

PRAISE ye the Lord; for it is good to sing praises unto our God;

**For it is pleasant; and praise is comely.**

The Lord doth build up Jerusalem: he gathereth together the outcasts of Israel.

**He healeth the broken in heart, and bindeth up their wounds.**

He counteth the number of the stars; he calleth them all by their names.

**Great is our Lord, and of great power; his understanding is infinite.**

The Lord lifteth up the meek; he casteth the wicked down to the ground.

**Sing unto the Lord with thanksgiving; sing praise upon the harp unto our God:**

Who covereth the heavens with clouds, who prepareth rain for the earth,

**Who maketh grass to grow upon the mountains.**

He giveth to the beast his food, and to the young ravens which cry.

**The Lord taketh pleasure in them that fear him, in those that hope in his mercy.**

Praise the Lord, O Jerusalem; praise thy God, O Zion.

**For he hath strengthened the bars of thy gates; he hath blessed thy children within thee.**

He maketh peace in thy borders, and filleth thee with the finest of the wheat.

**He sendeth forth his commandment upon earth: his word runneth very swiftly.**

He giveth snow like wool; he scattereth the hoar-frost like ashes.

**He casteth forth his ice like morsels; who can stand before his cold?**

He sendeth out his word, and melteth them; he causeth his wind to blow, and the waters flow.

**He showed his word unto Jacob, his statutes and his ordinances unto Israel.**

He hath not dealt so with any nation;

**And as for his ordinances, they have not known them.  Praise ye the Lord.**

### SELECTION 53

PSALM 148

PRAISE ye the Lord.   Praise ye the Lord from the heavens: praise him in the heights.

**Praise ye him, all his angels: praise ye him, all his hosts.**

Praise ye him, sun and moon: praise him, all ye stars of light.

**Praise him, ye heavens of heavens, and ye waters that are above the heavens.**

Let them praise the name of the Lord: for he commanded, and they were created.

**He hath also established them for ever and ever: he hath made a decree which shall not pass.**

Praise the Lord from the earth, ye dragons, and all deeps;

**Fire and hail; snow and vapors; stormy wind fulfilling his word;**

Mountains and all hills; fruitful trees and all cedars;

**Beasts and all cattle; creeping things and flying fowl;**

Kings of the earth, and all peoples; princes, and all judges of the earth;

**Both young men and maidens; old men and children;**

Let them praise the name of the Lord: for his name alone is excellent;

**His glory is above the earth and heaven.**

He also exalteth the horn of his people, the praise of all his saints;

**Even of the children of Israel, a people near unto him. Praise ye the Lord.**

Psalm 150

Praise ye the Lord. Praise God in his sanctuary:

**Praise him in the firmament of his power.**

Praise him for his mighty acts:

**Praise him according to his excellent greatness.**

Praise him with the sound of the trumpet:

**Praise him with the psaltery and harp.**

Praise him with the timbrel and dance:

**Praise him with stringed instruments and organs.**

Praise him upon the loud cymbals:

**Praise him upon the high sounding cymbals.**

Let every thing that hath breath praise the Lord.

**Praise ye the Lord.**

# Selection 54

Job 28: 12–28

BUT where shall wisdom be found?

**And where is the place of understanding?**

Man knoweth not the price thereof;

**Neither is it found in the land of the living.**

The deep saith, It is not in me; and the sea saith, It is not with me.

**It cannot be gotten for gold, neither shall silver be weighed for the price thereof.**

It cannot be valued with the gold of Ophir, with the precious onyx, or the sapphire.

**Gold and crystal cannot equal it, neither shall it be exchanged for jewels of fine gold.**

No mention shall be made of coral or of pearls;

**Yea, the price of wisdom is above rubies.**

The topaz of Ethiopia shall not equal it,

**Neither shall it be valued with pure gold.**

Whence then cometh wisdom? And where is the place of understanding?

**Seeing it is hid from the eyes of all living, and kept close from the birds of the air.**

Destruction and death say, We have heard a rumor thereof with our ears.

**God understandeth the way thereof, and he knoweth the place thereof.**

For he looketh to the ends of the earth, and seeth under the whole heaven;

**When he maketh a weight for the wind: yea, he meteth out the waters by measure.**

When he made a decree for the rain, and a way for the lightning of the thunder:

**Then did he see it, and declare it: he established it, yea, and searched it out.**

And unto man he said, Behold, the fear of the Lord, that is wisdom;

**And to depart from evil is understanding.**

## SELECTION 55

PROVERBS 3: 13-26

HAPPY is the man that findeth wisdom, and the man that getteth understanding.

**For the gaining of it is better than the gaining of silver, and the profit thereof than fine gold.**

She is more precious than rubies; and none of the things thou canst desire are to be compared unto her.

**Length of days is in her right hand; in her left hand are riches and honor.**

Her ways are ways of pleasantness, and all her paths are peace.

**She is a tree of life to them that lay hold upon her: and happy is everyone that retaineth her.**

The Lord by wisdom founded the earth; by understanding he established the heavens.

**By his knowledge the depths were broken up, and the skies drop down the dew.**

My son, let them not depart from thine eyes; keep sound wisdom and discretion:

**So shall they be life unto thy soul, and grace to thy neck.**

Then shalt thou walk in thy way securely, and thy foot shall not stumble.

**When thou liest down, thou shalt not be afraid;**

Yea, thou shalt lie down, and thy sleep shall be sweet.

**Be not afraid of sudden fear, neither of the desolation of the wicked, when it cometh;**

For the Lord will be thy confidence,

**And will keep thy foot from being taken.**

## Selection 56

Isaiah 9: 2; 6–7

THE people that walked in darkness have seen a great light;

**They that dwelt in the land of the shadow of death, upon them hath the light shined.**

For unto us a child is born, unto us a son is given;

**And the government shall be upon his shoulder;**

And his name shall be called Wonderful Counsellor, Mighty God, Everlasting Father, Prince of Peace.

**Of the increase of his government and of peace there shall be no end, upon the throne of David and upon his kingdom,**

To establish it, and to uphold it with justice and with righteousness from henceforth even forevermore.

**The zeal of the Lord of hosts will perform this.**

Isaiah 11: 1–9

And there shall come forth a shoot out of the stock of Jesse,

**And a branch out of his roots shall bear fruit.**

And the spirit of the Lord shall rest upon him,

**The spirit of wisdom and understanding, the spirit of counsel and might, the spirit of knowledge and of the fear of the Lord.**

And his delight shall be in the fear of the Lord;

**And he shall not judge after the sight of his eyes, neither decide after the hearing of his ears;**

But with righteousness shall he judge the poor,

**And decide with equity for the meek of the earth;**

And he shall smite the earth with the rod of his mouth, and with the breath of his lips shall he slay the wicked.

**And righteousness shall be the girdle of his waist, and faithfulness the girdle of his loins.**

And the wolf shall dwell with the lamb, and the leopard shall lie down with the kid; and the calf and the young lion and the fatling together;

**And a little child shall lead them.**

And the cow and the bear shall feed; their young ones shall lie down together; and the lion shall eat straw like the ox.

**And the sucking child shall play on the hole of the asp, and the weaned child shall put his hand on the adder's den.**

They shall not hurt nor destroy in all my holy mountain;

**For the earth shall be full of the knowledge of the Lord, as the waters cover the sea.**

## SELECTION 57

ISAIAH 35

THE wilderness and the dry land shall be glad; and the desert shall rejoice and blossom as the rose.

**It shall blossom abundantly, and rejoice even with joy and singing;**

The glory of Lebanon shall be given unto it, the excellency of Carmel and Sharon;

**They shall see the glory of the Lord, the excellency of our God.**

Strengthen ye the weak hands, and confirm the feeble knees.

**Say to them that are of a fearful heart, Be strong, fear not;**

Behold your God will come with vengeance, even God with a recompense; he will come and save you.

**Then the eyes of the blind shall be opened, and the ears of the deaf shall be unstopped.**

Then shall the lame man leap as a hart, and the tongue of the dumb shall sing;

For in the wilderness shall waters break out, and streams in the desert.

And the glowing sand shall become a pool, and the thirsty ground springs of water:

In the habitation of jackals, where they lay, shall be grass with reeds and rushes.

And a highway shall be there, and a way, and it shall be called the way of holiness;

The unclean shall not pass over it, but it shall be for the redeemed;

The wayfaring men, though fools, shall not err therein.

No lion shall be there, nor shall any ravenous beast go up thereupon;

They shall not be found there; but the redeemed shall walk there;

And the ransomed of the Lord shall return and come with singing unto Zion;

And everlasting joy shall be upon their heads;

They shall obtain gladness and joy, and sorrow and sighing shall flee away.

## SELECTION 58

ISAIAH 40: 1–11; 27–31

COMFORT ye, comfort ye my people, saith your God.

Speak ye comfortably to Jerusalem;

And cry unto her, that her warfare is accomplished, that her iniquity is pardoned,

That she hath received of the Lord's hand double for all her sins.

The voice of one that crieth: Prepare ye in the wilderness the way of the Lord;

Make level in the desert a highway for our God.

Every valley shall be exalted, and every mountain and hill shall be made low;

And the uneven shall be made level, and the rough places a plain;

And the glory of the Lord shall be revealed, and all flesh shall see it together;

For the mouth of the Lord hath spoken it.

The voice of one saying: Cry,

And one said: What shall I cry?

All flesh is grass, and all the goodliness thereof is as the flower of the field; the grass withereth, the flower fadeth, because the breath of the Lord bloweth upon it; surely the people is grass.

The grass withereth, the flower fadeth; but the word of our God shall stand forever.

O thou that tellest good tidings to Zion, get thee up on a high mountain;

O thou that tellest good tidings to Jerusalem, lift up thy voice with strength; lift it up, be not afraid; say unto the cities of Judah, Behold your God!

Behold, the Lord will come as a mighty one, and his arm will rule for him;

Behold, his reward is with him, and his recompense before him.

He will feed his flock like a shepherd,

He will gather the lambs in his arms, and carry them in his bosom, and will gently lead those that have their young.

Why sayest thou, O Jacob, and speakest, O Israel, My way is hid from the Lord, and the justice due to me is passed away from my God.

Hast thou not known? hast thou not heard?

The everlasting God, the Lord, the Creator of the ends of the earth, fainteth not, neither is weary;

There is no searching of his understanding.

He giveth power to the faint; and to him that hath no might he increaseth strength.

Even the youths shall faint and be weary, and the young men shall utterly fall:

But they that wait for the Lord shall renew their strength;

They shall mount up with wings as eagles; they shall run, and not be weary; they shall walk, and not faint.

## SELECTION 59

Isaiah 53: 1–7; 10–12

WHO hath believed our report? and to whom hath the arm of the Lord been revealed?

For he grew up before him as a tender plant, and as a root out of a dry ground;

He hath no form nor comeliness; and when we see him, there is no beauty that we should desire him.

He was despised, and rejected of men; a man of sorrows, and acquainted with grief;

And as one from whom men hide their face he was despised; and we esteemed him not.

Surely he hath borne our griefs, and carried our sorrows; yet we did esteem him stricken, smitten of God, and afflicted.

But he was wounded for our transgressions, he was bruised for our iniquities;

The chastisement of our peace was upon him; and with his stripes we are healed.

All we like sheep have gone astray; we have turned everyone to his own way;

And the Lord hath laid on him the iniquity of us all.

He was oppressed, yet when he was afflicted he opened not his mouth;

As a lamb that is led to the slaughter, and as a sheep that before its shearers is dumb, so he opened not his mouth.

Yet it pleased the Lord to bruise him; he hath put him to grief;

When thou shalt make his soul an offering for sin, he shall see his seed,

He shall prolong his days, and the pleasure of the Lord shall prosper in his hand.

He shall see of the travail of his soul, and shall be satisfied.

By his knowledge shall my righteous servant justify many; and he shall bear their iniquities.

Therefore will I divide him a portion with the great, and he shall divide the spoil with the strong;

Because he poured out his soul unto death, and was numbered with the transgressors;

Yet he bare the sin of many, and made intercession for the transgressors.

## SELECTION 60

ISAIAH 55

HO, everyone that thirsteth, come ye to the waters, and he that hath no money; come ye, buy and eat;

Yea, come, buy wine and milk without money and without price.

Wherefore do ye spend money for that which is not bread?

And your labor for that which satisfieth not?

Hearken diligently unto me, and eat ye that which is good,

And let your soul delight itself in fatness.

Incline your ear, and come unto me; hear, and your soul shall live;

And I will make an everlasting covenant with you, even the sure mercies of David.

Behold, I have given him for a witness to the peoples,

A leader and commander to the peoples.

Behold, thou shalt call a nation that thou knowest not; and a nation that knew not thee shall run unto thee,

Because of the Lord thy God, and for the Holy One of Israel; for he hath glorified thee.

Seek ye the Lord while he may be found;

Call ye upon him while he is near;

Let the wicked forsake his way,

And the unrighteous man his thoughts;

And let him return unto the Lord, and he will have mercy upon him;

And to our God, for he will abundantly pardon.

For my thoughts are not your thoughts,

Neither are your ways my ways, saith the Lord.

For as the heavens are higher than the earth,

So are my ways higher than your ways, and my thoughts than your thoughts.

For as the rain cometh down and the snow from heaven,

And returneth not thither, but watereth the earth,

And maketh it bring forth and bud, that it may give seed to the sower and bread to the eater;

So shall my word be that goeth forth out of my mouth;

It shall not return unto me void, but it shall accomplish that which I please,

And it shall prosper in the thing whereto I sent it.

For ye shall go out with joy, and be led forth with peace;

The mountains and the hills shall break forth before you into singing;

And all the trees of the field shall clap their hands.

**Instead of the thorn shall come up the fir-tree, and instead of the brier shall come up the myrtle-tree;**

And it shall be to the Lord for a name,

**For an everlasting sign that shall not be cut off.**

## SELECTION 61

MATTHEW 5: 3–16

BLESSED are the poor in spirit:

**For theirs is the kingdom of heaven.**

Blessed are they that mourn:

**For they shall be comforted.**

Blessed are the meek:

**For they shall inherit the earth.**

Blessed are they that hunger and thirst after righteousness:

**For they shall be filled.**

Blessed are the merciful:

**For they shall obtain mercy.**

Blessed are the pure in heart:

**For they shall see God.**

Blessed are the peacemakers:

**For they shall be called sons of God.**

Blessed are they that have been persecuted for righteousness' sake:

**For theirs is the kingdom of heaven.**

Blessed are ye when men shall reproach you, and persecute you, and say all manner of evil against you falsely, for my sake. Rejoice and be exceeding glad:

**For great is your reward in heaven; for so persecuted they the prophets that were before you.**

Ye are the salt of the earth; but if the salt have lost its savor, wherewith shall it be salted?

**It is thenceforth good for nothing, but to be cast out, and to be trodden under foot of men.**

Ye are the light of the world.

**A city that is set on a hill cannot be hid.**

Neither do men light a candle, and put it under a bushel, but on a candlestick; and it giveth light unto all that are in the house.

**Let your light so shine before men, that they may see your good works, and glorify your Father which is in heaven.**

# SELECTION 62

MATTHEW 6: 19–21; 24–34

LAY not up for yourselves treasures upon earth;

**Where moth and rust consume, and where thieves break through and steal.**

But lay up for yourselves treasures in heaven;

**Where neither moth nor rust doth consume, and where thieves do not break through nor steal; for where thy treasure is, there will thy heart be also.**

No man can serve two masters; for either he will hate the one, and love the other; or else he will hold to the one, and despise the other.

**Ye cannot serve God and mammon.**

Therefore I say unto you, Be not anxious for your life, what ye shall eat, or what ye shall drink; nor yet for your body, what ye shall put on.

**Is not the life more than the food, and the body than the raiment?**

Behold the birds of the heaven, that they sow not, neither do they reap, nor gather into barns; and your heavenly Father feedeth them.

**Are not ye of much more value than they?**

Which of you by being anxious can add one cubit unto the measure of his life? And why are ye anxious concerning raiment?

**Consider the lilies of the field, how they grow; they toil not, neither do they spin; yet I say unto you, that even Solomon in all his glory was not arrayed like one of these.**

But if God doth so clothe the grass of the field, which today is, and tomorrow is cast into the oven;

**Shall he not much more clothe you, O ye of little faith?**

Be not therefore anxious, saying, What shall we eat? or, What shall we drink? or, Wherewithal shall we be clothed?

**For after all these things do the Gentiles seek; for your heavenly Father knoweth that ye have need of all these things.**

But seek ye first the kingdom of God and his righteousness; and all these things shall be added unto you.

**Be not therefore anxious for the morrow; for the morrow will be anxious for itself. Sufficient unto the day is the evil thereof.**

## SELECTION 63

Luke 1: 46–55

MY soul doth magnify the Lord,

**And my spirit hath rejoiced in God my Saviour;**

For he hath regarded the low estate of his handmaiden.

**For behold, from henceforth all generations shall call me blessed;**

For he that is mighty hath done to me great things; and holy is his name.

**And his mercy is on them that fear him from generation to generation.**

He hath showed strength with his arm;

**He hath scattered the proud in the imagination of their hearts.**

He hath put down the mighty from their seats,

**And exalted them of low degree.**

He hath filled the hungry with good things;

**And the rich he hath sent empty away.**

He hath given help to his servant Israel, in remembrance of his mercy:

**As he spake to our fathers, to Abraham, and to his seed for ever.**

## SELECTION 64

Luke 1: 68–79

BLESSED be the Lord God of Israel; for he hath visited and redeemed his people;

**And hath raised up a horn of salvation for us in the house of his servant David;**

As he spake by the mouth of his holy prophets, which have been since the world began;

**That we should be saved from our enemies, and from the hand of all that hate us.**

To perform the mercy promised to our fathers, and to remember his holy covenant;

**The oath which he sware to our father Abraham: that he would grant unto us,**

That we being delivered out of the hand of our enemies might serve him without fear;

**In holiness and righteousness before him, all the days of our life.**

And thou, child, shalt be called the prophet of the Highest;

**For thou shalt go before the face of the Lord to prepare his ways;**

To give knowledge of salvation unto his people by the remission of their sins,

**Through the tender mercy of our God; whereby the dayspring from on high hath visited us;**

To give light to them that sit in darkness, and in the shadow of death,

**To guide our feet into the way of peace.**

Luke 2: 29–32

Lord, now lettest thou thy servant depart in peace, according to thy word:

**For mine eyes have seen thy salvation.**

Which thou hast prepared before the face of all peoples;

**A light to lighten the Gentiles, and the glory of thy people Israel.**

## Selection 65

Luke 2: 8–20

AND there were in the same country shepherds abiding in the field, keeping watch over their flock by night.

**And lo, the angel of the Lord came upon them, and the glory of the Lord shone round about them: and they were sore afraid.**

And the angel said unto them, Fear not: for, behold, I bring you good tidings of great joy, which shall be to all people.

**For unto you is born this day in the city of David a Saviour, which is Christ the Lord.**

And this shall be a sign unto you; Ye shall find the babe wrapped in swaddling clothes, lying in a manger.

**And suddenly there was with the angel a multitude of the heavenly host praising God, and saying,**

Glory to God in the highest, and on earth peace, good will toward men.

**And it came to pass, as the angels were gone away from them into heaven, the shepherds said one to another,**

Let us now go even unto Bethlehem, and see this thing which is come to pass, which the Lord hath made known unto us.

**And they came with haste, and found Mary, and Joseph, and the babe lying in a manger.**

And when they had seen it, they made known abroad the saying which was told them concerning this child.

**And all they that heard it wondered at those things which were told them by the shepherds.**

But Mary kept all these things, and pondered them in her heart.

**And the shepherds returned, glorifying and praising God for all the things that they had heard and seen, as it was told unto them.**


# SELECTION 66

JOHN 15: 1–17

I AM the true vine, and my Father is the husbandman.

**Every branch in me that beareth not fruit he taketh away:**

And every branch that beareth fruit, he purgeth it, that it may bring forth more fruit.

**Now ye are clean through the word which I have spoken unto you.**

Abide in me, and I in you.

**As the branch cannot bear fruit of itself, except it abide in the vine; no more can ye, except ye abide in me.**

I am the vine, ye are the branches:

**He that abideth in me, and I in him, the same bringeth forth much fruit: for without me ye can do nothing.**

If a man abide not in me, he is cast forth as a branch, and is withered;

**And men gather them, and cast them into the fire, and they are burned.**

If ye abide in me, and my words abide in you, ye shall ask what ye will, and it shall be done unto you.

**Herein is my Father glorified, that ye bear much fruit; and so shall ye be my disciples.**

Even as the Father hath loved me, so have I loved you: abide ye in my love.

**If ye keep my commandments, ye shall abide in my love; even as I have kept my Father's commandments, and abide in his love.**

These things have I spoken unto you, that my joy may be in you, and that your joy may be made full.

**This is my commandment, that ye love one another, even as I have loved you.**

Greater love hath no man than this, that a man lay down his life for his friends.

**Ye are my friends, if ye do whatsoever I command you.**

No longer do I call you servants; for the servant knoweth not what his lord doeth.

**But I have called you friends;**

For all things that I heard from my Father I have made known unto you.

**Ye did not choose me, but I chose you, and appointed you, that ye should go and bear fruit, and that your fruit should abide:**

That whatsoever ye shall ask of the Father in my name, he may give it you.

**These things I command you, that ye love one another.**

## SELECTION 67

ROMANS 12: 1–2; 9–21

I BESEECH you therefore, brethren, by the mercies of God, to present your bodies a living sacrifice, holy, acceptable to God, which is your spiritual service.

**And be not fashioned according to this world;**

But be ye transformed by the renewing of your mind,

**That ye may prove what is the good and acceptable and perfect will of God.**

Let love be without hypocrisy;

**Abhor that which is evil; cleave to that which is good.**

In love of the brethren be tenderly affectioned one to another; in honor preferring one another;

**In diligence not slothful; fervent in spirit, serving the Lord.**

Rejoicing in hope; patient in tribulation; continuing steadfastly in prayer;

Communicating to the necessities of the saints; given to hospitality.

Bless them that persecute you; bless and curse not.

Rejoice with them that rejoice; weep with them that weep.

Be of the same mind one toward another.

Set not your mind on high things, but condescend to things that are lowly.

Be not wise in your own conceits. Render to no man evil for evil.

Take thought for things honorable in the sight of all men.

If it be possible, as much as in you lieth, be at peace with all men.

Avenge not yourselves, beloved, but give place unto the wrath of God;

For it is written, Vengeance belongeth unto me; I will recompense, saith the Lord.

But if thine enemy hunger, feed him; if he thirst, give him to drink;

For in so doing thou shalt heap coals of fire upon his head.

Be not overcome of evil, but overcome evil with good.


## SELECTION 68

J CORINTHIANS 13

THOUGH I speak with the tongues of men and of angels,

But have not love, I am become as sounding brass, or a clanging cymbal.

And though I have the gift of prophecy and understand all mysteries and all knowledge; and though I have all faith, so that I could remove mountains,

But have not love, I am nothing.

And though I bestow all my goods to feed the poor, and though I give my body to be burned,

But have not love, it profiteth me nothing.

Love suffereth long, and is kind; love envieth not;

Love vaunteth not itself, is not puffed up;

Doth not behave itself unseemly, seeketh not its own,

**Is not easily provoked, thinketh no evil;**

Rejoiceth not in iniquity, but rejoiceth in the truth;

**Beareth all things, believeth all things, hopeth all things, endureth all things.**

Love never faileth:

**But whether there be prophecies, they shall fail;**

Whether there be tongues, they shall cease;

**Whether there be knowledge, it shall vanish away.**

For we know in part, and we prophesy in part;

**But when that which is perfect is come, that which is in part shall be done away.**

When I was a child, I spake as a child, I understood as a child, I thought as a child:

**But when I became a man, I put away childish things.**

For now we see in a mirror, darkly; but then face to face.

**Now I know in part; but then shall I know even as also I am known.**

But now abideth faith, hope, love, these three;

**And the greatest of these is love.**

## SELECTION 69

I CORINTHIANS 15: 20–26; 41–45; 47–49; 53–58

NOW is Christ risen from the dead, and become the firstfruits of them that slept.

**For since by man came death, by man came also the resurrection of the dead.**

For as in Adam all die, even so in Christ shall all be made alive.

**But each in his own order: Christ the firstfruits; then they that are Christ's, at his coming.**

Then cometh the end, when he shall deliver up the kingdom to God, even the Father;

**When he shall have abolished all rule and all authority and power.**

For he must reign, till he hath put all his enemies under his feet.

**The last enemy that shall be destroyed is death.**

There is one glory of the sun, and another glory of the moon, and another glory of the stars; for one star differeth from another star in glory.

**So also is the resurrection of the dead. It is sown in corruption; it is raised in incorruption:**

It is sown in dishonor; it is raised in glory:

**It is sown in weakness; it is raised in power:**

It is sown a natural body; it is raised a spiritual body.

**If there is a natural body, there is also a spiritual body.**

So also it is written, The first man Adam became a living soul.

**The last Adam became a life-giving spirit.**

The first man is of the earth, earthy:

**The second man is of heaven.**

As is the earthy, such are they also that are earthy:

**And as is the heavenly, such are they also that are heavenly.**

And as we have borne the image of the earthy,

**We shall also bear the image of the heavenly.**

For this corruptible must put on incorruption, and this mortal must put on immortality.

**So when this corruptible shall have put on incorruption, and this mortal shall have put on immortality,**

Then shall be brought to pass the saying that is written, Death is swallowed up in victory.

**O death, where is thy sting? O grave, where is thy victory?**

The sting of death is sin; and the strength of sin is the law.

**But thanks be to God, who giveth us the victory through our Lord Jesus Christ.**

Therefore, my beloved brethren, be ye steadfast, unmoveable, always abounding in the work of the Lord,

**Forasmuch as ye know that your labor is not in vain in the Lord.**

## SELECTION 70

I JOHN 4: 7–21

BELOVED, let us love one another: for love is of God; and every one that loveth is born of God, and knoweth God.

**He that loveth not knoweth not God; for God is love.**

In this was manifested the love of God toward us, because that God hath sent his only begotten Son into the world, that we might live through him.

**Herein is love, not that we loved God, but that he loved us, and sent his Son to be the propitiation for our sins.**

Beloved, if God so loved us, we also ought to love one another.

**No man hath seen God at any time: if we love one another, God abideth in us, and his love is perfected in us.**

Hereby we know that we abide in him and he in us, because he hath given us of his Spirit.

**And we have beheld and bear witness that the Father hath sent the Son to be the Saviour of the world.**

Whosoever shall confess that Jesus is the Son of God, God abideth in him, and he in God.

**And we know and have believed the love which God hath toward us.**

God is love; and he that abideth in love abideth in God, and God in him.

**Herein is love made perfect with us, that we may have boldness in the day of judgment;**

Because as he is, even so are we in this world.

**There is no fear in love: but perfect love casteth out fear, because fear hath torment; and he that feareth is not made perfect in love.**

We love, because he first loved us.

**If a man say, I love God, and hateth his brother, he is a liar: for he that loveth not his brother whom he hath seen, how can he love God whom he hath not seen?**

And this commandment have we from him,

**That he who loveth God love his brother also.**

## SELECTION 71

ACTS 17: 24–28

GOD that made the world and all things therein, he, being Lord of heaven and earth, dwelleth not in temples made with hands;

**Neither is he served by men's hands, as though he needed anything,**

Seeing he himself giveth to all life, and breath, and all things;

**And he made of one blood all nations of men to dwell on all the face of the earth,**

Having determined their appointed seasons, and the bounds of their habitation;

**That they should seek the Lord, if haply they might feel after him and find him,**

Though he is not far from each one of us;

**For in him we live, and move, and have our being.**

ROMANS 10: 12–15

There is no difference between the Jew and the Greek: for the same Lord over all is rich unto all that call upon him.

**For whosoever shall call upon the name of the Lord shall be saved.**

How then shall they call on him in whom they have not believed?

**And how shall they believe in him of whom they have not heard?**

And how shall they hear without a preacher?

**And how shall they preach, except they be sent?**

As it is written, How beautiful are the feet of them that preach the gospel of peace,

**And bring glad tidings of good things!**

MATTHEW 9: 37–38

The harvest truly is plenteous, but the laborers are few;

**Pray ye therefore the Lord of the harvest, that he will send forth laborers into his harvest.**

MATTHEW 28: 18–20

And Jesus came and spake unto them, saying:

**All power is given unto me in heaven and in earth.**

Go ye therefore, and teach all nations,

Baptizing them in the name of the Father, and of the Son, and of the Holy Spirit:

Teaching them to observe all things whatsoever I have commanded you:

And, lo, I am with you alway, even unto the end of the world.

## SELECTION 72

ISAIAH 1: 2, 11a, 12, 16b–17

HEAR, O heaven; and give ear, O earth; for the Lord hath spoken:

To what purpose is the multitude of your sacrifices unto me?

When ye come to appear before me, who hath required this at your hand, to tread my courts?

Cease to do evil; learn to do well; seek justice, relieve the oppressed, judge the fatherless, plead for the widow.

ISAIAH 58: 6–9a; 10–11

Is not this the fast that I have chosen? to loose the bands of wickedness, to undo the heavy burdens,

And to let the oppressed go free, and that ye break every yoke?

Is it not to deal thy bread to the hungry, and that thou bring the poor that are cast out to thy house?

When thou seest the naked, that thou cover him; and that thou hide not thyself from thine own flesh?

Then shall thy light break forth as the morning, and thine health shall spring forth speedily;

And thy righteousness shall go before thee: the glory of the Lord shall be thy rearward.

Then shalt thou call, and the Lord will answer;

Thou shalt cry, and he will say, Here I am.

If thou draw out thy soul to the hungry, and satisfy the afflicted soul;

Then shall thy light rise in obscurity, and thy darkness be as the noonday;

And the Lord will guide thee continually, and satisfy thy soul in drought, and make fat thy bones;

And thou shalt be like a watered garden, and like a spring of water, whose waters fail not.

MICAH 6: 8

He hath showed thee, O man, what is good;

**And what doth the Lord require of thee, but to do justly, and to love mercy, and to walk humbly with thy God?**

## SELECTION 73

MATTHEW 5: 38–48

YE have heard that it hath been said, An eye for an eye, and a tooth for a tooth:

**But I say unto you, Resist not him that is evil:**

But whosoever shall smite thee on thy right cheek, turn to him the other also.

**And if any man will go to law with thee, and take away thy coat, let him have thy cloak also.**

And whosoever shall compel thee to go a mile, go with him twain.

**Give to him that asketh thee, and from him that would borrow of thee turn not thou away.**

Ye have heard that it hath been said, Thou shalt love thy neighbor, and hate thine enemy.

**But I say unto you, Love your enemies, and pray for them that persecute you;**

That ye may be sons of your Father who is in heaven: for he maketh his sun to rise on the evil and on the good, and sendeth rain on the just and on the unjust.

**For if ye love them that love you, what reward have ye? do not even the publicans the same?**

And if ye salute your brethren only, what do ye more than others? do not even the Gentiles the same?

**Ye therefore shall be perfect, as your heavenly Father is perfect.**

MATTHEW 25: 34–40

Then shall the King say unto them on his right hand, Come ye blessed of my Father,

**Inherit the kingdom prepared for you from the foundation of the world:**

For I was hungry, and ye gave me to eat:

**I was thirsty, and ye gave me drink:**

I was a stranger, and ye took me in:

Naked, and ye clothed me:

I was sick, and ye visited me:

I was in prison, and ye came unto me.

Then shall the righteous answer him, saying, Lord, when saw we thee hungry, and fed thee? or thirsty, and gave thee drink?

When saw we thee a stranger, and took thee in? or naked, and clothed thee?

Or when saw we thee sick, or in prison, and came unto thee?

And the King shall answer and say unto them, Verily I say unto you, Inasmuch as ye did it unto one of these my brethren, even these least, ye did it unto me.

## SELECTION 74

MICAH 4: 1-4

IN the last days it shall come to pass, that the mountain of the house of the Lord shall be established in the top of the mountains, and it shall be exalted above the hills:

And peoples shall flow unto it.

And many nations shall come, and say, Come, and let us go up to the mountain of the Lord, and to the house of the God of Jacob;

And he will teach us of his ways, and we will walk in his paths:

For the law shall go forth of Zion,

And the word of the Lord from Jerusalem.

And he will judge between many peoples, and will decide concerning strong nations afar off;

And they shall beat their swords into ploughshares, and their spears into pruninghooks;

Nation shall not lift up sword against nation,

Neither shall they learn war any more.

But they shall sit every man under his vine and under his fig tree; and none shall make them afraid:

For the mouth of the Lord of hosts hath spoken it.

ISAIAH 65: 17-19; 21-25

Behold, I create new heavens and a new earth;

And the former shall not be remembered, nor come into mind.

But be ye glad and rejoice for ever in that which I create;

**For, behold, I create Jerusalem a rejoicing, and her people a joy.**

And I will rejoice in Jerusalem, and joy in my people;

**And the voice of weeping shall be no more heard in her, nor the voice of crying.**

They shall build houses, and inhabit them; and they shall plant vineyards, and eat the fruit of them.

**They shall not build, and another inhabit; they shall not plant, and another eat;**

For as the days of a tree are the days of my people,

**And mine elect shall long enjoy the work of their hands.**

They shall not labor in vain, nor bring forth for trouble;

**For they are the seed of the blessed of the Lord, and their offspring with them.**

And it shall come to pass, that before they call, I will answer;

**And while they are yet speaking, I will hear.**

The wolf and the lamb shall feed together, and the lion shall eat straw like the bullock: and dust shall be the serpent's meat.

**They shall not hurt nor destroy in all my holy mountain, saith the Lord.**

## SELECTION 75

JOHN 17: 3–6; 16–23

THIS is life eternal, that they should know thee the only true God, and Jesus Christ, whom thou hast sent.

**I have glorified thee on the earth: I have finished the work which thou gavest me to do.**

And now, O Father, glorify thou me with thine own self with the glory which I had with thee before the world was.

**I manifested thy name unto the men whom thou gavest me out of the world: thine they were, and thou gavest them me; and they have kept thy word.**

They are not of the world, even as I am not of the world.

**Sanctify them in the truth: thy word is truth.**

As thou hast sent me into the world, even so have I also sent them into the world.

**And for their sakes I sanctify myself, that they also may be sanctified in truth.**

Neither for these only do I pray, but for them also that believe on me through their word;

**That they all may be one;**

As thou, Father, art in me, and I in thee, that they also may be in us:

**That the world may believe that thou didst send me.**

And the glory which thou gavest me I have given them;

**That they may be one, even as we are one:**

I in them, and thou in me, that they may be perfected into one;

**And that the world may know that thou hast sent me, and hast loved them, as thou hast loved me.**

EPHESIANS 4: 1–6

I beseech you that ye walk worthy of the vocation wherewith ye are called,

**With all lowliness and meekness, with long-suffering,**

Forbearing one another in love;

**Endeavoring to keep the unity of the spirit in the bond of peace.**

There is one body, and one spirit, even as ye were called in one hope of your calling;

**One Lord, one faith, one baptism, one God and Father of all, who is above all, and through all, and in all.**